AF352490

THE HISTORY OF AL-ṬABARĪ

AN ANNOTATED TRANSLATION

VOLUME XXIII

The Zenith of the Marwānid House

THE LAST YEARS OF ʿABD AL-MALIK

AND

THE CALIPHATE OF AL-WALĪD

A.D. 700–715 / A.H. 81–96

The History of al-Ṭabarī

Editorial Board

Ihsan Abbas, University of Jordan, Amman

C. E. Bosworth, The University of Manchester

Franz Rosenthal, Yale University

Ehsan Yar-Shater, Columbia University (*General Editor*)

The preparation of this volume was made possible in part by a grant from the National Endowment for the Humanities, an independent federal agency.

Bibliotheca Persica

Edited by Ehsan Yar-Shater

The History of al-Ṭabarī

(Ta'rīkh al-rusul wa'l-mulūk)

VOLUME XXIII

The Zenith of the Marwānid House

translated and annotated

by

Martin Hinds

University of Cambridge

State University of New York Press

Published by
State University of New York Press, Albany
© 1990 State University of New York
All rights reserved
Printed in the United States of America
No part of this book may be used or reproduced
in any manner whatsoever without written permission
except in the case of brief quotations embodied in
critical articles and reviews.
For information, address State University of New York
Press, State University Plaza, Albany, N. Y. 12246

Library of Congress Cataloging in Publication Data
Ṭabarī, 838?–923.
 The zenith of the Marwanid House.
 (The history of al-Ṭabarī=Ta'rīkh al-rusul wa'l
mulūk; v. 23) (SUNY series in Near Eastern studies)
(Bibliotheca Persica)
 Translation of extracts from: Ta'rīkh al-rusul
wa-al-mulūk.
 Bibliography: p.
 1. Islamic Empire—History—661–750.
I. Hinds, Martin. II. Title. III. Series: Ṭabarī,
838?–923. Ta'rīkh al-rusul wa-al-mulūk. English;
v. 23. IV. Series: SUNY series in Near Eastern
studies. V. Series: Bibliotheca Persica (Albany, N.Y.)
DS38.2.T313   1985   vol. 23   909'.1 S   87-17997
[DS38.5]   [909'.097671]
ISBN 0-88706-721-2
ISBN 0-88706-722-0 (pbk.)
10 9 8 7 6 5 4 3 2 1

Preface

THE HISTORY OF PROPHETS AND KINGS (*Ta'rīkh al-rusul wa'l-mulūk*) by Abū Jaʿfar Muḥammad b. Jarīr al-Ṭabarī (839–923), here rendered as the *History of al-Ṭabarī*, is by common consent the most important universal history produced in the world of Islam. It has been translated here in its entirety for the first time for the benefit of non-Arabists, with historical and philological notes for those interested in the particulars of the text.

Al-Ṭabarī's monumental work explores the history of the ancient nations, with special emphasis on biblical peoples and prophets, the legendary and factual history of ancient Iran, and, in great detail, the rise of Islam, the life of the Prophet Muḥammad, and the history of the Islamic world down to the year 915. The first volume of this translation will contain a biography of al-Ṭabarī and a discussion of the method, scope, and value of his work. It will also provide information on some of the technical considerations that have guided the work of the translators.

The *History* has been divided into 38 volumes, each of which covers about two hundred pages of the original Arabic text in the Leiden edition. An attempt has been made to draw the dividing lines between the individual volumes in such a way that each is to some degree independent and can be read as such. The page numbers of the original in the Leiden edition appear on the margins of the translated volumes.

Al-Ṭabarī very often quotes his sources verbatim and traces the chain of transmission (*isnād*) to an original source. The chains of

transmitters are, for the sake of brevity, rendered by only a dash
(—) between the individual links in the chain. Thus, "according
to Ibn Ḥumayd—Salamah—Ibn Isḥāq" means that al-Ṭabarī received the report from Ibn Ḥumayd, who said that he was told by
Salamah, who said that he was told by Ibn Isḥāq, and so on. The
numerous subtle and important differences in the original Arabic
wording have been disregarded.

The table of contents at the beginning of each volume gives a
brief survey of the topics dealt with in that particular volume. It
also includes the headings and subheadings as they appear in al-
Ṭabarī's text, as well as those occasionally introduced by the
translator.

Well-known place names, such as, for instance, Mecca,
Baghdad, Jerusalem, Damascus, and the Yemen, are given in their
English spellings. Less common place names, which are the vast
majority, are transliterated. Biblical figures appear in the accepted
English spelling. Iranian names are usually translated according
to their Arabic forms, and the presumed Iranian forms are often
discussed in the footnotes.

Technical terms have been translated wherever possible, but
some, such as dirham and imām, have been retained in Arabic
forms. Others that cannot be translated with sufficient precision
have been retained and italicized as well as footnoted.

The annotation aims chiefly at clarifying difficult passages,
identifying individuals and place names, and discussing textual
difficulties. Much leeway has been left to the translators to include in the footnotes whatever they consider necessary and
helpful.

The bibliographies list all the sources mentioned in the
annotation.

The index in each volume contains all the names of persons
and places referred to in the text, as well as those mentioned in
the notes as far as they refer to the medieval period. It does not
include the names of modern scholars. A general index, it is
hoped, will appear after all the volumes have been published.

For further details concerning the series and acknowledgments,
see Preface to Volume I.

Ehsan Yar-Shater

Contents

Preface / v

Translator's Foreword / xi

Map: Khurasan and Transoxania in the Early Eighth
   Century / xvi

The Last Years of ʿAbd al-Malik

The Events of the Year 81 (cont'd) (700/701) / 3

What Led ʿAbd al-Raḥmān b. Muḥammad b. al-Ashʿath to Do
   What He Did . . . / 3

The Events of the Year 82 (701/702) / 14

[Operations at al-Baṣrah and al-Kūfah] / 14
The Reason for Ibn al-Ashʿath's Progress to Dayr al-Jamājim
   and [the Battle] between Him and al-Ḥajjāj / 20
[The Death of al-Mughīrah b. al-Muhallab] / 26
The Reason for al-Muhallab's Departure from Kish / 29
The Cause and Place of the Death [of al-Muhallab] / 31

The Events of the Year 83 (702/703) / 35

The Cause of [Ibn al-Ashʿath's] Defeat / 35
The Cause of the Battle [of Maskin], with a
   Description of It / 46
[The Breakup of Ibn al-Ashʿath's Defeated Army] / 49
[A Second Account of the Battle of Maskin] / 68
[The Reason Why al-Ḥajjāj Built Wāsiṭ] / 70

The Events of the Year 84 (703/704) / 72

The Reason Why [Yazīd b. al-Muhallab] Conquered [the
   Fortress of Nīzak] / 74

The Events of the Year 85 (704/705) / 77

What [Ibn al-Ashʿath] Died of and How It Came About / 77
The Reason Why al-Ḥajjāj Dismissed [Yazīd b. al-Muhallab]
   from Khurasan and Appointed al-Mufaḍḍal / 83
[Al-Mufaḍḍal's Conquest of Bādghīs] / 88
[Mūsā b. ʿAbdallāh's] Going to al-Tirmidh [and His Activities]
   until He Was Killed There / 90
[ʿAbd al-Malik's Desire to Remove His Brother
   from the Succession] / 108

The Events of the Year 86 (705) / 116

[The Death of ʿAbd al-Malik] / 116
Report on His Age When He Died / 117
His Descent and His Teknonym (*Kunyah*) / 117
His Children and Wives / 118

The Caliphate of al-Walīd b. ʿAbd al-Malik

The Events of the Year 86 (cont'd) (705) / 125

What Happened to Qutaybah in Khurasan in This Year / 127

The Events of the Year 87 (705/706) / 131

[The Appointment of ʿUmar b. ʿAbd al-ʿAzīz as
   Governor of Medina] / 131

[Qutaybah's Peace Agreement with the People of
  Bādghīs] / 133
Report of [Qutaybah's] Campaign [against Paykand] / 134

The Events of the Year 88 (706/707) / 140

[Reconstruction of the Mosque of Medina] / 141
[Qutaybah's] Campaign [against Tūmushkath
  and Rāmīthanah] / 143

The Events of the Year 89 (707/708) / 146

The Events of the Year 90 (708/709) / 149

[Qutaybah's Conquest of Bukhārā] / 150
[Renewed Peace between Qutaybah and the Soghdians] / 152
[Nīzak's] Perfidy and Why He Was Vanquished / 153
[Qutaybah's Retribution against the People of al-Ṭālaqān] / 155
The Reason for [the Muhallabids'] Escape from al-Ḥajjāj's
  Prison and Their Going to Sulaymān / 156

The Events of the Year 91 (709/710) / 164

[Qutaybah's Capture and Killing of Nīzak] / 164
[Qutaybah's Campaign in Transoxania] / 174
[Khālid al-Qasrī's Strict Governorship of Mecca] / 177
[Al-Walīd's Visit to Medina] / 179

The Events of the Year 92 (710/711) / 182

The Events of the Year 93 (711/712) / 184

[The Killing of the King of Khām Jird and Renewed Peace
  with Khwārazm] / 185
[Qutaybah's Conquest of Samarqand] / 189
[Mūsā b. Nuṣayr's Dismissal of Ṭāriq b. Ziyād] / 201
Why al-Walīd Dismissed ['Umar b. 'Abd al-'Azīz] / 201

The Events of the Year 94 (712/713) / 204

Qutaybah's Campaign [in al-Shāsh and Farghānah] / 205
['Uthmān b. Ḥayyān al-Murrī's] Governorship / 206
The Report of [Sa'īd b. Jubayr's] Death / 209

x   Contents

The Events of the Year 95 (713/714) / 215

The Report of [Qutaybah's] Campaign [in al-Shāsh] / 216

The Events of the Year 96 (714/715) / 218

[The Death of al-Walīd b. ʿAbd al-Malik] / 218
Report of Some of What He Did / 219
[Al-Walīd's Desire to Remove Sulaymān from
   the Succession] / 222
[Qutaybah in Kāshghar and China] / 224

Bibliography of Cited Works / 231

Index / 237

Translator's Foreword

The early years of the eighth century constitute what in retrospect can be seen as the high point of Marwānid Umayyad power. When, in 693, the prolonged war against the Zubayrids had finally come to an end, the Caliph ʿAbd al-Malik b. Marwān had been free to set about Umayyad consolidation; this took longest in Iraq, in a sequence of events culminating in the revolt led in 700–702 by the Iraqi *sharīf* ʿAbd al-Raḥmān b. Muḥammad b. al-Ashʿath al-Kindī (with which this volume begins), which seriously imperiled Marwānid control of Iraq and was countered with considerable difficulty. Thereafter, however, ʿAbd al-Malik presided over a strong and dynamic Arab kingdom, with al-Ḥajjāj b. Yūsuf al-Thaqafī as his powerful governor of Iraq and the East. When ʿAbd al-Malik died in 705, the kingdom passed to his son al-Walīd, during whose ten-year caliphate al-Ḥajjāj remained at his post and further Arab expansion took place: in Central Asia, in Sind, and in the Iberian Peninsula. To many of their contemporaries, the Arabs of that time must have looked like potential world conquerors. The volume ends in 715, shortly after the deaths of al-Ḥajjāj and al-Walīd, and just two years before the dispatch of the ill-fated Arab expedition to Constantinople.[1]

---

1. For general literature relating to this period, see J. Wellhausen, *The Arab Kingdom and Its Fall*, Calcutta 1927, pp. 232–57, 427–44; M. A. Shaban, *Islamic History A.D. 600–750 (A.H. 132): A New Interpretation*, Cambridge, 1971, pp. 110–26; H. Kennedy, *The Prophet and the Age of the Caliphates*, London and New York, 1986, pp. 100–4; G. R. Hawting, *The First Dynasty of Islam: The Umayyad Caliphate, A.D. 661–750*, London and Sydney, 1986, pp. 58–71.

In this volume, as is often the case in his chronicle, al-Ṭabarī's focus is on events in Iraq and the East, and he pays only fleeting attention to what was going on in Syria, Egypt, and the West; and it so happens that the central figure in the Arab history of this period was al-Ḥajjāj b. Yūsuf. Both of the subjects receiving the most attention in this volume involved him: (1) the revolt of Ibn al-Ashʿth and how al-Ḥajjāj managed to deal with it;[2] and (2) events in Khurasan and Transoxania, notably the conquests effected by al-Ḥajjāj's protégé and governor of Khurasan, Qutaybah b. Muslim.[3] In the case of the first of these subjects, much of what is relayed by al-Ṭabarī is also relayed by al-Balādhurī; in the case of the second, al-Ṭabarī is unquestionably the major source.

Ibn al-Ashʿath's revolt began in Sijistān and moved to Iraq; many grievances were involved, but the main reason why the revolt so nearly succeeded was that it brought together, on an unprecedented scale, highly disparate elements of Iraqi opposition to Syrian domination. The earlier Sufyānid Umayyad administration of Iraq had involved controlling the Iraqi Arab tribesmen through the local tribal *ashrāf*, and the Zubayrids tried similarly to involve them in the power structure (albeit with less success than the Sufyānids); on occasions when the established order in Iraq was exposed to any local threat or opposition, the *ashrāf* formally aligned themselves (or were required to align themselves) with the representatives of Umayyad/Zubayrid government there. It is therefore a telling comment on the state of affairs in Iraq under al-Ḥajjāj that the *sharīf* Ibn al-Ashʿath, supported by other *ashrāf*, led a revolt against the representative of Marwānid rule; it was a revolt that constituted a major departure from the earlier pattern of sharīfian behavior and provided a leadership capable of uniting the various disgruntled Iraqi interest groups.

---

2. On this, see Wellhausen, *Kingdom*, pp. 232–50; C. E. Bosworth, *Sīstān under the Arabs, from the Islamic Conquest to the Rise of the Saffārids (30–250/651–864)*, Rome, 1968, pp. 55–63; *EI*[2], s.v. Ibn al-Ashʿath (L. Veccia Vaglieri); ʿA. ʿA. Dixon, *The Umayyad Caliphate (65–86/684–705): A Political Study*, London, 1971, pp. 153–68; and, most recently, R. Sayed, *Die Revolte des Ibn al-Ašʿaṯ und die Koranleser: Ein Beitrag zur Religions- und Sozialgeschichte der frühen Umayyadenzeit*, Freiburg im Breisgau, 1977.

3. See Wellhausen, *Kingdom*, pp. 427–44; H. A. R. Gibb, *The Arab Conquests in Central Asia*, London, 1923, pp. 29–58; also *EI*[2], s.v. Ḳutayba b. Muslim (C. E. Bosworth).

Al-Ḥajjāj was able to counter it only by bringing in massive Syrian reinforcements for the Syrian troops already with him. Following the suppression of the revolt, the role of the Iraqi Arab tribesmen and their leaders was obviously to be diminished even more than it had been already, and al-Ṭabarī gives us detailed accounts of the stern measures then taken by al-Ḥajjāj in Iraq. In addition, he established Wāsiṭ (rather than making any more use of al-Baṣrah and/or al-Kūfah) as the base for his Syrian troops in Iraq. The Iraqi Arabs were for the time being well and truly subjugated to Syrian domination.

As for events in Khurasan and beyond, the period opens with Muhallabid governors of Khurasan, first al-Muhallab b. Abī Ṣufrah himself, then successively his sons Yazīd and al-Mufaḍḍal. Following the failure of Ibn al-Ashʿath's insurrection, the Muhallabids were the last Iraqi family of major importance, and al-Ḥajjāj soon succeeded in ousting them from Khurasan. Al-Ṭabarī goes on to regale us with the remarkable story of Mūsā b. ʿAbdallāh b. Khāzim, the Sulamī who for fifteen years operated independently from his base at al-Tirmidh, before proceeding to the most important part of his account: the conquests effected in Central Asia by Qutaybah b. Muslim al-Bāhilī, al-Ḥajjāj's governor of Khurasan from 86 (705). Between that date and 96 (715), Qutaybah brought the whole of Lower Ṭukhāristān and Transoxania under Arab sway and made important inroads beyond the Jaxartes. Despite the fact that the account of the expedition to Kāshghar in 96 (715) seems to be an exaggeration (as Gibb has shown), it is nonetheless clear that Qutaybah achieved more in Central Asia than any other Arab conqueror of the Umayyad period; "with Ḥajjāj at his back, [he] held his conquests together, and when he disappeared there was neither leader nor organization to take his place."[4] Al-Ṭabarī tells us a great deal about these important conquests, but he says almost nothing about the less important conquests in Sind effected at the same time by Muḥammad b. al-Qāsim al-Thaqafī,[5] who was a relative of al-Ḥajjāj's and was directly responsible to him; one might have thought that the Ḥajjāj

---

4. Gibb, *Arab Conquests*, p. 54.
5. See F. Gabrieli, "Muḥammad ibn Qāsim and the Arab Conquest of Sind," *East and West*, N.S. 15 (1965), pp. 281–95.

connection would have led al-Ṭabarī to say more about these operations, but it is necessary in fact to turn to al-Balādhurī's *Futūḥ al-buldān* for details about them. More predictably, al-Ṭabarī also pays very little attention to the third instance of Arab expansion at this time, namely, the conquest of much of the Iberian Peninsula by Mūsā b. Nuṣayr and Ṭāriq b. Ziyād.[6]

Of the other matters touched on in this volume, something may be said, first, about Arab operations against the Byzantines. Here, as is apparent from the digest made by Brooks,[7] al-Ṭabarī tells us more than any other single Arabic source; and it is clear that in general there was more activity on that front in the caliphate of al-Walīd than in that of ʿAbd al-Malik, which is scarcely surprising in view of ʿAbd al-Malik's more pressing concerns. Even so, the sum of information available is depressingly meager, and numerous contradictions and problematic place names remain to be resolved.[8]

Secondly, there were two attempts during this period to divert succession to the caliphate. The first of these, when ʿAbd al-Malik wished to divert it from his brother ʿAbd al-ʿAzīz to his son al-Walīd, was blocked by ʿAbd al-ʿAzīz; the matter was resolved for ʿAbd al-Malik when his brother predeceased him. The second, when al-Walīd wished to divert the succession from his brother Sulaymān to his son ʿAbd al-ʿAzīz, was blocked by Sulaymān, who outlived al-Walīd and succeeded to the caliphate. As Hawting has remarked, "In view of the potentiality for conflict inherent in the lack of a fixed order of succession to the caliphate in the Umayyad period, it is remarkable how seldom real trouble developed from it."[9]

Thirdly, it can be noted, too, that during this period there emerged into prominence two figures who would subsequently play roles of major importance. ʿUmar b. ʿAbd al-ʿAzīz b. Marwān, a son of ʿAbd al-Malik's brother mentioned in the preceding para-

---

6. E. Lévi-Provençal, *Histoire de l'Espagne musulmane*, new ed., Leiden and Paris, 1950–53, vol. I; also *EI*[2], s.v. al-Andalus (E. Lévi-Provençal).

7. E. W. Brooks, "The Arabs in Asia Minor (641–750) from Arabic Sources," *Journal of Hellenic Studies* 18 (1898), pp. 190–94.

8. See, most recently, R.-J. Lilie, *Die byzantinische Reaktion auf die Ausbreitung der Araber* (Miscellanea Byzantina Monacensia 22), Munich, 1976, pp. 113–22.

9. *First Dynasty of Islam*, p. 59.

graph, and later the Caliph 'Umar II, served as governor of Medina for six years under al-Walīd, until the latter was persuaded by al-Ḥajjāj to dismiss him; and Khālid al-Qasrī, who was to become the governor of Iraq for most of the caliphate of Hishām b. 'Abd al-Malik, served as governor of Mecca for perhaps as long as the last seven years of al-Walīd's caliphate.[10]

This was above all what Shaban had styled "the age of Ḥaj-jāj,"[11] and particularly so in the caliphate of al-Walīd, who, as Wellhausen has pointed out, "gave him a free hand, and even in his own sphere of government gave in to him and consulted his wishes."[12] This most unforgettable of Arab governors did more than any other individual to turn the period covered by the present volume into the pinnacle of the Marwānid achievement. Yet even he did not get his way in one important regard: in 90 (708–9), Yazīd b. al-Muhallab and other Muhallabids escaped from his custody in Iraq and gained the protection of the Caliph's brother, Sulaymān, in Palestine. Al-Ḥajjāj's attempts to put pressure on al-Walīd to remedy the matter came to nothing. Six years later, Sulayman was caliph and the Muhallabids were in the ascendant.

There remains only the agreeable task of thanking those who have been kind enough to put their expertise at my disposal in the course of making and annotating this translation. Professor Iḥsān 'Abbās not only gave freely of his time to provide me with *fatwā*s on all manner of queries that came up in the course of making the translation, but he also went through the penultimate draft and made further valuable suggestions. Professor Edmund Bosworth and Dr. Patricia Crone also went through the draft and made helpful comments and criticisms, for which I am grateful. All three scholars are of course to be absolved from any blame for such infelicities as may appear in the translation in its final form.

Martin Hinds

---

10. See *EI²*, s.v. Khālid b. 'Abd Allāh al-Ḳasrī (G. R. Hawting), where the chronological difficulties relating to Khālid's governorship of Mecca are discussed.
11. *Islamic History*, ch. 6; see also *EI²*, s.v. al-Ḥadjdjādj b. Yūsuf (A. Dietrich).
12. *Kingdom*, p. 251.

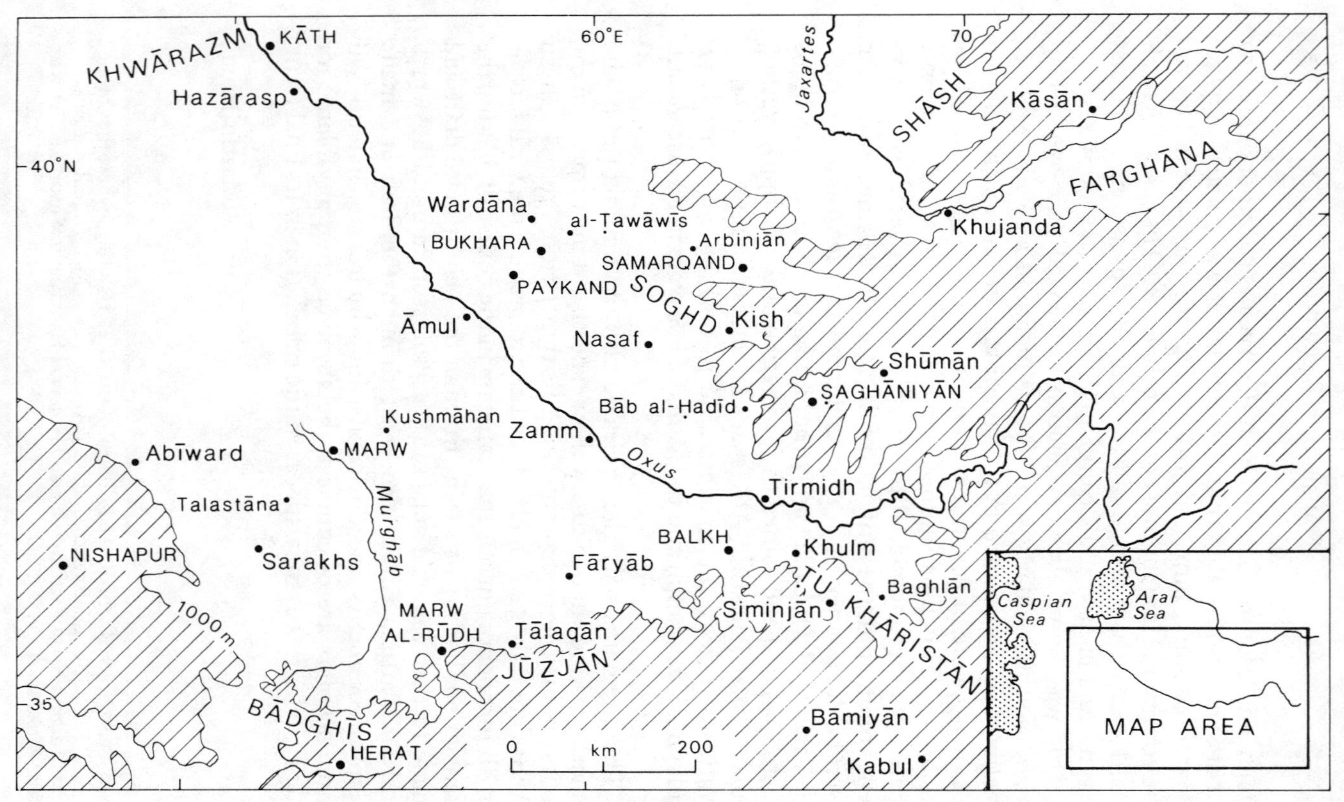

Khurasan and Transoxania in the Early Eighth Century

The Last Years of ʿAbd al-Malik

81 (cont'd)

(FEBRUARY 26, 700–FEBRUARY 14, 701)

[1052]

Abū Jaʿfar said: In this year ʿAbd al-Raḥmān b. Muḥammad b. al-Ashʿath and those of the Iraqi army who were with him disobeyed al-Ḥajjāj and advanced upon him to fight him. This is what Abū Mikhnaf said on the authority of Abū al-Mukhāriq al-Rāsibī; as for al-Wāqidī, he claimed that this took place in the year 82.

What Led ʿAbd al-Raḥmān b. Muḥammad b. al-Ashʿath to Do What He Did, with an Account of His Actions after Disobeying al-Ḥajjāj

We have already mentioned under the year 80 the presence of ʿAbd al-Raḥmān b. Muḥammad in the territory of the Zunbīl[1] and his letter to al-Ḥajjāj concerning what he had done there and what he proposed to do in the future. We shall now mention what happened to him in the year 81, this being the account of Abū Mikhnaf on the authority of Abū al-Mukhāriq.

---

1. The literature relating to the question of whether this title was Rutbīl (and variants) or Zunbīl (and variants) is listed by Sayed, *Die Revolte des Ibn al-Ašʿat und die Koranleser*, p. 148. The form Zunbīl has been preferred here and below (the text consistently gives the form Rutbīl).

According to Hishām—Abū Mikhnaf—Abū al-Mukhāriq al-Rāsibī: Al-Ḥajjāj wrote to 'Abd al-Raḥmān, in reply to his letter, "To continue: Your letter has reached me and I have understood what you have mentioned in it. Your letter is the letter of a man who wants a truce and is pleased with reconciliation, having blandished a lowly and slight foe. They have struck down Muslim troops whose performance was good and whose capacity in the cause of Islam was mighty. By your life, O son of the mother of 'Abd al-Raḥmān, if you hold back from the enemy with my troops and arms you will be heedless of those Muslims who were struck down. I do not consider the decision you claim to have reached to be based on a strategem; I think that all that impels you to do that is your weakness and your confused judgment. So do what I ordered you to do, penetrating far into their territory, destroying their fortresses, killing their fighting men, and taking their children captive."

[1053]

Then he sent after [that letter] another in which he said, "To continue: Order the Muslims who are with you to till the soil and settle. That is your abode until God grants [you] victory over them."

Then he sent after [that letter] a further one in which he said, "To continue: Do what I ordered you to do, and penetrate far into their territory. Otherwise your brother Isḥāq b. Muḥammad[2] is to be the amīr of the people, and you are to let him have that to which I have appointed him."

When ['Abd al-Raḥmān] read [this] letter, he said, "Shall I bear responsibility for Isḥāq?" and he showed [the letter] to him.[3] [Isḥāq] said, "Don't do it." ['Abd al-Raḥmān] said, "By the Lord of this," meaning the copy of the Qur'ān, "if you mention [this] to anyone, I'll kill you." [Isḥāq] thought that he meant the sword and put his hand on the pommel of his sword.

Then ['Abd al-Raḥmān] summoned the people, praised God, and said, "O people, I am one who gives you sincere advice, one who has your well-being at heart, and one who is watchful of all benefit that encompasses you. My view in the matter of your dealings

---

2. According to al-Balādhurī (*Anonyme arabische Chronik*, Band XI [henceforward *AAC*], p. 324), Isḥāq had been sent out by al-Ḥajjāj at the head of a separate army.

3. The drift of what immediately follows is not entirely clear, and it is likely that some text is missing.

with the enemy was a view about which I consulted [both] the discerning among you and those of you who are experienced in war. They were satisfied with it in respect of you, considering it to be conducive to your well-being, and in both the short term and the long. I wrote to your amīr al-Ḥajjāj [telling him this], and he responded with a letter in which he charged me with incompetence and weakness and ordered me to hasten the business of taking you far into the territory of the enemy, that being the territory in which your brethren perished but yesterday. I am one of you: I go on when you go on, and I balk when you do." [At this,] the people were stirred up in support of him and said, "No, we balk against the enemy of God: We shall not heed him, nor shall we obey."

[1054]

Abū Mikhnaf said: Muṭarrif b. ʿĀmir b. Wāthilah al-Kinānī told me that his father,[4] who was a poet and *khaṭīb*,[5] was the first to speak on that day. After praising God, he said, "To continue: Al-Ḥajjāj wants for you none other than what the sayer of yore[6] wanted when he said to his brother, 'Mount your servant on the mare: If he perishes he perishes, and if he escapes [then so much the better] for you.' By God, al-Ḥajjāj does not care that he is taking chances with you by forcing you into a territory of sheer cliffs and narrow passes. If you win and take booty, he will devour the territory and appropriate [its] wealth, thereby extending his dominion; while if your enemy wins, you will become hated enemies, whose distress will be of no concern to him and whom he will not pity. So disavow al-Ḥajjāj, the enemy of God, and give the oath of allegiance to ʿAbd al-Raḥmān. I [hereby] cause you to witness that I am the first to disavow [him]." [At this,] the people called out from every side, "We do so, we do so, we disavow the enemy of God."

ʿAbd al-Muʾmin b. Shabath b. Ribʿī al-Tamīmī,[7] who was in charge of [ʿAbd al-Raḥmān's] police force when he arrived [in Sijistān], stood up next and said, "O servants of God, if you obey al-Ḥajjāj he will make this land your land for as long as you live. He

---

4. Abū al-Ṭufayl ʿĀmir b. Wāthilah: see Sezgin, *Geschichte des arabischen Schrifttums* (henceforward *GAS*), vol. II, p. 412.

5. A term signifying a tribal spokesman in pre-Islamic times and subsequently the deliverer of the Friday sermon (see *EI²*, s.v.).

6. So rendering *al-qāʾil al-awwal*; al-Balādhurī, *AAC*, p. 325, gives simply *al-qāʾil*. I have not encountered elsewhere the piece of wisdom that follows.

7. Crone, *Slaves on Horses*, p. 118.

will keep you out in the field in the manner of Pharaoh, who, I have been informed, was the first to keep armies out in the field; I think that most of you will be dead before seeing your loved ones. So give the oath of allegiance to your amīr, set off against your enemy, and expel him from your land (that is, Iraq)." [At this] the people rose up to ʿAbd al-Raḥmān and gave him the oath of allegiance. He said, "Give me the oath of allegiance to disavow al-Ḥajjāj, the enemy of God, and to help me, and to fight against him along with me until God expels him from the land of Iraq"; and they rendered the oath of allegiance to him. No mention was made at that time of any disavowal of ʿAbd al-Malik.

[1055]

Abū Mikhnaf said: ʿUmar b. Dharr,[8] the qāṣṣ,[9] related to me that his father was there with him and that ʿAbd al-Raḥmān had flogged him and imprisoned him because of his attachment to his brother al-Qāsim b. Muḥammad.[10] But when he came out in revolt, he summoned Dharr, and gave him a mount, raiment, and gifts; [Dharr] was among those who set off with him, functioning as a qāṣṣ and khaṭīb.[11]

According to Abū Mikhnaf—Sayf b. Bishr al-ʿIjlī—al-Munakhkhal b. Ḥābis al-ʿAbdī: When Ibn Muḥammad set off from Sijistān, he appointed over Bust ʿIyāḍ b. Himyān[12] al-Bakrī, from the Banū Sadūs b. Shaybān b. Dhuhl b. Thaʿlabah, and over Zaranj ʿAbdallāh b. ʿĀmir al-Tamīmī al-Dārimī. Then he sent to the Zunbīl and made peace with him on the understanding that, if Ibn al-Ashʿath were to win, the Zunbīl would not be liable to tax (kharāj) as long as he lived, and, if Ibn al-Ashʿath were to be defeated and so desired it, the Zunbīl would give him refuge with him.

According to Abū Mikhnaf—Khushaynah b. al-Walīd: When ʿAbd al-Raḥmān left Sijistān heading for Iraq, al-Aʿshā went before him on a mare, saying (rajaz):[13]

---

8. Caskel, Ğamharat an-nasab, register.

9. Teller of popular stories (see EI², s.v. Ḳāṣṣ).

10. A slightly fuller account of this is given in al-Balādhurī, AAC, p. 326.

11. Cf. the account given by Khalīfah b. Khayyāṭ, Taʾrīkh, p. 279.

12. Thus too in Ibn al-Athīr, but ʿIyāḍ b. ʿAmr according to al-Balādhurī, AAC, p. 327.

13. This is Aʿshā Hamdān (see EI², s.v., and Sezgin, GAS, vol. II, pp. 345–46). Regarding the following verses, cf. von Goutta, Der Aġaniartikel über ʾAʿšà von Hamdān, pp. 38, 54; Geyer, The Díwán of al-Aʿshà, pp. 341–42 (Arabic text); al-Balādhurī, AAC, pp. 328–29; Aghānī,² vol. VI, p. 59; and al-Masʿūdi, Murūj, vol. V, p. 356 = par. 2109.

Distant is he whose residence is at the Īwān,[14]   [1056]
     the Īwān of Chosroes, the possessor of villages
     and sweet-smelling plants,
For a lover who has emerged in Zābulistān.
     There have been two liars from Thaqīf,
Their past liar[15] and a second one.
     May my Lord give power to Hamdān over Thaqīf,
For a day until nighttime, so consoling us for what took place
     [before].
     We betook ourselves to the devilish infidel,
When, in unbelief after belief, he exceeded the bounds
     with the noble lord ʿAbd al-Raḥmān.
He set forth with a throng of Qaḥṭān, like locusts,
     while from Maʿadd b. ʿAdnān he brought
A tumultuous and mighty multitude.
     So tell Ḥajjāj, Satan's friend, [if he can]
Stand steady against Madhḥij and Hamdān,
     that they will give him to drink from the
     goblet of poison,
And will send him off to the villages of Ibn Marwān.   [1057]

He (sc. Abū Mikhnaf) said: ʿAbad al-Raḥmān sent ʿAṭiyyah b. ʿAmr al-ʿAnbarī over his vanguard. Al-Ḥajjāj sent the cavalry against him, but he defeated it at each engagement. Al-Ḥajjāj asked who it was and was told that it was ʿAṭiyyah. This is why al-Aʿshā said (kāmil):

When you put the mountain roads of Fārs,
     one by one, behind them,
Then send ʿAṭiyyah with the cavalry
     to cast them down upon him.[16]

Then ʿAbd al-Raḥmān advanced with the people. He asked about Abū Isḥāq al-Sabīʿī,[17] whom he had inscribed among his companions, saying, "You are my maternal uncle"; [Abū Isḥāq] was told,

---

14. The Sasanian palace at Ctesiphon is meant here (see *EI²*, s.v.).
15. Presumably, al-Mukhtār b. Abī ʿUbayd is meant.
16. Reading ʿalayhi (von Goutta, *Aġaniartikel*, p. 55; Geyer, *The Dīwán of al-Aʿshà*, p. 312 [Arabic text]; al-Balādhurī, *AAC*, p. 320; and al-Masʿūdī, loc. cit.) in place of ʿalayka. Cf. Ibn Aʿtham, *Futūḥ*, vol. VII, p. 129.
17. Caskel, *Ġamharat an-nasab*, register, s.v. ʿAmr b. ʿAbd Allāh.

"Don't go to him, for he has asked about you," and he did not like
to go. ʿAbd al-Raḥmān then went on until he passed through
Kirmān and placed over them (sc. the people of Kirmān) Kharashah
b. ʿAmr al-Tamīmī. Abū Isḥāq stayed there and did not take part in
the civil war (*fitnah*) until [the battle of Dayr] al-Jamājim. When
[ʿAbd al-Raḥmān] entered Fārs, the people gathered together and
said, "If we have disavowed al-Ḥajjāj, the governor of ʿAbd al-
Malik, then we have [as a consequence] disavowed ʿAbd al-Malik";
and they gathered around ʿAbd al-Raḥmān.[18]

Abū Mikhnaf said: Among what Abū al-Ṣalt related to me [was
this]: [The first person who][19] disavowed ʿAbd al-Malik was Tayḥān b. Abjar of the Banū Taym Allāh b. Thaʿlabah. He stood up
[1058] and said, "O people, I have disavowed Abū Dhibbān[20] just as I
divest myself of my shirt." All but a few of the people then disavowed him, rose up to Ibn Muḥammad, and rendered the oath of
allegiance to him. His oath of allegiance was: "Do you swear
allegiance on [the basis of] the Book of God, the Sunnah of his
Prophet,[21] disavowal of the imāms of error, and struggle against
those who violate that which is sacred?" If they said "Yes," he
accepted the oath.

When it reached al-Ḥajjāj that he had been disavowed, he wrote
to ʿAbd al-Malik informing him about ʿAbd al-Raḥmān b. Muḥammad b. al-Ashʿath and asking him to hasten the sending of troops
to him. He sent his letter to ʿAbd al-Malik, citing at the end of it
these verses by al-Ḥārith b. Waʿlah (*basīṭ*):[22]

Ask the one who is the neighbor (or: under the protection,
> *mujāwir*) of Jarm, "Have I brought upon
> them a war that will divide neighbors of

---

18. Omitting the following *fa-kāna awwal al-nās*.

19. Inserting *kāna awwal man*, as given by manuscripts O and B.

20. Literally, "father of the flies," i.e., one who has stinking breath, an epithet
applied in particular to ʿAbd al-Malik (see Lane, *Lexicon*, p. 952b); see also al-
Thaʿālibī, *Laṭāʾif al-maʿārif*, p. 36 [English trans. pp. 56–57]).

21. On the significance of this wording, see Crone and Hinds, *God's Caliph*, pp.
59ff.

22. On the poet, see Sezgin, *GAS*, vol. II, p. 147. Regarding the following verses
(and their attribution), cf. al-Balādhurī, *AAC*, p. 333; *Aghānī*,[2] vol. XXII, p. 219;
Khalīfah, *Taʾrīkh*, p. 279; al-Mubarrad, *Kāmil*, p. 155; Ibn Ḥamdūn, *Tadhkirah*,
vol. II, p. 454; Yāqūt, *Muʿjam*, vol. III, p. 877. Ibn Aʿtham (*Futūḥ*, vol. VII, pp. 123–
24) has Ibn al-Ashʿath proclaiming these verses while in Fārs.

sincere and friendly conduct?
Have I risen up with a clamorous army full of
    neighing horses between the plain and the mountain?[23]
Have I left the women of the tribe exposed to the sun,
    out in the open, trying to make fires out of
    hawdaj saddles?"

And he went along until he stopped at al-Baṣrah.

[News of] the rebellion of ʿAbd al-Raḥmān while he was in Sijistān reached al-Muhallab,[24] who wrote to him, "To continue: O Ibn Muḥammad, you have put your foot in a stirrup that is very wrong for the community of Muḥammad. By God, look to yourself and do not destroy it; do not spill Muslim blood; do not sunder unity; do not violate the oath of allegiance. By God, if you say, 'I fear the people for myself (*nafs*),' [know that] God is more properly to be feared for it than the people. Do not expose it to God['s anger] by shedding blood or by deeming licit that which is not. Peace be upon you." [1059]

Al-Muhallab [also] wrote to al-Ḥajjāj, "To continue: The people of Iraq have advanced toward you, like a flood coming down from above, unstoppable until it reaches its resting place. The people of Iraq are fierce at the start of their exodus, desiring their sons and womenfolk; nothing will stop them getting to their families and embracing (lit. sniffing)[25] their children. So encounter them there. God willing, He will give you victory over them." When al-Ḥajjāj read this letter, he said, "God damn him; he is not looking to my interests but to those of his cousin."[26]

When al-Ḥajjāj's letter came to ʿAbd al-Malik, it appalled him. He descended from his throne, sent for Khālid b. Yazīd b. Muʿāwiyah,[27] called him [in], and had him read the letter. When

---

23. Reading *bayna 'l-sahli wa'l-furuṭi*, as given in other versions, rather than *bayna 'l-jammi wa'l-furuṭi* (which appears to have arisen by dittography).

24. Al-Muhallab b. Abī Ṣufrah, the governor of Khurasan at this time (see *EI*², s.v. [forthcoming]).

25. *Yashummū*: al-Balādhurī, *AAC*, p. 336, gives *yatakassamū*, which makes no obvious sense and is presumably a corruption of *yashummū*; cf. Khalīfah, *Taʾrīkh*, p. 280 (*shammū nisāʾahum wa-awlādahum*) and Ibn Kathīr, *Bidāyah*, vol. IX, p. 37, line 10 (*shammū awlādahum*).

26. Cf. al-Balādhurī, *AAC*, p. 336.

27. *EI*², s.v.

[Khālid] saw his concern, he said,[28] "O Commander of the Faithful, if this incident [arises from] the direction of Sijistān, do not fear it; [but] if it is from the direction of Khurasan, then I [myself] fear it." Then ['Abd al-Malik] went to the people, stood up among them, praised God, and said, "The people of Iraq have found my life too long and wish to hasten my demise. O God, empower the swords of the people of Syria over them, so that they may achieve Thy pleasure; if they do so, they will fall short of Thy displeasure." Then he descended.

Al-Ḥajjāj stayed in al-Baṣrah, prepared himself for the encounter with Ibn Muḥammad, and ignored the advice of al-Muhallab. At the same time Syrian horsemen were reaching him daily from 'Abd al-Malik, borne on post-mules in groups of one hundred, fifty, ten, and less, while he daily sent to 'Abd al-Malik letters and messages with information about Ibn Muḥammad—what district he had stopped in, what district he had set off from, which people had hastened to him [and so on].

Abū Mikhnaf said: Fuḍayl b. Khadīj[29] related to me that the place where he was registered [as a soldier] (maktab) was in Kirmān, where there were four thousand Kūfan and Baṣran horsemen, and that, when Ibn Muḥammad b. al-Ashʿath passed by them, [these forces] quickly went off with him. Al-Ḥajjāj [in the meantime] resolved to engage Ibn al-Ashʿath and went with the Syrians to Tustar; and [from there] he sent out advance parties led by Muṭahhar b. Ḥurr al-ʿAkkī—or al-Judhāmī—and 'Abdallāh b. Rumaythah al-Ṭāʾī, with Muṭahhar in overall command. These reached [the river] Dujayl, which had already been crossed by a troop sent by 'Abd al-Raḥmān—three hundred horsemen commanded by 'Abdallāh b. Abān[30] al-Ḥārithī—who formed a strongpoint for 'Abd al-Raḥmān and his army. When Muṭahhar b. 'Amr got to them, he ordered 'Abdallāh b. Rumaythah to advance on them; the cavalry of 'Abdallāh [b. Abān] was defeated and pushed back to [the river], and his companions were wounded.

According to Abū Mikhnaf—Abū al-Zubayr al-Hamdānī: I was among the companions of Ibn Muḥammad when he summoned

---

28. Preferring al-Balādhurī's *fa-lammā raʾā . . . qāl* to al-Ṭabarī's *wa-raʾā . . . fa-qāl.*

29. Al-Kindī (see the index to al-Ṭabarī's text).

30. Muḥammad b. Abān b. 'Abdallāh, according to al-Balādhurī, *AAC*, p. 339.

and gathered the people. Then he said, "Cross to [the enemy][31] from this place." So the people impelled their horses into the Dujayl from that place which he had designated, and, by God, no sooner had most, though not all, of our horses crossed than we attacked Muṭahhar b. Ḥurr and al-Ṭā'ī and defeated them, that being on the Day of Sacrifice, 81 (January 25, 701). We killed on a large scale and took their camp.[32]

[News of] the defeat reached al-Ḥajjāj while he was delivering the sermon. Abū Kaʿb b.[33] ʿUbayd b. Sarjis ascended [the pulpit] to him and informed him of the people's defeat, at which he said, "O people, go to al-Baṣrah for a camp and a place for fighting, for grain and supplies: This place in which we are cannot support us." Then he set off, returning, and the cavalry of the Iraqis[34] followed him; whenever they came upon a straggler, they killed him and [in this way] acquired [much] baggage, which they gathered together. Al-Ḥajjāj went on, without deviating, until he stopped at al-Zāwiyah.[35] He sent for the grain of the merchants at al-Kallā',[36] took it and [had it] transported to him, and left al-Baṣrah to the Iraqis [that is, the Iraqi army], his governor over it being al-Ḥakam b. Ayyūb b. Abī ʿAqīl al-Thaqafī;[37] and the Iraqis came on until they entered al-Baṣrah. When he had suffered this setback and retreated, al-Ḥajjāj called for al-Muhallab's letter and [re]read it. Then he said, "What a man! What a general! He advised us correctly, and we did not accept [what he said]."

According to authorities other than Abū Mikhnaf, al-Ḥakam b. Ayyūb was the civilian governor of al-Baṣrah, while ʿAbdallāh b. ʿĀmir b. Mismaʿ[38] was in command of the police.   [1062]

---

31. Al-Balādhurī, *AAC*, p. 339, gives *aṣḥāb al-Ḥajjāj*.

32. The account of this engagement given by al-Balādhurī, *AAC*, pp. 339–40, is rather fuller and clearer: *Inter alia*, it includes the information that Muṭahhar's force consisted of 7,000 Syrians; Ibn Aʿtham, on the other hand, opts for a force of 8,000 horsemen (*Futūḥ*, vol. VII, p. 130).

33. Al-Balādhurī, *AAC*, p. 340, omits "Abū Kaʿb b."

34. Ibn al-Athīr reads *aṣḥāb ʿAbd al-Raḥmān*.

35. Yāqūt (*Muʿjam*, vol. II, p. 911) knew this as no more than a place near al-Baṣrah.

36. The river port of al-Baṣrah and one of its markets (see Pellat, *Le milieu baṣrien*, pp. 20, 235).

37. A relative and son-in-law of al-Ḥajjāj (Crone, *Slaves on Horses*, p. 131).

38. A member of the important Baṣran Shaybānī family known as the Masāmiʿah (ibid, p. 117, and *EI²*, s.v. Masāmiʿah).

Then al-Ḥajjāj went with his army until he stopped at Rustā-qubādh,[39] which was part of Dastawā, one of the districts of al-Ahwāz, and pitched camp there. Ibn al-Ashʿath advanced and stopped at Tustar, [with the result that] there was a river between them. Al-Ḥajjāj sent Muṭahhar b. Ḥurr al-ʿAkkī with two thousand men,[40] and they rushed a strongpoint of Ibn al-Ashʿath's. Ibn al-Ashʿath proceeded swiftly and attacked them, this being in the evening of ʿArafah in the year 81 (January 24, 701). It is said that they killed fifteen hundred of the Syrians, the rest of whom returned to [al-Ḥajjāj] in defeat. He had with him one hundred fifty million [dirhams], which he distributed among his commanders, making them responsible for them, and went in defeat to al-Baṣrah. [Meanwhile,] Ibn al-Ashʿath addressed his companions, saying, "As for al-Ḥajjāj, he is nothing. We want to carry the war to ʿAbd al-Malik." [At the same time, news of] the defeat of al-Ḥajjāj reached the people of al-Baṣrah, and ʿAbdallāh b. ʿĀmir b. Mismaʿ wanted to cut the bridge to prevent his passage; but al-Ḥakam b. Ayyūb bribed him with one hundred thousand [dirhams], and he desisted from this [action]. [Then] al-Ḥajjāj entered al-Baṣrah: He sent to Ibn ʿĀmir and wrested the one hundred thousand [dirhams] from him.

The account reverts to that of Abū Mikhnaf on the authority of Abū al-Zubayr al-Hamdānī: When ʿAbd al-Raḥmān b. Muḥammad entered al-Baṣrah, all of its *qurrāʾ*[41] and middle-aged men rendered the oath of allegiance to him to fight al-Ḥajjāj and disavow ʿAbd al-Malik; and a Jahḍamī of al-Azd called ʿUqbah b. ʿAbd al-Ghāfir,[42] who was a Companion, jumped up and gave the oath of allegiance to ʿAbd al-Raḥmān, being strong in his conviction of the rightness of fighting al-Ḥajjāj. Al-Ḥajjāj entrenched himself against [ʿAbd al-Raḥmān],[43] and ʿAbd al-Raḥmān entrenched himself against al-Baṣrah. ʿAbd al-Raḥmān's entry into al-Baṣrah took place at the end of Dhū al-Ḥijjah 81 (mid-February 701).

[1063]

---

39. On the Dujayl river between al-Ahwāz and Tustar (see Le Strange, *Lands of the Eastern Caliphate*, p. 237, and *EI*², s.v. ʿAskar Mukram).

40. Cf. n. 32 above.

41. Generally held to have been Qurʾān reciters (see *EI*², s.v. Ḳurrāʾ). For a detailed discussion of these particular Baṣran *qurrāʾ*, see Sayed, *Revolte*, chap. v.

42. Sayed, *Revolte*, p. 350.

43. Where al-Ṭabarī has *ʿalayhi*, Ibn al-Athīr has *ʿalā nafsihi*.

Sulaymān b. ʿAbd al-Malik led the pilgrimage in this year: This is what Aḥmad b. Thābit related to me on the authority of he who mentioned it on the authority of Isḥāq b. ʿĪsā on the authority of Abū Maʿshar; and so too said al-Wāqidī. He (sc. al-Wāqidī) [also] said: Ibn Abī Dhiʾb[44] was born in this year; the governor of Medina in this year was Abān b. ʿUthmān;[45] over Iraq and the East was al-Ḥajjāj b. Yūsuf; over the military affairs (*ḥarb*) of Khurasan was al-Muhallab, and over its taxation (*kharāj*) was al-Mughīrah b. al-Muhallab,[46] [both of these being appointees acting] on behalf of al-Ḥajjāj; in charge of the judiciary of al-Kūfah was Abū Burdah b. Abī Mūsā,[47] and in charge of the judiciary of al-Baṣrah was ʿAbd al-Raḥmān b. Udhaynah.[48]

---

44. A traditionist who died in 158 (774) or 159 (775) (Ibn Ḥajar, *Tahdhīb*, vol. IX, p. 306).

45. A son of the Caliph ʿUthmān b. ʿAffān (see *EI²*, s.v.).

46. *EI²*, s.v. (Banū) ʾl-Muhallab (forthcoming).

47. *EI²*, s.v. al-Ashʿarī.

48. ʿAbd al-Raḥān b. Udhaynah b. al-Ḥārith al-ʿAbdī (see Caskel, *Ğamharat an-nasab*, register; Wakīʿ, *Akhbār al-quḍāh*, vol. I, pp. 304–7).

The
Events of the Year
82
(February 15, 701–February 3, 702)

[Operations at al-Baṣrah and al-Kūfah]

Among the events of this year were the battles that took place between al-Ḥajjāj and ʿAbd al-Raḥmān b. Muḥammad at al-Zāwiyah.

According to Hishām b. Muḥammad—Abū Mikhnaf—Abū al-Zubayr al-Hamdānī: ʿAbd al-Raḥmān's entry into al-Baṣrah took place at the end of Dhū al-Ḥijjah, and they fought in Muḥarram of the year 82 (February–March 702). They came together one day, and their fighting intensified. Then the Iraqis defeated [the Syrians], forcing them back to al-Ḥajjāj and fighting them in their trenches. The defeat of the whole of Quraysh and Thaqīf was such that ʿUbayd b. Mawhab, the mawlā and secretary of al-Hajjāj, said (ṭawīl):

Al-Barāʾ and his cousin Muṣʿab fled,
    and Quraysh fled, but for Āl Saʿīd.[49]

---

49. Cf. al-Balādhurī, *AAC*, p. 347, where it is clear that al-Ḥajjāj's relatives al-Barāʾ b. Qabīṣah b. Abī Aqīl and Muṣʿab b. ʿAbdallāh b. Abī ʿAqīl are meant; the Banū Saʿīd in question were probably the descendants of Saʿīd b. al-ʿĀṣ al-Umawī (see the reference to ʿAnbasah b. Saʿīd on p. 348).

Then they came together at the end of al-Muḥarram, on the day
when the Iraqis defeated the Syrians: The [Syrian] right and left
wings turned back, their spears were in disarray, and their [front]
line was routed, to the extent that [the Iraqis] drew near to us.
When al-Ḥajjāj saw that, he fell to his knees, drew his sword a
span, and said, "How admirable Muṣ'ab was! How noble he was
when there overtook him what overtook him, and I know, by
God, that he did not wish to flee."

He (sc. Abū al-Zubayr) said: I signaled to my father with my eye
to give me permission to smite [al-Ḥajjāj] with my sword, and he
signaled back firmly [that I should not], and I kept still. Then I
happened to turn, and, lo and behold, Sufyān b. al-Abrad al-
Kalbī[50] had attacked them and defeated them on the right wing.
So I said, "Rejoice, O amīr, for God has defeated the enemy." He
said to me, "Stand up and look," so I stood up and looked and
said, "God has defeated them." He said, "Stand up, Ziyād, and
look"; so Ziyād stood up and looked and said, "It's true, God has
certainly caused you to prosper; they have been defeated." And al-
Ḥajjāj cast himself down in prostration. When I returned, my
father reviled me and said, "Did you want to kill me and my
family?"

The following were killed in the battle: 'Abd al-Raḥmān b.
'Awsajah Abū Sufyān al-Nihmī[51] and 'Uqbah b. 'Abd al-Ghāfir al-
Azdī al-Jahḍamī,[52] among those *qurrā'* who were all killed in the
same place; 'Abdallāh b. Rizām al-Ḥārithī;[53] al-Mundhir b. al-
Jārūd;[54] and 'Abdallāh b. 'Āmir b. Misma'.[55] The head of this last-
named was brought to al-Ḥajjāj, who said, "I do not think that
this [fellow] left me in order to have his head brought to me."

Sa'īd b. Yaḥyā b. Sa'īd b. al-'Āṣ[56] fought a duel on that day with a

[1065]

---

50. Caskel, *Ǧamharat an-nasab*, register.

51. Sayed, *Revolte*, p. 357 (wrongly an-Nuhmī).

52. See above, n. 42.

53. This cannot be right, for we find him alive and well below (p. 25). It can be
noted that Mss. O and B (as well as al-Balādhurī, *AAC*, p. 346) omit the words *b.
Rizām . . . al-Mundhir b. al-Jārūd . . . 'Abd Allāh b.*

54. This cannot be al-Mundhir b. al-Jārūd, who had already been dead for twenty
years (Caskel, *Ǧamharat an-nasab*, register, and cf. preceding note); possibly one
of his sons is meant (cf. below, p. 69, where his son Bishr is killed at Maskin).

55. Cf. above, p. 11 and n. 38.

56. Al-Umawī (Caskel, *Ǧamharat an-nasab*, register).

man who killed him; they claimed that he was a mawlā of al-Faḍl[57] b. 'Abbās b. Rabī'ah b. al-Ḥārith b. 'Abd al-Muṭṭalib,[58] a brave man called Nuṣayr. [Al-Ḥajjāj] had earlier criticized his gait, and, when he saw him going about between the [battle] lines, he said, "Never again shall I criticize him for this gait."

Al-Ṭufayl b. 'Āmir b. Wāthilah was killed.[59] It was he who had said in Fārs, while advancing on al-Ḥajjāj with 'Abd al-Raḥmān from Kirmān (ṭawīl):[60]

[The phantom of] Janūb[61] paid us a night visit at
    al Ghariyyān,[62] after we,
    the distance being long, had become fatigued.
They (that is, our troops) have come to you leading the fates;
    our vanguard[63] has been guided to you by [your] sins.
[1066] There is no good on earth for anyone who does not have
    a share from God in the world to come.
Inform al-Ḥajjāj that there has drawn near to him
    chastisement that will strike [him] through
    the hands of the believers.
When we come to the two miṣrs (that is, al-Baṣrah and
    al-Kūfah), Muḥammad[64] will flee,
    but flight will not save the son of the accursed one.

[Al-Ḥajjāj] said [when he learned of al-Ṭufayl's death], "The fate [which you wanted for us] is a matter which God knew you to be more deserving of. He hastened it for you in this world and will chastise you in the next."

[The Iraqis] were defeated, and 'Abd al-Raḥmān set off toward al-Kūfah, followed by those Kūfans who were with him and the

---

57. Following the *Addenda et Emendanda.*
58. A Hāshimī who had been killed in 63 (683) (Caskel, *Ğamharat an-nasab,* register).
59. For his father, see above, n. 4.
60. The fourth of the following verses is given also by al-Balādhurī (*AAC,* p. 346).
61. I am grateful to Professor Iḥsān 'Abbās for pointing out to me that this is to be read as a woman's name; her identity, however, remains unclear.
62. "Two well-known buildings in El-Koofeh, at El-Thaweeyeh, where is the tomb of 'Alee, the Prince of the Faithful, asserted to have been built by one of the Kings of El-Ḥeereh" (Lane, *Lexicon,* p. 2254b). See the discussion by Fahd, *Le panthéon de l'Arabie centrale,* p. 91–94.
63. Preferring *ūlānā to awlānā.*
64. The son of al-Ḥajjāj (cf. below, p. 48).

strongest of the Baṣran horsemen. When he had gone, the Baṣrans flocked to ʿAbd al-Raḥmān b. ʿAbbās b. Rabīʿah b. al-Ḥārith b. ʿAbd al-Muṭṭalib[65] and swore allegiance to him. For five nights he fought al-Ḥajjāj with them; it was the fiercest fighting the people had seen. Then he went off and joined Ibn al-Ashʿath, and was followed and joined by a group of Baṣrans. There also went out [of al-Baṣrah] al-Ḥarīsh b. Hilāl al-Saʿdī,[66] from the Banū Anf al-Nā-qah,[67] who was wounded; he went to Safawān[68] and died of his wound. [Also] killed was Ziyād b. Muqātil b. Mismaʿ,[69] from the Banū Qays b. Thaʿlabah, who was in command of the *khums*[70] of Bakr b. Wāʾil with Ibn al-Ashʿath and was over the infantry. His daughter[71] Ḥamīdah stood up and lamented him, saying (*mutaqārib*):

[1067]

Ziyād defended his two banners,
    and the protector of the Banū al-ʿAnbar fled.[72]

Al-Baltaʿ[73] al-Saʿdī came and heard her lamenting her father and stigmatizing the Tamīmī. He had been selling clarified butter at al-Mirbad;[74] he left his clarified butter with his friends, came until he stood beneath her, and said (*mutaqārib*):

Why do you blame one who did not commit blameworthy
    actions?
May the night be long for a marriageable young lady such
    as you!

---

65. Al-Hāshimī (Caskel, *Ğamharat an-nasab*, register).

66. Who had earlier been a Tamīmī leader of importance in Khurasan (Caskel, loc. cit.).

67. I.e., the Banū Jaʿfar b. Qurayʿ b. ʿAwf of Saʿd/Tamīm (see Caskel, *Ğamharat an-nasab*, vol. I, chart 77).

68. A place one day's journey from al-Baṣrah on the road to the Ḥijāz (Yāqūt, *Muʿjam*, vol. III, pp. 98–99).

69. Crone, *Slaves on Horses*, p. 117.

70. One of the "fifths" into which the Baṣran fighting men were divided (Pellat, *Le milieu baṣrien*, p. 23).

71. According to al-Balādhurī, *AAC*, p. 351, she was Ḥamīdah (or Ḥumaydah) bt. Muqātil, i.e., the *sister* of Ziyād.

72. *Rāyatayhi*, "banners": al-Balādhurī, *AAC*, p. 351, reads *qawmihi*. Reading *muḥāmī* "protector," with *AAC* (rather than *judayy*,"small kid," with al-Ṭabarī), since al-Ḥarīsh was not himself a member of the Banū al-ʿAnbar.

73. The pointing is lacking or impressionistic; the name could also be al-Balīgh or al-Nābigh or al-Tabīʿ.

74. The Baṣran halting place for caravans (*EI²*, s.v. [forthcoming]).

If the spear point destroyed your father,
   the horses may reach he who was in flight
   (that is, the father)
And they may butt under the dust
   one who was not innocent[75] and had no excuse.
We defended the standard of al-Ḥarīsh,
   while the standard of the Banū Jaḥdar[76] went astray.

[1068]   ʿĀmir b. Wāthilah said, elegizing his son Ṭufayl (basīṭ):

Ṭufayl left care weighing upon me and departed this life,
   and that has crushed my strength signally.
I shall never forget the two sons of Sumayyah,[77]
   whatever else I may forget, [the loss of] each of
   whom was for me a source of fatigue.
The fates [earlier] missed me, not trying to come
   forward to me
   until my old age, when they left me with nothing.
After Ṭufayl I have become as one from whom the waters
   have dried up and the water has disappeared into
   the earth,[78]
One who has no camel to ride in the land and who,
   if he strives in the track of him who has escaped
   him, becomes weary.
There arose from the land of Khāqān,[79] which the sons
[1069]   of Fārs had subjugated like lions[80] in their squadrons,[81]
And from Sijistān a web of circumstances rendered attractive
   to you by fate, perdition brought for you
Until you reached the basins of death and the squadrons
   went away from you, leaving no one behind [alive].

---

75. *Al-barī: Al-shahīd,* "martyred," is given as a variant.

76. The Masāmiʿah were descendants of Jaḥdar b. Ḍubayʿah (Crone, *Slaves on Horses,* p. 116).

77. Presumably, the poet's wife.

78. The text has *al-miyāh,* "waters," while Ibn al-Athīr gives *al-suyūl,* "the floods." Reading *aw naḍabā,* "disappeared into the earth," as given by manuscripts O and B.

79. A title used by the Turks to signify "[supreme] ruler" (*EI*[2], s.v. Khāḳān).

80. Reading *ghulubā* in place of the *ghalabā* given by the editor.

81. *Fī arbāʿihā:* see Ibn Manẓūr, *Lisān al-ʿarab,* vol. XIX, p. 20, who gives the definition *jamāʿāt min al-nās.*

They left you felled, a hostage to the battlefield,
    where you see the vultures in groups over the dead.
They made a compact and then did not fulfill what
    they had undertaken,
    [instead] handing the captives and the plunder
    over to the enemy.
What a disgrace it is for a people when their women
    are taken captive,
    when they are numerous and they experience
    disgrace and destitution!

According to Abū Mikhnaf—Hishām b. Ayyūb b. ʿAbd al-Raḥmān b. Abī ʿAqīl: Al-Ḥajjāj stayed put for the rest of al-Muḥarram and the beginning of Ṣafar. Then he appointed over al-Baṣrah Ayyūb b. al-Ḥakam b. Abī ʿAqīl.[82] Ibn al-Ashʿath went to al-Kūfah, where al-Ḥajjāj had left in charge ʿAbd al-Raḥmān b. ʿAbdallāh b. ʿĀmir al-Ḥaḍramī, a confederate (ḥalīf) of Ḥarb b. Umayyah.[83]

Abū Mikhnaf said: As Yūnus b. Abī Isḥāq related it to me, he was in command of four thousand Syrians.

Abū Mikhnaf said: Sahm b. ʿAbd al-Raḥmān al-Juhanī related to me that there were two thousand of them. Ḥanẓalah b. al-Warrād al-Tamīmī,[84] from the Banū Riyāḥ b. Yarbūʿ, and Ibn ʿAttāb b. Warqāʾ[85] were over al-Madāʾin, while Maṭar b. Nājiyah,[86] from the Banū Yarbūʿ, was in charge of the maʿūnah.[87] When [news of] the Ibn al-Ashʿath affair reached [Maṭar b. Nājiyah], he advanced until he came near to al-Kūfah. Ibn al-Ḥaḍramī fortified himself in the citadel, and the Kūfans rose up with Maṭar b. Nājiyah

[1070]

---

82. Here, and below (pp. 46, 130), "Ayyūb b. al-Ḥakam" should be taken to signify "al-Ḥakam b. Ayyūb" (see above, n. 37, and cf. Khalīfah, *Taʾrīkh*, pp. 295, 314).

83. The text gives ʿAbd al-Raḥmān b. ʿAbd al-Raḥmān b. ʿAbdallāh b. ʿĀmir, but the second "ʿAbd al-Raḥmān" appears to have arisen by dittography (cf. Ms O; al-Balādhurī, *AAC*, p. 353; Crone, *Slaves on Horses*, p. 132).

84. About whom al-Ṭabarī has nothing else to say.

85. Presumably Khālid b. ʿAttāb (see the index to the Ṭabarī text and Caskel, *Ǧamharat an-nasab*, register).

86. Caskel, loc. cit.

87. The exact responsibilities of such an appointment at this time remain unclear; they may have included fiscal duties, in addition to general administration and/or the maintenance of law and order (see *EI*², s.v. [forthcoming]).

against Ibn al-Ḥaḍramī and the Syrians who were with him. [Maṭar] besieged him, and they offered peace with him in return for getting out and leaving him the citadel; so he made peace with them.

Abū Mikhnaf said: Yūnus b. Abī Isḥāq related to me that he saw them coming down from the citadel in haste. The door of the citadel was opened for Maṭar b. Nājiyah, the people crowded up to it, and Maṭar was crushed against it.[88] He drew his sword and with it smote the lip of one of the mules of the Syrians; then he cast its lip aside and entered the citadel. The people gathered to him, and he gave them two hundred dirhams [each].

Yūnus said: I saw [the dirhams] being divided among them; Abū al-Saqr[89] was among those who were given them. [Then] Ibn al-Ashʿath came in defeat to al-Kūfah, followed thither by the people.

Abū Jaʿfar said: In this year, according to one [of the authorities], there took place between al-Ḥajjāj and Ibn al-Ashʿath the battle of Dayr al-Jamājim. Al-Wāqidī said: The battle of Dayr al-Jamājim was in Shaʿbān of this year (September–October 701). Others have said that it took place in the year 83.

The Reason for Ibn al-Ashʿath's Progress to Dayr al-Jamājim and [the Battle] between Him and al-Ḥajjāj

According to Hishām—Abū Mikhnaf—Abū al-Zubayr al-Ham-dānī al-Arḥabī: I had sustained a wound. The Kūfans went out to receive Ibn al-Ashʿath when he came, and received him after he had crossed the Zabārā[90] bridge. As he was drawing near to it, he said to me, "I'd be grateful if you would turn off the road, so that the people will not see your wound. I don't want the wounded to receive them." I did so,[91] and the people entered al-Kūfah.

[1071]

---

88. According to al-Balādhurī, *AAC*, p. 353, he was crushed against the door by a mule.

89. If this is how the name is to be read.

90. Yāqūt (*Muʿjam*, vol. II, p. 912) knew this as a place ("I think it was one of the *nawāḥī* of al-Kūfah") mentioned in connection with the Qarāmiṭah in the time of al-Muqtadir (see de Goeje, *Mémoire sur les Carmathes*,[2] p. 97).

91. Reading *faʿaltu*, as proposed in the *Addenda et Emendanda*.

When he entered al-Kūfah, all the Kūfans inclined to him—
Hamdān got to him first[92]—and surrounded him at the residence
of ʿAmr b. Ḥurayth, except for a group from Tamīm which was
not great in number; these last had gone to Maṭar b. Nājiyah and
had wanted to fight for him, but were unable to take on the
people. ʿAbd al-Raḥmān called for ladders of various kinds,[93] and
these were placed in position so that the people might climb up
the citadel; they did this and took [Maṭar], who was brought to
ʿAbd al-Raḥmān and said to him, "Spare me, for I am the worthiest of your horsemen and the most able of them to replace you."
[ʿAbd al-Raḥmān] ordered that he be imprisoned. Then he called
for him subsequently and pardoned him, and Maṭar rendered the
oath of allegiance to him. The people entered into [ʿAbd al-
Raḥmān's] presence and rendered the oath of allegiance to him.
The Baṣrans came to him, and the strongpoints and frontier ways
of access fell to him; among those Baṣrans who came to him was
ʿAbd al-Raḥmān b. al-ʿAbbās b. Rabīʿah b. al-Ḥārith b. ʿAbd al-
Muṭṭalib—so he was known—who had fought al-Ḥajjāj for three
[nights][94] at al-Baṣrah after the exodus of Ibn al-Ashʿath. [News of]
that reached ʿAbd al-Malik, who said, "May God fight ʿUdayy al-
Raḥmān![95] He has fled, and some of the young men of Quraysh   [1072]
have fought for three [nights] after him."

Al-Ḥajjāj set off from al-Baṣrah and went through the land until
he passed between al-Qādisiyyah and al-ʿUdhayb.[96] [The Iraqis]
prevented him from stopping at al-Qādisiyyah: ʿAbd al-Raḥmān b.
Muḥammad b. al-Ashʿath sent against him ʿAbd al-Raḥmān b.
al-ʿAbbās with a large force made up of cavalry from the two *miṣrs*
(that is, al-Baṣrah and al-Kūfah), and they prevented him from
stopping at al-Qādisiyyah. Then they kept pace with him until
they came out at the top of Wādī al-Sibāʿ;[97] they kept pace with

---

92. Al-Balādhurī, *AAC*, p. 356, notes that they were his maternal uncles (see
also above, p. 7, and below, note 237).

93. So rendering *al-salālim wa-al-ʿajal*.

94. Cf. above (p. 17), where we are told that he had fought him for five nights.

95. Literally, "the small enemy of the Merciful," this being a play on the name
ʿAbd al-Raḥmān, "the servant of the Merciful."

96. To the south-southwest of al-Kūfah. For discussion of their exact location,
see *EI*², s.v. al-Ḳādisiyya (p. 384b).

97. Which receives passing attention from Yāqūt (*Muʿjam*, vol. IV, p. 876) as one
of the *nawāḥī* of al-Kūfah.

each other until al-Ḥajjāj stopped at Dayr Qurrah[98] and ʿAbd al-Raḥmān b. al-ʿAbbās stopped at Dayr al-Jamājim.[99] Then Ibn al-Ashʿath came and stopped at Dayr al-Jamājim, while al-Ḥajjāj was [still] at Dayr Qurrah. Al-Ḥajjāj used to say subsequently, "Couldn't ʿAbd al-Raḥmān augur from the birds when he saw that I had stopped at Dayr Qurrah and he had stopped at Dayr al-Jamājim?"[100]

There gathered together at Dayr al-Jamājim the Kūfans, the Baṣrans, the people of the frontier ways of access and the strongpoints, and the *qurrāʾ* of the two *miṣr*s. They were unanimous in making war on al-Ḥajjāj, being united in that by their hatred and loathing of him. They were at that time one hundred thousand stipendiary fighting men, accompanied by a like number of their mawlās.

Al-Ḥajjāj's reinforcements from ʿAbd al-Malik had come to him before he stopped at Dayr Qurrah; before stopping there, he had wanted to go up to Hīt[101] and the area of the Jazīrah, out of a desire to be near[er] to Syria and the Jazīrah and so that he could be close to the *rafāghah*[102] of the price [of the foodstuffs] of the Jazīrah. But when he passed by Dayr Qurrah, he said, "This place isn't far from the Commander of the Faithful, and al-Falālīj[103] and ʿAyn al-Tamr[104] are nearby"; and he stopped there and entrenched himself in his camp, [just as] Ibn Muḥammad had in his.

[1073] The people would make sorties every day and fight, while at the same time advancing their trenches toward each other; and the fighting intensified. When [news of] that reached the heads of Quraysh and the Syrians with ʿAbd al-Malik and his mawlās, they said, "If the only thing that will please the people of Iraq is the

---

98. Yāqūt, *Muʿjam*, vol. II, p. 685, where its location is described simply as "opposite Dayr al-Jamājim"; also *EI²*, s.v. Dayr Ḳurra.

99. Yāqūt, *Muʿjam*, vol. II, p. 652, where it is said to have been seven parasangs from al-Kūfah. For further details, see *EI²*, s.v. Dayr al-Djamādjim; and Sayed, *Revolte*, p. 211.

100. Dayr Qurrah means literally "the monastery of satisfaction," while Dayr al-Jamājim means literally "the monastery of the skulls" (for all that other explanations are volunteered).

101. An Iraqi town situated on the right bank of the Euphrates and generally regarded as the border town between Iraq and the Jazīrah (*EI²*, s.v. al-Djazīra).

102. "Ampleness, or abundance, of the means of subsistence" (Lane, *Lexicon*, p. 1124c); presumably, "cheapness" is meant here (cf. below, n. 109).

103. According to Yāqūt (*Muʿjam*, vol. III, p. 908), the *falālīj* of the Sawād were its villages.

104. A settlement some eighty miles to the west of al-Kūfah (see *EI²*, s.v.).

removal of al-Ḥajjāj from them, that is easier than fighting them; so remove him from them, and that will secure obedience and spare our blood and theirs." [At this, 'Abd al-Malik] sent his son 'Abdallāh b. 'Abd al-Malik to his brother, Muḥammad b. Marwān, [who was] in the territory of al-Mawṣil, ordering him to come to him. Both joined him, with their armies, and he ordered them to put it to the people of Iraq that al-Ḥajjāj would be removed from them, that they would be assigned the same stipends as those assigned to the Syrians, and that Ibn Muḥammad could stop in any part of Iraq he wished and could be governor of it for as long as he wished and as long as 'Abd al-Malik was ruler.[105] If they accepted this, al-Ḥajjāj would be dismissed and Muḥammad b. Marwān would be amīr of Iraq; and if they refused to accept it, al-Ḥajjāj would [remain] amīr of the Syrian army and war commander, with Muḥammad b. Marwān and 'Abdallāh b. 'Abd al-Malik responsible to him.[106]

No order ever came to al-Ḥajjāj that was harder or more vexatious and hurtful to him than this, on account of [his] fear that they would accept and he would be dismissed. He wrote to 'Abd al-Malik, "O Commander of the Faithful, if you present the Iraqis with my removal, it will not be long before they disobey you and go against you. That will simply make them bolder against you. Did you not see and hear of the uprising of the Iraqis with al-Ashtar against Ibn 'Affān? When he asked them what they wanted, they said, 'The removal of Saʿīd b. al-ʿĀṣ'; and, when he had removed him, the year was not out before they went to him and killed him.[107] It takes iron to cleave iron.[108] May God be propitious to you in your deliberations. Peace be upon you." 'Abd al-Malik[, however,] insisted on proposing these conditions to the Iraqis, desiring freedom from war.

[1074]

When [Muḥammad b. Marwān and 'Abdallāh b. 'Abd al-Malik] had joined up with al-Ḥajjāj, 'Abdallāh went forth and said, "O people of Iraq, I am 'Abdallāh, son of the Commander of the Faithful. He will give you such-and-such," and he mentioned the

---

105. *Wāliyan*: Ibn al-Athīr reads *khalīfatan*, "caliph."

106. Ibn Aʿtham, *Futūḥ*, vol. VII, p. 137, gives a different version: According to him, 'Abd al-Malik's offer to the Iraqis consisted of (i) the dismissal of al-Ḥajjāj, (ii) the evacuation of the Syrians, and (iii) the appointment over them of whomever they might want.

107. Cf. Hinds, "Kûfan Political Alignments," pp. 360–61.

108. Cf. Freytag, *Arabum Proverbia*, vol. I, pp. 9–10.

conditions which we have mentioned. [Then] Muḥammad b. Marwān said, "I am the messenger of the Commander of the Faithful to you, and he proposes to you such-and-such," and he mentioned these conditions.

They said, "We shall come back this evening," and went back and joined Ibn al-Ashʿath. Every single commander, chief, and horseman came to him. Ibn al-Ashʿath praised God and then said, "To continue: You have been presented with something which, if you take it today, [appears to be] an opportunity, and I am not sure that it will tomorrow [prove to] be a [matter for] regret for one possessed of insight. You are today all square [with them]. If they take al-Zāwiyah into account [against you], you may take the battle day of Tustar into account against them. Accept what they have offered you while you are mighty and strong, while the [Syrians] are fearful of you and you are still able to look down on them; and, by God, you will remain bold against them and mighty in their eyes if you accept, forever, as long as you live."

[1075]   The people rose up on every side and said, "God has destroyed them. They are in a state of anguish, distress, famine, dearth, and abasement, while we have large numbers, [foodstuffs at] a cheap[109] price, and supplies nearby. No, by God, we shall not accept." And they repeated their disavowal of [ʿAbd al-Malik]. The first to do so at al-Jamājim were ʿAbdallāh b. Dhuʾāb and ʿUmayr b. Tayḥān. Their disavowal of him at al-Jamājim was more united than it had been in Fārs. [At this], Muḥammad b. Marwān and ʿAbdallāh b. ʿAbd al-Malik returned to al-Ḥajjāj and said, "Your camp and your army are your affair, so do as you think best. We have been ordered to heed and obey you." He said, "I told you that none other than the two of you are wanted for this command." Then he said, "I shall fight for you, and my authority is yours," and, whenever they met him, they greeted him as the amīr; [however,] it has been claimed by Abū Yazīd al-Saksakī that he also greeted them as amīrs when he met them. They let him get on with the war, which he took charge of.

According to Abū Mikhnaf—al-Kalbī, Muḥammad b. al-Sāʾib: When the people gathered at al-Jamājim, I heard ʿAbd al-Raḥmān b. Muḥammad say, "The Banū Marwān are reviled on account of

---

109. *Al-rafīgh* (cf. above, n. 102): Ibn al-Athīr reads *al-rakhīṣ*.

[their] blue-eyed (that is, non-Arab) [mother].[110] By God, they have a lineage no better than that; and the Banū Abī al-ʿĀs[111] [are worse still, being] *aʿlāj*[112] from the people of Saffūriyyah![113] If this matter (that is, the caliphate) is among Quraysh, then I can adduce an origin from Quraysh,[114] and, if it is among the Arabs, I am the son of al-Ashʿath b. Qays!"[115] He said this at the top of his voice, to make the people hear.

They went forth to fight. Al-Ḥajjāj placed over his right wing ʿAbd al-Raḥmān b. Sulaym al-Kalbī,[116] over his left wing ʿUmārah   [1076]
b. Tamīm al-Lakhmī,[117] over his cavalry Sufyān b. al-Abrad al-Kalbī,[118] and over his infantry ʿAbd al-Raḥmān[119] b. Ḥabīb[120] al-Ḥakamī. Ibn al-Ashʿath placed over his right wing al-Ḥajjāj b. Jāriyah al-Khathʿamī,[121] over his left wing al-Abrad b. Qurrah al-Tamīmī,[122] over his cavalry ʿAbd al-Raḥmān b. ʿAbbās b. Rabīʿah b. al-Ḥārith al-Hāshimī,[123] over his infantry Muḥammad b. Saʿd b. Abī Waqqāṣ,[124] and over his cataphracts ʿAbdallāh b. Rizām al-Ḥārithī.[125] He placed Jabalah b. Zaḥr b. Qays al-Juʿfī—who was accompanied by fifteen men from Quraysh—over the *qurrāʾ*, among whom were ʿĀmir al-Shaʿbī, Saʿīd b. Jubayr, Abū al-Bakhtarī, and ʿAbd al-Raḥmān b. Abī Laylā.[126]

---

110. *Al-zarqāʾ*: see Glossarium, p. CCLXXVII.

111. On this Qurashī group, see *EI²*, suppl., s.v. Aʿyāṣ.

112. Singular *ʿilj*, a term signifying a man who is strong, sturdy, non-Arab, and an unbeliever.

113. A district in al-Urdunn, near al-Ṭabariyyah (Yāqūt, *Muʿjam*, vol. III, p. 402). For some of the background to this piece of abuse, see Crone, *Meccan Trade*, p. 102, n. 70.

114. *Fa-ʿannī fuqiʾat* (or *taqawwabat*) *bayḍat Quraysh*. His grandmother, the wife of al-Ashʿath, was a sister of Abū Bakr's (*EI²*, s.v. al-Ashʿath).

115. Cf. Ibn Aʿtham's (somewhat similar) version of this outburst (*Futūḥ*, vol. VII, p. 140).

116. Crone, *Slaves on Horses*, pp. 130–31.

117. Ibid., p. 140.

118. See above, n. 50.

119. "ʿAbdallāh" according to Mss. O and B, as well as Ibn al-Athīr.

120. "Khubayb" according to Ibn al-Athīr.

121. Caskel, *Ğamharat an-nasab*, register.

122. Crone, *Slaves on Horses*, pp. 112–13.

123. See above, n. 65.

124. Who, oddly, does not figure in Ibn al-Kalbī's *Jamharah*; see the index to al-Ṭabarī's text.

125. For all that we have been told above (p. 15 and n. 53) that he had been killed at the battle of al-Zāwiyah; he also reappears below (pp. 39, 43).

126. See the list of *qurrāʾ* provided by Sayed (*Revolte*, pp. 35off., nos. 44, 15, 14, 23, and 17, respectively).

Then they began to engage each other every day and to fight. The supplies of the Iraqis came to them from al-Kūfah and its Sawād, and they were abundantly provided for as they wanted, [both the Kūfans] and their brethren the Baṣrans. The Syrians[, on the other hand,] were in dire straits: Prices went up to their disadvantage, food supplies became scarce for them, and they lacked meat; it was as if they were under siege. But, for all that, they took on the Iraqis throughout the day, fighting very fiercely. First al-Ḥajjāj would advance his trench, and then [the Iraqis] would [advance theirs, and so it went on] until the day on which Jabalah b. Zaḥr was struck down; then ['Abd al-Raḥmān] sent [word] to Kumayl b. Ziyād al-Nakha'ī,[127] who was a grave man, steadfast in war, possessed of courage, and a voice among the people. His (that is, Jabalah's) squadron was called "The Squadron of the Qurrā'." When attacked, they would scarcely move, and, when attacking, they would not retreat; they were known for that. One day, they made a sortie as usual, and the people made a sortie with them. Al-Ḥajjāj deployed his companions and then marched among his battle ranks. Ibn Muḥammad made a sortie with seven battle ranks, one after another. Al-Ḥajjāj deployed against Jabalah b. Zaḥr's squadron of *qurrā'* three squadrons, over which he placed al-Jarrāḥ b. 'Abdallāh al-Ḥakamī;[128] they advanced against them.

[1077]

Abū Mikhnaf said: Abū Yazīd al-Saksakī related to me: I, by God, was among the cavalry deployed against Jabalah b. Zaḥr. We attacked him and his companions three times, one attack per squadron, and, by God, we found them in no way wanting.

[The Death of al-Mughīrah b. al-Muhallab]

In this year al-Mughīrah b. al-Muhallab[129] died in Khurasan.

According to 'Alī b. Muḥammad—al-Mufaḍḍal b. Muḥammad: Al-Mughīrah b. al-Muhallab was his father's deputy at Marw over the whole of his province; then he died in Rajab 82 (August–September 701). The news reached Yazīd [b. al-Muhallab], and the army learned of it, but they did not inform al-Muhallab. Yazīd

---

127. See Sayed's list, p. 357, no. 27.
128. *EI²*, s.v. al-Djarrāḥ b. 'Abd Allāh; Crone, *Slaves on Horses*, pp. 132–33.
129. See above, n. 46.

wanted to let [al-Muhallab] know, so he instructed the women to cry out. Al-Muhallab said, "What is this?" and he was told, "al-Mughīrah has died." At this, he exclaimed, "Verily to God we belong, and verily unto Him we return!" and he grieved until his grief became apparent upon him and one of his intimates took him to task. He summoned Yazīd and sent him to Marw, having advised him as to what he should do, while his tears poured down onto his beard. Al-Ḥajjāj wrote to al-Muhallab, offering his condolences in respect of al-Mughīrah, who had been a *sayyid*. On the day when al-Mughīrah died, al-Muhallab was stationed at Kish[130] in Transoxania, for the purpose of making war on its people.

[1078]

['Alī b. Muḥammad] continued: Yazīd went off with sixty—also put at seventy—horsemen, including Mujjāʿah b. ʿAbd al-Raḥmān al-ʿAtakī, ʿAbdallāh b. Muʿammar b. Shumayr[131] al-Yashkurī, Dīnār al-Sijistānī, al-Haytham b. al-Munakhkhal al-Jurmūzī, Ghazwān al-Iskāf the lord of Zamm[132]—who had converted to Islam at al-Muhallab's hand—Abū Muḥammad al-Zammī, and ʿAṭiyyah, [who was] a mawlā of ʿAtīk. They were encountered in the desert of Nasaf by 150 Turks, who said to them, "Who are you?" and they replied, "Merchants." "Where are [your] loads?" asked [the Turks], and they replied, "We have sent them on ahead." "Well, give us something," said [the Turks]. Yazīd refused, but Mujjāʿah gave them a garment, some pieces of cloth, and a bow, and they departed. Then they acted treacherously and returned to them, and Yazīd said, "[There,] I knew best about them—fight them." The fighting between them intensified. Yazīd was on a horse near to the ground,[133] and with him was a Khārijī man whom he had taken [prisoner]. [This man] said [to him], "Allow me to live," and [Yazīd] acceded to that. Then he said to [the man], "What are you capable of?" and [the man] charged upon [the Turks] until he mingled with them; then he was behind them, having killed a man, then he rushed again and mingled with them until he came out in front of them, having killed [another] man; then he returned to Yazīd, who had [in the meantime] killed one of their lords and

---

130. *EI*[2], s.v.
131. Following the *Addenda et Emendanda*.
132. See below, n. 346.
133. Presumably, he was on a small horse or pony; Ibn al-Athīr omits the phrase.

been shot in the leg. [The Turks now] put on more pressure, and Abū Muḥammad al-Zammī fled; but Yazīd doggedly faced up to them, until they ultimately abstained from fighting [Yazīd and his companions]. They said, "We acted treacherously, but we shall not depart until either we all die, or you die, or you give us something."

[1079] Yazīd swore that he would not give them anything, but Mujjāʿah said, "For heaven's sake! Al-Mughīrah has perished, and you saw what an effect his death had on al-Muhallab. I beseech you by God not to be struck down today." [Yazīd] said [to him], "Al-Mughīrah did not exceed his allotted span, and I shall not exceed mine." Then Mujjāʿah threw them a yellow turban, and they took it and departed, [after which] Abū Muḥammad al-Zammī came with horsemen and food. Yazīd said to him, "You deserted us, O Abū Muḥammad," to which he replied, "I simply went off to bring reinforcements and food." The *rajaz* poet said:

Yazīd, you sword of Abū Saʿīd,[134]
    peoples and armies, together with
The throng on the gathering day which is witnessed, know
    that you, on the battle day with the Turks,
    are made of stern stuff.

And al-Ashqarī[135] said (*basīṭ*):

The Turks know, when [Yazīd] encounters their throngs,
    that they have met one who is [like] a meteor that
    dispels darkness,
[One accompanied] by young men like lions of the thicket,
    who know no refuge save patience and endurance.
We see streaks of blood covering the people,
    but I do not see any sign of them shrinking back
    or fearing to advance.
Beneath them are full-grown horses that endure the adversity
    that they (the riders) endure, until they (the horses)
    are shoed[136] with blood.
[1080] In the turmoil of death, until nighttime envelops them,
    neither side either flees or suffers defeat.

---

134. I.e., al-Muhallab.
135. Kaʿb b. Maʿdān al-Ashqarī (see Sezgin, *GAS*, vol. II, pp. 377–78).
136. Following the *Addenda et Emendanda*.

In this year al-Muhallab made peace with the people of Kish in return for tribute[137] and left it, heading for Marw.

The Reason for al-Muhallab's Departure from Kish

According to ʿAlī b. Muḥammad—al-Mufaḍḍal b. Muḥammad: Al-Muhallab was suspicious of some people from Muḍar. He accordingly imprisoned them and departed from Kish, leaving them [there]; he also left Ḥurayth b. Quṭbah, the mawlā of Khuzāʿah, saying to him, "When you have exacted the whole of the tribute, return the[ir] hostages to them." He crossed the river [Oxus] and, when he got to Balkh, he stopped there. He wrote to Ḥurayth, "I cannot be sure that, if you return the hostages to them, they will not attack you; accordingly, when you take possession of the tribute, do not set the hostages free until you reach Balkh territory." Ḥurayth said to the king of Kish, "Al-Muhallab has written to me [telling me] to detain the hostages until I reach Balkh territory." If you hasten [to let me have] what you owe, I shall hand your hostages over to you and go and tell him that his letter arrived after I had exacted the whole of what was owing and had handed the hostages over to you." [At this, the king] hastened [to pay] to [Ḥurayth and those with him the sum stipulated in] their peace agreement, and [Ḥurayth] returned to them those of them whom he held. [Ḥurayth] then set off and [was en route when he] was confronted by the Turks, who said, "Ransom yourself and those who are with you; we encountered Yazīd b. al-Muhallab, and he ransomed himself." Ḥurayth said, "Do you imagine that Yazīd's mother gave birth to me?" and he fought them and killed [some of] them and took prisoners, whom [the Turks] then ransomed; he treated them with favor, released them, and returned the ransom to them. His words, "Do you imagine that Yazīd's mother gave birth to me?" reached al-Muhallab, who said, "That slave is disdainful of [the idea] that he might have been born of his kinsmen,"[138] and he became angry.

[1081]

---

137. So rendering *fidyah* (see Wellhausen, *Kingdom*, p. 434).

138. So rendering *an talidahu raḥimuhu* (Ibn al-Athīr says *an talidahu ummu Yazīd*); it is difficult to understand what al-Ṭabarī's version is driving at here, since Ḥurayth was a mawlā of Khuzāʿah and not of al-Azd.

When [Ḥurayth] came to [al-Muhallab] at Balkh, the latter said to him "Where are the hostages?" [Ḥurayth] replied, "I took possession of what was owing and let them go." [Al-Muhallab] said, "Didn't I write to you [telling you] not to let them go?" "Your letter reached me after I had let them go," [Ḥurayth] replied, "and after I had been spared what you feared." "You are lying," said [al-Muhallab], "you approached them and their king, and you apprised him of my letter to you," and he ordered that [Ḥurayth] be stripped. The latter exhibited much distress at being stripped, to such an extent that al-Muhallab thought that he must have leprosy; then he stripped him and gave him thirty lashes. Ḥurayth said, "I should have preferred you to have given me three hundred lashes without having stripped me," out of modesty and shame at being stripped; and he swore that he would kill al-Muhallab.

Al-Muhallab rode forth one day, and Ḥurayth also rode. While he was going along behind al-Muhallab, he ordered two ghulāms[139] of his to smite him; one of them refused and left him and departed, while the other did not dare to advance on [al-Muhallab] on his own. When he returned, [Ḥurayth] said to his ghulām, "What prevented you from [attacking] him?" [The ghulām] replied, "Fear for you, by God. I did not fear for myself, by God. I knew that, if we killed him, both you and we would be killed. My consideration was for you: Had I known that you would be safe from being killed, I should have killed him."

[Alī b. Muḥammad] continued: Ḥurayth left off coming to al-Muhallab and made a show of being in pain. It reached al-Muhallab that he was feigning illness and that he wished to murder him, and he said to Thābit b. Quṭbah, "Bring me your brother, for he is to me as one of my sons. I did what I did to him only out of consideration for him and as a matter of discipline, just as I might give one of my sons a hiding in order to discipline him." Thābit accordingly came to his brother and besought him and asked him to ride to al-Muhallab. But he refused, being fearful of [al-Muhallab], and said, "I shall not go to him after he has done to me what he has done. I do not trust him, and he does not trust me." When his brother Thābit saw that, he said to him, "If that is

[1082]

---

139. This term has been translated as "young man" or "youth" when it clearly means no more than that, but has sometimes been left untranslated when some sort of servile or subservient status is implied (see *EI²*, s.v.).

your view, set forth with us to Mūsā b. ʿAbdallāh b. Khāzim," for Thābit feared that Ḥurayth would murder al-Muhallab and that they would then all be killed. They accordingly set forth with three hundred of their *shākiriyyah*[140] and Arab adherents.

Abū Jaʿfar said: In this year al-Muhallab b. Abī Ṣufrah died.

The Cause and Place of the Death [of al-Muhallab]

ʿAlī b. Muḥammad said: Al-Mufaḍḍal related to me: When he departed from Kish, al-Muhallab went off heading for Marw, and, when he was at Zāghūl[141] [in the territory of] Marw al-Rūdh, he was struck by pleurisy—some people say by plague.[142] He summoned Ḥabīb and those of his [other] sons who were present, called for some arrows that were tied in a bundle, and said, "Do you think that you could break these while they are gathered together?" They said, "No." He said, "Do you think that you could break them when they are separated?" They said, "Yes." He said, "Thus is the collective body (*jamāʿah*). My testamentary command to you is pious fear of God and [respect for] the bond of kinship. The bond of kinship prolongs the allotted span, multiplies wealth, and increases numbers. I forbid you the forsaking of relations, for that occasions [hell]fire and brings about abasement and destitution. Love one another, relate to one another in a friendly fashion, be united and not at variance, and do good for one another; in this way your affairs will be as one. When the sons of a single mother fall out with one another, what hope is there for the sons of co-wives?! Incumbent upon you are obedience and [respect for] the collective body. Let your good-doing be nobler than your words. I like it in a man that his action be superior to [what] his tongue [says]. When answering, be on your guard against slips of the tongue: A man's foot may slip, and he

[1083]

---

140. "Personal guard" (Barthold, *Turkestan*[3], p. 180); from Persian *chākar*, "servant."

141. Yāqūt (*Muʿjam*, vol. II, p. 907) knows it simply as one of the villages of Marw al-Rūdh, its only claim to fame being the presence there of al-Muhallab's tomb.

142. Following Lane in the rendering of *shawkah*; Dozy, however, defines it as "a painful ulcer, usually in the thumb" (*Supplément*, s.v.), which fits well with al-Yaʿqūbī's *akilah waqaʿat fī rijlihi*, "an ulcer which manifested itself in his foot" (*Buldān*, p. 299).

can recover himself; but his tongue may slip, and he can be destroyed. Acknowledge the entitlement of everyone who comes to you. A man's coming to you, whether in the morning or the evening, suffices to commend him to you. Prefer generosity to miserliness. Love the Arabs and do good [to them]. An Arab is a man to whom you can make [no more than] a promise and he will die in defense of you; how then [do you think] he will behave [if you have done him good]? In war, exercise patience together with trickery, which is more beneficial in war than courage. When the battle encounter takes place, [God's] decree domes down: If a man is resolute and then triumphs over his enemy, people say, 'He went about things head-on and then triumphed,' and he is praised; but if, after exercising patience, he does not triumph, people say, 'He was not remiss, nor did he throw away his chances, but [God's] decree prevailed.' Recite the Qur'ān and learn the established practices and the discipline of the virtuous. Beware of levity and of too much talking in your gatherings. I have deputed Yazīd over you and have put Ḥabīb in command of the army until he takes it to Yazīd. Do not oppose Yazīd."[143] Al-Mufaḍḍal said to him, "[Even] if you had not preferred him, we should have."

Al-Muhallab died, having made his testament to Ḥabīb. Ḥabīb prayed over him and then went to Marw. Yazīd wrote to 'Abd al-Malik with [news of] the death of al-Muhallab and his deputing of him; and al-Ḥajjāj confirmed him [in his position]. It is said that [al-Muhallab] said on the occasion of his death and testament, "If it were up to me, I should appoint Ḥabīb as the chief of my sons."

['Alī b. Muḥammad] said: He died in Dhū al-Ḥijjāh 82 (January 702); and Nahār b. Tawsi'ah al-Taymī[144] said (ṭawīl):

The campaigning that brought riches nigh has ended,
    and generosity and munificence have died
      after al-Muhallab.

[1084]

---

143. For another version of this *wasiyyah*, see Ibn A'tham, *Futūḥ*, vol. VII, pp. 119ff.

144. The text wrongly says "al-Tamīmī" (a common error on the part of copyists). On this poet, see Sezgin, *GAS*, vol. II, p. 379. The first two of the following verses are much cited: Cf., for example, al-Ṭabarī, *Ta'rīkh*, ser. ii, p. 1251 (below, p. 199); al-Zubayr b. Bakkār, *al-Akhbār al-muwaffaqiyyāt*, p. 386; Ibn 'Abd Rabbihi, *'Iqd*, vol. III, p. 298; Yāqūt, *Mu'jam*, vol. IV, p. 506; Ibn Khallikān, *Wafayāt al-a'yān*, vol. V, p. 354; Hinds, *Early Islamic Family*, par. 54.

They have stayed at Marw al-Rūdh as two pledges
     at his sepulcher
     and have been rendered totally absent from
     east and west.
If anyone says, "Who of all people most deserves
     a blessing?"
     we name him, without fear [of contradiction].
He made both flat and rugged territory available to us,
     with cavalry like flocks of swift sandgrouse,
Exposing them to the thrusting of spears until
     it was as if
     he were honoring them with dyed purple.
He is surrounded by Qaḥṭān, who have bound
     themselves to him,
     and by their allies from the tribe[s] of
     Bakr and Taghlib.
The two tribes of Maʿadd take refuge with his
     standard,
     offering themselves and their mothers and
     fathers as ransoms for him.

In this year al-Ḥajjāj b. Yūsuf appointed Yazīd b. al-Muhallab   [1085]
over Khurasan after the death of al-Muhallab.

In it, too, ʿAbd al-Malik dismissed Abān b. ʿUthmān[145] from
Medina. Al-Wāqidī said: He dismissed him from it on 13 Jumādā
II (25 July 701).

He (sc. al-Wāqidī) said: In it, too, ʿAbd al-Malik appointed Hishām b. Ismāʿīl al-Makhzūmī[146] over Medina. When he was appointed there, Hishām b. Ismāʿīl dismissed from the judiciary of
Medina Nawfal b. Musāḥiq al-ʿĀmirī,[147] who had been appointed
to that position by Yaḥyā b. al-Ḥakam; when Abān b. ʿUthmān
took over there after the dismissal of Yaḥyā, he confirmed
[Nawfal in his position] in charge of the judiciary. Abān's tenure
of office lasted seven years, three months, and thirteen nights.
When Hishām b. Ismāʿīl dismissed Nawfal b. Musāḥiq from the

---

145. See above, n. 45.
146. Caskel, *Ǧamharat an-nasab*, register; *EI²*, s.v. Makhzūm.
147. From ʿĀmir b. Luʾayy of Quraysh (Caskel, *Ǧamharat an-nasab*, register).

judiciary, he appointed in his place 'Amr b. Khālid al-Zuraqī.[148]

The leader of the pilgrimage in this year was Abān b. 'Uthmān: Thus it has been related to me by Aḥmad b. Thābit on the authority of him who mentioned it on the authority of Isḥāq b. 'Īsā on the authority of Abū Ma'shar. Over al-Kūfah and al-Baṣrah and the East was al-Ḥajjāj, while over Khurasan was Yazīd b. al-Muhallab, acting on behalf of al-Ḥajjāj.

---

148. 'Amr b. Khaldah al-Zuraqī according to Khalīfah (*Ta'rīkh*, p. 299 [and 'Umar b. Khuldah al-Z., according to the 1968 Damascus edition by Zakkār, p. 390]); the clan in question is presumably Zurayq b. 'Āmir of Khazraj of the Anṣār (see Caskel, *Ğamharat an-nasab*, chart 192, where a certain Khaldah b. 'Āmir is to be found, albeit without a son named 'Amr/'Umar).

The
Events of the Year

83

(FEBRUARY 4, 702–JANUARY 23, 703)

In it there took place the defeat of ʿAbd al-Raḥmān b. Muḥammad b. al-Ashʿath at Dayr al-Jamājim.

[1086]

The Cause of [Ibn al-Ashʿath's] Defeat

According to Hishām b. Muḥammad—Abū Mikhnaf—Abū al-Zubayr al-Hamdānī: I was among the cavalry of Jabalah b. Zaḥr. When the Syrians attacked him time after time, ʿAbd al-Raḥmān b. Abī Laylā, the specialist in religious law (faqīh), called to us, saying,[149] "O body of qurrāʾ, for no one is flight more unseemly than for you. I heard ʿAlī—may God raise his station among the virtuous and grant him the best reward of martyrs and those who are veracious—say on the day when we encountered the Syrians [at Ṣiffīn]: 'O Believers, he who sees aggression being committed and something disliked being enjoined and denies it in his heart, he is safe and secure; he who denies [it] with his tongue is rewarded, he being worthier than his companion [who simply de-

---

149. According to Ibn al-Athīr (and al-Maqrīzī—see the *Addenda et Emendanda*), it was Jabalah who said this, to ʿAbd al-Raḥmān and the qurrāʾ.

nied it in his heart]; and he who denies it with the sword, so that the Word of God may be uppermost and the word of the oppressors the lowest,[150] he is the one who achieves the path of right guidance, the one whose heart is illuminated with certainty.' So fight these innovators, who deem licit that which is illicit, who neither know nor acknowledge that which is right, and who have committed an aggression which they do not deny."

Abū al-Bakhtarī said, "Fight for your religion and for [this] world of yours. By God, if they triumph over you, they will corrupt your religion for you and take over your worldly interests."

Al-Sha'bī said, "O people of Islam, fight them. No harm will overtake you in fighting them. By God, I know of no people on the face of the earth more oppressive or tyrannical in rule than they. [1087] So hasten against them."

Sa'īd b. Jubayr said, "Fight them. You will not sin by fighting against them and their sins with [firm] intention and certitude. Fight against their tyranny in rule, their insolent behavior in [matters pertaining to] religion, their abasing of the weak, and their 'causing the death of' ritual prayer."[151]

According to Abū Mikhnaf—Abū al-Zubayr: We prepared to charge them, and Jabalah said to us, "When you charge them, make the charge a true one: Do not turn your faces away from them before you fall upon their line." [Abū al-Zubayr] continued: We charged them single-mindedly and strongly. We smote the three squadrons until they split up; then we went on until we fell on their line and smote them until we removed them from [their position]; then we withdrew and passed by Jabalah, fallen, and we did not know how he had been killed.

[Abū al-Zubayr] said: That shook us. We became faint-hearted and stopped where we were. Our *qurrā'* were numerous,[152] and

---

150. Cf. Qur'ān 9:40.

151. *Imatātihim al-ṣalāt*. Cf. Hawting, *First Dynasty of Islam*, p. 70, to which it may be added that it was known in Baṣran and Omani Ibāḍī circles of the late second/early third century A.H. that al-Ḥajjāj had sometimes delayed the Friday prayer until sunset, when the noon, afternoon, and sunset prayers were performed together (*al-Siyar wa-al-jawābāt li-'ulamā' wa-a'immat ahl 'Umān*, vol. I, pp. 291, 309–10 [the source being Abū Sufyān Maḥbūb b. al-Raḥīl]); and the seventeenth-century chronicler Ibn al-'Imād (*Shadharāt al-dhahab*, vol. I, p. 92) was aware that al-Ḥajjāj *kāna yumītu al-ṣalāt ḥattā yakhruja waqtuha*, literally, "he used to cause the death of ritual prayer until the [proper] time for its performance passed."

152. According to Ibn A'tham (*Futūḥ*, vol. VII, p. 139), there were over 8,000 *min al-qurrā' wa-al-zuhhād wa-al-'ubbād mimman yarā qatl al-Ḥajjāj jihād*[an].

we passed the news of the death of Jabalah b. Zaḥr from one to
another. For each of us, it was as if he had lost his father or his
brother; indeed, on that battlefield it was an even more grievous
loss. Then Abū al-Bakhtarī al-Ṭā'ī said to us, "Do not let the
killing of Jabalah b. Zaḥr show its effect upon you. He was simply
a man among you whose fate came to him on its [appointed] day;
there was no way his [death] day could have been put either
forward or back. Each of you will taste what he has tasted: [Each   [1088]
will be] called and will answer." [Abū al-Zubayr] continued: I
looked at the faces of the *qurrā'*, and despondency was clearly
written on them. Their tongues were tied. [A sense of] failure was
manifest among them. The Syrians, glad and joyful, called out,
"O enemies of God, you are destroyed. God has killed your wayward leader."[153]

According to Abū Mikhnaf—Abū Yazīd al-Saksakī: When Jabalah and his companions charged, we were put to flight, and they
followed us. A group split off from us and was to one side, and we
looked, and, lo and behold, his companions were following our
companions, and he had stopped on top of an elevated piece of
ground, [waiting] for his companions to return to him. One of us
said, "That, by God, is Jabalah b. Zaḥr. Charge him while his
companions are distracted from him by the fighting; perhaps you
will strike him down." [Abū Yazīd] continued: So we charged
him. I testify that he did not flee: Rather, he charged us with his
sword. When he came down from the elevation, we transfixed
him with spears and dislodged him from his horse; he fell down
dead. His companions returned, and, when we saw them coming,
we turned aside from them. When they saw him dead, we saw
from their exclamations[154] and grief what gladdened our eyes. He
continued: We distinguished that plainly [too] in their [manner
of] fighting us and their coming out against us.

According to Abū Mikhnaf—Sahm b. ʿAbd al-Raḥmān al-
Juhanī: When Jabalah was struck down, his death shook the people. Then Bisṭām b. Maṣqalah b. Hubayrah al-Shaybānī came, and
his arrival encouraged the people. They said, "This man can take
the place of Jabalah." Abū al-Bakhtarī heard such talk from one of

---

153. So rendering *ṭāghūt* (which seems preferable to the variant *ṭāghiyah*).
154. *Istirjāʿihim*, i.e., their exclamation of the words *innā li-Allāh wa-innā
ilayhi rājiʿūn*, "To God we belong and to Him we return!"

them and said, "How foul that you have been made [by God]! If one man among you is killed, you think that you are surrounded; if Ibn Maṣqalah is now killed, will you surrender yourselves to destruction, and will you say that there is no one left to fight alongside? How fit you are for our hope of you to be altered!" Bisṭām had come from al-Rayy, and on the way he and Qutaybah [b. Muslim] had encountered each other. Qutaybah had invited him to [side with] al-Ḥajjāj and the Syrians, while Bisṭām had invited [Qutaybah] to [side with] ʿAbd al-Raḥmān and the Iraqis. Each had declined the other's proposal, and Bisṭām had said, "I would rather die with the Iraqis than live with the Syrians"; he had stopped at Māsabadhān.[155]

When [Bisṭām] arrived, he said to Ibn Muḥammad, "Give me the command of the cavalry of Rabīʿah"; and he did so. Then [Bisṭām] said to them, "O band of Rabīʿah, I have a bad disposition in war; please tolerate it for me." He was a brave man. One day, the people went out to fight and he attacked with the cavalry of Rabīʿah until he entered the [Syrian] camp. They took, among others, about thirty women—slave girls and concubines—and he brought them back with him until he drew near to his [own] camp, when he let them go, and they went off and entered al-Ḥajjāj's camp. "Woe to them!" said [al-Ḥajjāj], "Let [the Iraqis] protect their women! Had they not returned [our women], I would be taking their women captive[156] tomorrow when I triumph." Then they fought on a subsequent day, and ʿAbdallāh b. Mulayl al-Hamdānī made an attack with his cavalry, entered [the Syrian] camp, and took eighteen women captive. With him was Ṭāriq b. ʿAbdallāh al-Asadī, who was an archer. An old Syrian man came out of his tent, and the Asadī began to say to one of his companions, "Conceal this old man from me, lest I shoot him or attack him and transfix him." The old man said, raising his voice, "O God, gather us and them together with well-being"; the Asadī said, "I do not want to kill someone like this," and he left him. [At this] Ibn Mulayl brought the women [to a place] not far [from the Syrian camp] and let them go too. Al-Ḥajjāj said [by way of

[1089]

[1090]

---

155. A district of Jibāl bordering Iraq (Le Strange, *Lands of the Eastern Caliphate*, p. 202).

156. Preferring Ibn al-Athīr's *la-sabaytu nisāʾahum* to al-Ṭabarī's *la-subiyat nisāʾuhum*.

reaction] something similar to what he had said on the first occasion [when women were taken].

According to Hishām [b. Muḥammad al-Kalbī]—his father: Al-Walīd b. Naḥīt[157] al-Kalbī, from the Banū ʿĀmir, advanced in a squadron upon Jabalah b. Zaḥr. Al-Walīd, who was a huge man, got down from his riding animal,[158] and he and Jabalah, who was a man of middling size, engaged each other. [Al-Walīd] smote [Jabalah] on the head, and he fell. His companions were defeated, and his head was brought.

According to Hishām—Abū Mikhnaf and ʿAwānah al-Kalbī: When the head of Jabalah b. Zaḥr was brought to al-Ḥajjāj, he carried it on two spears and then said, "O people of Syria, rejoice. This is the beginning of victory. No sedition has ever been put down without a leading Yemeni being killed in it, and this is one of their leading men."

Then they made a sortie one day, and a Syrian came forth calling for a duel. Al-Ḥajjāj b. Jāriyah went out to him, attacked him, transfixed him, and brought him off his mount. His companions charged and saved him, he being a man from Khathʿam called Abū al-Dardāʾ. Al-Ḥajjāj b. Jāriyah said, "I didn't recognize him until he fell. Had I done so, I should not have fought him; I do not want someone like him from my people to be struck down."

ʿAbd al-Raḥmān b. ʿAwf al-Ruʾāsī, Abū Ḥumayd, went forth and   [1091] called for a duel. A cousin (ibn ʿamm) of his among the Syrians went out to him, and they exchanged blows with their swords. Each of them said, "I am the champion (lit. 'young man') of Kilāb," and then each said to the other, "Who are you?" When they had questioned each other, they abstained from fighting.

ʿAbdallāh b. Rizām al-Ḥārithī went out to the squadron of al-Ḥajjāj and said, "Come out to me one by one." A man was sent out to him, and he killed him. He did this for three days, killing a man each day. Then he arrived on the fourth day and they said, "He has come, would that God had not brought him!" He called for a duel. Al-Ḥajjāj said to al-Jarrāḥ [sc. b. ʿAbdallāh al-Ḥakamī], "Go out to him," so he went out to him. ʿAbdallāh b. Rizām, who

---

157. The text gives "Nukhayt," and it can be seen from the variants that the form of this name is uncertain.
158. Preferring the variant dābbatihi to rāyatihi.

was a friend of his, said to him, "Woe to you, O Jarrāḥ, whatever made you come out to me?" He said, "I have been put to the test with you." [ʿAbdallāh] said to him, "Are you in favor of something good?" [Al-Jarrāḥ] said, "What is that?" [ʿAbdallāh] said, "I shall lose for you, and you [will be able to] go back to al-Ḥajjāj having done well in his eyes, and he will praise you. As for me, I shall [be able to] put up with people's talk about you concerning my defeat, out of love for your safety. I do not want someone like you from my people to be killed." [Al-Jarrāḥ] said, "Do [that]," and attacked him; [ʿAbdallāh] began to simulate flight, running in front of him. The Ḥārithī's uvula had been cut,[159] and he was very thirsty; with him was a lad who had a skin of water and gave him to drink whenever he was thirsty. Al-Ḥārithī ran in front of him and al-Jarrāḥ [caught up and] attacked him in earnest, wanting nothing more than to kill him. The lad shouted to him, "The man is serious about killing you." But the Ḥārithī felt compassion for him, smote him on the head with an iron bar, felled him, and said to the lad, "Sprinkle some of the water in the skin on his face and give him to drink"; the lad did so. Then [the Ḥārithī] said, "O Jarrāḥ, you rewarded me badly. I wanted well-being for you, and you wanted to make me visit destiny." [Al-Jarrāḥ] said, "I did not want that." He said, "Go; I have left you on account of our kinship and [for the sake of] the clan."

[1092]   According to Muḥammad b. ʿUmar al-Wāqidī—Ibn Abī Sabrah—Ṣāliḥ b. Kaysān—Saʿīd al-Ḥarashī:[160] I was in the battle line on that day when an Iraqi called Qudāmah b. al-Ḥarish al-Tamīmī came out and stood between the two lines and said, "O band of the Jarāmiqah[161] of the Syrians, we call you to the Book of God and the Sunnah of His Messenger;[162] if you refuse [to accept this], let a man come out to me." A Syrian man went out to him, and he killed him, [and more went out] until he had killed four. When al-Ḥajjāj saw that, he ordered a crier to call out, "Let no one

---

159. Not in the fighting, of course, but previously; presumably, because it had become swollen. Professor Iḥsān ʿAbbās informs me that this practice still persists in Middle Eastern village life.

160. Caskel, *Ğamharat an-nasab*, register.

161. A term signifying natives (i.e., non-Arabs) of al-Jazīrah (see *EI²*, s.v. Djarādjima [vol. II, p. 457b]), and hence clearly intended here as an insult.

162. See above, n. 21.

go out to this dog"; and the people held back.

Saʿīd al-Ḥarashī continued: I drew near to al-Ḥajjāj and said, "May God cause the amīr to prosper! You have decided that no one should go out to this dog, at a time when these people have perished according to their allotted spans. This man too has his allotted span, and I hope that it has now run its course. Give permission to my companions who have come with me that one of them may go against him." Al-Ḥajjāj said, "This dog has turned the thing into a habit and has frightened [our] people. [But] I [nonetheless] give permission to your companions; he who wishes to stand up may do so." Al-Ḥarashī accordingly returned to his companions and informed them [of this], and, when Qudāmah called out for a duel, one of al-Ḥarashī's companions went out against him, only to be killed by him. That distressed Saʿīd and weighed heavily upon him, on account of what he had said to al-Ḥajjāj. Then Qudāmah called out [yet again] for a duel, and Saʿīd drew near to al-Ḥajjāj and said, "May God cause the amīr to prosper! Give me permission to go against this dog." He said, "Are you up to it?" Saʿīd said, "Yes, I am just as you want." Al-Ḥajjāj said, "Show me your sword," and he gave it to him. Al-Ḥajjāj said, "I have with me a sword that is heavier than this one," and he ordered that the sword be his and gave it to him. Then he looked at Saʿīd and said, "You have fine armor and a strong horse, [but even so] I do not know how the matter will turn out with this dog." Saʿīd said, "I hope that God will give me victory over him." Al-Ḥajjāj said, "Go forth with God's blessing."

Saʿīd said: So I went out to him and, when I drew near to him, he said, "Stop, O enemy of God!" and I stopped, pleased. He said, "Choose: Either you let me strike you three times [first], or I let you strike me three times and then you let me." I said, "Let me [go first]," and he placed his chest on his saddle bow and said, "Strike." I grasped my sword with both hands and struck [him] on the helmet as hard as I could; he did nothing, and I was displeased with both my sword and my blow. Then I decided to strike him at the base of his neck,[163] hoping thereby either to cut right through or [at the very least] to disable his hand. I struck it and did noth-

[1093]

---

163. So rendering *aṣl al-ʿātiq*.

ing, so displeasing both myself and those who were remote from me in the area of the camp, when what I had done reached them. The third [attempt was] similarly [unsuccessful]. Then he unsheathed a sword and said, "[Now] let me [have a go]." I let him and he struck me a blow with which he felled me. Then he dismounted from his horse, sat on my chest, pulled a dagger or knife out of his boot and placed it on my throat, intending to slay me. I said to him, "I beseech you by God, you will not acquire the nobility and renown by killing me that you will acquire by sparing me." He said, "Who are you?" I said, "Sa'īd al-Harashī." He said, "Woe, enemy of God! Depart, and inform your master of what you have encounterịd." Sa'īd said: I accordingly departed, [1094] hastening, until I got to al-Hajjāj. He said, "What do you think?" I said, "The amīr knew better."

The account returns to that of Abū Mikhnaf on the authority of Abū Yazīd [al-Saksakī]: Abū al-Bakhtarī al-Ṭā'ī and Sa'īd b. Jubayr used to say, "It is not given to any soul to die, save by the leave of God, at an appointed time," to the end of the verse,[164] and then they charged until they fell upon the battle line.

Abū al-Mukhāriq said: We fought them for a full hundred days, which I counted. He went on: We stopped at Dayr al-Jamājim with Ibn Muhammad on the morning of Tuesday, 1 Rabī' I, 83 (April 4, 702), and we were defeated on Wednesday, 14 Jumādā II (July 15, 702),[165] when the sun was at the highest point of the day. We were never bolder against them, nor they weaker against us, than on that day.

He continued: We went out to them, and they to us, on Wednesday, 14 Jumādā II, and we fought them for most of the day the best we had ever fought them. We felt safe from defeat, gaining the upper hand, when Sufyān b. al-Abrad al-Kalbī sallied forth with the cavalry from the [Syrian] right wing until he drew near to al-Abrad b. Qurrah al-Tamīmī, who was in command of 'Abd al-

---

164. Qur'ān 3:145 = 139.
165. Ibn al-Athīr gives the same dates and correctly arrives at a total of 103 days. Ibn A'tham (Futūḥ, vol. VII, p. 138) knows the hundred-day report and another report to the effect that the fighting lasted for four months; cf. Khalīfah (Ta'rīkh, pp. 284–85), who states that the defeat took place on 14 Jumādā (sic) 82 (sic). For further discussion, see Périer, Vie d'al-Hadjdjadj ibn Yousof, p. 186n.; Sayed, Revolte, pp. 220–21.

Raḥmān b. Muḥammad's left wing. Then, by God, after not much fighting, [al-Abrad b. Qurrah] was defeated. This was something on his part that the people disapproved of, since he was a brave man and flight was not a habit of his; they suspected that he had been granted an assurance of safety and that an agreement had been reached with him [by the Syrians] that he would be defeated with the people. When he did that, the battle lines near him were routed, and the people rode off in all directions. ʿAbd al-Raḥmān b. Muḥammad ascended the pulpit and began to call to the people, "To me, O servants of God! I am Ibn Muḥammad!" ʿAbdallāh b. Rizām al-Ḥārithī came to him and stopped under his pulpit; and ʿAbdallāh b. Dhuʾāb al-Sulamī came with his cavalry. [ʿAbd al-Raḥmān] stood near him and stayed put until the Syrians were close to him and their arrows began to get the better of him. At this, [ʿAbd al-Raḥmān] said, "O Ibn Rizām, attack these men and cavalry," and he did so until they ran off. Then more Syrian cavalry came, together with infantry, and he said, "Attack them, O Ibn Dhuʾāb," and he did so until they ran off. [ʿAbd al-Raḥmān himself] stayed where he was, not leaving his pulpit, and the Syrians entered [his] camp and cried out, "God is great!" ʿAbdallāh b. Yazīd b. al-Mughaffal al-Azdī—whose brother's daughter Mulaykah was the wife of ʿAbd al-Raḥmān[166]—climbed up to him and said, "Come down. I am afraid you will be taken captive if you do not come down. Maybe, if you leave [now], you will [be able to] gather together a force with which God will destroy them on another day." ʿAbd al-Raḥmān then came down, and the Iraqis left the camp in defeat and disorder. ʿAbd al-Raḥmān b. Muḥammad went off with Ibn Jaʿdah b. Hubayrah,[167] accompanied by members of his family, and, when they were opposite the village of the sons of Jaʿdah at al-Fallūjah,[168] they summoned a ferryboat and crossed in it. Bisṭām b. Maṣqalah joined them and said, "Is ʿAbd al-Raḥmān b. Muḥammad in the boat?" but they did not

[1095]

---

166. Mulaykah would thus be the granddaughter of Yazīd b. al-Mughaffal, rather than his daughter, as Ibn al-Kalbī thought (Caskel, *Ğamharat an-nasab*, vol. I, chart 218, and vol. II, p. 427); in Ibn al-Athīr "al-Mughaffal" is wrongly rendered as "al-Mufaḍḍal."

167. Presumably, either Jaʿfar b. Jaʿdah or ʿAbdallāh b. Jaʿdah (see Caskel, *Ğamharat an-nasab*, register).

168. A locality on the Euphrates downstream from al-Anbār (*EI²*, s.v.).

speak to him. [Bisṭām] suspected that ['Abd al-Raḥmān] was among them and said (ṭawīl):

May a soul for which you are cautious not find refuge.

[and (mutaqārib)]:[169]

[1096]   Qays set the country on fire against me,
                until, when it blazed, he desisted.

Then he went off until he reached his house, wearing arms and riding his horse, from which he had not dismounted. His daughter came out to him, and he clasped her; and his family came out to him, weeping. He made his testament to them and said, "Do not weep. Don't you know, if I do not leave you, how long I am likely to remain with you before I die? If I do die, then He who grants you sustenance now is alive and will not die. He will sustain you after my death, just as He sustains you in my lifetime." Then he bade his family farewell and left al-Kūfah.

According to Abū Mikhnaf—al-Kalbī, Muḥammad b. al-Sāʾib: When they were defeated, the sun was at its highest point in the day. He went on: I set off, straining, with my spear, sword, and shield, until I reached my family on the same day without having discarded any of my arms. Al-Ḥajjāj had said, "Leave them. Let them scatter and do not follow them," and a crier called out, "Whoever returns will be given safe-conduct."

After the battle, Muḥammad b. Marwān returned to al-Mawṣil and 'Abdallāh b. 'Abd al-Malik to Syria, leaving Iraq to al-Ḥajjāj. He went on until he entered al-Kūfah, seated beside him Maṣ-qalah b. Karib b. Raqabah al-'Abdī, who was a khaṭīb,[170] and said, "Revile in all possible ways every man to whom we have done good; revile [each one] for ingratitude and disloyalty. Stigmatize in all possible ways everyone you know to have a defect and make him slight in his own eyes." No one rendered [al-Ḥajjāj] the oath of allegiance but that he [first] said to him, "Do you testify that [1097]   you have been in a state of unbelief?" If he acknowledged this, [al-Ḥajjāj] accepted the oath of allegiance; if not, he killed him. There

---

169. This verse is ascribed to al-Rabīʿ b. Ziyād (see, for example, Ibn Manẓūr, Lisān al-ʿarab, vol. XIV, p. 356).
    170. See above, n. 5.

came to him a man from Khath'am, who had kept himself apart from all [the Iraqis], on the other side of the Euphrates, and [al-Ḥajjāj] asked him what he had been up to. [The man] said, "I stayed apart, on the other side of this river, waiting to see what would happen to [the Iraqi army], until you were victorious. Then I came to you in order to render you the oath of allegiance along with the people." [Al-Ḥajjāj] said, "Were you waiting [to see the result]? Do you testify that you are an unbeliever?" [The man] said, "What a bad man I would be—I, who have worshiped God for eighty years—if I were now to testify against myself to unbelief." [Al-Ḥajjāj] said, "In that case, I shall kill you." He said, "If you kill me, well, by God, there is very little life left in me anyway. I wait for death morning, noon, and night." [Al-Ḥajjāj] said, "Behead him!" and he was beheaded. [People] have claimed that no Qurashī or Syrian or anyone of the two sides remained around [that man] but that he felt compassion for him and deplored the killing of him.[171]

[Al-Ḥajjāj] summoned Kumayl b. Ziyād al-Nakha'ī[172] and said to him, "You are the one who retaliated by killing 'Uthmān, the Commander of the Faithful. I have [long] wanted to find a way of getting at you." [Kumayl] said, "I do not know which of us you are getting angry with: With him, when he laid himself open to retaliation, or with me, when I turned away from punishing him." Then he said, "O you man of Thaqīf, do not gnash your fangs at me, do not come down on me like a sand dune, do not bare your wolfish teeth at me! By God, there is very little life left in me anyway.[173] Carry out what you have decided; the appointment [will be with] God; the killing will be followed by [divine] judgment." Al-Ḥajjāj said, "The decisive proof [will be] against you." He said, "That [will be the case only] if you are sitting in judgment." [Al-Ḥajjāj] said, "O yes, you were among those who killed 'Uthmān and disavowed the Commander of the Faithful. Kill him!" and he was killed, his killer being Abū al-Jahm b.

[1098]

---

171. Dixon (*Umayyad Caliphate*, pp. 167–68, n. 109) correctly observes that this sentence was misunderstood by Veccia Vaglieri (*EI²*, s.v. Ibn al-Ash'ath [vol. III, p. 719a]).

172. See above, n. 127.

173. Literally, "all that has remained of my life is the period between the two drinkings of the ass: He drinks in the morning and dies in the evening, and he drinks in the evening and dies in the morning."

Kinānah al-Kalbī, of the Banū 'Āmir b. 'Awf, the cousin (*ibn 'amm*) of Manṣūr b. Jumhūr.[174] After him, somebody else was brought, and al-Ḥajjāj said, "I see a man who will not, I think, testify against himself to unbelief." [The man] said, "Do you [think you can] trick me as if I did not know myself? I am the most unbelieving person on earth. I am even more of an unbeliever than Pharaoh, the master of the stakes!"[175] Al-Ḥajjāj laughed and let him go. He stayed in al-Kūfah for a month and kept the Syrians away from the houses of the Kūfans.[176]

In this year there took place the battle at Maskin between al-Ḥajjāj and Ibn al-Ashʿath, after [the latter] had been put to flight from Dayr al-Jamājim.

The Cause of the Battle [of Maskin], with a Description of It

According to Hishām [b. Muḥammad al-Kalbī]—Abū Mikhnaf—Abū Yazīd al-Saksakī: Muḥammad b. Saʿd b. Abī Waqqāṣ went off after the battle of [Dayr] al-Jamājim until he stopped at al-Madāʾin; there he was joined by a great many people. [At about the same time] 'Ubaydallāh b. 'Abd al-Raḥmān b. Samurah b. Ḥabīb b. 'Abd Shams al-Qurashī went off to al-Baṣrah, in which was Ayyūb b. al-Ḥakam b. Abī 'Aqīl,[177] the cousin of al-Ḥajjāj, and took it. 'Abd al-Raḥmān b. Muḥammad [thereupon] went to al-Baṣrah, while ['Ubaydallāh] was there; the people rallied to him, and he stopped there. At this, 'Ubaydallāh went to Ibn Muḥammad b. al-Ashʿath and said to him, "It was not my intention to be separate from you; I took [the city] for you." Al-Ḥajjāj [now] set forth and started with al-Madāʾin. He stopped opposite it for five [nights], during which time he readied [his] men in ferryboats. When it reached Muḥammad b. Saʿd that they had crossed to them, [he

[1099]

---

174. Who rose to prominence as a general at the very end of the Umayyad period (Crone, *Slaves on Horses*, p. 158).

175. This being a form of reference to Pharaoh occurring in the Qur'ān (89:10 = 9 and 38:12 = 11); for some discussion of it, see *EI²*, s.v. Firʿawn.

176. *'Azala ahl al-Sha'm 'an buyūt ahl al-Kūfa*. Ibn al-Athīr, on the other hand, tells us just the opposite: *anzala ahl al-Sha'm buyūt ahl al-Kūfah*, and he goes on to say: *anzalahum al-Ḥajjāj fīhā maʿa ahlihā, wa-huwa awwal man anzala al-jund fī buyūt ghayrihim*. . . .

177. For 'Ubaydallāh see Caskel, *Ǧamharat an-nasab*, register. On Ayyūb see above, n. 82.

and] all [who were with him] set off and joined Ibn al-Ash'ath. Al-Ḥajjāj advanced toward him, and the people [at al-Baṣrah] went out with ['Abd al-Raḥmān] to Maskin[178] on [the] Dujayl [river]. [There] the Kūfans and the fugitive elements from the peripheral areas came to him. The people reproved each other for having taken to flight, and most of them rendered an oath of allegiance to Bisṭām b. Maṣqalah to fight to the death. 'Abd al-Raḥmān dug in around his companions and protected one flank by flooding, so making fighting [possible] in [only] one direction; he was also joined by Khālid b. Jarīr b. 'Abdallāh al-Qasrī,[179] who came from Khurasan with people from the Kūfan contingent [there]. They fought most furiously for fifteen nights in Sha'bān (September), until Ziyād b. Ghunaym al-Qaynī, who was in charge of al-Ḥajjāj's strong-points, was killed; that shook [al-Ḥajjāj] and his companions very considerably.

According to Abū Mikhnaf—Abū Jahḍam al-Azdī: Al-Ḥajjāj stayed awake all night, going about among us and saying to us, "You are people of obedience, and they are people of disobedience; you are striving after God's pleasure, while they are striving after His displeasure. God's wont with you concerning them is good. You will never fight them gallantly on any battlefield or show endurance against them but that God will requite you with victory against them and triumph over them. So go against them in the morning aggressively, earnestly. I do not doubt victory, God willing."

[Abū Jahḍam] continued: we went against them in the morning, [1100] having made our dispositions shortly before daybreak. We were afoot earlier than they were, and we fought them the hardest we had ever fought them. 'Abd al-Malik b. al-Muhallab came to us on an armored horse[180] at a time when the cavalry of Sufyān b. al-

---

178. This is not the better-known Maskin (watered by the Dujayl canal) to the north of what would later be the city of Baghdad (Le Strange, *Lands of the Eastern Caliphate*, map II and p. 51), but a more obscure Maskin somewhere on or near the Dujayl (Kārūn) river (see Sayed, *Revolte*, p. 225, for further details; Yāqūt, *Mu'jam*, vol. IV, p. 531, seems himself to be mistaken when he says, "al-Ḥāzimī mentioned that Maskin is also [a place] at the Dujayl of al-Ahwāz where al-Ḥajjāj's battle with Ibn al-Ash'ath took place, and that is a mistake on his part").

179. This appears to be the one and only reference to a person of this name (cf. Crone, *Slaves on Horses*, p. 114); Wellhausen's reference to this name (*Kingdom*, p. 251) should be changed to Khālid b. 'Abd Allāh al-Qasrī.

180. Reading *mujaffifan* where the text has *muḥaffifan*.

Abrad was without armor. Al-Ḥajjāj said to him, "Join these odd-ments to you[r men], O ʿAbd al-Malik; I may be making an at-tack." He did so, and the Iraqis were attacked from every side and put to flight. Abū al-Bakhtarī al-Ṭāʾī and ʿAbd al-Raḥmān b. Abī Laylā were killed. Before being killed, they said, "Flight is always odious to us"; then they were struck down.

[Abū Jahdam] continued: Bisṭām b. Maṣqalah al-Shaybānī went with four thousand of the most steadfast [people] from the two *miṣrs* (that is, al-Baṣrah and al-Kūfah); they broke the sheaths of their swords. Ibn Maṣqalah said to them, "If, in fleeing from death, we might escape it, we would flee; but we know that it will come upon us soon, and where can one take oneself away from what is inevitable? O you people, you are manifesting what is right, so fight for what is right. By God, [even] if you were not in the right, death with honor would [still] be better than life in a state of abasement." He and his companions then fought fiercely and put the Syrians to flight several times. Eventually al-Ḥajjāj said, "Bring in the archers: No one else can fight them." When the archers came and the [Syrians] surrounded them on every side, all but a few of them were killed. Bukayr b. Rabīʿah b.[181] Tharwān al-Ḍabbī was taken captive and was brought to al-Ḥajjāj, who killed him.

According to Abū Mikhnaf—Abū al-Jahdam: I brought a cap-tive known to al-Ḥajjāj for his bravery. Al-Ḥajjāj said, "O Syrians, [1101] it is part of God's favor to you that this young man has brought the horseman of the Iraqis as a captive. Behead him!" And he killed him.

[Abū al-Jahdam] continued: Ibn al-Ashʿath and those who had been put to flight with him went in the direction of Sijistān. Al-Ḥajjāj sent after him ʿUmārah b. Tamīm al-Lakhmī, together with his son Muḥammad b. al-Ḥajjāj, with ʿUmārah as the amīr over the people. ʿUmārah b. Tamīm went to ʿAbd al-Raḥmān and caught up with him at al-Sūs.[182] [ʿUmārah] fought him for one hour in the daytime; then he and his companions were defeated and went off until they reached Sābūr.[183] ʿAbd al-Raḥmān b.

---

181. Omitting "Abī," as proposed in the *Addenda et Emendanda*.
182. Ancient Susa, in Khūzistān (Le Strange, *Lands of the Eastern Caliphate*, p. 240).
183. I.e., Shāpūr in Fārs (ibid., p. 262).

Muḥammad was [in the meantime] joined by the Kurds, together with the routed troops who were with him. ʿUmārah b. Tamīm next fought them fiercely in the narrow pass, until he and many of his companions were wounded; then they were defeated and left the mountain road to ʿAbd al-Raḥmān, who went on until he passed through Kirmān.

Al-Wāqidī said: The battle of al-Zāwiyah at al-Baṣrah was in Muḥarram 83 (February 702).

[The Breakup of Ibn al-Ashʿath's Defeated Army]

According to Abū Mikhnaf—Sayf b. Bishr al-ʿIjlī—al-Munakhkhal b. Ḥābis al-ʿAbdī: When ʿAbd al-Raḥmān b. Muḥammad entered Kirmān, he was met by ʿAmr b. Laqīṭ al-ʿAbdī, who was his governor over it; [this ʿAmr] prepared hospitality for him, and he stopped. A shaykh of ʿAbd al-Qays called Maʿqil then said to him, "By God, it has reached us concerning you, O Ibn al-Ashʿath, that you were a coward." ʿAbd al-Raḥmān said, "By God, I was not a coward. By God, I have advanced with infantry upon infantry, and I have wrapped up cavalry with cavalry; I have fought both horseman and infantryman, and I have not been defeated. I have not left the battlefield to the enemy at any time until I found no place in which to fight and saw no one to fight along with me; rather, [far from being a coward,] I sought a premature sovereignty."[184] Then he went with those who were with him until he entered the desert of Kirmān.

According to Abū Mikhnaf—Hishām b. Ayyūb b. ʿAbd al-Raḥmān b. Abī ʿAqīl: When Ibn Muḥammad went into the desert of Kirmān, followed by the Syrians, one of the Syrians entered a residence in the desert, and there he found, inscribed by one of the Kūfans, some of the poetry of Abū Jildah al-Yashkurī, [from] a long ode [of his] (*wāfir*).[185]

O woe and all [-embracing] sorrow,
    what anguish [there is] at what we have encountered!

[1102]

---

184. So rendering *zāwaltu mulk*an *mu'ajjal*an.
185. On this poet, see Sezgin, *GAS*, vol. II, pp. 375–76 (also Bosworth, *Sīstān*, p. 59 and n. 6). Regarding the following verses, cf. *Aghānī*², vol. XI, pp. 312–13; verses 3 and 4 also occur in Ibn Aʿtham, *Futūḥ*, vol. VII, p. 143.

We have left both the religion and this world,
　　and we have abandoned [our] wives and children.
We were not religious people,
　　that we might endure tribulation when tested,
Nor were we people of this world,
　　able to protect it, even though we did not
　　aspire to religion.
We have left our homes to the rabble of ʿAkk
　　and [to] the indigenous villagers and the Ashʿarīs.[186]

Then Ibn Muḥammad went on until he reached Zaranj, the [chief] city of Sijistān, in which was a man from the Banū Tamīm whom he had put in charge of it, namely, ʿAbdallāh b. ʿĀmir al-Naʿʿār,[187] from the Banū Mujāshiʿ b. Dārim. When ʿAbd al-Raḥmān b. Muḥammad came to him in defeat, he shut the gate of the city in his face and prevented him from entering it. ʿAbd al-Raḥmān stayed put for some days in the hope of gaining access to it, but, when he saw that he would not achieve this, he went off to Bust, in charge of which he had appointed a man from Bakr b. Wāʾil called ʿIyāḍ b. Himyān Abū Hishām b. ʿIyāḍ al-Sadūsī.[188] [This ʿIyāḍ] received him and invited him to stop [at Bust], which he accordingly did; [ʿIyāḍ] thereupon waited until ʿAbd al-Raḥmān's companions were off guard and had strayed away from him, and then pounced upon him and put him in bonds, desiring thereby to be secure vis-à-vis al-Ḥajjāj and to achieve [good] standing in his eyes.

News of ʿAbd al-Raḥmān's arrival had in the meantime reached the Zunbīl, who went to meet him. When ʿIyāḍ took [ʿAbd al-Raḥmān], the Zunbīl moved on Bust[189] and invested it, sending [word] to the Bakrī [as follows]: "By God, if you harm as much as a hair of his head,[190] I shall not leave the battlefield until I bring you

---

186. As Wellhausen points out (*Kingdom*, p. 249), "ʿAkk and Ashʿar as *pars pro toto* . . . seems to be an insulting phrase to dub [the Syrian troops] barbarians."

187. Reading "al-Naʿʿār" here and below, with the *Naqāʾiḍ* (p. 751, line 2) and Sayed (*Revolte*, pp. 228, 241: an-Naʿār [sic]); naʿʿār means "clamorous," while the form baʿʿār appears to be unattested.

188. Ibn al-Athīr names him as ʿIyāḍ b. Himyān b. Hishām, while al-Yaʿqūbī (*Taʾrīkh*, vol. II, p. 333) knows him as ʿIyāḍ b. ʿAmr (cf. above, n. 12).

189. Al-Ṭabarī's text is confused at this point; I have drawn inspriation from Ibn al-Athīr.

190. Literally, "If you hurt him with what casts a mote in his eye, or harm him in any way, or deprive him of a single hair."

down and kill you and all who are with you; I shall take your offspring captive and divide all you own among the troops." The Bakrī sent [word] to him [as follows]: "Give us a safe-conduct for ourselves and for what we own, and we shall hand him over to you safe and sound, together with what he owns in its entirety." [The Zunbīl] made peace with them on [that basis] and gave them a safe-conduct, and they in turn opened the gate for Ibn al-Ashʿath and set him free. He came to the Zunbīl and said to him, "This [man] was my governor over this city, and I trusted him and was satisfied with him when I appointed him; he, however, acted treacherously toward me and perpetrated against me what you have seen, so let me kill him." [The Zunbīl] said, "I have given him a safe-conduct and dislike [the idea of] acting treacherously toward him." [ʿAbd al-Raḥmān] said, "In that case, let me push him and punch him in the chest and neck and demean him." [The Zunbīl] agreed to this, and ʿAbd al-Raḥmān b. Muḥammad did so.[191]

[1104]

[ʿAbd al-Raḥmān] then went off with the Zunbīl until they entered the latter's territory, [where] the Zunbīl lodged him and did him honor. With [ʿAbd al-Raḥmān] were numerous routed troops. There were [in addition] large numbers of [other] routed troops, together with companions of ʿAbd al-Raḥmān and those chiefs and leaders who had stood with Ibn al-Ashʿath against al-Ḥajjāj in every battlefield, did not hope for a safe-conduct, did not accept al-Ḥajjāj's safe-conduct[192] when it was first offered,[193] and strove wholeheartedly against him. [These people] set off after Ibn al-Ashʿath, in search of him, until they fetched up in[194] Sijistān; they, together with those of the [Arabs] of Sijistān and of the indigenous inhabitants[195] who followed them, numbered about sixty thousand. They went against ʿAbdallāh b. ʿĀmir al-Naʿʿār and besieged him; they also wrote to ʿAbd al-Raḥmān, who was [still] with the Zunbīl, informing him of their advance, their

---

191. In Ibn Aʿtham's account (*Futūḥ*, vol. VII, p. 152), ʿAbd al-Raḥmān kills the Bakrī.

192. Where al-Ṭabarī has *wa-lam yaqbalū amān al-Ḥajjāj*, Dhahabī (*Taʾrīkh al-Islām*, vol. III, p. 229) reads *mimman lam yathiq bi-amān al-Ḥajjāj*, "of those who did not trust al-Ḥajjāj's safe-conduct."

193. The text reads *fī awwali marrah*, which seems otiose; it is omitted by Ibn al-Athīr.

194. *Ḥattā saqaṭū bi-* in al-Ṭabarī; Ibn al-Athīr has *fa-balaghū*.

195. So rendering *ahl Sijistān wa-ahl al-balad*, following Bosworth (*Sīstān*, p. 61); *wa-ahl al-balad* is omitted by Ibn al-Athīr.

number, and their being together. The person who led them in ritual prayer was ʿAbd al-Raḥmān b. al-ʿAbbās b. Rabīʿah b. al-Ḥārith b. ʿAbd al-Muṭṭalib. They [then] wrote [again] to [Ibn al-Ashʿath]: "Come to us. Perhaps we shall go to Khurasan. Many [Iraqi][196] troops are there, and they may swear allegiance to us in fighting the Syrians. It is a broad and spacious land, containing men and fortresses." At this, ʿAbd al-Raḥmān b. Muḥammad and those who were with him went forth to them, and they besieged ʿAbdallāh b. ʿĀmir al-Naʿʿār until they dislodged him; on ʿAbd al-Raḥmān's orders, he was beaten, tortured, and imprisoned.

[Next,] ʿUmārah b. Tamīm advanced toward them with [an army of] Syrians, and the companions of ʿAbd al-Raḥmān b. [1105] Muḥammad said to ʿAbd al-Raḥmān, "Take us out of Sijistān; let us leave it to [ʿUmārah] and betake ourselves to Khurasan." ʿAbd al-Raḥmān b. Muḥammad said, "Over Khurasan is Yazīd b. al-Muhallab, who is a resolute and bold young man who is not going to let his authority pass to you. If you were to enter [Khurasan], you would find him hastening toward you. Nor will the Syrians leave off pursuing you. I dislike [the idea of] the Khurasanis and the Syrians combining against you, and I fear that you will not achieve what you seek." They said, "The people of Khurasan are from us,[197] and we hope that, if we were to enter it, those of them who would follow us would outnumber those who would fight us. It is a very extensive land, in which we may direct ourselves wherever we wish and remain until God destroys al-Ḥajjāj and[198] ʿAbd al-Malik, or [until] we decide otherwise."[199] ʿAbd al-Raḥmān said to them, "Go [relying] on [the mention of] the name of God," and they went off until they reached Herat. [Next, those who remained with ʿAbd al-Raḥmān were taken unawares when][200] ʿUbaydallāh b. ʿAbd al-Raḥmān b. Samurah al-Qurashī departed from [ʿAbd al-Raḥmān's] camp with two thousand [men] and left him, taking a road different from the road [taken by those who had left for Herat]. On the following morning, Ibn Muḥammad

---

196. So understanding *minnā*; cf. Ibn al-Athīr's reference to *man bihā min ʿashāʾirihim*.

197. I.e., Iraqis; see the preceding note.

198. Reading the variant *wa-*, rather than *aw*.

199. So understanding *narā min raʾyinā* (or *mā raʾyunā*).

200. So rendering *fa-lam yashʿurū bi-shayʾin ḥattā*.

stood up among [those who remained with him], praised God, and said, "To continue: I have witnessed you in these battlefields, and among them there has been no place of witnessing but that in it I have steeled myself for you[r sakes] until no one of you has remained in it. When I saw that you would neither fight nor show fortitude in adversity, I came to a refuge and place of safety. Once I was there, there came to me your letters to the effect that I should come to you and that we were as one and would perhaps fight our enemy. So I came to you. Then you were of the opinion that I should go to Khurasan, and you claimed that you were united with me and that you would not separate from me. Now this [man] ʿUbaydallāh b. ʿAbd al-Raḥmān has done what you have seen, and today I have had enough of you. Do as you see fit. As for me, I am going off to the friend from whom I came to you. Those of you who want to follow me may do so, and those who do not wish to do that may go wherever they want, seeking protection from God."

[1106]

One group detached itself from them, and another group went off with [ʿAbd al-Raḥmān b. Muḥammad], but the bulk of the army stayed put. When ʿAbd al-Raḥmān [b. Muḥammad] had departed, they rallied to ʿAbd al-Raḥmān b. al-ʿAbbās and gave the oath of allegiance to him. Ibn Muḥammad went to the Zunbīl, and they went to Khurasan, ending up in Herat, where they encountered al-Ruqād al-Azdī—from [the clan of] al-ʿAtīk—and killed him; [at this,] Yazīd b. al-Muhallab moved against them.

As for ʿAlī b. Muḥammad al-Madāʾinī, he mentioned on the authority of al-Mufaḍḍal b. Muḥammad that Ibn al-Ashʿath, when he had been defeated at Maskin, went to Kābul and that ʿUbaydallāh b. ʿAbd al-Raḥmān b. Samurah came to Herat and blamed and stigmatized Ibn al-Ashʿath for his flight. ʿAbd al-Raḥmān b. ʿAbbās [then] came to Sijistān, was joined by Ibn al-Ashʿath's routed forces, proceeded to Khurasan with a body [of men] put at twenty thousand, and stopped at Herat; [there] they encountered al-Ruqād b. ʿUbayd[201] al-ʿAtakī and killed him. With ʿAbd al-Raḥmān [b. ʿAbbās] from [the tribe of] ʿAbd al-Qays was ʿAbd al-Raḥmān b. al-Mundhir b. al-Jārūd,[202] to whom Yazīd b. al-

---

201. Or "Ziyād" (cf. al-Ṭabarī's text, ser. ii, p. 1004).
202. On his father, see above, n. 54.

Muhallab sent [the following message]: "You could have a lot of leeway in the territory, and [could be dealing with] someone a lot less sharp and strong than I. Move to a territory in which I have no authority, for I do not like [the idea of] fighting you. If you want me to support you with the wherewithal for your journeying, I shall help you." [ʿAbd al-Raḥmān b. al-Mundhir] responded to him: "We have not stopped in this territory in order to wage war, nor in order to settle; all we want to do is rest up and then move on, God willing. We have no need of what you have proposed." Yazīd's messenger went off [bearing this message] to [Yazīd].

[1107]

Then [ʿAbd al-Raḥmān b. ʿAbbās] al-Hāshimī started levying taxes. [This] reached Yazīd, who said, "He who wants to rest and then pass on does not collect tax (kharāj)." He sent out al-Mufaḍḍal [b. al-Muhallab] over an advance party of four thousand—also put at six thousand—and then sent four thousand [men] after him. Yazīd weighed himself in his armor, which came to four hundred riṭls,[203] and said, "I think that I am too heavy to fight. What horse could carry me?" Then he called for his horse al-Kāmil,[204] deputed over Marw his maternal uncle, Judayʿ b. Yazīd,[205] and set forth for Marw al-Rūdh, where he visited the tomb of his father, stayed there for three days, and gave one hundred dirhams to each of those who were with him. Then he went to Herat and sent [word] to the Hāshimī [as follows]: "You have rested, fattened yourself, and collected taxes. You may keep the taxes you have collected. If you want more, we shall give you more. But leave, by God. I do not want to fight you."

[Al-Madāʾinī] said: [ʿAbd al-Raḥmān b. ʿAbbās al-Hāshimī, now] accompanied by ʿUbayd Allāh b. ʿAbd al-Raḥmān b. Samurah, insisted on fighting. Al-Hāshimī clandestinely subverted the army of Yazīd, making them promises and calling them to himself. One of them informed Yazīd, who said, "This is no longer a matter of mere reproof: I'll have him for lunch before he has me for dinner," and he went against him. In due course, the two armies drew near to each other and prepared for battle. A chair

---

203. Assuming an Umayyad riṭl (or raṭl) of 400 g. (see EI², s.v. Makāyil and Mawāzīn), it weighed approximately 80 lbs.

204. "The Perfect."

205. Possibly Judayʿ b. Saʿīd is meant (see al-Ṭabarī's text, ser. ii, p. 856, and Caskel, Ǧamharat an-nasab, register).

was set up for Yazīd, and he sat upon it; he put his brother al-Mufaḍḍal in command of the fighting. There advanced one of the companions of al-Hāshimī, called Khulayd ʿAynayn[206] from [the tribe of] ʿAbd al-Qays, mounted on his horse, and he raised his voice and said (ṭawīl):   [1108]

She[207] made a call, O Yazīd b. al-Muhallab,
     a grief-stricken call; then her eyes filled
     with tears.
If the caller were to make the call heard, [Yazīd]
     would respond to it
     with compact spears and with swords, the
     scabbards of which would be cast aside.
The ashrāf of Iraq have fled and have left
     hornless cattle there to meet their fate.

He wanted [thereby] to incite Yazīd. Yazīd remained silent for a long time, until the people thought that the poetry had moved him. Then he said to a man, "Call out and let them hear. . . ."[208] They imposed that upon them, despite its difficulty, and Khulayd said (ṭawīl):

Bad is the one whose name is called and extolled;
     the virgins and non-virgins of Iraq call to him.
When Yazīd is called to a grievous battle day involving
     the defense of those whom he is honor-bound to defend,
     sexual organs are protected only by their real
     protectors.
I think that he will soon be
     committed, just as he used to commit others.
No free-born women will weep for him, only hired
     wailing women,
     the spotted and the black (that is, the slaves)
     among them will be weeping over him.

Yazīd said to al-Mufaḍḍal, "Take your cavalry forward," and he did so and they rushed upon one another. After not much fighting   [1109]

---

206. Yāqūt, Muʿjam, vol. III, p. 755, explains that the ʿAynayn in question was a well or watering place in al-Baḥrayn; cf. al-Mubarrad, Kāmil, p. 498 and n. i).

207. Judging by the verses that follow these, "she" would appear to be the Arab women of Iraq.

208. It looks as if some of the text has been lost here.

between them, the people separated from ʿAbd al-Raḥmān, and he held out, together with a group of those who were most steadfast and the ʿAbdīs. Saʿd b. Najd al-Qurdūsī[209] charged Ḥulays al-Shaybānī, who was [positioned] in front of ʿAbd al-Raḥmān, and Ḥulays speared him and unseated him from his horse; his companions protected him, and then [Yazīd's] people outnumbered [ʿAbd al-Raḥmān's, who] were put to flight. Yazīd ordered [his men] to desist from following them; they took what was in their camp, and they took [some] of them captive. Yazīd put ʿAṭāʾ b. Abī al-Sāʾib in charge of the camp and instructed him to collect together what was in it. They came across thirteen women, whom they brought to Yazīd; he made them over to Murrah b. ʿAṭāʾ b. Abī al-Sāʾib, who transported them [first] to al-Ṭabasayn[210] and then[ce] to Iraq. Yazīd said to Saʿd b. Najd, "Who speared you?" and [Saʿd] replied, "Ḥulays al-Shaybānī, and I, by God, as a foot soldier am stronger than he is as a cavalryman." [This] reached Ḥulays, who said, "He lies, by God! I am stronger than he is, both as a cavalryman and as a foot soldier."

ʿAbd al-Raḥmān b. Mundhir b. Bishr b. Ḥārithah[211] fled and went to Mūsā b. ʿAbdallāh b. Khāzim.

[Al-Madāʾinī] continued: Among the prisoners were Muḥammad b. Saʿd b. Abī Waqqāṣ; ʿUmar b. Mūsā b. ʿUbaydallāh b. Maʿmar; ʿAyyāsh b. al-Aswad b. ʿAwf al-Zuhrī; al-Hilqām b. Nuʿaym b. al-Qaʿqāʿ b. Maʿbad b. Zurārah; Fayrūz Ḥusayn; Abū al-ʿIlj, [who was] the mawlā of ʿUbaydallāh b. Maʿmar; a man from [1110] the Āl Abī ʿAqīl;[212] Sawwār b. Marwān; ʿAbd al-Raḥmān b. Ṭalḥah b. ʿAbdallāh b. Khalaf; and ʿAbdallāh b. Fuḍālah al-Azhrānī.[213] [ʿAbd al-Raḥmān b. al-ʿAbbās] al-Hāshimī made it to Sind, while Ibn Samurah reached Marw. Then Yazīd departed to Marw and sent the prisoners to al-Ḥajjāj with Sabrah b. Nakhf b. Abī Ṣufrah,[214] having [first] let Ibn Ṭalḥah and ʿAbdallāh b. Fuḍālah go; [in addition, some] people calumniated ʿUbaydallāh b. ʿAbd al-

---

209. Caskel, *Ǧamharat an-nasab*, register.

210. Two towns, each called Ṭabas, in Qūhistān (see Le Strange, *Lands of the Eastern Caliphate*, pp. 359ff.).

211. Possibly ʿAbd al-Raḥmān b. al-Mundhir b. al-Jārūd (Bishr) is meant.

212. This identification is striking, since the Āl Abī ʿAqīl was the family of al-Ḥajjāj; it is omitted by Ibn al-Athīr.

213. On these prisoners, see Sayed, *Revolte*, pp. 239–41.

214. I.e., a first cousin of Yazīd b. al-Muhallab's.

Rahmān b. Samurah, and Yazīd took him and imprisoned him.

According to Hishām [b. Muhammad al-Kalbī]—al-Qāsim b. Muhammad al-Hadramī—Hafs b. 'Umar b. Qabīsah—a man from the Banū Hanīfah called Jābir b. 'Umārah: Yazīd b. al-Muhallab detained 'Abd al-Rahmān b. Talhah with him and kept him safe; [this] Talhī had sworn an oath that he would never see Yazīd b. al-Muhallab on any occasion without going to him to kiss his hand by way of thanks for what he had done.

[Hishām also] said: Muhammad b. Sa'd b. Abī Waqqās said to Yazīd, "I ask you [to free me] in return for my father's invocation for your father," and he let him go;[215] there is rather a long story behind Muhammad b. Sa'd's words to Yazīd.[216]

According to Hishām—Abū Mikhnaf—Hishām b. Ayyūb b. 'Abd al-Rahmān b. Abī 'Aqīl al-Thaqafī: Yazīd b. al-Muhallab sent the rest of the prisoners to al-Hajjāj b. Yūsuf. [First,] 'Umar b. Mūsā b. 'Ubaydallāh b. Ma'mar ⟨was brought forward⟩[217] and [al-Hajjāj] said, "You are the police chief of 'Udayy al-Rahmān."[218]   [1111]
He said, "May God cause the amīr to prosper! It was a sedition that engulfed both the righteous and the unrighteous, and we entered into it. God has [now] given you power over us. If you forgive, then that will be by virtue of your moderation[219] and graciousness; if you punish, you will punish sinning wrong-doers." Al-Hajjāj said, "As for your words 'that engulfed both the righteous and the unrighteous,' you have lied; it engulfed the unrighteous, while the righteous were preserved from it. As for your acknowledgment of your sin, perhaps it will benefit you," and he was removed; people entertained hopes for his well-being until al-Hilqām b. Nu'aym was brought forward and [al-Hajjāj] said to him, "Tell me what you hoped for in following 'Abd al-Rahmān b. Muhammad. Did you hope that he would become caliph?" He said, "Yes, I did hope that, and it was my aspiration that he would cause me to occupy a position the like of yours vis-à-vis 'Abd al-Malik."

---

215. But cf. below, p. 65.
216. Sa'd made the invocation after al-Muhallab had distinguished himself on al-Hakam b. 'Amr al-Ghifārī's expedition to Khurasan in the late 40s (660s) (see Hinds, *Early Islamic Family*, pars. 24–25).
217. Inserting something like *fa-quddima* before *bi-'Umar*; the *Addenda et Emendanda* suggest *fa-lammā qadimū 'alayhi da'ā*.
218. See above, n. 95.
219. So rendering *hilm* here and in what follows; see *EI*², s.v.

[Hishām] continued: Al-Ḥajjāj became angry and said, "Behead him!" and he was killed.

[Hishām] continued: He looked at ʿUmar b. Mūsā[220] b. ʿUbaydallāh b. Maʿmar, who had been set away from him to one side, and said, "Behead him!"; and the rest of them were [all] killed. He had [earlier] given a safe-conduct to ʿAmr b. Abī Qurrah al-Kindī of the clan of Ḥujr,[221] who was a *sharīf* from an old family. He said to him, "O ʿAmr, you used to tell me of and relate to me your dislike of Ibn al-Ashʿath and of al-Ashʿath before him. Then you followed ʿAbd al-Raḥmān b. Muḥammad b. al-Ashʿath. By God, there [was] not in you [any] dislike of following them; I don't believe a word you say."[222]

[Hishām] continued: When al-Ḥajjāj had defeated the people at [Dayr] al-Jamājim, his crier had called out, "Whoever reaches Qutaybah b. Muslim at al-Rayy will be given a safe-conduct."[223] Many people reached Qutaybah, among them ʿĀmir al-Shaʿbī. Al-Ḥajjāj remembered al-Shaʿbī one day and said, "Where is he, and what has he been doing?" Yazīd b. Abī Muslim[224] said to him, "It has come to my attention, O amīr, that he has reached Qutaybah b. Muslim at al-Rayy." [Al-Ḥajjāj] said, "I shall send [word] to [Qutaybah]; let [al-Shaʿbī] be brought to us," and he wrote to Qutaybah: "To continue: Send al-Shaʿbī to me when you read this letter of mine. Peace be upon you." [Al-Shaʿbī] was sent to him.

According to Abū Mikhnaf—al-Sarī b. Ismāʿīl—al-Shaʿbī: I was a friend of Ibn Abī Muslim's. When I was brought to al-Ḥajjāj, I met Ibn Abī Muslim and said to him, "Advise me." He said, "I don't know how to advise you except [to say] that you should excuse youself as much as you can"; and I was similarly advised by [other] counselors and brethren. When I entered into his presence, [however,] I adopted a view different from theirs. I saluted him as amīr and then said, "O amīr, people have told me to excuse myself to you, adducing other than what God knows to be the truth. By God, in this situation I shall not say other than what

[1112]

---

220. The text wrongly gives "Mūsā b. ʿUmar."

221. See Caskel, *Ǧamharat an-nasab*, register, s.v. ʿAmr b. Salama.

222. Ibn al-Athīr makes it clear that al-Ḥajjāj killed him.

223. So rendering *fa-huwa amānuhu* (lit. "he (sc. Qutaybah) will be his safe-conduct").

224. A mawlā and foster brother of al-Ḥajjāj (Crone, *Slaves on Horses*, p. 243, n. 420).

is true. By God, we have set up a chief against you,[225] have urged
[people to oppose you], and have struggled against you as hard as
we could, without falling short. We were neither strong and sin-
ful, nor pious and innocent. God gave you victory over us. If you
act violently, then that is by reason of our sins and the measures
we took; if you forgive us, that will be by reason of your moderation and after clear proof you possess against us." Al-Ḥajjāj said to
him, "By God, you are dearer to me in respect of what you say
than one who enters into our presence with his sword dripping
with our blood and then says, 'I did nothing and witnessed nothing.' You are safe with us, O Shaʿbī. Depart."

[1113]

[Al-Shaʿbī] said: So I departed. When I had walked a little way,
he said, "Come here, O Shaʿbī."

[Al-Shaʿbī] said: At that my heart sank. Then I remembered his
words "You are safe, O Shaʿbī," and I felt tranquil. He said, "How
did you find the people, O Shaʿbī, after me?"

[Al-Shaʿbī] said: He had [earlier] treated me with honor,[226] and I
said, "May God cause the amīr to prosper. After you, by God, I
had no kohl but sleeplessness;[227] I found my place of habitation
difficult, and I was in a state of unending fear; I lost upright
brethren, and I found no [adequate] substitute for the amīr." He
said, "Depart, O Shaʿbī," and I departed.

According to Abū Mikhnaf—Khālid b. Qaṭan al-Ḥārithī: Al-
Ḥajjāj was brought al-Aʿshā—[that is,] Aʿshā Hamdān[228]—and
said to him, "Well now, O enemy of God, recite to me your words
'bayna al-ashajj ⟨wa-⟩bayna Qays':[229] Deliver your verse." He
said, "I would rather recite what I said regarding you." [Al-Ḥajjāj]
said, "Very well, recite that to me," and he recited to him
(ṭawīl):[230]

God insisted on bringing His light to fulfillment
    and on extinguishing the light of evildoers,
Making the people of truth victorious in every

---

225. So rendering qad sawwadnā ʿalayka.
226. Ibn Kathīr (Bidāyah, vol. IX, p. 49) adds qabla 'l-khurūj ʿalayhi.
227. So rendering qad iktaḥaltu baʿdaka'l-sahar.
228. See above, n. 13.
229. See below, p. 62 and n. 237.
230. For the following verses, cf. Geyer, The Dīwán of al-Aʿshà, pp. 320–21
(Arabic texts); Aghānī², vol. VI, pp. 60–61 (which differs considerably); von Goutta, Aġaniartikel, pp. 39–41, 56–58.

　　　　　battlefield;
　　　　　the sword blow will straighten the inclining
　　　　　neck of the one who was a proud king,
[1114]　And bring down abasement on Iraq and its people,
　　　　　because of their breaking of the certain and
　　　　　firm compact,
[Because of] their innovation and their big words,
　　　　　which do not ascend to God,
And [because of] their breaking of an oath of allegiance:
　　　　　They make [such an oath] today and break it tomorrow.
Their Lord has filled their hearts with cowardice,
　　　　　and they only approach people as if threatened.
They are bereft of veracity and of fortitude in adversity;
　　　　　they are full of boasting and bravado.
How do you think God disunited them
　　　　　and scattered them far and wide?
Their dead are the dead of waywardness and sedition,
　　　　　while their living have become abased and pursued.
When we advanced on Ibn Yūsuf in the early morning
　　　　　and the two armies flashed and thundered,
[1115]　We crossed toward him, over the two trenches;
　　　　　we just crossed and reached the death that was waiting.
Al-Ḥajjāj confronted our lines,
　　　　　without having given warning,
With a line which was as if it had lightning in its ranks,
　　　　　when its helmets shone and gleamed.
We moved toward it in lines which were like
　　　　　the mountains of Sharawrā,[231] if they could
　　　　　be brought to move.
Al-Ḥajjāj forthwith drew his sword
　　　　　against us, and our army fled and broke up.
Al-Ḥajjāj never fights but that you see him
　　　　　well supported (i.e., by God) and provided for,
　　　　　accustomed to victories.
Ibn ʿAbbās[232] is in a state of indecision,
　　　　　which we liken to a black portion of the night:
They neither pointed a spear at him nor unsheathed;

---

231. To the east of Tabūk (Yāqūt, *Muʿjam*, vol. III, p. 282).
232. I.e., ʿAbd al-Raḥmān b. al-ʿAbbās al-Hāshimī, as Ibn al-Athīr points out.

surely the coward often encountered [a foe]   [1116]
   and unsheathed?
The cavalry of Sufyān[233] wheeled round against us
   with its horsemen, their lances broken (i.e.,
   from much use).
Sufyān led them, and it was as if his standard,
   from [much] piercing, was a red cloth stiff
   with dye.
Around him were mature men and beardless youths
   from Quḍāʿah,
   furious heroes in situations where the coward
   would turn aside.
When he said, "Attack!" they charged as one,
   ʾand the spear points were brought to their
   drinking places
By the troops and cavalry of the Commander of the
   Faithful,
   and his authority became mighty and supported.
May the Commander of the Faithful be given joy by
   his victory
   over a community [of people] who were
   oppressors and enviers!
They leapt up complaining of oppression from
   their amīrs,
   while it was they who were the most oppressive
   and obdurate of the oppressors.
We have found the Banū Marwān to be the best imāms,
   and the worthiest of these people in moderation
   and the exercise of authority,
And the best of Quraysh by way of origin,   [1117]
   and the noblest of them, except for the Prophet
   Muḥammad.
When we reflect on the consequences of his rule,
   we find the Commander of the Faithful to have
   been directed aright.
People who have openly contended with God will be
   overcome,[234]

---

233. I.e., Sufyān b. al-Abrad al-Kalbī.
234. Al-Ṭabarī has *sa-yughlabu qawm*^{un}, while Ibn al-Athīr gives *sa-yaghlibu qawm*^{an}.

> if they try to deceive Him, He [proves to be]
> stronger and more crafty.
> Thus does God mislead him whose heart is
> sick and him who espouses hypocrisy and blasphemes.
> They have left families and property behind them,
> and fair virgins clad in gowns,
> Who call to them, shedding tears on their account,
> and allowing those tears, together with
> antimony, to fall on their cheeks.
> If you do not offer them compassion,
> they will become captives and the[ir] menfolk slaves.
> Will you perpetrate the braking of compacts,
> disobedience, perfidy, and abasement?
> May God despise and make distant those who are
> despicable!
> Muhammad's chick[235] has brought ill luck upon the
> two *misr*s [of al-Basrah and al-Kūfah]—
> justly so—and he did not encounter anything
> more propitious from the bird of omen,

[1118] > Just as God brought ill luck upon al-Nujayr[236]
> and its people,
> by reason of a grandfather of his who was
> [even] more wretched and troublesome.

The Syrians said, "He has done well, may God cause the amīr to prosper!" Al-Ḥajjāj said, "He has not done well. You do not know what he meant by it." Then he said, "O enemy of God, we do not praise you for these words. You only said [what you did] out of sorrow that he was not victorious and by way of incitement of your companions against us. It is not about this that we have asked you. Deliver to us your words (*kāmil*):

> 'Between the man with the scarred face and Qays is a
> proud and lofty [glory].' "[237]

---

235. I.e., 'Abd al-Raḥmān b. Muḥammad.

236. The castle in Ḥaḍramawt where 'Abd al-Raḥmān's grandfather al-Ashʿath finally surrendered after staging a revolt following the death of the Prophet (see *EI*², s.v. al-Ashʿath).

237. Cf. *Aghānī*², vol. VI, pp. 46, 61; al-Masʿūdī, *Murūj*, vol. V, p. 358 = par. 2110; and Ibn Aʿtham, *Futūḥ*, vol. VII, p. 147. "The man with the scarred face" (*al-*

He did so, and, when he said (that is, reached the words) "Say, 'bravo' for his father and for the son," al-Ḥajjāj said, "No, by God, you won't say 'bravo' after this for anyone ever again"; and he sent him forward, and he was beheaded.

Regarding the matter of the prisoners taken by Yazīd b. al-Muhallab and sent by him to al-Ḥajjāj, and regarding, too, the matter of Ibn al-Ashʿath's troops routed on the battle day of Maskin, there is information other than that mentioned by Abū Mikhnaf on the authority of his sources. It is mentioned on their authority in that connection that, when Ibn al-Ashʿath was defeated, these [troops] went with the rest of the routed troops to al-Rayy, which had been taken by ʿUmar b. Abī al-Ṣalt b. Kanārā,[238] a mawlā of the Banū Naṣr b. Muʿāwiyah, who was one of the finest of horsemen, and they joined him. Then Qutaybah b. Muslim arrived in al-Rayy on behalf of al-Ḥajjāj, who had appointed him over it. The people whom I have mentioned as being sent by Yazīd b. al-Muhallab to al-Ḥajjāj in bonds, and the rest of the routed troops of Ibn al-Ashʿath who had gone to al-Rayy, said to ʿUmar b. Abī al-Ṣalt, "We put you in command of us; with us you will wage war on Qutaybah." ʿUmar consulted his father, Abū al-Ṣalt, and his father said to him, "By God, my son, if these people will go under your standard, I do not care if you are killed tomorrow," and he tied his standard. Then [ʿUmar] went forth and was defeated together with his companions. They fled to Sijistān, where the routed troops gathered, and wrote to ʿAbd al-Raḥmān b. Muḥammad, who was with the Zunbīl. Then there happened to them with Yazīd b. al-Muhallab what I have mentioned.

[1119]

Abū ʿUbaydah [Maʿmar b. al-Muthannā][239] mentioned: When Yazīd wanted to send the captives to al-Ḥajjāj, his brother Ḥabīb said to him, "How do you regard the Yamaniyyah, given that you

---

ashajj) was ʿAbd al-Raḥmān's paternal grandfather, al-Ashʿath, while "Qays" refers to the father of his maternal grandfather, Saʿīd b. Qays al-Hamdānī (see Wellhausen, *Kingdom*, p. 247; *EI²*, s.v. Ibn al-Ashʿath); Ibn al-Athīr mistakenly thought that *al-ashajj* referred to ʿAbd al-Raḥmān's father, Muḥammad, and that ʿAbd al-Raḥmān's maternal grandfather was Maʿqil b. Qays al-Riyāḥī.

238. This being the form proposed (to replace "Kannāz") in the *Addenda et Emendanda* (in which connection see the references given by Justi, *Iranisches Namenbuch*, p. 155, s.v. Kanarang 4); it is also given by Khalīfah (*Taʾrīkh*, pp. 284, 288, where "ʿAmr" is read in place of "ʿUmar").

239. Died in 209 (824–25), or thereabouts (*EI²*, s.v.).

have sent Ibn Ṭalḥah?" Yazīd said, "He is al-Ḥajjāj and he should not be thwarted." [Ḥabīb] said, "Habituate yourself to [the idea of] being dismissed, and do not send him; we do owe him a favor." [Yazīd] said, "How so?" [Ḥabīb] said, "Al-Muhallab was dunned for two hundred thousand [dirhams][240] in the congregational mosque, and Ṭalḥah[241] paid them for him." So [Yazīd] set Ibn Ṭalḥah free and sent the remaining [prisoners to al-Ḥajjāj]; al-Farazdaq said (kāmil):

Ibn Ṭalḥah found the best grouping on the day when
> his people
encountered Qaḥṭān on the battle day of Herat.[242]

It has been said that al-Ḥajjāj, when he was brought the prisoners from Yazīd b. al-Muhallab, said to his chamberlain, "If I call upon you to bring their leader, bring me Fayrūz." Then he put his throne in a prominent position—he was at that time at Wāsiṭ al-Qaṣab, [this being] before the city of Wāsiṭ had been built—and said to his chamberlain, "Bring me their leader." [The chamberlain] said to Fayrūz, "Stand up," and al-Ḥajjāj said to him, "Abū ʿUthmān, what made you rebel with these people? By God, you are not from the same flesh and blood." He said, "[It was] a sedition in which everyone was caught up, including us." [Al-Ḥajjāj] said, "Write down for me [a list of] your assets." He said, "Then what?" [Al-Ḥajjāj] said, "[Just] write them down first." He said, "Will my life then be safe?" [Al-Ḥajjāj said], "Write them down; then I'll see." He said, "O ghulām,[243] write down one million [dirhams] and[244] two million [dirhams]," and he mentioned much money. Al-Ḥajjāj said to him, "Where are these assets?" He said, "With me." [Al-Ḥajjāj] said, "So hand them over." He said, "Will my life then be safe?" [Al-Ḥajjāj] said, "By God, you will hand them over, and I shall then kill you." He said, "By God, you're not going to have both my money and my life." Al-Ḥajjāj then said to the chamberlain, "Put him to one side,"

[1120]

---

240. 100,000 dirhams, according to Ibn al-Athīr.

241. He being the distinguished Khuzāʿī general Ṭalḥah b. ʿAbdallāh (Ṭalḥat al-Ṭalaḥāt), "der freigebigste Araber seiner Zeit" (see Caskel, Ǧamharat an-nasab, register).

242. This verse does not appear in al-Farazdaq's Dīwān.

243. See above, n. 139.

244. This "and" is given by Ms B and Ibn al-Athīr.

and he did so.

Then [al-Ḥajjāj] said, "Bring me Muḥammad b. Saʿd b. Abī Waq-qāṣ." [The chamberlain] called him and al-Ḥajjāj said to him, "You shadow of Satan,[245] you most wayward and arrogant of people, you decline to take the oath of allegiance to Yazīd b. Muʿāwiyah, you liken yourself[246] to Ḥusayn and Ibn ʿUmar, and then you become muezzin for Ibn Kanārā,[247] the slave of the Banū Naṣr"—meaning ʿUmar b. Abī al-Ṣalt—and he struck him on the head with a stick [which he held] in his hand until he caused it to bleed. Muḥammad said to him, "[Easy,] man! You have [already] won; so be forgiving,"[248] and [al-Ḥajjāj] stayed his hand. Then [Muḥammad] said, "If you see fit, you can write to the Commander of the Faithful; if a pardon [for me] comes to you, you will have been party to that and [will be duly] praised; and if there comes to you other than that, you will [at least] have gone to great lengths." [Al-Ḥajjāj] remained silent for a long time with downcast eyes; then he said, "Behead him!" and he was beheaded.

Then he called for ʿUmar b. Mūsā and said to him: "You philanderer,[249] will you stand with an iron bar protecting the head of the son of the weaver,[250] drink [intoxicating] drink with him in the bathhouse of Fārs, and say what you said?[251] Where is al-Farazdaq? Stand and recite to him what you said about him?" And [al-Farazdaq] recited to him (kāmil):[252]

You dyed your penis for fornication and you were
    not about
    to dye the heroes (i.e., with blood) on the
    day of battle.

---

245. *Ẓill al-shayṭān*, a sobriquet explained by al-Thaʿālibī with reference to Ibn Saʿd's height, swarthiness, and stout build (*Laṭāʾif al-maʿārif*, p. 40 [English trans., p. 59]).

246. Reading *tatashabbahu*, with Ibn al-Athīr (cf. Ibn Aʿtham, *Futūḥ*, vol. VII, p. 155: *yatashabbahu*); the Ṭabarī text has *t.sh.b.h.*

247. See above, n. 238.

248. Cf. Freytag, *Arabum Proverbia*, vol. II, p. 630.

249. If this is how *ʿabd al-marʾah* is to be understood.

250. I.e., Ibn al-Ashʿath, this being an insult because weaving was a despised occupation (see Brunschvig, "Métiers vils en Islam," pp. 5off.) and one which Yemenis were stereotypically mocked for engaging in (al-Thaʿālibī, *Laṭīʾif al-maʿārif*, p. 40 [English trans., p. 59]).

251. This allusion remains in need of clarification.

252. This verse does not appear in al-Farazdaq's *Dīwān*.

[ʿUmar] said, "By God, I have kept it away from your secluded women." Then [al-Ḥajjāj] ordered that he be beheaded.

Then he called for Ibn ʿUbaydallāh b. ʿAbd al-Raḥmān b. Samurah, [who proved to be just] a young man. He said, "May God cause the amīr to prosper! I am guiltless. I was a young lad with my father and mother, with no say whatever, being with them wherever they happened to be." [Al-Ḥajjāj] said, "Was your mother with your father in all of these seditions?" He said, "Yes." [Al-Ḥajjāj] said, "May God's curse be upon your father!"

Then he called for al-Hilqām b. Nuʿaym and said [to him], "Supposing that[253] Ibn al-Ashʿath sought what he sought, what did you hope for with him?" He said, "I hoped that he would gain mastery and appoint me over Iraq, just as ʿAbd al-Malik has appointed you." [Al-Ḥajjāj] said (addressing one of his staff), "Stand up, O Ḥawshab, and behead him." [Ḥawshab] moved toward him, and al-Hilqām said to him, "You son of a bitch";[254] [Ḥawshab] beheaded him.

Then ʿAbdallāh b. ʿĀmir[255] was brought. When he stood before [al-Ḥajjāj], he said, "May your eyes never see Paradise, O Ḥajjāj, if you forgive[256] Ibn al-Muhallab for what he has done." [Al-Ḥajjāj] said, "What has he done?" and ʿAbdallāh replied (basīṭ):[257]

Because he cleverly set his family free
    and drove Muḍar to you in fetters.
With your people he protected his family from death's onset,
    and your people were of less consequence to him.

Al-Ḥajjāj remained silent for a long time with downcast eyes, and [these words] rested in his heart. [Then] he said, "What does that have to do with you? Behead him!" and he was beheaded. [But the

---

253. Ibn al-Athīr reads *aḥbabta anna* where the Ṭabarī text gives *ijʿal*.

254. Reading *yā ibna laṭīfati iskatay al-farj*, "you son of a woman with (?)tight *labia majora*," and translating freely; I cannot take the credit for this inspired reconstruction of the text (which rests on what survives in Ms B).

255. Presumably, the ʿAbdallāh b. ʿĀmir al-Naʿʿār who had earlier been at Zaranj (see above, p. 00).

256. *Aqalta*, while Ibn al-Athīr has *aflatta*; cf. Khalīfah (*Taʾrīkh*, p. 284) and the Omani version of this story (see Hinds, *Early Islamic Family*, par. 61 and n. 135).

257. In Khalīfah's version and in the Omani version of this, al-Ḥajjāj's interlocutor is al-Hilqām; the following verses are given in both of these versions.

words] remained in al-Ḥajjāj's soul until he dismissed Yazīd from
Khurasan and imprisoned him.

Then he gave the order and Fayrūz was tortured. As part of his
torture, split Persian cane was tied to him, and he was dragged on it
until it pierced his body in many places; then [a mixture of] vinegar
and salt was sprinkled onto him. When he felt [the onset of] death,
he said to [his] torturer, "The people will not doubt that I have been
killed; owing to me are deposits of wealth with the people that will
never be handed over to you. Show me to the people, that they may
know that I am alive and hand over the money." Al-Ḥajjāj was
informed [of this] and said, "Put him on view." So he was taken out
to the city gate, and he called to the people, "Those who know me
know me; [as for] those who do not know me, I am Fayrūz Ḥuṣayn.
[Some] people have money owing to me. Anyone who has anything
owing to me may keep it, perfectly legally. Let not anyone hand
over a [single] dirham of it. Let those who have witnessed this
inform those who are not present." Al-Ḥajjāj gave the order and
[Fayrūz] was killed. This is part of what al-Walīd b. Hishām b.
Qaḥdham related on the authority of Abū Bakr al-Hudhalī.

Ḍamrah b. Rabīʿah related on the authority of Ibn Shawdhab
that al-Ḥajjāj's governors[258] wrote to him, "The land tax has
become depleted. The *ahl al-dhimmah* have become Muslims
and have gone off to the garrison cities." [Al-Ḥajjāj] wrote to al-
Baṣrah and elsewhere, "Whoever originates from a village must
go out [and return] to it." The people went out and camped and
began to weep and call out, "O Muḥammad! O Muḥammad!" and
they had no idea of where to go. Then the *qurrāʾ* of the Baṣrans
began to go out to them, masked,[259] and to weep at what they
heard from them and what they saw. [Ḍamrah] continued: Then
Ibn al-Ashʿath came in the wake of that, and the *qurrāʾ* of the
Baṣrans committed themselves to fighting al-Ḥajjāj with ʿAbd al-
Raḥmān b. Muḥammad b. al-Ashʿath.

According to Ḍamrah b. Rabīʿah—al-Shaybānī: On the battle
day of al-Zāwiyah, al-Ḥajjāj killed eleven thousand [people] and
spared only one, whose son was one of al-Ḥajjāj's secretaries. [Al-

[1122]

[1123]

---

258. ʿUmmāl: This may be an early example of the term in the sense of "fiscal
intendants" (cf. *EI*², s.v. ʿĀmil).
259. So rendering *mutaqanniʿīn*.

Ḥajjāj] said to [the secretary], "Do you want us to forgive your
father for you?" He said, "Yes," and [al-Ḥajjāj] left [the father] to
his son. [Al-Ḥajjāj] deceived them by means of the safe-conduct:
He gave orders to a crier, who called out at the defeat, "There is no
safe-conduct for so-and-so, nor for so-and-so," and he named men
from those *ashrāf*, without saying, "The people will be safe." The
rank and file then said, "He has given safe-conduct to all the people
except those individuals," and they advanced to his compound.
When they had gathered together, he ordered them to lay down
their arms. Then he said, "Today I shall order to deal with you a
man to whom you are not related." He ordered ʿUmārah b. Tamīm
al-Lakhmī to deal with them; [ʿUmārah] brought them near and
then killed them.

It has been related on the authority of al-Naḍr b. Shumayl that
Hishām b. Ḥassān said: The number of people killed in bonds by
al-Ḥajjāj reached 120,000 or 130,000.

[A Second Account of the Battle of Maskin]

Concerning the defeat of Ibn al-Asʿath at Maskin, an account
other than that of Abū Mikhnaf has been mentioned: Ibn al-
Ashʿath and al-Ḥajjāj met at Maskin, in the territory of Abazqubādh.[260] The camp of Ibn al-Ashʿath was next to a river called
Kh.dāsh[261] at the back part of al-Nahr—[that is,] Nahr Tīrā.[262]
[1124] Al-Ḥajjāj stopped at the river Afr.y.dh,[263] and the two camps were
in their entirety between the Tigris, al-Sīb,[264] and al-Karkh.[265]
They fought for a month—also said to be less than that—and al-
Ḥajjāj did not know of any way to them other than the way on
which they were engaging each other. Then he was brought an old
man who was a herdsman called Zawraq, and he showed him a

---

260. A place lying between al-Baṣrah and Wāsiṭ and not far from Maysān and
Dast-i Maysān, associated in the chronicles of the early conquests with al-Madhār
(Yāqūt, *Muʿjam*, vol. I, pp. 90–91).
261. Which remains to be identified.
262. A right-bank affluent of the lower Karkhah river in Khūzistān (Le Strange,
Lands of the Eastern Caliphate, p. 241).
263. Which remains to be identified.
264. Yāqūt (*Muʿjam*, vol. III, p. 209) knew this as "the Baṣran river" (*nahr al-
Baṣrah*), which had a large settlement in it (*fīhi qaryah kabīrah*).
265. Yāqūt (*Muʿjam*, vol. IV, p. 253) knew Karkh al-Baṣrah as a place in Maftaḥ
(which was itself a place between al-Baṣrah and Wāsiṭ [vol. IV, p. 586]).

way round behind al-Karkh, six parasangs long,[266] through a thicket and some shallow water. [Al-Ḥajjāj] selected four thousand of the most eminent of the Syrians and said to their leader, "Let this unbeliever (ʿilj) be in front of you. Here are four thousand dirhams for you to take with you. If he gets you to their camp, pay the money to him; if he [proves to have] lied to us,[267] behead him. If you see them, attack them with those who are with you. Let your battle cry be 'O Ḥajjāj! O Ḥajjāj!'" The leader set off at the time of the afternoon prayer, and al-Ḥajjāj's army and that of Ibn al-Ashʿath met when the leader moved off with those who were with him at the time of the afternoon prayer. They fought until nighttime, and al-Ḥajjāj withdrew until he crossed [the] al-Sīb [river], which he had bridged;[268] Ibn al-Ashʿath entered his camp and plundered what was in it. He was asked, "Why not follow him?" He said, "We are worn out," and he returned to his camp; his companions cast down their weapons and passed the night sure that they had won. The people [making up the force of four thousand] attacked them halfway through the night, shouting their battle cry, and the companions of Ibn al-Ashʿath did not know where to direct themselves: Dujayl to the left [or] the Tigris, with its awful eroded bank, straight ahead? Those who drowned were more numerous than those who were killed. Al-Ḥajjāj heard the noise and crossed [the] al-Sīb to his camp. Then he sent his cavalry to the [other force], and the two armies met at the camp of Ibn al-Ashʿath. [The latter] fled with three hundred [men] and went along the bank of the Tigris until he reached [the] Dujayl [river], which he crossed in boats. They hocked their riding animals and went downstream in the boats to [1125] al-Baṣrah. Al-Ḥajjāj entered [Ibn al-Ashʿath's] camp and plundered what was in it. He killed anyone he found, until he had killed four thousand [people]. It is said that among those he killed was ʿAbdallāh b. Shaddād b. al-Hād;[269] also killed were Bisṭām b. Maṣqalah b. Hubayrah; ʿUmar[270] b. Ḍubayʿah al-Raqāshī; Bishr b. al-Mundhir b. al-Jārūd[271] and al-Ḥakam b. Makhramah, who were

---

266. About 36 kilometers.
267. Reading kadhabanā, as proposed in the Addenda et Emendanda.
268. So rendering ʿaqada.
269. Sayed, Revolte, p. 355, no. 16.
270. ʿAmr, according to Ibn al-Athīr.
271. See above, n. 54.

both ʿAbdīs; and Bukayr b. Rabīʿah b. Tharwān al-Ḍabbī. Al-Ḥajjāj was brought their heads on a shield. He began to look at the head of Bisṭām and recited (basīṭ):[272]

If you pass along the valley of a male serpent,
  go and leave me to deal with[273] the serpent
  of the valley.

Then he looked at the head of Bukayr and said, "How did this wretch get to be with these? Take hold of his ear, boy, and cast it away from them." Then he said, "Place this shield in front of Mismaʿ b. Mālik b. Mismaʿ."[274] It was placed before him, and he wept. Al-Ḥajjāj said, "What has made you weep? Is it out of sorrow for them?" He said, "No, rather out of fear of hell fire for them."

[*The Reason Why al-Ḥajjāj Built Wāsiṭ*]

In this year al-Ḥajjāj built Wāsiṭ. The reason for his building it, in among what has been mentioned, was that al-Ḥajjāj raised Kūfan levies [to go] to Khurasan, and they camped at Ḥammām ʿUmar.[275] A young Kūfan man from the Banū Asad, who had recently married his paternal uncle's daughter, departed from the camp to his cousin at night. Somebody knocked hard on the door, and, lo and behold, it was a drunken Syrian. The cousin said to the [Asadī] man, "We've had a lot of trouble from this Syrian. He does this sort of thing every night, wanting something not very nice. I have complained about him to the shaykhs among his companions, and they know about it." [The Asadī] said, "Let him in," and they did so. Then he locked the door, the woman having [first] seen to the house and made it pleasant. The Syrian said, "Your time has come," and the Asadī killed him and struck off his head. When the dawn call to prayer was made, the [Asadī]

[1126]

---

272. The poet is Ḥārithah b. Badr al-Ghudānī (Sezgin, *GAS*, vol. II, p. 326) and another version of the following verse can be found (with others) in *Aghānī*[1], vol. XXI, p. 44 (= p. 425 of the supplement to vol. VIII of *Aghānī*[2]).

273. The *Aghānī* here gives *umāris*, which is preferred in the *Addenda et Emendanda* to the *uqāsī* given in the text.

274. Crone, *Slaves on Horses*, p. 117.

275. A place between Jāmiʿān (later al-Ḥillah) and Niffār (Le Strange, *Lands of the Eastern Caliphate*, p. 73).

went out to the camp, saying to his wife, "When the dawn prayer has been prayed, send [word] to the Syrians that they should remove their man. They will take you to al-Ḥajjāj; tell him the truth, just as it was." She did so, and the dead man was borne off to al-Ḥajjāj. The woman was brought into his presence; with him on his throne was ʿAnbasah b. Saʿīd.[276] [Al-Ḥajjāj] said to her, "What happened?" She told him, and he said, "You have told the truth." Then he said to the blood claimants[277] of the Syrian, "Bury your relative. He has been killed by God [and is headed] for hell fire; there will be no retaliation and no blood money." Then his crier called out, "No one [of the Syrians] may stop off with any one [of the Iraqis]. Move out and make camp." [Al-Ḥajjāj] sent out scouts to reconnoiter [and find] for him a place to settle. He worked assiduously until he stopped at the fringes of Kaskar, and, while he was at the site of Wāsiṭ, lo and behold, a monk advanced on a donkey of his and crossed the Tigris. When he was at the site of Wāsiṭ, the she-ass parted her legs and urinated; the monk dismounted and dug up the urine and then carried it and threw it into the Tigris, during all of which time al-Ḥajjāj was watching. Al-Ḥajjāj said, "Bring him to me," and he was brought. [Al-Ḥajjāj] said, "What possessed you to do what you did?" [The monk] said, "We find [it written] in our books that there will be built in this place a mosque in which God will be worshiped as long as there remains on earth anyone who proclaims His oneness." Al-Ḥajjāj marked out the city of Wāsiṭ and built the mosque at that place.

In this year, according to what al-Wāqidī said, ʿAbd al-Malik dismissed Abān b. ʿUthmān from Medina and appointed over it Hishām b. Ismāʿīl al-Makhzūmī. [1127]

Hishām b. Ismāʿīl led the pilgrimage in this year: Thus it was related to me by Aḥmad b. Thābit on the authority of he who related it to him on the authority of Isḥāq b. ʿĪsā on the authority of Abū Maʿshar.

The governors of the amṣār in this year, apart from Medina were [the same as] the governors of the preceding year. As for Medina, we have mentioned those who were over it in [this year].

---

276. I.e., ʿAnbasah b. Saʿīd b. al-ʿĀṣ al-Umawī (cf. above, n. 49).
277. So rendering wulāt in this context.

The
Events of the Year

84

(JANUARY 24, 703–JANUARY 13, 704)

In [this year] there took place the campaign of ʿAbdallāh b. ʿAbd al-Malik b. Marwān against the Byzantines, in [the course of] which he conquered al-Maṣṣīṣah.[278] Thus it was mentioned by al-Wāqidī.

In [this year, too,] al-Ḥajjāj killed Ayyūb b. al-Qirriyyah,[279] who was one of those who had been with Ibn al-Ashʿath. The reason why he killed him—in among what has been mentioned—was that, after his departure from Dayr al-Jamājim, he used to enter into the presence of Ḥawshab b. Yazīd, who was al-Ḥajjāj's governor of al-Kūfah, and Ḥawshab would say, "Look at this fellow standing with me. Tomorrow or the day after there will arrive from the amīr a letter [containing orders] that I shall have to implement." [Then] one day, while he was standing, there came to him a letter from al-Ḥajjāj [which said]: "To continue: You have become a haven and a refuge for the hypocrites of Iraq. When you read this letter of mine, send Ibn al-Qirriyyah to me with his hand tied to his neck in the company of one of your confidants." When Ḥawshab

[1128]

---

278. Ibn al-Athīr here gives additional information on these Arab operations at al-Maṣṣīṣah.

279. See *EI²*, s.v. Ibn al-Ḳirriyya.

had read the letter, he threw it to [Ibn al-Qirriyyah], who read it and
said, "To hear is to obey"; [Ḥawshab] sent him in bonds to al-
Ḥajjāj. When [Ibn al-Qirriyyah] entered into al-Ḥajjāj's presence,
[the latter] said to him, "O Ibn al-Qirriyyah, what have you prepared for this situation?" He said, "May God cause the amīr to
prosper, three words, like riders at a standstill:[280] this world, the
next world, and doing good." [Al-Ḥajjāj] said, "Explain yourself;
otherwise you will be in trouble."[281] He said, "I shall do so. As for
this world, it [consists of] available wealth, to be consumed by both
the righteous and the unrighteous; as for the next world, it is a just
scale and a place of assembly in which there is nothing false; as for
doing good, if I am asked to do it I shall accept, and, if others are
asked to do it to me, I shall take it with both hands." [Al-Ḥajjāj]
said, "In that case, accept the sword when it falls upon you." He
said, "May God cause the amīr to prosper, forgive me my slip and
grant me some delay.[282] Every fleet steed takes a fall, and every
brave man [at some time] underachieves."[283] Al-Ḥajjāj said, "Certainly not. By God, I shall make you visit[284] hell." He said, "Then
let me be at rest, for I [almost] feel its heat." [Al-Ḥajjāj] said, "Take
him forward, guard, and behead him!" When al-Ḥajjāj looked at
him floundering in his own blood, he said, "If only we had left off
Ibn al-Qirriyyah, so that we might hear [more] of his words." Then
he gave the order and [the cadaver of Ibn al-Qirriyyah] was removed
and discarded.

According to Hishām—ʿAwānah: When al-Ḥajjāj prohibited Ibn   [1129]
al-Qirriyyah from speaking, Ibn al-Qirriyyah said to him, "By
God, if you and I had been on an equal footing, we should both
have fallen[285] or you would have found me unassailable."

---

280. Cf. the account given by al-Masʿūdī, *Murūj*, vol. V, pp. 323–24 = par. 2081.
If, here and in what follows, Ibn al-Qirriyyah's remarks seem stilted, it is because
they are in rhyming prose in the original.

281. So rendering *ukhruj mimmā qulta*.

282. So rendering *wa-asighnī* (which is rightly preferred in the *Addenda et
Emendanda* to *wa-asqinī*) *rīqī*.

283. *Laysa jawād illā lahu kabwah wa-lā shujāʿ illā lahu habwah*; Ibn al-Athīr
adds *wa-lā ṣārim illā lahu nabwah*. Cf. al-Dīnawarī, *Kitāb al-akhbār al-ṭiwāl*, pp.
326–27 (*li-kulli jawādin kabwah wa-li-kulli ḥalīmin hafwah wa-li-kulli shujāʿin
nabwah*), and Freytag, *Arabum Proverbia*, vol. II, p. 430 (*li-kulli ṣārimin nabwah
wa-li-kulli jawādin kabwah*).

284. Reading *la-uzīrannaka*, with the *Addenda et Emendanda* (and Ibn al-
Athīr), in preference to *la-uriyannaka*.

285. Following the *Addenda et Emendanda* (*la-shiknā*).

In this year Yazīd b. al-Muhallab conquered the fortress of Nīzak[286] at Bādghīs.

The Reason Why [Yazīd b. al-Muhallab] Conquered [the Fortress of Nīzak]

According to 'Alī b. Muḥammad—al-Mufaḍḍal b. al-Muhallab: Nīzak was staying in a fortress at Bādghīs, and Yazīd watched for a good time to campaign against him and set spies on him. [News] reached him that [Nīzak] had sallied forth, and Yazīd went to [the fortress] in his absence. [News of this] reached Nīzak, who returned, and [Yazīd] made peace with him on condition that he would hand over to him the treasures that were in the fortress and would leave it with his dependents. [In this connection,] Ka'b b. Ma'dān al-Ashqarī said (basīṭ):[287]

Bādghīs—which [is such that] he who occupies its
> upper part
> overcomes kings and, if he wishes, may act
> tyrannically and oppressively—
Is well fortified: No king before [Yazīd] has
> taken it by guile;
> [it can be taken] only when it is faced by
> a vast army of his.
Its fires, viewed from a distance, could be imagined
> to be
> stars, in the first third of the night.
When [Yazīd] circled round it, their hearts sank
> until they left it to him to judge, and he decided.
He humbled its inhabitant (that is, Nīzak) after his
> [previous] greatness
> [by making him] pay poll tax,[288] [he thereby]
> acknowledging abasement and oppression.
[1130]   A few days thereafter,
> before which you had revealed grief and

---

286. See Gibb, *The Arab Conquests in Central Asia*, p. 26; Ghirshman, *Les Chionites-Hephtalites*, p. 102; *EI²*, s.v. Bādghīs.

287. On the poet, see above, n. 135. Some of the following verses appear also in Ibn A'tham, *Futūḥ*, vol. VII, p. 225.

288. So rendering *al-jizā*.

oppression,
The Provider gave you that, dividing it
    among [God's] creatures; and the deprived one
    is he who is deprived.
With one of your hands you give the enemy poison
    to drink, while the generosity of the other
    is ceaseless.
Can the gift and grace of Yazīd be compared with
    anything other than the Euphrates and the
    Nile in spate?
When they are at their high points, they are no
    more generous than he,
    [even] when they rise above elevated ground
    and hillocks.

And he said (*ṭawīl*):

My praise for the clan of al-ʿAtīk is that they
    are generous in hospitality and noble of origin.
When they make an agreement with one they protect,
    he occupies an elevated place of safety,
    securely high and well defended.
He expelled Nīzak from Bādghīs, and Nīzak
    was in a position which was too difficult for
    kings to snatch from him,
[A position] soaring beneath the sky, like
    a white summer cloud from which the rain clouds
    have passed away.
Not even the mountain goats reach its uppermost parts,   [1131]
    nor birds, save its eagle and osprey.
The children of its people have not been frightened
    by the wolf,
    nor have its dogs barked at anything save the
    stars.
I have desired to encounter al-ʿAtīk, the possessors
    of wisdom,
    made to have mastery, with their riding camels
    protected,
Just as the son of the soil whose lands are parched
    desires rain from abundant clouds,

Then, after despair, he is given to drink, to the
    point where [his land's] conduits cannot cope
    and the billows [of water] gurgle.
God has gathered together those who were remote from
    one another, and there have come together
    groups from many and varied distant places.

['Alī b. Muḥammad] said: Nīzak used to glorify the fortress; when he saw it, he prostrated himself to it. Yazīd b. al-Muhallab wrote to al-Ḥajjāj concerning the conquest; Yazīd's letters to al-Ḥajjāj were written by Yaḥyā b. Ya'mar al-'Adwānī,[289] who was a confederate (ḥalīf) of Hudhayl. He wrote: "We encountered the enemy, and God gave us the upper hand.[290] We killed some and took some captive, while others took themselves to the tops of the mountains, the bottoms[291] of the valleys, the low-lying fields, and the bends of the rivers." Al-Ḥajjāj asked who it was who acted as Yazīd's secretary and was told that it was Yaḥyā b. Ya'mar. He wrote to Yazīd [telling him to send Yaḥyā to him], and [Yazīd] sent him via the messenger service. Then [this] most eloquent of people came to him, and [al-Ḥajjāj] said, "Where were you born?" He said, "In al-Ahwāz." "And this eloquence?" "I memorized the speech of my father, who was an eloquent man." "Now tell me, does 'Anbasah b. Sa'īd make grammatical mistakes?" "Yes, often." "And so-and-so?" "Yes." "Tell me about myself; do I make grammatical mistakes?" "Yes, you make a barely perceptible mistake. You add a letter and you drop a letter: You [also] say 'inna' instead of 'anna' and 'anna' instead of 'inna.'" [Al-Ḥajjāj] said, "I'll give you three days. If, after three days, I find you in Iraqi territory, I'll kill you." [Yaḥyā] returned to Khurasan.[292]

[1132]

The pilgrimage in this year was led by Hishām b. Ismā'īl al-Makhzūmī: Thus it was related to me by Aḥmad b. Thābit on the authority of him who mentioned it to him on the authority of Isḥāq b. 'Īsā on the authority of Abū Ma'shar.

The governors of the amṣār in this year were the same as those I have named above under the year 83.

---

289. Caskel, *Ğamharat an-nasab*, register.
290. Lit. "God gave us their shoulders."
291. *'Arā'ir*: See the *Addenda et Emendanda* and the learned note in the *Glossarium*.
292. A briefer version of this story is given by al-Mubarrad (*Kāmil*, p. 158).

The
Events of the Year

85

(JANUARY 14, 704–JANUARY 1, 705)

In [this year] the death of ʿAbd al-Raḥmān b. Muḥammad b. al-Ashʿath took place.

What [Ibn al-Ashʿath] Died of
and How It Came About

According to Hishām b. Muḥammad—Abū Mikhnaf: When Ibn al-Ashʿath departed from Herat, returning to the Zunbīl, there was with him a man from [the tribe of] Awd called ʿAlqamah b. ʿAmr. [This man] said to him, "I do not want to enter [the territory of the Zunbīl] with you." ʿAbd al-Raḥmān said to him, "Why?" [1133] He said, "Because I fear for you and for those who are with you. By God, in my mind's eye it is as if the letter of al-Ḥajjāj has already arrived, coming to the Zunbīl and filling him with fear, and he has either sent you (sing.) off in submission or he has killed you (pl.). Here [we] are five hundred [men]; you could make an oath with us to the effect that we shall enter the city, entrench ourselves in it, and fight until we are either given a safe-conduct or die nobly." ʿAbd al-Raḥmān said to him, "If you were to enter with me, I should be munificent to you and honor you." But ʿAlqamah refused, and ʿAbd al-Raḥmān entered into the presence of the Zunbīl. These five hundred [men] went off, placed over themselves[293] Mawdūd al-Naḍrī[294] and then stayed put until ʿUmārah b. Tamīm al-Lakhmī advanced upon them; [ʿUmārah] besieged them and they fought him and resisted him until he gave them a safe-conduct and they went forth to him. He kept his word to them.

[Hishām] continued: One letter of al-Ḥajjāj's after another came to the Zunbīl concerning ʿAbd al-Raḥmān b. Muḥammad, saying, "Send him to me; otherwise, by the One other than Whom there is no god, I shall cause a million[295] fighting men to trample your land." With the Zunbīl there was a man from the Banū Tamīm, from [the clan of] the Banū Yarbūʿ, called ʿUbayd b. Abī Subayʿ,[296] and he said to the Zunbīl, "I shall obtain for you from al-Ḥajjāj a compact [to the effect that] he will refrain from taxing your land for seven years on condition that you hand ʿAbd al-Raḥmān b. Muḥammad over to him." The Zunbīl said to ʿUbayd, "If you do that, you will have of me what you ask." [ʿUbayd] then wrote to al-Ḥajjāj, [telling him] that the Zunbīl would not disobey him and that he would keep on at the Zunbīl until he sent ʿAbd al-Raḥmān b. Muḥammad to him. At that, al-Ḥajjāj gave him money, and he [1134] took money from the Zunbīl in that regard. The Zunbīl sent ʿAbd al-Raḥmān b. Muḥammad's head to al-Ḥajjāj, [who] for seven years let him keep [the taxation stipulated in] the peace agreement that he [normally] took from him. Al-Ḥajjāj used to say, "The Zunbīl sent the enemy of God to me after he [had] cast himself off a roof and died."

According to Abū Mikhnaf—Sulaymān b. Abī Rāshid—Mulaykah the daughter of Yazīd:[297] When ʿAbd al-Raḥmān died—

---

293. Reading *jaʿalū ʿalayhim*, with Ibn al-Athīr; the Ṭabarī text gives *baʿathū ʿalayhim*.

294. Ibn al-Athīr reads "al-Baṣrī," which seems unlikely. We are told below (p. 79) that he was from the Banū al-ʿAnbar, but that clan does not appear to have had any subclan by the name of Naḍr; it is just possible that "al-Naḍrī" is a scribal distortion of "al-ʿAnbarī."

295. 100,000, according to al-Yaʿqūbī (*Taʾrīkh*, vol. II, p. 333).

296. The "Abī" is missing in Ibn al-Athīr; according to the *Naqāʾiḍ* (p. 413, ll. 1–2 [in an account that differs somewhat]), he was ʿAbd Allāh or ʿUbayd Allāh b. Abī Subayʿ of the Banū Rabīʿah b. Ḥanẓalah b. Mālik b. Zayd[manāt] Tamīm.

297. Wife of ʿAbd al-Raḥmān; see above, p. 43, where she is identified as the daughter of the brother of ʿAbd Allāh b. Yazīd b. al-Mughaffal al-Azdī; Ibn Aʿtham, on the other hand, identifies her as the daughter of a certain Yazīd al-ʿĀmirī (*Futūḥ*, vol. VII, p. 157). Cf. Sayed, *Revolte*, p. 236.

and his head was [at the time resting] on my thigh—he was suffering from tuberculosis. When he died and they wanted to bury him, the Zunbīl sent for him, cut off his head, and sent it to al-Ḥajjāj.[298] He [also] took eighteen male descendants of al-Ashʿath and detained them with him, while leaving all [the rest of] his companions who had been with [ʿAbd al-Raḥmān]. He wrote to al-Ḥajjāj about his taking of the eighteen men from ʿAbd al-Raḥmān's family, and al-Ḥajjāj wrote to him instructing him to execute them and send their heads to him. He disliked [the idea of] their being brought to him alive, [lest] a petition be made to ʿAbd al-Malik about them and [any] one of them be set free.

On the matter of Ibn Abī Subayʿ and Ibn al-Ashʿath, there has been said other than what I have mentioned on the authority of Abū Mikhnaf. This is what has been mentioned on the authority of Abū ʿUbaydah Maʿmar b. al-Muthannā, who used to say: It has been claimed that ʿUmārah b. Tamīm set forth from Kirmān and came to Sijistān, over which was a man from the Banū al-ʿAnbar called Mawdūd. He [first] besieged him and then gave him a safe-conduct. Then he gained mastery of Sijistān and sent [word] to the Zunbīl, to whom al-Ḥajjāj wrote:[299] "To continue: I have sent to you ʿUmārah b. Tamīm with [a force of] thirty thousand Syrians who have neither forsaken obedience, nor disavowed a Caliph, nor followed an imām of waywardness. He pays each of them one hundred dirhams a month. War is very much to their taste. They seek Ibn al-Ashʿath." But the Zunbīl refused to hand him over.

With Ibn al-Ashʿath was ʿUbayd b. Abī Subayʿ al-Tamīmī, whom he had singled out for his special favor. He was a messenger to the Zunbīl, for whose special favor he was also singled out and to whom he gave cheer. Al-Qāsim b. Muḥammad b. al-Ashʿath said to his brother ʿAbd al-Raḥmān, "I can't be sure that this Tamīmī will not betray you; do kill him," and [ʿAbd al-Raḥmān] intended to do so. [News of this] reached Ibn Abī Subayʿ, who feared him and misrepresented him to the Zunbīl; he put [the latter] in fear of al-Ḥajjāj and called upon him to betray Ibn al-Ashʿath. [The Zunbīl] responded positively to him, and [Ibn Abī

[1135]

---

298. Al-Dhahabī's personal view of this report is dismissive (hādhā qawl shādhdh wa-Abū Mikhnaf kadhdhāb: Taʾrīkh al-Islām, vol. III, p. 235).

299. Ibn Aʿtham (Futūḥ, vol. VII, p. 156) gives a slightly fuller version of this letter.

Subay'] went out clandestinely to 'Umārah b. Tamīm[300] and stipulated a reward[301] in respect of Ibn al-Ash'ath. He specified one
million [dirhams] and stayed with ['Umārah]. 'Umārah wrote of
this to al-Ḥajjāj, who replied: "Give 'Ubayd and the Zunbīl what
they ask for: Come to terms [with them]." The Zunbīl stipulated
that his territory should not be campaigned against for ten years
and that he should thereafter pay [annual tribute in the amount
of] nine hundred thousand [dirhams].[302] [The Zunbīl] and 'Ubayd
were given what they asked for, and the Zunbīl sent [word] to Ibn
al-Ash'ath. He had him brought into his presence together with
thirty of his relatives, having prepared neck collars[303] and fetters
for them. He put a neck collar on each of ['Abd al-Raḥmān] and al-
Qāsim and sent them all to the nearest to him of 'Umārah's strong
points; to the body of people who had been with Ibn al-Ash'ath he
said, "Split up to wherever you wish." When Ibn al-Ash'ath came
near to 'Umārah, he cast himself from the top of a residence[304]
and died. His head was cut off, and it and the prisoners were
brought to 'Umārah. He executed them and sent the head of Ibn
al-Ash'ath and the heads of his relatives, together with his wife, to
al-Ḥajjāj. Concerning that, one of the poets said (kāmil):[305]

[1136]   How far away the place of the cadaver is from its head:
          a head in Egypt and a cadaver at al-Rukhkhaj.[306]

Al-Ḥajjāj [had] sent [the head] to 'Abd al-Malik, and he [had] sent
it to [his brother] 'Abd al-'Azīz, who was at that time over
Egypt.[307]

---

300. Who was at Bust at this time, according to al-Ya'qūbī.
301. This being the definition given in the *Glossarium*.
302. Ibn Kathīr (*Bidāyah*, vol. IX, p. 53) says 100,000.
303. *Al-jawāmi'*, i.e., neck collars fitted with hand manacles (see Lane, *Lexicon*,
s.v. *jāmi'ah*).
304. So rendering *qaṣr*; he is also said to have cast himself from a mountain (al-
Balādhurī, *Futūḥ*, p. 400).
305. Ibn Khurradādhbih (*al-Masālik wa'l-mamālik*, p. 40) cites this verse and
puts it into the mouth of 'Abd al-Malik. Al-Mas'ūdī (*al-Tanbih wa'l-ishrāf*, p. 316)
gives this and a second verse, but not the name of the poet.
306. The area in Sijistān watered by the Qandahār river (Le Strange, *Lands of
the Eastern Caliphate*, p. 339).
307. Ibn Kathīr (*Bidāyah*, vol. IX, p. 54) says that 'Abd al-Raḥmān's head was
buried in Egypt; according to Ibn A'tham (*Futūḥ*, vol. VII, p. 158), the heads of 'Abd
al-Raḥmān and others were taken from Egypt to Ḥaḍramawt and dropped into a
well there.

According to 'Umar b. Shabbah—Ibn 'Ā'ishah—Sa'd b. 'Ubaydallāh: When 'Abd al-Malik was brought the head of Ibn al-Ash'ath, he sent it with a eunuch to a woman from [the family of al-Ash'ath] who was married to a man from Quraysh. When it was put in front of her, she said, "Welcome to a visitor who does not speak. He is one of the kings, who sought something of which he was worthy, but the fates decreed otherwise." The eunuch made to go off with the head, but she drew it out of his hand, saying, "No, by God, [not] until I have done what is necessary." Then she called for [some] althea[308] [with which] she washed it and smeared it[s beard]; then she said, "Now you may have it," and he took it. He informed 'Abd al-Malik [of this], and, when her husband entered into his presence, he said, "If you are able to produce a daughter[309] by her[, that will be a very good thing]."

It has been mentioned that Ibn al-Ash'ath looked at one of his companions while he was fleeing to the territory of the Zunbīl and recited (mutaqārib):[310]

Fear pursues him, and he has lost his course:
    Thus is one who dislikes the heat of battle.
His boots are full of holes, [and] he complains of chafing;
    the edges of sharp pumice stones[311] hurt his feet.
There would have been rest for him in death,
    and death is inevitable for [God's] servants.

[The man] turned to him and said, "O you insignificant blamer [of others],[312] why were you not steadfast in one of the battlefields, so that we might die in front of you? That would have been better for you than what you have come to."

According to Hishām—Abū Mikhnaf: Al-Ḥajjāj set forth in   [1137]

---

308. *Khiṭmī*: see Lane, *Lexicon*, p. 768a.

309. *Sakhlah*, literally "a kid."

310. Lines 2 and 3 of the following verses are given by Ibn A'tham (*Futūḥ*, vol. VII, p. 151), where another verse is also given. Cf. also al-Ya'qūbī, *Ta'rīkh*, vol. II, p. 391, and al-Ṭabarī, *Ta'rīkh*, ser. iii, p. 167 (in the contexts of Zayd b. 'Alī and Muḥammad al-Nafs al-Zakiyyah respectively).

311. See Dozy (*Supplément*, s.v.) for this definition of the term *marw*.

312. Reading *luḥayyah* (rather than *liḥyah*), i.e., the diminutive of (the feminine) *lāḥiyah*.

those days of his, going about accompanied by Ḥumayd al-Arqaṭ,[313] who said (*rajaz*):

He still constructs a trench and destroys it,
    in protection of an army that he leads and betrays,
Until his plunder is in your hands;
    how far from his place of mustering is his
    place of defeat!
He who is fitted for vehement striving for mastery
    is he who does not turn away from it in disgust.[314]

Al-Ḥajjāj said, "This is truer than what the wicked Aʿshā Hamdān
said (*kāmil*):

I have been informed [that] al-Ḥajjāj b.[315] Yū-
    suf slipped, fell, and perished.

Now it is clear to him who it was who slipped and perished,[316]
feared and failed, and doubted and suspected." He raised his voice,
and there was no one who did not fear his anger. Al-Urayqiṭ[317] was
silent, and al-Ḥajjāj said to him, "Go back to what you were saying.
What is the matter with you, O Arqaṭ?" He said, "May I be made
your ransom, O amīr; and the authority of God is mighty. You
became angry, and my muscles became aquiver, my joints tight,
my sight dim, and I felt giddy." Al-Ḥajjāj said to him, "Yes indeed,
the authority of God is mighty. Go back to what you were doing."
And he did so.

One day, when al-Ḥajjāj was going along accompanied by Ziyād
b. Jarīr b. ʿAbdallāh al-Bajalī,[318] who was one-eyed, he said, "What
was it you said to Ibn Samurah?" He said, "I said (*rajaz*):

O one-eyed man, may I be the ransom of the one-eyed;
    you thought that the dug trench

---

313. See *EI*², s.v. Ḥumayd al-Arḳaṭ; Sezgin, *GAS*, vol. II, p. 333.
314. Freytag, *Arabum Proverbia*, vol. I, p. 85; Lane, *Lexicon*, p. 2615a.
315. Reading *Ḥajjāja 'bna* in place of *anna bunayya* (see Geyer, *The Dīwán of
al-Aʿshà*, p. 312, line 6 [Arabic text], and p. 310 of his apparatus; *Aghānī*², vol. VI,
p. 59); Ibn Aʿtham (*Futūḥ*, vol. VII, p. 129) reads *anna 'bna* at this point.
316. The arabic is wordier: *zalaqa wa-tabba wa-daḥaḍa wa-ankabba.*
317. Sic, being the diminutive form of al-Arqaṭ.
318. Crone, *Slaves on Horses*, p. 114.

Would repel from you what fate had in store
   and [stop] calamities befalling."

It has been said that the death of 'Abd al-Raḥmān b. Muḥammad [1138]
took place in the year 84.

In this year al-Ḥajjāj b. Yūsuf dismissed Yazīd b. al-Muhallab
from Khurasan and appointed over it al-Mufaḍḍal b. al-Muhallab,
the brother of Yazīd.

The Reason Why al-Ḥajjāj Dismissed
[Yazīd b. al-Muhallab] from Khurasan
and Appointed al-Mufaḍḍal

'Alī b. Muḥammad mentioned on the authority of al-Mufaḍḍal b.
Muḥammad that al-Ḥajjāj went on a delegation to 'Abd al-Malik
and on his way back stopped at a monastery. He was told that in
the monastery there was a learned old man of the People of the
Books;[319] so he summoned him and said, "O shaykh, do you find
in your books [any reference to] our current situation?" He said,
"Yes, we find [references to] your past, your present, and your
future." [Al-Ḥajjāj] said, "Are names given or [just] general de-
scriptions?" He said, "Both: [You can find] a description without
a name and a name without a description." [Al-Ḥajjāj] said,
"Don't you find a description of the Commander of the Faithful?"
He said, "We find it in [respect of] the time in which we are
living: A bald king—whoever gets in his way is felled." [Al-Ḥajjāj]
said, "Then who?" He said, "A man called al-Walīd." [Al-Ḥajjāj]
said, "Then what?" He said, "A man whose name is the name of a
prophet,[320] through whom the people will be possessed of good
fortune." [Al-Ḥajjāj] said, "Do you know me?" He said, "I have
been told about you." [Al-Ḥajjāj said], "Do you know what I
govern?" He said, "Yes." [Al-Ḥajjāj] said, "Who will govern it
after me?" He said, "A man called Yazīd." [Al-Ḥajjāj] said, "In my
life[time] or after my death?" He said, "I don't know." [Al-Ḥajjāj] [1139]
said, "Do you know his description?" He said, "He will commit
an act of perfidy. I don't know anything other than that."

---

319. *Min ahl al-kutub;* Ibn al-Athīr omits the phrase, while Ibn Kathīr
(*Bidāyah*, vol. IX, pp. 55) has *ahl al-kitāb* here and below.
320. I.e., Sulaymān (b. 'Abd al-Malik).

[ʿAlī b. Muḥammad] continued: Yazīd b. al-Muhallab came to his mind and he set off. He traveled for seven [nights], fearful of what the old man had said, and arrived [at Wāsiṭ]. Then he wrote to ʿAbd al-Malik, asking to be relieved of Iraq. [ʿAbd al-Malik] wrote to him, "O son of the mother of al-Ḥajjāj, I know what you are getting at and that you want to know my opinion of you. By my life, I see the influence of Nāfiʿ b. ʿAlqamah.[321] Divert yourself from this until God brings you what is coming."

Al-Farazdaq said, mentioning his journey (ṭawīl):[322]

If birds had been charged with making the like of
    his journey
    from Jerusalem to Wāsiṭ, they would have
    become weary!
He went by night on fleet camels from Palestine, after
    nighttime had drawn near to the sun of the
    day and [the sun] had set.
That day was not out[323] before he made [the camels] kneel
    in Maysān, weary and weak from their night journey.
It was as if a hungry falcon were in the saddle,
    when the deep gloom revealed him.

[ʿAlī b. Muḥammad] continued: One day, when al-Ḥajjāj was unoccupied, he summoned ʿUbayd b. Mawhab,[324] who entered striking the ground [with a stick]. [Al-Ḥajjāj] raised his head and said, "Woe, O ʿUbayd, the people of the Books mention that what I govern will be governed by a man called Yazīd. I have thought of Yazīd b. Abī Kabshah and Yazīd b. Ḥusayn b. Numayr and Yazīd b. Dīnār,[325] and it can't be any of those, since they are not up to it. It must be Yazīd b. al-Muhallab." ʿUbayd said to him, "You have ennobled [the Muhallabids] and have made their dominion mighty. They are possessed of numbers, endurance, obedience,

[1140]

---

321. Presumably, this was the name of the learned old man.

322. Cf. al-Farazdaq, Dīwān, vol. I, p. 116 (where an extra verse is given and we are told that the journey took seven days), and Yāqūt, Muʿjam, vol. I, p. 424 (where the verses are ascribed to baʿd al-aʿrāb).

323. Preferring Yaqut's ghāba to al-Ṭabarī's (and the Dīwān's) ʿāda.

324. See above, p. 14.

325. For the first two of these, see Crone, Slaves on Horses, pp. 96 and 97, respectively; the third is mentioned only at this point by al-Ṭabarī.

and good fortune. How worthy [Yazīd] is." [But] al-Ḥajjāj decided
to dismiss Yazīd; he did not, however, find any way of proceeding
against him until the arrival of al-Khiyār b. Sabrah b. Dhu'ayb b.
'Arfajah b. Muḥammad b. Sufyān b. Mujāshi',[326] who had been
one of al-Muhallab's horsemen and was with Yazīd. Al-Ḥajjāj said
to him, "Tell me about Yazīd." He said, "He is good in obedience
and easygoing in his way of proceeding." [Al-Ḥajjāj] said, "You are
lying! Tell me the truth." He said, "God is most sublime and
great, [Yazīd] has saddled up without a bridle." [Al-Ḥajjāj] said,
"You speak truly," and he thereafter appointed al-Khiyār over
'Umān.[327]

['Alī b. Muḥammad] continued: Then [al-Ḥajjāj] wrote to 'Abd
al-Malik, blaming Yazīd and the family of al-Muhallab for [their]
adherence to the Zubayrids, and 'Abd al-Malik wrote to him: "I
do not consider the obedience of the Muhallabids to the
Zubayrids to be a shortcoming; rather, I see it as loyalty on their
part to them, and that loyalty will induce them to be loyal to
me." Al-Ḥajjāj wrote to him making him fearful of their perfidy,
on account of what the old man had told him, and 'Abd al-Malik
wrote to him: "You have said a lot about Yazīd and the
Muhallabids. Give me the name of a man who would be suitable
for Khurasan," and he gave him the name of Mujjā'ah b. Si'r al-
Sa'dī.[328] 'Abd al-Malik wrote to him: "The opinion that induced
you to regard the Muhallabids as corrupt is the same as that
which induced you [to name] Mujjā'ah. Look out for me a tough   [1141]
man who will carry out your orders," and he named Qutaybah b.
Muslim. ['Abd al-Malik] wrote to him: "Appoint him."

It reached Yazīd that al-Ḥajjāj had dismissed him, and he said to
his family, "Whom do you think al-Ḥajjāj will appoint over
Khurasan?" They said, "A man from Thaqīf." He said, "By no
means. He will write to one of you with his appointment. [Then,]
when I reach him, he will dismiss [that man], and he will appoint
a man from Qays: How worthy Qutaybah would be."

---

326. Crone, *Slaves on Horses*, p. 133 (wrongly Khiyār b. *Abī* Sabrah).

327. For a rather fuller (if somewhat confused) account of this episode, see
Hinds (*Early Islamic Family*, pars. 62–67), where "[Yazīd] has saddled up without
a bridle" (i.e., acted without adequate preparation) comes out as "a people who
have saddled up without bridles" (par. 66).

328. Crone, *Slaves on Horses*, p. 136.

['Alī b. Muḥammad] continued: When 'Abd al-Malik gave permission to al-Ḥajjāj to dismiss Yazīd, [al-Ḥajjāj] did not like to write to [Yazīd] about his dismissal; so he wrote to him [saying], "Appoint al-Mufaḍḍal as your deputy and come." Yazīd sought the advice of Ḥuḍayn b. al-Mundhir,[329] who said, "Stay, and make an excuse, for the Commander of the Faithful has a good opinion of you. The order has only come from al-Ḥajjāj.[330] If you stay [here] and do not hurry off, I hope that [the Commander of the Faithful] will write to [al-Ḥajjāj instructing him] to confirm [you in your position]." Yazīd said, "We are a family that has been blessed in [respect of] obedience; I do not like disobedience and conflict," and he began to get ready. But he did so too slowly for the liking of al-Ḥajjāj, who wrote to al-Mufaḍḍal, "I have put you over Khurasan." [At this,] al-Mufaḍḍal began to nag Yazīd, and Yazīd said to him, "Al-Ḥajjāj will not confirm you in your position after I [have gone]. It was only fear that I might resist him that induced him to act as he has." [Al-Mufaḍḍal] said, "No, you are envious of me." [Yazīd] said, "O son of Bahlah![331] Would I envy you? You'll see." Yazīd went off in Rabī' II 85 (April–May 704), and al-Ḥajjāj then dismissed al-Mufaḍḍal. The poet said to al-Mufaḍḍal and to his full brother 'Abd al-Malik (kāmil):

[1142]　O two sons of Bahallah, my Lord disgraced you
　　　　on the morning when the shining hero went off.
You forsook your brother and fell
　　　　to the bottom of a dark place, the denizen of
　　　　which is exposed to harm.
Repent much and sincerely; it is only
　　　　the greatest loser who refuses and disdains to repent.

Ḥuḍayn said to Yazīd (ṭawīl):

I gave you a prudent instruction and you defied me,
　　　　only to become stripped of office and regretful.

---

329. The poet (al-)Ḥuḍayn b. al-Mundhir al-Raqāshī: See EI[2], s.v.; Sezgin, GAS, vol. II, p. 376.

330. So understanding innama utīta min al-Ḥajjāj.

331. Bahlah (or Bahallah), as becomes apparent in the first of the following verses, was the mother of al-Mufaḍḍal. It is specified below, p. 157, that she was an Indian woman.

I am not going to weep over you out of longing,
  and I am not going to pray for you to return safely.[332]

When Qutaybah arrived in Khurasan, he said to al-Ḥuḍayn, "What was it you said to Yazīd?" He said, "I said:

I gave you a prudent instruction and you defied me:
  if you blame, you yourself are more deserving of blame.
If it reaches al-Ḥajjāj that you have defied him,
  you will find yourself in deep trouble with him."[333]

[Qutaybah] said, "What was it you instructed him to do that he disobeyed?" [Al-Ḥuḍayn] said, "I instructed him to take to the amīr all the gold and silver he could find." A man said to 'Iyāḍ b. Ḥuḍayn, "As for your father, when Qutaybah tested him, he found him wise when he said, 'I instructed him to take to the amīr all the gold and silver he could find.'"

'Alī [b. Muḥammad] said, and Kulayb b. Khalaf [also] related to us: Al-Ḥajjāj wrote to Yazīd, "Campaign in Khwārazm." [Yazīd] wrote to him, "O amīr, it has little plunder and fierce dogs."[334] Al-Hajjāj wrote to him, "Appoint a deputy and come [to me]." [Yazīd] wrote to him, "I want to campaign in Khwārazm." [Al-Ḥajjāj wrote to him, "Do not campaign in it. It is as you have described it." [Yazīd] then campaigned [there] and did not obey [al-Ḥajjāj]. The people of Khwārazm made a peace agreement with him; he took captives according to the peace terms and made his return journey in the winter. The cold became intense for [Yazīd and his men], and they took the clothes of the prisoners and put them on. Those captives died of cold.

[1143]

['Alī b. Muḥammad] continued: Yazīd stopped at Talastānah,[335] and a plague afflicted the people of Marw al-Rūdh that year. Al-Ḥajjāj wrote to him, "Come," and he set off: He did not pass through any place but that [its people] spread out aromatic plants for him.

---

332. Cf. Hinds, *Early Islamic Family*, par. 68.
333. Ibid., par. 71.
334. A piece of rhyming prose difficult to replicate in English.
335. "A halting place six parasangs before Dandānaqān on the road from Sarakhs to Marw" (Cornu, *Atlas: Répertoires*, p. 155).

Yazīd was given his appointment in the year 82 and was dismissed in the year 85. He set out [to Iraq] from Khurasan in Rabīʿ II 85 (April–May 704), and Qutaybah was appointed.

As for Hishām b. Muḥammad, he mentioned on the authority of Abū Mikhnaf, concerning al-Ḥajjāj's dismissal of Yazīd from Khurasan, a cause other than the one mentioned by ʿAlī b. Muḥammad. He mentioned in that connection on the authority of Abū Mikhnaf—Abū al-Mukhāriq al-Rāsibī and others: Al-Ḥajjāj, when he had finished with ʿAbd al-Raḥmān b. Muḥammad, had no concern save Yazīd b. al-Muhallab and his family. Al-Ḥajjāj had humbled all the Iraqis except for Yazīd and his family and those of the people of the two *miṣr*s who were with them in Khurasan; after ʿAbd al-Raḥmān b. Muḥammad, he feared in Iraq only Yazīd b. al-Muhallab. Al-Ḥajjāj [accordingly] began to try to deceive Yazīd, in an attempt to extract him from Khurasan. He would send to [Yazīd] to come to him, and [Yazīd] would adduce to him the excuse of the enemy and the war in Khurasan. He kept on in this wise until the last part of the rule of ʿAbd al-Malik. Then al-Ḥajjāj wrote to ʿAbd al-Malik, advising him to dismiss Yazīd b. al-Muhallab and informing him of the obedience of the Muhallabids to Ibn al-Zubayr, [as a result of which] they would not be loyal to him. ʿAbd al-Malik wrote to him: "I do not consider the obedience and loyalty of the sons of al-Muhallab to the Zubayrids to be a shortcoming; their obedience and loyalty to them is what has induced them to be obedient and loyal to me." Then [Hishām b. Muḥammad] mentioned the rest of the report along the lines mentioned by ʿAlī b. Muḥammad.

[1144]

In this year al-Mufaḍḍal campaigned against Bādghīs and conquered it.

[Al-Mufaḍḍal's Conquest of Bādghīs]

ʿAlī b. Muḥammad mentioned on the authority of al-Mufaḍḍal b. Muḥammad: Al-Ḥajjāj dismissed Yazīd and wrote in the year 85 to al-Mufaḍḍal concerning his appointment over Khurasan, which lasted for nine months. He campaigned against Bādghīs and conquered it. He took plunder, which he divided among the people: Every man received eight hundred dirhams. Then he campaigned against Akharūn and Shūmān,[336] where he was victorious, took plunder, and divided what he had taken among the people. Al-Mufaḍḍal had no treasury; he [simply] gave out to the people when anything came [his way], and, if he took anything as plunder, he divided it among them. Ka'b al-Ashqarī said, in praise of al-Mufaḍḍal (ṭawīl).[337]

You see rich and poor from every [tribal] grouping,
    bands of all sorts heading for al-Mufaḍḍal.
One visitor [comes] hoping for the benefits of
    his generosity,
    while another goes off having had his needs attended to.
If we head for a land other than yours, we shall not find
    in it a better place to head for nor [shall
    we find] a place of contentment.
If we enumerate the noblest ones, those who are
    sagacious,
    those who have provided good for themselves
    [with God], you are the first!
By my life, al-Mufaḍḍal has made an overpowering assault,   [1145]
    which has made available the watering places
    and herbage in Shūmān.
On the battle day of Ibn 'Abbās,[338] you received
    the like of that,
    and it was for us [as] a sharp sword between
    the two sides.
All of al-Muhallab's moral qualities have become
    clear in you,[339]
    you have been clad with the same means of
    attaining honor as that with which he clad
    himself—
[He,] your father, who strove as no one else did
    and passed on a glory that was not falsely claimed.

---

336. To the southeast of Samarqand (see Barthold, *Turkestan*³, p. 74, for details); Shaban, (*The 'Abbāsid Revolution*, p. 62) judges these operations to have been "minor raids."

337. The following verses appear not to occur elsewhere.

338. Presumably, 'Abd al-Raḥmān b. 'Abbās al-Hāshimī is meant.

339. Taking *laka* to signify *fīka*.

In this year Mūsā b. 'Abdallāh b. Khāzim al-Sulamī was killed at al-Tirmidh.[340]

[Mūsā b. 'Abdallāh's] Going to al-Tirmidh [and His Activities] until He was Killed There

It has been mentioned that the reason for his going to al-Tirmidh was that, when his father, 'Abdallāh b. Khāzim, killed those of the Banū Tamīm whom he killed at Fartanā[341]—an account of his killing of them has been mentioned above[342]—the bulk of those who had remained with him separated from him. He went out to Nishapur and feared [what] the Banū Tamīm [might do] to his baggage[343] in Marw. He therefore said to his son Mūsā, "Move my baggage from Marw and cross the Balkh river (that is, the Oxus), so that you may take refuge with one of the kings or in a fortress where you may stay." Mūsā accordingly set off from Marw with two hundred and twenty horsemen. By the time he reached Āmul,[344] some down-and-out robbers[345] had taken refuge with him, and his party numbered four hundred; [at Āmul] he was joined by [some] men from the Banū Sulaym, including [1146] Zur'ah b. 'Alqamah. He then reached Zamm,[346] [whose people] fought him, and he defeated them, acquired money, and crossed the river. He then reached Bukhārā and asked its lord for refuge. [The latter] refused, fearing him, and said, "[He is] a murderer, and his companions are like him, people given to war and evil; I do not feel secure from him," and he sent him a present of gold coins and riding animals, and a set of clothes. [Mūsā next] de-

---

340. Cf. Gibb, *Arab Conquests*, pp. 27–28; Shaban, *The 'Abbāsid Revolution*, pp. 59ff.; al-Balādhurī, *Futūḥ*, pp. 417–19.

341. Described by Yāqūt (*Mu'jam*, vol. III, p. 868) as a *qaṣr* at Marw al-Rūdh.

342. See al-Ṭabarī, *Ta'rīkh*, ser. II, pp. 593ff. and 695ff.

343. The concern about *thaqal* or *athqāl* exhibited here and in subsequent instances makes it plain that the "baggage" in question contained items of value (cf. the observation made by Shaban, *The 'Abbāsid Revolution*, p. 127, n. 2).

344. A town three miles from the left bank of the Oxus, near the crossing on the way from Marw to Bukhārā (Barthold, *Turkestan*³, p. 80; *EI*², s.v.).

345. So rendering *qawm min al-ṣa'ālīk*.

346. A town on the left bank of the Oxus, 125 miles upstream of Āmul (Barthold, *Turkestan*³, p. 80; *EI*², s.v. Āmul).

scended on one of the lords of the people of Bukhārā in Nūqān,[347] and [this man] said to him, "No good will come to you from staying in this place; the people are afraid of you and do not feel secure from you." He stayed with the dihqān of Nūqān for a few months and then went off looking for [either] a king with whom he might take refuge or a fortress; but he did not come to any place but that [its people] did not want him to stay among them and asked him to move away from them.

'Alī b. Muḥammad said: Then he reached Samarqand and stayed there. Ṭarkhūn,[348] its king, honored him and allowed him to stay, and he stayed for a long time. Now the people of Soghd have a table on which are put greasy meat,[349] bread, and a ewer of something to drink. On a [particular] day every year that is set out for the Horseman of Soghd,[350] and no one but he may go near it; it is his food on that day. If anyone else eats from it, he fights a duel with him, and the table goes to whichever one kills the other. One of Mūsā's companions said, "What is this table?" and he was told about it and fell silent. Then Mūsā's companion said, "I shall eat what is on this table, and I shall fight a duel with the Horseman of Soghd; if I kill him, I shall be their Horseman"; and he sat and ate what was on it. [The Horseman of Soghd] was told [of this] and came, much angered, and said, "O Arab, fight a duel with me." The Arab said, "Yes. I don't want anything other than a duel"; [the Horseman] fought him, and Mūsā's companion killed him. [At this,] the king of Soghd said [to Mūsā and his companions], "I accommodated you and honored you, and you have killed the Horseman of Soghd. Had I not given you and your companions a safe-conduct, I would kill you. Get out of my territory," and he gave [Mūsā] a gift.

[Mūsā next] reached Kish, and the lord of Kish wrote to Ṭarkhūn asking him for help. [Ṭarkhūn] came to him, and Mūsā went out to [Ṭarkhūn] with a force of seven hundred and fought

[1147]

---

347. This is what the text says, but Nūqān (Mashhad), to the east of Nishapur, does not fit the context.

348. The Ikhshīd of Soghd and the "leader of the native princes" (Barthold, *Turkestan*[3], p. 184).

349. *Laḥm wadik*; on the other hand, Ms. B and Ibn al-Athīr read *laḥm wa-khall*, "meat and vinegar."

350. Noted by Barthold, *Turkestan*[3], pp. 181–82.

them until evening. Then they abstained from fighting, Mūsā's companions having sustained many wounds. In the morning, Mūsā gave them the order, and they shaved their heads, just as the Khārijīs do,[351] and cut their tent poles,[352] just as the [Iranian] foreigners do when they [decide to] fight to the death. Mūsā said to Zur'ah b. 'Alqamah, "Set off to Ṭarkhūn and try a ruse on him." He came to him, and Ṭarkhūn said to him, "Why have your companions done what they have done?" He said, "They have chosen to defy death, and what need do you have, O king, of killing Mūsā and [yourself] being killed? You will not get to him before there is killed among you[r] people the like of their number. If you were to kill him and all of them, you would not [thereby] gain good fortune, because he has high standing among the Arabs and no one will govern Khurasan without seeking to avenge his blood. If you get away safely from one [governor], you will not get away safely from another." [Ṭarkhūn] said, "There is no way that I am going to leave Kish in his hand[s]." [Zur'ah] said, "Well, desist from him, so that he may depart." He desisted, and Mūsā came to al-Tirmidh, in which was a fortress next to the river, looking out over it. Mūsā happened upon one of the dihqāns of al-Tirmidh coming from the fortress, [this] dihqān being someone who was avoiding the Tirmidh Shāh. He said to Mūsā, "The lord of al-Tirmidh is reticent and extremely shy. If you treat him kindly and give him presents, he will let you into his fortress; for he is weak." [Mūsā] said, "Certainly not. I shall ask him to let me into his fortress." He then asked him, and [the Tirmidh Shāh] refused. [At this,] Mūsā used guile on him,[353] giving him presents and treating him kindly, until relations between them became good and [the Tirmidh Shāh] came out [of his fortress]. They went out hunting together, with Mūsā going to great lengths in treating him kindly. The lord of al-Tirmidh prepared some food and sent to Mūsā, "I want to honor you. So take lunch with me and bring one hundred of your companions." Mūsā chose one hundred of his companions, and they entered [the city] on their horses. When

[1148]

---

351. For two examples, see Ibn Durayd, *Ishtiqāq*, p. 217, and Ibn al-Jawzī, *Sīrat 'Umar b. 'Abd al-'Azīz*, p. 78.

352. So understanding ṣ.f.n.ā.t. *akhibiyatihim*; see the comments in the *Glossarium*.

353. Reading *mākarahu* (not *mā k.r.h.*), with Ibrāhīm.

[the horses] were in the city, they neighed to one another, and the people of al-Tirmidh augured evil and said to them, "Dismount! Dismount!" Then they were brought into a house fifty by fifty and given lunch. When they had finished the lunch, Mūsā reclined, and they[354] said to him, "Get out!" He said, "I shall not [in the future be able to] take a house like this one; I shall not leave it until it is either my house or my grave," and they fought them in the city. A number of the people of al-Tirmidh were killed, the others fled, and [Mūsā and his companions] entered their dwellings. Mūsā took control of the city and said to the Tirmidh Shāh, "Go forth! I shall confront neither you nor any of your companions." So the king and the people of the city set forth and went to the Turks, seeking their help. [The Turks] said to them, "A hundred men came in to you and expelled you from your land. We fought them at Kish. We shall not fight these [people again]." Mūsā stayed in al-Tirmidh, and his companions, who numbered seven hundred, came in to him. When his father was killed, he was joined by his father's companions, [they being] four hundred horsemen. He became strong and took to going out and making raids on those who were around him.

['Alī b. Muḥammad] continued: The Turks sent some people to the companions of Mūsā to find out what he was up to. When they arrived, Mūsā said to his companions, "There has to be a stratagem for [dealing with] these [people]."

['Alī b. Muḥammad] continued: That was [at a time of] the most intense heat. Mūsā then gave an order for fire, and it was kindled; he gave an order to his companions, and they put on winter clothes, and saddlecloths on top of those, and stretched out their hands to the fire as if warming themselves at it. Mūsā [now] gave permission to the Turks [to come in], and they entered and were fearful at what they saw. They said, "Why have you done this?" They said, "We find it cold at this time [of the year], and we find it hot in winter." [The Turks] returned and said, "[They are] jinn; we shall not fight them."

['Alī b. Muḥammad] continued: The chief of the Turks wanted to campaign against Mūsā. He sent messengers to him, and he

[1149]

---

354. In Ibn al-Athīr's version, they are in the fortress, and it is the Tirmidh Shāh who says what follows.

sent poison together with arrows in musk. He meant by the poison that fighting them was hard; the arrows [represented] war and the musk peace, [and his message was,] "Choose war or peace." [Mūsā] burned the poison, broke the arrows, and scattered the musk. The [Turks] said, "They don't want peace. [Mūsā] is letting [us] know that fighting them is like fire and that he will break us," and they did not campaign against them.

['Alī b. Muḥammad] continued: Bukayr b. Wishāḥ, as governor of Khurasan, neither confronted him nor sent anyone against him. Then Umayyah [b. 'Abdallāh b. Khālid b. Asīd] came [as governor] and went in person seeking [Mūsā]; but Bukayr rebelled against him and renounced allegiance and he returned to Marw.[355] When Umayyah made peace with Bukayr, he stayed put for that year. In the following year, he sent to Mūsā a man from Khuzā'ah with a large force. The people of al-Tirmidh went back to the Turks and asked for their help, but [the Turks] refused. [The people of al-Tirmidh] then said to them, "Some of their own people have campaigned against them and have besieged them; if you help us against them, we shall overcome them." [At this,] the Turks went with the people of al-Tirmidh in a large force, and Mūsā [found himself] surrounded by the Turks and the Khuzā'ī. He would fight the Khuzā'ī in the first part of the day and the Turks in the latter part; and [in this way] he fought them for two or three months. Mūsā then said to 'Amr b. Khālid b. Ḥusayn, who was a horseman, "This has gone on long [enough]. I have

[1150] decided to make a night attack on the camp of the Khuzā'ī, for they think that they are safe at night. What do you think?" ['Amr] said, "A night action would be good, but let it be against the foreigners, for the Arabs are more wary, faster at repelling, and braver at night than the foreigners. So attack them by night, and I hope that God will help us against them. Then we shall be free to fight the Khuzā'ī, we being in the fortress and they being in the open; they are no abler in fortitude or more knowledgeable in war than we are."

['Alī b. Muḥammad] continued: Mūsā decided to make a night attack on the Turks. When a third of the night had passed, he set out with four hundred [men] and said to 'Amr b. Khālid, "Set out

---

355. For the background on Bukayr and Umayyah (a Tamīmī and a Qurashī, respectively), see Shaban, *The 'Abbāsid Revolution*, pp. 44–47.

after us and keep near us. When you hear our *takbīr* (that is, our
call "God is great"), make one yourselves." He went along the
riverbank until he was upstream of the camp. Then he went by
way of the district of Guftān,[356] and, when he came near to their
camp, he made his companions into "fourths" (*arbāʿ*). Then he
said, "Circle their camp, and, when you hear our *takbīr*, make
one yourselves," and he went on, with ʿAmr in front of him and
[the others] going behind him. When the lookouts saw them, they
said, "Who are you?" They replied, "People passing through."

[ʿAlī b. Muḥammad] continued: When they had passed the lookout post, they split up, circled the camp, and made a *takbīr*; the
next thing the Turks knew was swords falling [upon] them, and
they were stirred up, [began] killing one another, and fled. There
were sixteen Muslim casualties. [The Muslims] then took possession of their camp and acquired arms and money. In the morning,
the Khuzāʿī and his companions were shaken by that, feared a
similar night attack, and were on their guard. ʿAmr b. Khālid said
to Mūsā, "You'll only win with a stratagem. They have supplies,   [1151]
and they are numerous. Let me go to them. Maybe I shall gain the
opportunity to be alone with their leader and kill him. [First] give
me a beating." [Mūsā] said, "You [want to] rush into being beaten
and to expose yourself to being killed?" [ʿAmr] said, "As for exposing myself to being killed, I do that every day. As for being beaten,
how easy that is in comparison with what I intend." So [Mūsā]
gave him a beating, fifty lashes, and [ʿAmr] left Mūsā's camp and
went to the camp of the Khuzāʿī, seeking safety. He said, "I am
one of the people of the Yemen, and I was with ʿAbdallāh b.
Khāzim. When he was killed, I went to his son and stayed with
him. I was the first to go to him. When I reached him, he suspected me, acted in a partisan fashion against me,[357] and disliked
me, saying to me, 'Your partisanship is with the enemy, and you
are a spy of his.' He beat me, and I was not sure that I would not
be killed; so I fled." The Khuzāʿī gave him a safe-conduct, and he
stayed with him.

[ʿAlī b. Muḥammad] continued: One day [ʿAmr] entered [into

---

356. If this is how *k.ftān* is to be rendered; Barthold (*Turkestan*[3], p. 74) says that
it "was probably in the southern part of the Surkhān valley, or somewhere west of
it, in the present district of Shirabad." Shaban (*ʿAbbāsid Revolution*, p. 64) opts for
"Kiftān (Kifyāin)" (?).

357. So rendering *taʿaṣṣaba ʿalayya*.

the Khuzā'ī's presence] when he was unoccupied, and he saw no weapon with him. He said, as though offering him good advice, "May God cause you to prosper, someone like you, in a situation like yours, should at no time be without a weapon." [The Khuzā'ī] said, "I have a weapon with me," and he lifted the top part of his bedding, and there was an unsheathed sword. 'Amr took it, struck him, and killed him; [then] he set off, riding his horse. [The Khuzā'ī's companions only] realized what ['Amr] had been up to when he was far away. They sought him, but he gave them the slip and reached Mūsā. That army [of the Khuzā'ī] then broke up: Some of them crossed the river, while others came to Mūsā seeking safe-conduct, which he granted.

Umayyah [b. 'Abdallāh] did not send anyone against [Ibn Khāzim]. ['Alī b. Muḥammad] continued: Umayyah was dismissed, and al-Muhallab came as amīr. He did not confront Ibn Khāzim and said to his sons, "Beware of Mūsā. You will remain [1152] governors of this march as long as this heavy-bellied[358] [fellow] stays in his place. If he is killed, the first person to come against you as amīr of Khurasan will be a man from Qays." Al-Muhallab died without having sent anyone against [Mūsā]. Then Yazīd b. al-Muhallab took over, and he did not confront him. Al-Muhallab had beaten Ḥurayth b. Quṭbah al-Khuzā'ī, and [Ḥurayth] and his brother Thābit had gone off to Mūsā. When Yazīd b. al-Muhallab became governor, he took their property and their womenfolk and killed their uterine brother al-Ḥārith b. Munqidh, together with an affine of theirs who was the husband of Umm Ḥafṣ, the daughter of Thābit. What Yazīd had done reached [Ḥurayth and Thābit].

['Alī b. Muḥammad] continued: Thābit went to Ṭarkhūn and complained to him of what [Yazīd] had done to him. [Now] Thābit was much loved among the non-Arabs, enjoying wide renown; they honored him and guarded themselves [from anything untoward] by [invoking his name]. If one them made a compact which he wished to fulfill, he would swear by the life of Thābit and would not break his word. Ṭarkhūn became angry on his account and gathered Nīzak, al-Sabal,[359] and the people of Bukhārā and al-

---

358. So rendering *thaṭṭ*, which can also mean "thin-bearded"; Ibn al-Athīr gives *thabiṭ*, "stupid."
359. The title of the ruler of al-Khuttal (Marquart, *Ērānšahr*, pp. 69–70, 302).

Ṣaghāniyān;[360] they went, together with Thābit, to Mūsā b. ʿAbdallāh. [In the meantime,] there had fetched up with Mūsā the routed troops of ʿAbd al-Raḥmān b. al-ʿAbbās from Herat, the routed troops of Ibn al-Ashʿath from Iraq and the vicinity of Kābul, and Khurasani Tamīmīs who had been among those fighting Ibn Khāzim in the civil war. Gathered with Mūsā were eight thousand [men] from Tamīm, Qays, Rabīʿah, and Yemen. Thābit and Ḥurayth said to him, "Go until you cross the river and expel Yazīd b. al-Muhallab from Khurasan; then we shall make you governor. Ṭarkhūn, Nīzak, al-Sabal, and the people of Bukhārā are with you." He intended to do so, but his companions said to him, [1153] "Thābit and his brother acted unfaithfully to[361] Yazīd. If you expel Yazīd from Khurasan and they become safe, they will take charge and overcome you. So stay where you are." He accepted their opinion and stayed at al-Tirmidh. He said to Thābit, "If we expel Yazīd, a[nother] governor of ʿAbd al-Malik's will come; we shall [instead] expel Yazīd's governors in Transoxania, in the areas adjacent to us, and the region will be ours to devour." Thābit was satisfied with that and expelled those of Yazīd's governors who were in Transoxania. The revenues[362] were transported to them, and they and Mūsā became strong. Ṭarkhūn, Nīzak, the people of Bukhārā, and al-Sabal departed to their territories; Ḥurayth and Thābit ran affairs, while Mūsā was no more than nominal amīr. Mūsā's companions said to him, "We don't see that you are any more than nominal amīr, while Ḥurayth and Thābit are running affairs. Kill them and take charge." But he refused, saying, "I am not going to betray them after they have strengthened my rule." They, however, envied [Ḥurayth and Thābit] and pressed Mūsā in respect of them until they turned his heart [against them], making him fearful of their treachery. He [then] intended to help them in rising against Thābit and Ḥurayth, and matters became confused. While this was going on, there came against them the Hephthalites,[363] the Tibetans,[364] and the Turks, advancing in [an army numbering] seventy thousand, not counting those without

---

360. See *EI²*, s.v. Čaghāniyān.
361. Preferring the variant *khāʾināni li-* to the reading *khāʾifāni li-*.
362. So rendering *al-amwāl*.
363. Al-Hayāṭilah (see *EI²*, s.v.).
364. Al-Tubbat: See Dunlop, "Arab Relations with Tibet in the 8th and Early 9th Centuries A.D.," *Islâm Tetkikleri Enstitüsü Dergisi*, 5 (1973), p. 304.

helmets and coats of mail and those with plain helmets, but counting only those with tapering helmets.[365]

['Alī b. Muḥammad] continued: Ibn Khāzim went out to the suburb of the city with three hundred cataphracts. A chair was set up for him, and he sat upon it.

['Alī b. Muḥammad] continued: Ṭarkhūn ordered that the wall [1154] of the suburb be breached. Mūsā said, "Let them be," and they demolished [part of] it, and the first of them entered. Mūsā said, "Let them become [more] numerous," and he started to rotate an ax in his hand. When they had become numerous, he said, "Now resist them," and he rode and attacked them and fought them until he expelled them through the breach. Then he returned and sat on the chair. The king urged his companions to return, but they refused. He said, "This is Satan! He who wishes to look at Rustam should look at the man on the chair . . . ;[366] and he who refuses should advance upon him." Then the non-Arabs moved to the district of Guftān.

['Alī b. Muḥammad] said: [The Turks and their allies] made a raid on Mūsā's cattle; he grieved, did not eat, and began to play with his beard. Then he went by night with seven hundred [men] by way of a river[bed] which led to their trench; [this riverbed] had plants on both sides[367] and contained no water. In the morning, they were at the camp [of the enemy]. [Mūsā's] cattle came out, and [Mūsā himself] pounced on them and led them off; some of the [enemy] followed him and Sawwār, a mawlā of Mūsā's, turned on them and speared one of them and felled him. [The others] turned back from them, and Mūsā was safe with the cattle.

['Alī b. Muḥammad] continued: The non-Arabs renewed the fighting in the morning. Their king stood on a hill with ten thousand perfectly equipped [men]. Mūsā said [to his followers], "If you remove these [enemies], the rest will be [as] nothing." Ḥurayth b. Quṭbah headed for them, fought them in the first part of the day, and pressed them hard until he removed them from the hill; [he] was on that day shot in the forehead by an arrow. They abstained from fighting [for a time], and Mūsā then staged a

---

365. So rendering *bayḍah dhāt qūnus* (see Lane, *Lexicon*, p. 1440a, s.v. *sunbuk*); the exaggeration is obvious.

366. The text seems to be corrupt here.

367. Reading *ḥāfatayhi* (rather than *ḥāf.y.t.h*), as proposed in the *Addenda et Emendanda*.

night attack. His brother, Khāzim b. ʿAbdallāh b. Khāzim, charged until he reached their king's candle bearers[368] and stabbed one of them with the pommel of his sword; his horse was speared, ran off with him, and threw him into the Balkh river, where he drowned, wearing two coats of mail. The non-Arabs[369] were killed quickly, and those who escaped were in a bad way. Ḥurayth b. Quṭbah died after two days and was buried in his yurt.[370]   [1155]

[ʿAlī b. Muḥammad] continued: Mūsā set off, and they carried the heads to al-Tirmidh, where they made them face each other in two pyramids.[371] News of the battle reached al-Ḥajjāj, who said, "Praise be to God, who has helped the hypocrites against the unbelievers." Mūsā's companions said, "We had had enough of Ḥurayth being in charge; [now] relieve us of Thābit." [Mūsā] refused. [Meanwhile,] some of what they were getting up to reached Thābit, who infiltrated into Mūsā's service Muḥammad b. ʿAbdallāh b. Marthad al-Khuzāʿī, the paternal uncle of Naṣr b. ʿAbd al-Hamīd, [who was later] Abū Muslim's governor of al-Rayy.[372] [Thābit] said to him, "Beware of speaking Arabic. If they ask you where you are from, say, 'From the captives of al-Bāmiyān.'"[373] [This Muḥammad, then,] used to serve Mūsā and carry news about them to Thābit. [Thābit] said to him, "Remember what they say." Thābit was on his guard and used not to sleep until the young man returned. He ordered some of his *shākiriyyah* to guard him and spend the night with him in his house, they being accompanied by some Arabs.

The people put pressure on Mūsā and vexed him. One night he said to them, "You are going on at me too much. In what you desire [lies] your [own] destruction. You have wearied me. On what pretext will you murder him? I shall not act treacherously toward him." Nūḥ b. ʿAbdallāh, the brother of Mūsā, said, "Leave him to us. When he comes to you in the morning, we shall take

---

368. Taking *shamaʿah* to be the plural of *shāmiʿ*, as proposed in the *Glossarium* and the *Addenda et Emendanda*.

369. Ibn al-Athīr reads *al-turk* where Ṭabarī has *al-ʿajam*.

370. So rendering *qubbah* here and in what follows in the contexts of Khurasan and Transoxania (i.e., the round tent-like structure used by Turkomans and others).

371. Literally, "two pavilions" (*jawsaqayni*).

372. This would have been in the early 130s (747ff.); al-Ṭabarī makes no other reference to him.

373. *EI*², s.v.

him off to one of the houses and behead him in it before he can reach you." [Mūsā] said, "By God, it will be the end of you, and you know best." The young man heard [all this], and he went to Thābit and told him. [Thābit] set off on that same night with twenty horsemen and went on his way. In the morning, [Mūsā's men] found that he had gone and did not know how they had been outmaneuvered. [Then] they missed the young man and knew that he had spied on them for [Thābit].

Thābit reached H.shwrā[374] and stopped at the city. There came out to him many people, both Arab and non-Arab. [When] Mūsā [learned of this, he] said to his companions, "You have opened a door against yourselves; close it," and [he] went against [Thābit].

[1156]   Thābit came out to him in a large group and fought them. Mūsā ordered that the stockade be set on fire, and he fought them until [his men] forced Thābit and his companions to take refuge in the city and to fight [to repel] them from the city. Raqabah b. al-Ḥurr al-'Anbarī[375] advanced, plunged through the fire, and reached the door of the city. One of Thābit's companions was standing there guarding his companions, and [Raqabah] killed him. Then he returned, passing through the blazing fire, which caught the edges of a piece of dyed clothing he was wearing; he cast it from him and stopped. Thābit fortified himself in the city, and Mūsā stayed in the suburb.

When he was traveling to H.shwrā, Thābit had sent [word] to Ṭarkhūn, and Ṭarkhūn [now] came to help him. [News of the advent of Ṭarkhūn reached Mūsā, who returned to al-Tirmidh. ⟨Thābit and Ṭarkhūn went after him, accompanied by⟩[376] the people of Kish, Nasaf, and Bukhārā, with [an army of] eighty thousand [men]. They besieged Mūsā and cut off his supplies, until [he and his followers] were severely affected. In going against Mūsā, the companions of Thābit used to cross a river in

---

374. Thus, too, in al-Balādhurī, *Futūḥ*, p. 418; Kh.shwrā in Ms. P. This place remains to be identified; Shaban (*The 'Abbāsid Revolution*, p. 60) has it from Wellhausen that this was Khushwāragh (Wellhausen, *Kingdom*, p. 425, in fact says Khushwarâgh), but in neither case are we told where that may have been.

375. Caskel, *Gamharat an-nasab*, register.

376. This rendering is inspired by Ibn al-Athīr, where "Mūsā returned to al-Tirmidh" is followed by *wa-aqbala Thābit wa-Ṭarkhūn wa-ma'ahumā*; in al-Ṭabarī, however (and similarly in al-Balādhurī, *Futūḥ*, p. 418.17), it is followed simply by *a'ānahu*, which suggests (wrongly, judging by the context) that the people of Kish, etc., were supporting Mūsā.

the daytime and go back to their camp at night. One day, Raqabah, who was a friend of Thābit's and had advised the companions of Mūsā against doing what they had done, came out, wearing a tunic of silk (*khazz*), and called Thābit to a duel. [Thābit] said to him, "How are you, O Raqabah?" [Raqabah] said, "Do not ask about a man wearing a garment made of silk in the most intense of the summer heat," and he complained to him of their condition. [Thābit] said, "You brought this upon yourselves." [Raqabah] said, "I did not [willingly] take part in what they did. I did not like what they wanted." Thābit said, "Where will you be until there comes to you what has been foreordained for you?" [Raqabah] said, "I shall be with al-Muḥill al-Ṭufāwī, a man from [the] Yaʿṣur[377] [branch] of Qays"; al-Muḥill was a drinker, and Raqabah stopped with him.

[ʿAlī b. Muḥammad] continued: Thābit sent five hundred dirhams to Raqabah via ʿAlī b. al-Muhājir al-Khuzāʿī, [together with the message], "We have [some] merchants coming from Balkh. When it reaches you that they have arrived, send [word] to me and what you need will come to you." ʿAlī came to al-Muḥill's door, and there were Raqabah and al-Muḥill sitting with a large bowl of drink between them, together with a table on which were chickens and loaves of bread. Raqabah was tousle-headed and wearing a red waist wrapper around his middle. [ʿAlī] handed him the bag [of dirhams] and delivered the message. [Raqabah] did not speak to him. He took the bag, gestured to him with his hand to get out, and did not speak to him.

[ʿAlī b. Muḥammad] continued: Raqabah was a heavily built [man], sunken-eyed, prominent-cheeked, and gap-toothed, with a face [round? flat?] like a shield.

[ʿAlī b. Muḥammad] continued: When Mūsā's companions were in dire straits and the siege had intensified, Yazīd b. Huzayl said, "These people will stay on [besieging us] with Thābit [as long as he is alive], and it is better to be killed than to die of hunger. By God, I shall murder Thābit or die [in the attempt]," and he went out to Thābit and asked him for a safe-conduct. Zuhayr said to [Thābit], "I know more about this [man] than you do. He has not come to you because he likes you or because he

[1157]

---

377. Synonymous with Aʿṣur (on this, see al-Zabīdī, *Tāj al-ʿarūs*, vol. III, p. 406, line 38), the father of the Banū al-Ṭufāwah, Bāhilah, and Ghanī (see Caskel, *Ǧamharat an-nasab*, vol. I, chart 92).

fears you. He has come to you in order to act treacherously. Beware of him and leave him to me." [Thābit] said, "I am not going to take measures against a man who has come to me without my knowing whether he is like that or not." [Ẓuhayr] said, "Let me take hostages from him," and Thābit sent [word] to Yazīd, saying, "As for myself, I am not given to suspecting a man of treachery after he has asked for a safe-conduct, [but] your cousin knows more about you than I. So see to what he requires in order to deal with you." Yazīd said to Ẓuhayr, "O Abū Saʿīd, you are raising objections out of envy. Don't you think I have been humbled enough already? I had to leave Iraq and my family and came to [1158] Khurasan as you see. Doesn't [our] kinship make you sympathetic?" Ẓuhayr said to him, "By God, if I had had my own way, this would not have happened; but[, as it is,] give us your sons Qudāmah and al-Ḍaḥḥāk as hostages." [Yazīd] handed them over to them, and they were held by Ẓuhayr.

[Alī b. Muḥammad] continued: Yazīd kept looking out for inadvertency on the part of Thābit, and he was not able to do to him what he desired until one of the sons of Ziyād al-Qaṣīr al-Khuzāʿī died. News of his death reached [Ziyād] from Marw, and Thābit courteously went out to console [him], accompanied by Ẓuhayr and a group of his companions, including Yazīd b. Huzayl. The sun had set. When [Thābit] reached the river of al-Ṣaghāniyān, Yazīd b. Huzayl and two men who were with him tarried, Ẓuhayr and his companions having gone ahead. Yazīd then drew near to Thābit and smote him: The sword bit into his head and reached the brain.

[ʿAlī b. Muḥammad] continued: Yazīd and his two companions cast themselves into the river of al-Ṣaghāniyān. [Ẓuhayr and his companions] shot at them: Yazīd escaped by swimming, while his two companions were killed. Thābit was carried to his house. In the morning, Ṭarkhūn sent [word] to Ẓuhayr, "Bring me the two sons of Yazīd," and he brought them. Ẓuhayr [first] presented al-Ḍaḥḥāk b. Yazīd, and [Ṭarkhūn] killed him and threw [his cadaver] and his head into the river. [Ẓuhayr then] presented Qudāmah so that [Ṭarkhūn] might kill him. [Qudāmah] turned and the sword hit his chest instead of cutting [his head off]; [Ṭarkhūn] threw him into the river alive, and he drowned. Ṭarkhūn said, "Their father and his treachery killed them." Yazīd b. Huzayl said, "[In vengeance] for my sons, I shall kill every Khuzāʿī

in the city." 'Abdallāh b. Budayl b. 'Abdallāh b. Budayl b. Warqā',
who was one of the routed troops of Ibn al-Ash'ath who had come
to Mūsā, said to him, "If you want to do that to Khuzā'ah, it will
be difficult for you." Thābit lived for seven days and then died.
Yazīd b. Huzayl was a brave and generous [man], a poet, who
governed the island of Ibn Kāwan[378] in the days of Ibn Ziyād. He   [1159]
said (ṭawīl):

I used to call upon God secretly and sincerely
    to grant me taxes and legal income[379]
So that I might thereby leave Ṭalḥah[380] forgotten
    and my gifts and actions might thereby be praised.

['Alī b. Muḥammad] continued: After the death of Thābit, Ṭarkhūn took charge of the non-Arabs, and Zuhary took charge of the
companions of Thābit. However, they were weak, and this became well known. Mūsā decided to attack them by night, and a
man came and informed Ṭarkhūn [of this]. Ṭarkhūn laughed and
said, "Mūsā is too weak to enter his [own] privy [unaided]! How
can he stage a night attack against us? You have lost courage. No
one will guard the camp tonight." When a third of the night had
elapsed, Mūsā set out with eight hundred [men] whom he had
mobilized in the daytime and had made into "fourths."

['Alī b. Muḥammad] continued: He placed in charge of one
fourth Raqabah b. al-Ḥurr, over another his brother Nūḥ b.
'Abdallāh b. Khāzim, over [the third] Yazīd b. Huzayl, while he
himself was over the fourth. He said to them, "When you enter
their camp, spread out. Let no one of you pass anything without
striking it." The entered their camp from four directions and did
not pass any riding animal or man or tent or sack without striking
it. Nīzak heard the commotion, donned his arms, stood in the
dark night, and said to 'Alī b. al-Muhājir al-Khuzā'ī, "To to Ṭarkhūn, let him know where I am, and ask him what he thinks I
should do with [Mūsā]." ['Alī] came to Ṭarkhūn and lo, he was in a
tent, sitting on a chair, and his *shākiriyyah*[381] had lit fires before

---

378. I.e., Abarkāwan or Barkāwan or Kāwan or Banī Kāwan; also called Lāft and
now Qishm, being a large island near the mouth of the Persian Gulf (see Yāqūt,
Mu'jam, vol. II, p. 79, and vol. III, p. 837; Le Strange, *Lands of the Eastern Caliphate*, p. 261); *EI²*, s.v. Ḳishm.
379. Reading *wa-ḥalālī* (instead of *wa-rijālī*), with Ms. P.
380. See n. 241 above.
381. See above, n. 140.

him. [ʿAlī] delivered Nīzak's message to him, and [Ṭarkhūn] said, "Sit." He was raising his eyes in the direction of their camp and the noise when Maḥmiyah al-Sulamī came saying, "*Ḥā*ʾ, *mīm*,[382] they will not be given victory."[383] The *shākiriyyah* scattered, and Maḥmiyah entered the tent. Ṭarkhūn rose to [resist] him, and [Maḥmiyah] came to him quickly. [Ṭarkhūn] smote him and put him out of action.

[1160]

[ʿAlī b. Muḥammad] said; Ṭarkhūn wounded him in the chest with the sharp edge of [his] sword, felled him, returned to his chair, and sat on it; Maḥmiyah went out at a run.

[ʿAlī b. Muḥammad] said: The *shākiriyyah* returned, and Ṭarkhūn said to them, "You fled from a [single] man. Do you think, if it had been a fire, it would have burned more than one of you?" No sooner had he finished speaking than his slave girls entered the tent and the *shākiriyyah* fled out. He said to the slave girls, "Sit," and to ʿAlī b. al-Muhājir, "Stand."

[ʿAlī b. Muḥammad] said: The two of them went out and lo, there was Nūḥ b. ʿAbdallāh b. Khāzim in the ancillary tent. They wheeled about for a time and exchanged a couple of blows, but did nothing, and Nūḥ fled. Ṭarkhūn followed [Nūḥ] and wounded his horse in its flank. [The horse] reared up, and both it and Nūḥ fell into the river of al-Ṣaghāniyān. Ṭarkhūn returned with his sword dripping with blood. He and ʿAlī b. al-Muhājir went into the ancillary tent and then into the main tent. Ṭarkhūn said to the slave girls, "Go back," and they went back into the ancillary tent. Ṭarkhūn sent [word] to Mūsā, "Restrain your companions. We are moving out in the morning." Mūsā returned to his camp, and in the morning Ṭarkhūn and all the non-Arabs moved out. Each people returned to its country.

[ʿAlī b. Muḥammad] said: The people of Khurasan used to say, "We have never seen or heard of the like of Mūsā b. ʿAbdallāh b. Khāzim. He fought along with his father for two years. Then he went roaming about in the land of Khurasan until he came to a king and relieved him of his city and expelled him from it. Then

---

382. Seven sūrahs of the Qurʾān begin with this pair of "mysterious letters" (see *EI*[2], s.v. al-Ḳurʾān [vol. V, pp. 412ff.]), but the words that follow it here are not matched by the words that follow it there.

383. Qurʾān 3:111=107, 28:41, 41:16=15, 59:12. Al-Balādhurī (*Futūḥ*, p. 414) identifies *ḥā*ʾ *mīm lā yunṣarūna* as the battle cry of ʿAbdallāh b. Khāzim.

Arab and Turkish troops went to [fight] him, and he fought the Arabs in the first part of the day and the non-Arabs in the latter part of the day. He stayed in his fortress for fifteen years. Transoxania was his and no one strove with him to gain mastery over it." [1161]

['Alī b. Muḥammad] said: In Qūmis there was a man called 'Abdallāh at whose place young men (*fityān*) would gather to keep one another company at his trouble and expense. [This man] incurred a debt, and he came to Mūsā b. 'Abdallāh, who gave him four thousand [dirhams]; he took them to his companions. The poet said, reproving a man called Mūsā (*ṭawīl*):

You are not Moses, when he confided in his God,
    nor [are you] the giver [to] young men,[384] Mūsā b.
    Khāzim.

['Alī b. Muḥammad] said: When Yazīd [b. al-Muhallab] was dismissed and al-Mufaḍḍal took over, [al-Mufaḍḍal] wanted to enjoy al-Ḥajjāj's favor by fighting Mūsā b. 'Abdallāh. He sent out 'Uthmān b. Mas'ūd,[385] whom Yazīd had imprisoned, saying to him, "I want to send you against Mūsā b. 'Abdallāh." ['Uthmān said, "By God, he has killed people related to me without my having obtained revenge. I seek revenge for Thābit—the son of my paternal aunt—and for the Khuzā'ī. The treatment meted out to me and my family by your father and your brother has not been good. You (pl.) have imprisoned me and scared away my cousins and appropriated their property." Al-Mufaḍḍal said to me, "Put [all] this aside. Go and exact your revenge," and he sent him off with three thousand [men] saying to him, "Order a crier to cry out, 'Whoever joins us will have a regular place in the army.'"[386] He had that called out in the market, and people hastened to him. Al-Mufaḍḍal wrote to [his brother] Mudrik, who was at Balkh, instructing him to go with ['Uthmān]. ['Uthmān] set forth and, when he was at Balkh, he went out one night touring the camp and heard a man say, "I have killed him, by God." [At this,] he returned to his companions and said, "Surely I shall kill Mūsā, by [1162]

---

384. The text reads *al-qaynāt*, "singing girls," while the *Addenda et Emendanda* propose *al-qinyān*, which is presumably to be regarded as a misprint for *al-fityān* ("young men") in view of the preceding story.

385. On him, cf. Ibn A'tham, *Futūḥ*, vol. VII, pp. 215–17, 229–30.

386. So rendering *fa-lahu dīwān*.

the Lord of the Ka'bah."

['Alī b. Muḥammad] said: In the morning he set off from Balkh—Mudrik went out sluggishly with him—crossed the river and stopped with fifteen thousand [men] at an island at al-Tirmidh which is today called the Island of 'Uthmān,[387] on account of [his] stopping there. He wrote to al-Sabal and to Ṭarkhūn, and they came to him. They besieged Mūsā and rendered him and his companions in straitened circumstances. Mūsā went out at night to Guftān, supplied himself with provisions from it, and then returned and remained for two months in a straitened condition. 'Uthmān had dug a trench and was watching out for a night attack, so that Mūsā was not able to catch him off guard. [Mūsā] said to his companions, "How much longer? Let us make a sortie and make our battle day one of either victory or death"; and he said, "Head for Soghd and the Turks." Then he made a sortie, having left al-Naḍr b. Sulaymān b. 'Abdallāh b. Khāzim in the city; he had said to him, "If I am killed, do not hand the city over to 'Uthmān; hand it over to Mudrik b. al-Muhallab." He sortied and placed a third of his companions opposite 'Uthmān, saying [to them], "Do not engage him unless he fights you." He [himself] headed for Ṭarkhūn and his companions, and fought them gallantly. Ṭarkhūn and the Turks were defeated, and [Mūsā and his men] took their camp and began to carry it off.

Mu'āwiyah b. Khālid b. Abī Barzah looked at 'Uthmān, who was on a non-Arabian horse belonging to Khālid b. Abī Barzah al-Aslamī, and said, "Dismount, O amīr." But Khālid said, "Do not dismount, Mu'āwiyah brings ill luck.

The Soghdians and the Turks returned the charge and interposed themselves between Mūsā and the fortress. He fought them, and [his horse] was hamstrung and he fell. He said to a mawlā of his, "Carry me." [The Mawlā] said, "Death is disagreeable. Ride mounted behind me. If we escape, we shall both escape; if we perish, we shall both perish."

['Alī b. Muḥammad] said: [Mūsā] mounted behind him. 'Uthmān looked at him when he jumped up and said, "A jump [by] Mūsā, by the Lord of the Ka'bah." [Mūsā was] wearing a helmet of his which was adorned with red silk (*khazz*) and had a blue sapphire at its top.

[1163]

---

387. According to Barthold (*Turkestan*[3], p. 75), this is "undoubtedly Aral-Payghambar."

'Uthmān came out of the trench and [he and his men] put Mūsā's companions to flight. Then ['Uthmān] headed for Mūsā. Mūsā's riding animal stumbled, and he and his mawlā fell. ['Uthmān and his men] ran up to him, gathered around him, and killed him. 'Uthmān's crier called out, "Do not kill anyone you encounter; take him prisoner."

['Alī b. Muḥammad] continued: The companions of Mūsā scattered. Some of them were taken prisoner and were paraded before 'Uthmān. When he was brought an Arab prisoner, he said, "Our blood is licit for you and your blood illicit for us," and he ordered that he be killed. When he was brought a mawlā prisoner, he abused him and said, "These Arabs fight me. Why did you not become angry on my account?" and he ordered that he be beaten.[388] He was rough and coarse. No prisoner greeted him on that day apart from 'Abdallāh b. Budayl b. 'Abdallāh b. Budayl b. Warqā'—whose mawlā he was; when ['Uthmān] saw him, he turned away from him and gestured with his hand that he should be released—and Raqabah b. al-Ḥurr;[389] when he was brought [the latter], he looked at him and said, "There was no great sin against us from this [fellow]; he was a friend of Thābit's and was with people to whom he acted loyally. The wonder is that you took him prisoner." They said, "His horse was wounded, and he fell off it into a deep hole and was taken prisoner." ['Uthmān] set him free and gave him a mount, saying to Khālid b. Abī Barzah, "Let him stay with you."

['Alī b. Muḥammad] said: The person who despatched Mūsā b. 'Abdallāh was Wāṣil b. Ṭaysalah al-'Anbarī. One day 'Uthmān looked at Zur'ah b. 'Alqamah al-Sulamī, al-Ḥajjāj b. Marwān, and Sinān al-A'rābī, [who were standing] to one side, and said to them, "You have a safe-conduct." The people suspected that he did not give them a safe-conduct until they wrote to him [and made an arrangement with him].

['Alī b. Muḥammad] said: The city remained in the hands of al-Naḍr b. Sulaymān b. 'Abdallāh b. Khāzim. He said, "I shall not hand it over to 'Uthmān b. Muḥammad, but I shall hand it over to Mudrik." He did so, and [Mudrik] gave him a safe-conduct and [1164]

---

388. Ibn al-Athīr makes it clear that the mawlās were set free after being beaten.
389. Al-Balādhurī (Futūḥ, p. 419) renders this name "Raqyah b. Al-Ḥ.rfānah."

handed [the city] over to ʿUthmān. Al-Mufaḍḍal wrote of the conquest to al-Ḥajjāj. Al-Ḥajjāj said, "What an astonishing fellow Ibn Bahlah is! I order him to kill Ibn Samurah, and he writes to me that he is at death's door,[390] and he [then] writes to me that he has killed Mūsā b. ʿAbdallāh b. Khāzim."[391]

[ʿAlī b. Muḥammad] said: Mūsā was killed in the year 85. Al-Bakhtarī[392] mentioned that Maghrā b. al-Mughīrah b. Abī Ṣufrah killed Mūsā. He said (ṭawīl):

The cavalry crushed Khāzim, Nūḥ, and Mūsā at
    al-Tirmidh, as if crushed under the[ir] chests.

One of the army struck Mūsā's leg. When Qutaybah became governor, he was told about him and said, "What induced you to [do] what you did to the young man of the Arabs after his death?" [The man] said, "He had killed my brother." [Qutaybah] gave the order, and [the man] was killed in front of him.

In this year ʿAbd al-Malik b. Marwān wanted to remove his brother ʿAbd al-ʿAzīz [from the succession].[393]

[ʿAbd al-Malik's Desire to Remove His Brother from the Succession]

Al-Wāqidī mentioned that ʿAbd al-Malik intended that [removal] and Qabīṣah b. Dhuʾayb[394] advised him against it, saying, "Do not do this; you will raise a rebellious voice against yourself. Maybe death will come to him and you will be relieved of him." ʿAbd al-Malik desisted from that, while yet yearning in his heart to remove [ʿAbd al-ʿAzīz]. [Then] there entered into his presence Rawḥ b. Zinbāʿ al-Judhāmī,[395] who was the person most respected by ʿAbd al-Malik. He said, "O Commander of the Faithful, if you remove him, there will be no discord." [ʿAbd al-

---

390. Reading li-mā bi-hi in place of li-maʾābihi.

391. Ibn al-Athīr adds at this point, "the killing of Mūsā did not please him because he was from Qays."

392. Correctly proposed in the Addenda et Emendanda in preference to the form given in the text.

393. See al-Yaʿqūbī (Taʾrīkh, vol. II, pp. 334–35) for a different account.

394. ʿAbd al-Malik's secretary and brother-in-law (Crone, Slaves on Horses, p. 128).

395. Ibid., pp. 99–100 (where the form "Zanbā" is wrongly preferred).

Malik] said, "Do you think so, O Abū Zurʿah?" He said, "Yes, by   [1165]
God. I shall be the first to acquiesce in that." [ʿAbd al-Malik] said,
"You advise me well, God willing."

[Al-Wāqidī] said: While this was going on—and ʿAbd al-Malik
and Rawḥ b. Zinbāʿ had fallen asleep—Qabīṣah b. Dhuʾayb entered into their presence at night. ʿAbd al-Malik had previously
instructed his chamberlains, "Qabīṣah is not to be kept from me,
whatever time he may come, by night or by day, whether I am
unoccupied or have a man with me. Even if I am with the women,
he is to be brought into the session and I am to be informed of his
position," and he would come in. He was in charge of the seal and
the coinage; reports came to him before [they came to] ʿAbd al-
Malik, and he would read letters before him; he would bring a
letter to ʿAbd al-Malik unrolled and [ʿAbd al-Malik] would read
it—[all of this] being in honor of Qabīṣah. [Qabīṣah] entered into
[ʿAbd al-Malik's] presence, greeted him, and said, "May God reward you,[396] O Commander of the Faithful in respect of your
brother!" He said, "Has he died?" [Qabīṣah] said, "Yes." ʿAbd al-
Malik said, "We belong to God and to Him we return!" Then he
advanced upon Rawḥ and said to him, "God has sufficed us, O
Abū Zurʿah, with what we wanted and what we had decided on.
That was contrary to [what] you [advised], O Abū Isḥāq." Qabīṣah
said, "What was that?" and [ʿAbd al-Malik] informed him of what
had taken place. Qabīṣah said, "O Commander of the Faithful,
the right opinion always lies in patience; in haste there is what
there is."[397] ʿAbd al-Malik said, "Many a time there can be much
good in haste. You saw the affair of ʿAmr b. Saʿīd al-Ashdaq.
Wasn't haste in that better than patience?

In this year ʿAbd al-ʿAzīz b. Marwān died in Egypt in Jumādā I
(May–June 704). ʿAbd al-Malik assigned his governorship to his
son ʿAbdallāh b. ʿAbd al-Malik and put him in charge of Egypt.

As for al-Madāʾinī, he said in among what was related to us by
Abū Zayd on his authority: Al-Ḥajjāj wrote to ʿAbd al-Malik com-   [1166]
mending to him the oath of allegiance to al-Walīd [as heir to the
caliphate], and he sent in that regard a delegation led by ʿImrān b.

---

396. *Ājaraka Allāh (fī-),* a standard form of condolence.
397. A polite expression of objection or contradiction (see Lane, *Lexicon,* p.
2466c).

'Imrān b. 'Iṣām al-'Anazī.[398] 'Imrān stood up and gave an address, and the delegation spoke, and they urged 'Abd al-Malik and asked him to do that. 'Imrān b. 'Iṣām said (*wāfir*):[399]

O Commander of the Faithful, to you we bring
    from a distance a greeting and a salutation!
Acquiesce in what I want concerning your sons. Let
    your response to me
    be a noble action[400] for them and a support
    for us.
If I am to be obeyed in respect of al-Walīd,
    I make the caliphate and rule[401] over to him.
He resembles you. Quraysh surround his *qubbah*;[402]
    through him the people seek rain from the clouds,
And he is like you in piety. He has not acted
    childishly since the day
    when he took off his necklaces and amulets.
If you prefer your brother for [the caliphate], we,
    by your grandfather, are not able to level any
    accusation against that;
But we are on our guard lest, through his sons,
    the sons by different mothers, we be given
    poison to drink.[403]
And we fear, if you place dominion among them,
    clouds coming back to them without water.
Let not what you have milked [belong] tomorrow to
    people [who are such that]
    after tomorrow, your [own] sons will thirst.

---

398. Sayed, *Revolte*, pp. 351–52, no. 7.

399. Cf. al-Balādhurī, *AAC*, p. 241; *Aghānī*², vol. XVII, p. 275; Ibn Kathīr, *Bidāyah*, vol. IX, p. 59.

400. The Balādhurī and *Aghānī* variant *ukrūmat*ᵃⁿ seems preferable to 'ādiyyat*ᵃⁿ or 'āriyyat*ᵃⁿ.

401. The Balādhurī and *Aghānī* variant *wa'l-zimāmā* seems preferable to *wa'l-dhimāmā*.

402. Presumably, some sort of audience tent is meant.

403. The *Addenda et Emendanda* point out that the word *ma'tharat*ᵃⁿ, which is given in the text at this point, "corrupta videtur," and propose instead *mā'i-dat*ᵃⁿ, i.e., "we are on our guard against . . . poisoned fare"; al-Balādhurī's *an nusqā* seems preferable.

I swear, if 'Iṣām[404] were to go beyond me[405]
   in that regard, I should not forgive him that.
If I gave my brother [something] for the sake of merit,
   desiring thereby good repute and standing,
[That brother] would cause it to return to my sons,
   to the exclusion of his [own] sons;
     such [would be the case], or I would find some
     [other] way of dealing with him.
He who has cleavages among his relatives,
   the cleavage of dominion is the slowest to mend.

'Abd al-Malik said, "O 'Imrān, it is 'Abd al-'Azīz [whom you are talking about]." He said, "Use artifice on him, O Commander of the Faithful!"

'Alī [b. Muḥammad] said: 'Abd al-Malik wanted to have the oath of allegiance to al-Walīd [as heir] taken before the Ibn al-Ashʿath affair, because al-Ḥajjāj had sent 'Imrān b. 'Iṣām [to him] in that [connection]. When 'Abd al-'Azīz refused, 'Abd al-Malik turned away from what he wanted until 'Abd al-'Azīz died. When he wanted to remove 'Abd al-'Azīz and have the oath of allegiance taken to his son al-Walīd, he wrote to his brother, "If you think it right to make this matter over to your nephew. . . ." ['Abd al-'Azīz] refused, and ['Abd al-Malik] wrote to him, "Well, let [the caliphate] be his after you, for he is the dearest of creation to the Commander of the Faithful." 'Abd al-'Azīz wrote to him, "I see in Abū Bakr b. 'Abd al-'Azīz what you see in al-Walīd." 'Abd al-Malik said, "O God, 'Abd al-'Azīz has severed his relationship with me, and I shall sever mine with him," and he wrote to him, "Transport the revenue[406] of Egypt [to me]." 'Abd al-'Azīz wrote to him, "O Commander of the Faithful, you and I have both reached an age that no one in your family has reached without having only a little time left. Neither of us knows which of us will be reached by death first. If you are minded to make the rest of my life unpleasant for me, [by all means] do [so, but I would prefer otherwise]." [At this,] 'Abd al-Malik became gentle and said, "By my

[1167]

---

404. The poet's father.
405. Reading *takhaṭṭānī* instead of *takhaṭṭaʾanī*.
406. Thus rendering *kharāj* here; Ibn Kathīr (*Bidāyah*, vol. IX, p. 59) notes that 'Abd al-'Azīz used to remit nothing.

life, I shall not make the rest of his life unpleasant for him," and he said to his two sons, "If God wants to give you [the caliphate], no one of his servants will be able to avert that"; and he said to [1168] his two sons, al-Walīd and Sulaymān, "Have you ever committed anything forbidden?" They said, "No, by God." He said, "God is great! You will gain it, by the Lord of the Kaʿbah."

[ʿAlī b. Muḥammad] said: When ʿAbd al-ʿAzīz refused to acquiesce in what ʿAbd al-Malik wanted, ʿAbd al-Malik said, "O God, ʿAbd al-ʿAzīz has cut his relationship with me, and I shall cut mine with him," and, when ʿAbd al-ʿAzīz died, the Syrians said, "[ʿAbd al-ʿAzīz] has returned the Commander of the Faithful's affair to him; he made an invocation against him, and his call was answered."

[ʿAlī b. Muḥammad] said: Al-Ḥajjāj wrote to ʿAbd al-Malik advising him to use Muḥammad b. Yazīd al-Anṣārī as a secretary. He wrote to him, "If you want a discreet, submissive, easy-tempered, intelligent, worthy, and trusty man, whom you may take for yourself and with whom you may lodge your secret[s] and that which you do not wish to be manifest, then take Muḥammad b. Yazīd." ʿAbd al-Malik [accordingly] wrote to [al-Ḥajjāj], "Convey him to me," and he did so, and ʿAbd al-Malik took him as a secretary.

Muḥammad said: No letter reached [ʿAbd al-Malik] but that he passed it to me, and he concealed nothing but that he informed me of it, while keeping it from the people; nor did he write to any one of his governors but that he told me of it. I was sitting one day, in the middle of the daytime, when an official courier came from Egypt. He said, "[I request] permission to [meet] the Commander of the Faithful." I said, "This is not a time [when] permission [can be given]. Tell me what you have come for." He said, "No." I said, "If you have a letter, give it to me." He said, "No."

[Muḥammad] continued: One of those who were present with me informed the Commander of the Faithful, and he came out and said, "What is this?" I said, "A messenger who has come from Egypt." He said, "Well, take the letter." I said, "He has claimed that he has no letter." He said, "Then ask him what he has come for." I said, "I have asked him, and he did not tell me." He said, "Bring him in," so I took him in and the messenger said, "May God reward you, O Commander of the Faithful, in respect

of ʿAbd al-ʿAzīz!" [ʿAbd al-Malik] said, "We belong to God and to   [1169]
Him we return!" and wept, and [then] remained silent with downcast eyes for a time. Then he said, "May God have mercy on ʿAbd
al-ʿAzīz! By God, ʿAbd al-ʿAzīz has passed on and left us and this
life of ours," and the women and the people of the house wept.
Then he summoned me on the next day and said, "ʿAbd al-ʿAzīz,
may God have mercy on him, has gone on his way, and the people
must have a waymark and someone to be in charge after me. Who
do you think?" I said, "O Commander of the Faithful, the lord of
the people and the most pleasing and most worthy of them, al-
Walīd b. ʿAbd al-Malik." He said, "You are right, may God grant
you success! Who do you think should be after him?" I said, "O
Commander of the Faithful, who other than Sulaymān,[407] the
young man of the Arabs?" He said, "May you be granted success!
If we were to leave [the caliphate] to Al-Walīd, he would make it
over to his sons. Write a covenant for al-Walīd and [for] Sulaymān
after him!" So I wrote an oath of allegiance to al-Walīd and then
Sulaymān after him. [At this,] al-Walīd became angry with me.
He did not put me in charge of anything after I had advised Sulaymān's succession to him.

ʿAlī [b. Muḥammad] said on the authority of Ibn Juʿdubah: ʿAbd
al-Malik wrote to Hishām b. Ismāʿīl al-Makhzūmī to summon the
people [of Medina] to the oath of allegiance to al-Walīd and Sulaymān. They took the oath of allegiance, apart from Saʿīd b. al-
Musayyab,[408] who refused and said, "I shall not take the oath of
allegiance while ʿAbd al-Malik is alive." Hishām beat him violently, clad him in haircloth, and sent him to Dhubāb,[409] a mountain pass at Medina where they used to kill and crucify[410] [people].
He thought that they intended to kill him; but, when they got to
that place with him, they brought him back, and he said, "Had I
thought that they would not crucify me, I should not have worn   [1170]
haircloth drawers; but I said [to myself], 'They will crucify me,

---

407. Literally, "Where will you turn it away from Sulaymān?"

408. For a view of Saʿīd's role in the nascent religious law of the time, see
Juynboll, *Muslim Tradition*, pp. 15–17 and index.

409. Or Dhibāb, which Yāqūt knows simply as a mountain at Medina (*Muʿjam*,
vol. II, p. 716).

410. As Nöldeke pointed out (*ZDMG* 56 [1902], p. 433), Arab crucifixion appears
usually to have involved headless cadavers; for an apparent exception, see Ibn
Aʿtham, *Futūḥ*, vol. VII, p. 232.

and [the drawers] will cover up [my private parts].'" News [of that] reached 'Abd al-Malik, who said, "May God remove Hishām from all that is good! He should have summoned [Sa'īd] to the oath of allegiance, and, on his refusing [to take it], he should [either] have beheaded him or have desisted from him."

In this year 'Abd al-Malik had the oath of allegiance taken to al-Walīd and then, after him, to Sulaymān; and he made them the two heirs of the covenant of the Muslims. He sent his oath for them out in writing to [all Muslim] territories, and the people took the oath. Sa'īd b. al-Musayyab[, however,] refrained from that, and Hishām b. Ismā'īl, who was 'Abd al-Malik's governor of Medina, beat him, paraded him around, and imprisoned him. 'Abd al-Malik wrote to Hishām, blaming him for what he had done in that regard. The beating consisted of sixty lashes, and he paraded him as far as the top of the mountain pass [clad] in breeches made of hair.

According to al-Ḥārith—Ibn Sa'd—Muḥammad b. 'Umar al-Wāqidī—'Abdallāh b. Ja'far and other companions of ours: 'Abdallāh b. al-Zubayr appointed over Medina Jābir b. al-Aswad b. 'Awf al-Zuhrī, who summoned people to the oath of allegiance to Ibn al-Zubayr. Sa'īd b. al-Musayyab said, "No. Not until the people are united," and Jābir gave him sixty lashes. That reached Ibn al-Zubayr, who wrote to Jābir blaming him and saying, "Why should we bother with Sa'īd? Leave him."

[1171] According to al-Ḥārith—Ibn Sa'd—Muḥammad b. 'Umar—'Abdallāh b. Ja'far and other companions of ours: 'Abd al-'Azīz b. Marwān died in Egypt in Jumādā (sic) 84 (sic: May–June or June–July 703). 'Abd al-Malik then made the covenant to his two sons al-Walīd and Sulaymān, and sent the written oath to them to the territories. His governor [of Medina] at the time was Hishām b. Ismā'īl al-Makhzūmī, who summoned the people to the oath. They took it, and he summoned Sa'īd b. al-Musayyab to take the oath. He refused, saying, "No. I'll see." Hishām b. Ismā'īl gave him sixty lashes and paraded him in breeches made of hair as far as the top of the mountain pass. When they brought him back, he said, "Where are you bringing me back to?" They said, "To prison." He said, "By God, had I not thought it was going to be crucifixion, I should never have worn these breeches." [Hishām] returned him to the prison and detained him, and he wrote to

'Abd al-Malik informing him of [Saʿīd's] disobedience and what
had happened. ʿAbd al-Malik wrote to him blaming him for what
he had done and saying, "There is more need to draw Saʿīd close
[to you] by kind treatment of his kindred than to beat him. We
know that he has no dissension or disobedience in him."[411]

The pilgrimage was led in this year by Hishām b. Ismāʿīl al-
Makhzūmī: Thus it was related to us by Aḥmad b. Thābit on the
authority of him who mentioned it on the authority of Isḥāq b.
ʿĪsā on the authority of Abū Maʿshar; and al-Wāqidī said the same.
The governor of the East, together with Iraq, in this year was al-
Ḥajjāj b. Yūsuf.

---

411. Cf. the accounts of this episode given by Khalīfah (Taʾrīkh, pp. 290–91).

The
Events of the Year

86

 (JANUARY 2–DECEMBER 22, 705)

[*The Death of 'Abd al-Malik*]

One of [the events that took place] in [this year] was the death of
'Abd al-Malik b. Marwān in the middle of Shawwāl (early–mid
October).

According to Aḥmad b. Thābit—him who mentioned it on the
authority of Isḥāq b. 'Īsā—Abū Ma'shar: 'Abd al-Malik b. Marwān
died on Thursday in the middle of Shawwāl in the year 86. His
caliphate [lasted] ten years and five months.

As for al-Ḥārith, he related to me on the authority of Ibn Sa'd on
the authority of Muḥammad b. 'Umar, who said: Shuraḥbīl b. Abī
'Awn related to me on the authority of his father: The people
became unanimous about 'Abd al-Malik b. Marwān in the year 73
(692–93).

According to Ibn 'Umar—Abū Ma'shar Najīḥ: 'Abd al-Malik died
in Damascus on Thursday in the middle of Shawwāl in the year 86.
His rule, from the day when the oath of allegiance was taken to
him until the day he died, was twenty-one years and one and a half
months. For nine of these years, he was fighting Ibn al-Zubayr and
was recognized as caliph in Syria; then [he was recognized as
caliph] in Iraq, after Muṣ'ab had been killed, and remained [so

recognized] after 'Abdallāh b. al-Zubayr had been killed. The people were unanimous about him for thirteen years and four months,
less seven nights.

As for 'Alī b. Muḥammad al-Madā'inī, he, according to what
Abū Zayd related to us on his authority, said: 'Abd al-Malik died   [1173]
in Damascus in the year 86. His rule [lasted] thirteen years, three
months and fifteen days.

Report on His Age When He Died

The biographers (ahl al-siyar) differ in that [regard]. According to
al-Ḥārith—Ibn Saʿd—Muḥammad b. 'Umar—Abū Maʿshar Najīḥ:
'Abd al-Malik b. Marwān died aged sixty.

Al-Wāqidī said: It has been related to us that he died when he
was fifty-eight.[412]

[Abū Jaʿfar] said: The first [of these reports] is more secure,
[since] it conforms with his birth date. He was born in the year 26,
in the caliphate of 'Uthmān b. 'Affān, may God be pleased with
him, and he witnessed the Yawm al-Dār[413] with his father when
he was ten.

Al-Madā'inī, 'Alī b. Muḥammad, said, in among what Abū Zayd
mentioned on his authority: 'Abd al-Malik died at the age of sixty-
three.

His Descent and His Teknonym (Kunyah)[414]

As for his descent, [he was] 'Abd al-Malik b. Marwān b. al-Ḥakam
b. Abī al-ʿĀṣ b. Umayyah b. 'Abd Shams b. 'Abd Manāf. As for his
kunyah, [it was] Abū al-Walīd. His mother [was] 'Ā'ishah bt.
Muʿāwiyah b. al-Mughīrah b. Abī al-ʿĀṣ b. Umayyah. To ['Abd al-
Malik] Ibn Qays al-Ruqayyāt says (kāmil):[415]

---

412. Cf. al-Balādhurī (AAC, p. 152), who cites al-Wāqidī to the effect that 'Abd
al-Malik was fifty-three when he died.

413. I.e., the occasion of the murder of the Caliph 'Uthmān in Dhū 'l-Ḥijjah 35
(June 656).

414. See EI², s.v.

415. On the poet, see EI², s.v. Ibn Ḳays al-Ruḳayyāt, and Sezgin, GAS, vol. II, pp.
418–19; regarding the following verses, cf. al-Balādhurī, AAC, pp. 152–53; Ibn
'Abd Rabbihi, 'Iqd, vol. IV, p. 399; and Der Dîwân des 'Ubayd-Allâh Ibn Ḳais ar-
Rukajjât, pp. 215–16 (where further parallels are given).

You are the son of ʿĀʾishah, who
    excelled her fellow women in descent.
She paid no attention to her coevals
    and went off on her own sweet way.

[1174]   *His Children and Wives*

Among them were al-Walīd, Sulaymān, Marwān al-Akbar (who
was without issue), and ʿĀʾishah: Their mother was Wallādah bt.
al-ʿAbbās b. Jazʾ b. al-Ḥārith b. Zuhayr b. Jadhīmah b. Rawāḥah b.
Rabīʿah b. Māzin b. al-Ḥārith b. Quṭayʿah b. ʿAbs b. Baghīḍ.

Yazīd, Marwān, Muʿāwiyah (who was without issue), and Umm
Kulthūm: Their mother was ʿĀtikah bt. Yazīd b. Muʿāwiyah b.
Abī Sufyān.

Hishām, whose mother was Umm Hishām bt. Hishām b. Ismāʿīl b. Hishām b. al-Walīd b. al-Mughīrah al-Makhzūmī. Al-
Madāʾinī said: Her name was ʿĀʾishah bt. Hishām.

Abū Bakr, whose name [was] Bakkār. His mother was ʿĀʾishah
bt. Mūsā b. Ṭalḥah b. ʿUbaydallāh.

Al-Ḥakam, who died without issue. His mother was Umm
Ayyūb bt. ʿAmr b. ʿUthmān b. ʿAffān.

Fāṭimah bt. ʿAbd al-Malik, whose mother was Umm al-
Mughīrah bt. al-Mughīrah b. Khālid b. al-ʿĀṣ b. Hishām b. al-
Mughīrah.

ʿAbdallāh, Maslamah, al-Mundhir, ʿAnbasah, Muḥammad, Saʿīd
al-Khayr, and al-Ḥajjāj, who [were born] to *ummahāt awlād*.[416]

Al-Madāʾinī said: His wives, other than those we have mentioned, were (a) Shaqrāʾ bt. Salamah b. Ḥalbas al-Ṭāʾī, (b) a
daughter of ʿAlī b. Abī Ṭālib's,[417] peace be upon him, and (c)
Umm Abīhā bt. ʿAbdallāh b. Jaʿfar.

Al-Madāʾinī mentioned on the authority of ʿAwānah and others
than him that Salamah b. Zayd b. Wahb b. Nubātah al-Fahmī
[1175]   entered into ʿAbd al-Malik's presence and [ʿAbd al-Malik] said to

---

416. Plural of *umm walad*, a "female slave who has borne a child to her owner"
(Schacht, *An Introduction to Islamic law*, index).
417. Thus, too, in al-Balādhurī, *AAC*, p. 160, but according to Ibn al-Athīr this is
untrue.

him, "Which time you have experienced is the noblest and which
of the kings the most endowed with perfection?" [Salamah] said,
"As for kings, I have only seen those who can be both blamed and
praised; as for time, it raises some people and lays others low.
Everyone blames his own time, because it wears out the new and
renders the young decrepit; all that is in it becomes cut short,
except for hope." ['Abd al-Malik] said, "Tell me about Fahm."
[Salamah] said, "They are just as the one who said [the following
verses] said (khafīf):[418]

Night and day crept over Fahm
    b. 'Amr and they became like old bones.
Their abode became desolate,
    after glory, wealth and ease.
Thus does time put an end to
    people; their abodes remain like traces."

['Abd al-Malik] said, "And which of you says (wāfir):

I have seen people since time began,
    liking him who is rich among men,
Even if the rich man does little good
    and is niggardly, giving out small amounts.
I do not know why this should be so,
    and what people can hope for from misers.
Is it for material gain? There is no material gain,
    nor can he be hoped [to help] when the nights
    bring disaster."

[Salamah] said, "I."

'Alī [b. Muḥammad] said: Abū Qaṭīfah 'Amr b. al-Walīd b.
'Uqbah b. Abī Mu'ayṭ said to 'Abd al-Malik b. Marwān (ṭawīl):[419]

I have been informed that Ibn al-Qalammas[420] has
    stigmatized me,

---

418. Cf. al-Balādhurī, AAC, pp. 198–99.

419. On the poet, see Sezgin, GAS, vol. II, pp. 424–25; regarding the following
verses, cf. al-Balādhurī, AAC, pp. 212–13; Aghanī², vol. I, p. 34.

420. Or al-'Amallas; according to Ibn Manẓūr (Lisan al-'arab, s.vv.), qalammas
means "great lord" or "bountiful," while 'amallas means "vicious wolf" or
"vicious dog." It is not clear who is meant here.

and who among people is wholly free of fault?
[1176]   The chief of his people sees the paths of what is right,
           and the beturbaned leader may see what is right.
           [But] who are you? Tell me, who are you,
           when things are now visible, now concealed?

ʿAbd al-Malik said, "I did not think that the likes of us would have 'Who are you?' said to him. By God, but for what I know, I should have said something which would have caused you to join your base ancestors and should have had you beaten to death."

ʿAbdallāh b. al-Ḥajjāj al-Thaʿlabī said to ʿAbd al-Malik (rajaz):[421]

O Ibn Abī al-ʿĀṣ, O best of young men,
       you are the preserver of the religion if the
       religion becomes frail.
You are the one who does not let rule be of no avail;
       Quraysh are rent from you, just as the mill
       stone is rent [from its pivot].[422]
Abū al-ʿĀṣ—and in this he excelled—
       gave his sons advice which they heeded,
That they should kindle war and reject what he rejected,
       [sons] who thrust fiercely at necks and kidneys,
And advance boldly with swords
       to the fighting, and gather together [the like
       of] what he gathered.

[1177]   Aʿshā Banī Shaybān said (kāmil):[423]

All of Quraysh acknowledge
       that rule belongs to the sons of Abū al-ʿĀṣ,
To the most pious and deserving of them,
       as determined by consultation.
They defend what they govern,

---

421. On this poet, see Sezgin, *GAS*, vol. II, pp. 353–54; regarding the following verses, cf. *Aghānī*[2], vol. XIII, p. 169.

422. Reading *jība* and *jawba* in place of *ḥība* and *ḥawba*, as is suggested in the *Addenda et Emendanda*, the signification being that "you" are the center and "Quraysh" are around "you"; cf. Lane, *Lexicon*, p. 479b.

423. On the poet, see Sezgin, *GAS*, vol. II, p. 330; regarding the following verses, cf. al-Balādhurī, *AAC*, p. 213; Geyer, *The Dīwān of al-Aʿshà*, p. 280.

and benefit those who are in distress.
Of Quraysh they are the most deserving of it
      (i.e., the Caliphate),
      in good times and in bad.

ʿAbd al-Malik said, "I do not know that anyone had a stronger hold on this rule than I. Ibn al-Zubayr prayed long and fasted much, but, because of his avarice, he was not fitted to be a leader."

The Caliphate of
al-Walīd b. ʿAbd al-Malik

The
Events of the Year
86 (cont'd)
(JANUARY 2–DECEMBER 22, 705)

In this year the oath of allegiance was taken to al-Walīd b. ʿAbd al-Malik as caliph. It has been mentioned that, when he had buried his father, he departed from his grave, entered the mosque, and ascended the pulpit. The people gathered to him, and he made an address. He said, "To God we belong and to Him shall we return. God is the One Whose aid is sought against our loss at the death of the Commander of the Faithful. Praise be to God for having bountifully bestowed the caliphate on us. Stand and take the oath of allegiance." The first to stand for the oath was ʿAbdallāh b. Hammām al-Salūlī. He stood, saying (rajaz):[424]

God has given you that which cannot be excelled;
    heretics have wished to divert it
From you, but God insisted on leading it
    to you, until he invested you with its neck ring.

And he took the oath of allegiance to him. Then the people fol- [1178] lowed one another in taking the oath.

As for al-Wāqidī, he mentioned that al-Walīd, when he came back from the burial of his father—he was buried outside Bāb al-

---

424. Cf. al-Balādhurī, *AAC*, p. 27; Ibn ʿAbd Rabbihi, *ʿIqd*, vol. IV, p. 411; Ibn Kathīr, *Bidāyah*, vol. IX, p. 70.

Jābiyah[425]—did not go into his house but [instead] ascended the pulpit of Damascus, praised God and extolled Him as He deserves, and then said,[426] "O people, there can be no hastening of that which God has delayed, nor any delaying of that which God has hastened. Death is part of God's decree, of His prior knowledge, and of what He has written for His prophets and the bearers of His throne. The one charged with this community has taken to the dwelling places of the pious that which justifies for God [whatever He may dispense] by way of severity toward him who occasions doubt and gentleness toward the people of right and merit, [the people who] establish such of the beacon of Islam and its waymarks as God has established, by making the pilgrimage to this House, campaigning against these frontier ways of access, and waging these wars on the enemy of God. He (i.e., ʿAbd al-Malik) was neither incapable nor remiss. O people, incumbent upon you are obedience and cleaving to the collective body, for Satan is with the individual. O people, he who reveals to us his inner thoughts (that is, of opposition), we shall smite that in which his eyes are; and he who remains silent will die of his malady (that is, of his rancor)."[427] Then he descended, looked at what there was of the . . .[428] of the caliphate, and took it for himself. He was a froward tyrant.[429]

In this year Qutaybah b. Muslim arrived in Khurasan as governor on behalf of al-Ḥajjāj.

[1179] According to ʿAlī b. Muḥammad—Kulayb b. Khalaf—Ṭufayl b. Mirdās al-ʿAmmī and al-Ḥasan b. Rushayd—Sulaymān b. Kathīr al-ʿAmmī—his paternal uncle: I saw Qutaybah b. Muslim when he arrived in Khurasan in the year 86. He arrived while al-Mufaḍḍal, who intended to campaign in Akharūn and Shūmān,[430] was reviewing the army. Qutaybah addressed the people and urged them

---

425. The west gate of Damascus (*EI²*, s.v. Dimashḳ [vol. II, p. 279]), al-Jābiyah itself being situated about 80 km to the south of Damascus (*EI²*, s.v. al-Djābiya).

426. Cf. Ibn ʿAbd Rabbihi, *ʿIqd*, vol. IV, p. 91, for what follows.

427. Also in al-Yaʿqūbī, *Taʾrīkh*, vol. II, p. 338, and *Kitab al-ʿuyūn waʾl-ḥadāʾiq*, p. 2.

428. The text gives here *al-dawābb*, "the riding animals" (as does Ibn Kathīr, *Bidāyah*, vol. IX, p. 70), which can hardly be right.

429. To use Arberry's rendering of the expression *jabbār ʿanīd*, which occurs in the Qurʾān (11:59=62, 14:15=18); cf. al-Masʿūdi, *Murūj*, vol. V, p. 360 = par. 2114.

430. See above, n. 336 (first part).

to wage holy war. He said, "God has caused you to alight in this place so that He may make His religion strong, protect sacred things by means of you, and through you increase the abundance of wealth and the meting out of harsh treatment to the enemy. He promised His Prophet, may God bless him, in true speech and an articulate book and said, 'It is He who has sent His Messenger with the guidance and the religion of truth, that He may make it victorious over all religion, though the unbelievers be averse';[431] and He promised those who strive on His path the best reward and the greatest resource with Him. He said, 'That is because they are smitten neither by thirst, nor fatigue, nor emptiness on the path of God' up to where He says, 'the best of what they were doing.'[432] Then He gave the information concerning him who is killed on His path, that he is alive and provided for. He said, 'Count not those who were slain on God's path as dead, but rather living with their Lord, by Him provided.'[433] So fulfill the promise of your Lord and habituate yourselves to the greatest of distances and the sharpest[434] of pains; and beware of looking for easy ways out."[435]

What Happened to Qutaybah in Khurasan in This Year[436]

Qutaybah then reviewed the army, complete with weapons and animals, and went off, having deputed at Marw over its military affairs (*harb*) Iyās b. 'Abd Allāh b. 'Amr and over its taxation (*kharāj*) 'Uthmān b. al-Sa'dī. When he was at al-Ṭālaqān, he was met by the dihqāns of Balkh and some of their dignitaries, who went with him. When he crossed the river, he was met with gifts and a gold key[437] by Tīsh[438] al-A'war, the king of al-Ṣaghāniyān, who invited him to his country. Then there came to him[439] with

[1180]

---

431. Qur'ān, 9:33, 61:9.
432. Qur'ān, 9:120f. = 121–22.
433. Qur'ān, 3:169 = 163.
434. Reading *amaḍḍ* in place of *amḍā*.
435. This address is given in abbreviated form by Ibn A'tham (*Futūḥ*, vol. VII, p. 217).
436. Cf. Gibb, *Arab Conquests*, pp. 31–32.
437. Thus too in al-Balādhurī (*Futūḥ*, p. 419); "keys," according to Ibn al-Athīr.
438. Following the *Addenda et Emendanda* (see Marquart, *Ērānšăhr*, pp. 70, 226–27); see also the remarks of Bosworth, "The Rulers of Chaghāniyān in Early Islamic Times," *Iran* 19 (1981), p. 17, n. 10.

gifts and wealth the king of Guftān,[440] who [also] invited him to
his country. He went with Tīsh to al-Ṣaghāniyān and handed his
country [back] to him. [Now] the king of Akharūn and Shūmān
had been a bad neighbor to Tīsh, having campaigned against him
and hemmed him in; Qutaybah went to Akharūn and Shūmān,
which [formed part] of Ṭukhāristān,[441] and Ghushtāsbān[442] came
to him and made peace with him in return for tribute which he
made over to him. Qutaybah accepted it and was satisfied.

Then he departed for Marw and deputed over the army his
brother, Ṣāliḥ b. Muslim; he went ahead of his troops and reached
Marw before them. After Qutaybah's return [to Marw], Ṣāliḥ conquered . . . ;[443] he was accompanied by Naṣr b. Sayyār, who
showed valor on that day, and he gave him a village called Tinjānah.[444] Then Ṣāliḥ went to Qutaybah, who appointed him over
al-Tirmidh.

[ʿAlī b. Muḥammad] said: As for the Bāhilīs, they say [that]
Qutaybah arrived in Khurasan in the year 85. He reviewed the
army and the total of the coats of mail they counted was 350. He
campaigned against Akharūn and Shūmān, and then came back;
he embarked in boats, went downstream to Āmul, and left the
army, which took the Balkh road to Marw. [News of that] reached
al-Ḥajjāj, who wrote to him blaming him and impugning his decision to leave his army. He wrote to him, "If you are on campaign,
be at the head of the people; if you come back, be among the last
of them and [in] the rear guard."

[1181]

---

439. Ignoring the second component of *fa-atā-hu wa-atā*.

440. See above, n. 356.

441. In this connection, Wellhausen noted (*Arab Kingdom*, p. 430) that, while
Ṭukhāristān was "properly speaking, the mountainous country on both sides of
the middle Oxus as far as Badakhshân . . . usually only the country south of the
Oxus is understood under this name." Barthold states simply that "the term
'Ṭurkhāristān' was also used in a much broader sense to embrace all the provinces
on both shores of the Amu-Darya which were economically dependent on Balkh"
(*Turkestan*[3], p. 68).

442. Following Marquart's reading (*Ērānšahr*, p. 226), rather than the form given
in the text (cf. Justi, *Iranisches Namenbuch*, p. 372).

443. Two unclear components. According to the *Addenda et Emendanda*, the
first of these is to be read as Bāsārā or Bāsārān, on which see Marquart, *Ērānšahr*,
p. 227 (for further discussion, see Barthold, *Turkestan*[3], p. 70, n. 1); note, however,
that the parallel passage in al-Balādhurī's *Futūḥ* (p. 420) reads "Kāsān and Ūrasht
(leg. Ūrast) in Farghānah."

444. Not even Marquart knows more about this place.

It has been said that, before he crossed the river, Qutaybah in this year stayed [to take action] against Balkh, because some of it was in revolt against him and had waged open war against the Muslims. He accordingly fought its people, and one of the captives was the wife of Barmak, the father of Khālid b. Barmak; Barmak was in charge of al-Nawbahār.[445] [This woman] fell to the lot of 'Abdallāh b. Muslim, called al-Faqīr ("the poor one"),[446] the brother of Qutaybah b. Muslim, and he had sexual relations with her; he suffered from elephantiasis. Then the people of Balkh made peace on the day after Qutaybah had made war on them, and Qutaybah ordered that the captives be returned. Barmak's wife said to 'Abdallāh b. Muslim, "O Arab, I have conceived by you," and 'Abdallāh, who was at death's door, made a testamentary disposition that what was in her womb should be brought to him. She was returned to Barmak.

It has been mentioned that, in the days of al-Mahdī, when [the latter] arrived at al-Rayy, the descendants of 'Abdallāh b. Muslim went to Khālid [b. Barmak] and asserted his relationship to them. Muslim b. Qutaybah said to them, "If you claim him as a relative and that is formalized, you will have to provide him with a wife [from your family]," so they left him and turned away from their claim.

Barmak was a physician: He subsequently cured Maslamah [b. 'Abd al-Malik] of a malady he was suffering from.

In this year Maslamah b. 'Abd al-Malik made a campaign in Byzantine territory.

In it, too, al-Ḥajjāj imprisoned Yazīd b. al-Muhallab; he also [1182] dismissed Ḥabīb b. al-Muhallab from Kirmān and 'Abd al-Malik b. al-Muhallab from [the command of] his police.

The leader of the pilgrimage in this year was Hishām b. Ismā'īl al-Makhzūmī: Thus it was related to me by Aḥmad b. Thābit on the authority of him who mentioned it on the authority of Isḥāq b. 'Īsā on the authority of Abū Ma'shar; and al-Wāqidī said the

---

445. See *EI²*, s.v. al-Barāmika, and R. W. Bulliet, "Naw Barār and the Survival of Iranian Buddhism," *Iran* 14 (1976), pp. 140–45.

446. According to al-Tha'ālibī, he acquired this sobriquet because of his persistent pleading of poverty when importuning Qutaybah for extra shares of booty (*Laṭā'if al-ma'ārif*, p. 40 [English trans., p. 59]).

same. The amīr over the whole of Iraq and the whole of the East was al-Ḥajjāj b. Yūsuf; over civilian affairs (*ṣalāt*) at al-Kūfah was al-Mughīrah b. ʿAbdallāh b. Abī ʿAqīl, and over military affairs (*ḥarb*) there, on behalf of al-Ḥajjāj, was Ziyād b. Jarīr b. ʿAbdallāh; over al-Baṣrah was Ayyūb b. al-Ḥakam;[447] and over Khurasan was Qutaybah b. Muslim.

---

447. See above, n. 82.

The
Events of the Year

87

(DECEMBER 23, 705–DECEMBER 11, 706)

In this year al-Walīd b. ʿAbd al-Malik dismissed Hishām b. Ismāʿīl from Medina. [Notice of] his dismissal arrived [there], according to what has been mentioned, on the night of Sunday, 7 Rabīʿ I (February 26) in the year 87. His governorship there lasted four years, less a month or so.

[The Appointment of ʿUmar b. ʿAbd al-ʿAzīz as Governor of Medina]

In this year, too, al-Walīd put ʿUmar b. ʿAbd al-ʿAzīz in charge of Medina.

Al-Wāqidī said: He arrived there as governor in the month of Rabīʿ I, aged twenty-five, having been born in the year 62 (681–82). [Al-Wāqidī also] said: He arrived [with his baggage] on thirty camels and stopped at Dār Marwān.[448]

According to [al-Wāqidī]—ʿAbd al-Raḥmān b. Abī al-Zinād—

---

448. Which apparently served as the governor's residence. The Marwān in question was Marwān b. al-Ḥakam, who had himself served two terms as governor of Medina (de Zambaur, *Manuel*, p. 24); for an earlier reference to his *dār*, see al-Ṭabarī, *Taʾrīkh*, ser. ii, p. 164, 1.6.

[1183]   his father: When ʿUmar b. ʿAbd al-ʿAzīz arrived at Medina and stopped at Dār Marwān, the people came into his presence and greeted [him]. When he had prayed the noontime prayer, he summoned ten of the jurisprudents of Medina, [namely,] ʿUrwah b. al-Zubayr, ʿUbaydallāh b. ʿAbdallāh b. ʿUtbah, Abū Bakr b. ʿAbd al-Raḥmān, Abū Bakr b. Sulaymān b. Abī Ḥathmah,[449] Sulaymān b. Yasār, al-Qāsim b. Muḥammad, Sālim b. ʿAbdallāh b. ʿUmar, ʿAbdallāh b. ʿAbdallāh b. ʿUmar, ʿAbdallāh b. ʿĀmir b. Rabīʿah, and Khārijah b. Zayd. They entered into his presence and sat down. He then praised God and extolled Him as He deserves, and said, "I have summoned you for a matter for which you will be rewarded and in which you will be helpers [in achieving] what is right. I do not wish to make any decision without [knowing] your opinion or [at least] the opinion of those of you who are present. If you see anyone transgressing, or [information about] injustice on the part of [any] [sub]governor of mine reaches you, I entreat you, in such circumstances, to inform me." Then they went out, saying, "May God reward you with good," and dispersed.

[Abū Jaʿfar?] said: Al-Walīd wrote to ʿUmar, instructing him to make Hishām b. Ismāʿīl stand before the people; [al-Walīd] had a poor opinion of [Hishām].

Al-Wāqidī said: Dāwūd b. Jubayr said: The *umm walad*[450] of Saʿīd b. al-Musayyab informed me that Saʿīd summoned his son and his mawlās and said, "This man will be made to stand before the people, or has been, and let no one confront him or harm him with a [single] word; we shall leave that to God and [his] kindred, even if what I know is no good for him. As for speaking to him, I shall never speak to him."

[Al-Wāqidī] said: Muḥammad b. ʿAbdallāh b. Muḥammad b. ʿUmar related to me on the authority of his father: Hishām b.
[1184]   Ismāʿīl used to be a bad neighbor and harm us; ʿAlī b. al-Ḥusayn[451] met with serious harm from him. When [Hishām] was dismissed, al-Walīd ordered that he be made to stand before the people, and he said, "I fear only ʿAlī b. al-Ḥusayn." ʿAlī b. al-Ḥusayn went past him when he had been made to stand at Dār Marwān, having previously told his intimates that no one of them should confront

---

449. Ḥathmah is proposed by the *Addenda et Emendanda* in preference to Khaythamah. For Khārijah cf. Juynboll, *Muslim Tradition*, pp. 41–42.
450. Cf. above, n. 416.
451. I.e., ʿAlī b. al-Ḥusayn Zayn al-ʿĀbidīn, grandson of ʿAlī b. Abī Ṭālib.

Hishām with a [single] word. When [ʿAlī] passed, Hishām b. Ismāʿīl called out to him, "God knows very well where to place His
messages."[452]

In this year Nīzak went to Qutaybah, and Qutaybah made
peace with the people of Bādghīs on the basis that he would not
enter it.

[Qutaybah's Peace Agreement with the People of Bādghīs][453]

ʿAlī b. Muḥammad mentioned that Abū al-Ḥasan al-Jushamī informed him on the authority of Khurasani shaykhs and Jabalah b.
Farrūkh on the authority of Muḥammad b. al-Muthannā that there
were Muslim prisoners in the hands of Nīzak Ṭarkhān. When
Qutaybah made peace with the king of Shūmān, he wrote to
[Nīzak] concerning those Muslim prisoners whom he had, [telling
him] to release them and threatening him in his letter. Nīzak
feared him, set the prisoners free, and sent them to Qutaybah.
Qutaybah then sent to him Sulaym al-Nāṣiḥ, mawlā of
ʿUbaydallāh b. Abī Bakrah, calling him to peace and a safe-conduct.
[Qutaybah] also sent him a letter in which he swore by God that, if
[Nīzak] did not go to him, he would campaign against him and
pursue him wherever he might be, not turning back from him until
he either defeated him or died before so doing. Sulaym brought   [1185]
Qutaybah's letter to Nīzak, and [Nīzak] took to seeking [Sulaym's]
advice. He said to him, "O Sulaym, I do not think that your friend
has any good [in mind]. He has written to me a letter [of the sort]
that should not be written to someone like me." Sulaym said to
him, "O Abū al-Hayyāj, this man is severe in his government,
easygoing when he is treated gently, and difficult when he is
treated badly. Do not let the coarseness of his letter prevent you
from [going to] him. You will be very well treated by him and by all
of Muḍar." Nīzak accordingly went with Sulaym to Qutaybah and,
the people of Bādghīs made peace with [Qutaybah] in the year 87 on
the basis that he would not enter Bādghīs.

In this year Maslamah b. ʿAbd al-Malik campaigned in Byzan-

---

452. Thus, too, in al-Yaʿqūbī, *Taʾrīkh*, vol. II, p. 339; cf. Qurʾān, 6:124 (which has
risālatahu, in the singular). The remark was presumably intended as a compli-
ment to ʿAlī b. al-Ḥusayn in his capacity as a member of the Ahl al-Bayt.
453. Cf. Gibb, *Arab Conquests*, p. 32.

tine territory accompanied by Yazīd b. Jubayr.[454] He encountered a large force of Byzantines at Sūsanah[455] in the region of al-Maṣṣīṣah.

Al-Wāqidī said: In [this year] Maslamah encountered Maymūn al-Jurjumānī[456]—with Maslamah there were about one thousand fighting men from the people of Anṭākiyah[457]—at Ṭuwānah.[458] He killed many of [the enemy], and at his hands God conquered fortresses.

It has been said that the person who campaigned against the Byzantines in this year was Hishām b. ʿAbd al-Malik, at whose hands God conquered the fortress of Būlaq, the fortress of al-Akhram, and the fortress of Būlus and Qumqum.[459] He killed about one thousand mustaʿribah[460] fighting men and took their offspring and women captive.

In this year Qutaybah campaigned against Paykand.[461]

Report of [Qutaybah's] Campaign [against Paykand]

According to ʿAlī b. Muḥammad—Abū ʾl-Dhayyāl—al-Muhallab
[1186] b. Iyās—his father—Ḥusayn b. Mujāhid al-Rāzī and Hārūn b. ʿĪsā—Yūnus b. Abī Isḥāq and others: When Qutaybah made peace with Nīzak, he stayed [put] until the time for campaigning,[462] and then in that year—the year 87—he campaigned against

---

454. Who seems to be otherwise unknown.

455. I.e., Sision: See Brooks, "The Arabs in Asia Minor," p. 191, and Lilie, *Byzantinische Reaktion*, p. 115, from which it emerges (i) that this action must have taken place earlier than A.H. 87, and (ii) that the Arabs suffered a serious defeat.

456. Thus in the *Addenda et Emendanda*, in preference to the "al-Jurijānī" given in the text. This is Maymūn the Mardaite, who, contrary to what is implied here, was fighting on the Arab side against the Byzantines: See Brooks, "The Arabs in Asia Minor," pp. 191, 203; Lilie, *Byzantinische Reaktion*, p. 116; *EI*², s.v. Djarādjima (vol. II, p. 457a).

457. I.e., Antioch (see *EI*², s.v. Anṭākiya).

458. I.e., Tyana: See Brooks, "The Arabs in Asia Minor," p. 191; Lilie, *Byzantinische Reaktion*, p. 116.

459. The rendering of these place names is tentative, and they appear to be unidentified (Khalīfah gives *twl.q*, and Ibn Kathīr gives *q.myq.m*).

460. Defined by Lammens (in a somewhat earlier context) as "tribus arabes raliées à Byzance at au christianisme" ("Le califat de Yazīd 1 er," pp. 606–7).

461. Cf. Gibb, *Arab Conquests*, pp. 33–34; Narshakhī, *The History of Bukhara*, (trans. Frye), pp. 43ff.

462. Which, as becomes apparent below, was at the very beginning of spring.

Paykand. He went from Marw to Marw Rūdh to Āmul to Zamm,[463] crossed the river, and went to Paykand, which is the nearest of the cities of Bukhārā to the river and is called the City of the Merchants; it is at the end of the desert [adjacent to?] Bukhārā. When he stopped in the surrounding area, [the people of Paykand] asked the Soghdians for help and sought reinforcements from around them, and large numbers came to them, taking the road. No messenger of Qutaybah's could be sent off, nor could [any] messenger get to him; for two months no news reached him. Al-Ḥajjāj found news of him slow [in coming] and feared for the army. He ordered the people to make invocations for them in the mosques and wrote to this effect to the *amṣār*. [Qutaybah and his men] were fighting every day.

['Alī b. Muḥammad] continued: Qutaybah had a non-Arab spy called Tīdhar,[464] to whom the people of Upper Bukhārā gave money on [the understanding] that he would remove Qutaybah from them. [Tīdhar] came to [Qutaybah] and said, "Let me be alone with you," and the people [present] stood up [and left, although] Qutaybah kept Ḍirār b. Ḥuṣayn al-Ḍabbī back. Tīdhar said, "[There is] a [new] governor coming to you, for al-Ḥajjāj has been dismissed; you ought to go off with the people to Marw." Qutaybah called for Siyāh, his mawlā, and said, "Behead Tīdhar!" and he killed him. Then he said to Ḍirār, "There remains no one who knows this report but you and me, and I give God a covenant that, if this story comes out before this war of ours is finished, I shall make you join [Tīdhar]. Control your tongue, for the spreading of this story will weaken the forearms of the people."[465]

['Alī b. Muḥammad] continued: Then [those who had earlier been present] came in and were alarmed by the killing of Tīdhar. They stayed silent, with downcast eyes, and Qutaybah said, "Do not be alarmed by the killing of a slave who has been destroyed by God." They said, "We thought that he was a sincere adviser to the Muslims." He said, "On the contrary, he was advising insincerely. God has destroyed him for his crime, and he has gone on his way. Go and fight your enemies, and encounter them with

[1187]

---

463. See above, nn. 344 and 346.

464. This seems to be the likeliest rendering (see Justi, *Iranisches Namenbuch*, p. 324), the other forms given being T.ndh.r, Y.tdh.r, T.nd.r, and B.nd.r.

465. Ibn A'tham, *Futūḥ*, vol. VII, p. 219, gives a longer account of this.

[something] other than that with which you have been encountering them."[466]

The people then went off, readying themselves, and formed their lines. Qutaybah went and spurred on the flag bearers, and there was some fighting with spears. [The fighters] then came together, and swords were used to good effect; God sent fortitude down to the Muslims, and they fought them until the sun had set. Then God gave the Muslims the upper hand, and [their opponents] were routed, heading for the city. The Muslims followed them and distracted them from entering [the city]. They scattered, and the Muslims came upon them, killing and taking prisoners at will.

The few who had entered the city preserved themselves in it, and Qutaybah set workmen onto the foundation [of its wall] in order to demolish it. They asked him for a peace, and he made peace with them, appointing over them one of his sons.[467] [Then] he went away from them, intending to return [to Khurasan], but, when he had gone a stage or two and was five parasangs distant from them, they broke faith, killed the governor and his companions, and cut off their noses and ears. [This] reached Qutaybah, who returned to them, they having fortified themselves, and fought them for a month. Then he set the workmen onto the foundation of [the wall of] the city, and they [excavated it and]

[1188]   propped it up with wood; [Qutaybah] intended, when the [work of excavating and] propping was finished, to set fire to the wood so that [the wall] might be demolished. But the wall fell down while they were still propping it up, and forty of the workmen were killed. [The people in the city now] sought peace, but he refused, fought them, took [the city] by force of arms, and killed those fighting men who were in it. Among those taken in the city was a one-eyed man who had been responsible for mobilizing the Turks against the Muslims, and he said to Qutaybah, "I shall ransom myself." Sulaym al-Nāṣiḥ said, "What will you give?" He said, "Five thousand pieces of Chinese silk worth one million [dirhams]." Qutaybah said [to his men], "What do you think?"

---

466. That is, fight them more strongly.

467. So rendering *rajulan min banī Qutaybah*; thus too *apud* Khalīfah (*Taʾrīkh*, p. 303); however, Narshakhī (*The History of Bukhara*, p. 44) names the man appointed as Warqāʾ b. Naṣr al-Bāhilī, a name known also to al-Yaʿqūbī (*Taʾrīkh*, vol. II, p. 342), albeit not specifically in the context of Paykand.

They said, "We think that his ransom will augment the booty of the Muslims. What mischief can this [fellow] possibly do?" Qutaybah said [to the man], "No, by God, no Muslim woman will ever be frightened by you," and he gave the order, and he was killed.[468]

According to ʿAlī [b. Muḥammad]—Abū al-Dhayyāl—al-Muhallab b. Iyās—his father and al-Ḥasan b. Rushayd—Ṭufayl b. Mirdās: When Qutaybah conquered Paykand, they there came upon innumerable gold and silver vessels. He put in charge of the booty and the division ʿAbdallāh b. Waʾlān al-ʿAdawī, [who was] one of the Banū al-Malakān and was called by Qutaybah "the trustworthy one, the son of the trustworthy one," and Iyās b. Bayhas al-Bāhilī. They melted down the vessels and the idols and presented [the resultant bullion] to Qutaybah. They also presented to him the dross of what they had melted down, and he gave it to them. They were then given forty thousand [dirhams] for it, and they told [Qutaybah]. [At this, Qutaybah] changed his mind and ordered them to melt down [the dross]. They did so, and there emerged from it one hundred fifty thousand *mithqāls*, or fifty thousand *mithqāls*.[469]

They acquired much at Paykand. From Paykand there came into the hands of the Muslims [booty] the like of which they had never acquired in Khurasan. Qutaybah returned to Marw, and the Muslims became strong. They bought weapons and horses, and riding animals were procured for them. They competed with one another in fine attire and equipment, and they bought weapons at high prices, until the [price of a] spear reached seventy [dirhams].[470] Al-Kumayt said (*basīṭ*):[471]

[1189]

And the battle day of Paykand, the wonders of which
    cannot be enumerated,
    and Bukhārā did not fall short of that.

---

468. A similar account of this one-eyed prisoner is given by Ibn Aʿtham (*Futūḥ*, vol. VII, p. 224).

469. A *mithqāl* being approximately 4.4 g (see *EI*², s.v. Makāyil and Mawāzīn). The figure of 150,000 *mithqāls* is reflected in Narshakhī's report (p. 45) of the total amount of treasure taken (rather than what issued from the dross, which he does not mention).

470. Ibn Aʿtham (*Futūḥ*, vol. VII, p. 221) adds here that the price of a coat of mail reached 700 dirhams (cf. Narshakhī's remark that "a spear was worth fifty *dirhams*, a shield fifty or sixty, and a coat of mail seven hundred *dirhams*" [p. 46]).

471. *EI*², s.v. al-Kumayt b. Zayd al-Asadī; Sezgin, *GAS*, vol. II, pp. 347ff. The following verse is also given in *Shiʿr al-Kumayt*, no. 147.

In the treasuries were many weapons and much war matériel. Qutaybah wrote to al-Ḥajjāj seeking his permission to hand out these weapons to the troops, and he gave him permission. They brought out such war matériel and traveling equipment as was in the treasuries; he divided it out, and they equipped themselves. When springtime came, he summoned the people and said, "I am going to take you on campaign [now], before you need to carry provisions, and I shall bring you back before you need warm clothes"; and he set off finely equipped with riding animals and weapons. He went to Āmul and crossed from Zamm to Bukhārā; he went to Tūmushkath,[472] in Bukhārā [territory], and [its people] made peace with him.

According to ʿAlī [b. Muḥammad]—Abū al-Dhayyāl—shaykhs from the Banū ʿAdī: [Qutaybah's father,] Muslim al-Bāhilī, [had earlier] said to Waʾlān, "I have [some] money I should like to deposit with you." [Waʾlān] said, "Do you want it to be kept secret, or do you not mind the people knowing?" [Muslim] said, [1190] "I should like to keep it secret." [Waʾlān] said, "Send it with a man you trust to such-and-such a place and tell him that, when he sees a man in that place, he is to put down what he has with him and depart." "Yes," said Muslim, and he put the money in a saddlebag, loaded it on a mule, and said to a mawlā of his, "Set off with this mule to such-and-such a place and, when you see a man sitting, leave the mule and depart." The man set off with the mule. [Meanwhile] Waʾlān had reached the place at the appointed time, while Muslim's messenger was slow in getting to him. The time appointed by Waʾlān was past, and he thought that [Muslim must have] changed his mind; so he departed. There [now] came to that place a man from the Banū Taghlib and, [when] Muslim's mawlā came, he saw [the Taghlibī] sitting, left the mule, and returned [home]. The Taghlibī went up to the mule and, when he saw the money and did not see anyone with the mule, he led it to his house and took possession of both the mule and the money. Muslim thought that the money had gone to Waʾlān, and he did not ask him about it until he needed it. Then he met him and said, "My money." [Waʾlān] said, "I did not receive anything. I don't have any money of yours."

---

472. So reading *nūmushakath*, following Wellhausen (*Kingdom*, p. 434) and Gibb (*Arab Conquests*, p. 34); Barthold (*Turkestan*[3], p. 132, citing Yāqūt) identifies it as a "neighbourhood of Bukhara."

['Alī b. Muḥammad] continued: Muslim used to complain of [Wa'lān] and speak ill of him.

['Alī b. Muḥammad] continued: He came one day to a gathering (*majlis*) of the Banū Ḍubay'ah and complained of him. The Taghlibī was sitting [there], went up to him, spoke to him in private and asked him about the money, and then told him [that he had it]. He took [Muslim] to his house, brought out the saddlebag, and said, "Do you recognize it?" "Yes," said Muslim. "And the seal?" "Yes," said Muslim. "Take your money," said [the Taghlibī], and he told him the story [of how he had come by it]. Muslim went to the people and the tribes to whom he had complained of Wa'lān, exonerating him and telling them the story. Concerning Wa'lān, the poet says (*ṭawīl*):

I am not like Wa'lān, who was a leader in piety,   [1191]
    and I am not like 'Imrān or like al-Muhallab.

[This] 'Imrān [was 'Imrān] b. al-Faḍīl al-Burjumī.[473]

The leader of the pilgrimage in this year, according to what Aḥmad b. Thābit related to me on the authority of him who mentioned it on the authority of Isḥāq b. 'Īsā on the authority of Abū Ma'shar, was 'Umar b. 'Abd al-'Azīz, who was the amīr over Medina. Over the judiciary of Medina in this year was Abū Bakr b. 'Amr b. Ḥazm, on behalf of 'Umar b. 'Abd al-'Azīz. Over Iraq and the whole of the East was al-Ḥajjāj; his deputy over al-Baṣrah in this year was, according to what has been said, al-Jarrāḥ b. 'Abdallāh al-Ḥakamī, while 'Abdallāh b. Udhaynah was in charge of the judiciary [there]; his governor over military affairs (*ḥarb*) at al-Kūfah was Ziyād b. Jarīr b. 'Abdallāh, while Abū Bakr b. Abī Mūsā al-Ash'arī was over the judiciary [there]; over Khurasan was Qutaybah b. Muslim.

---

473. An early Arab campaigner in the East (al-Ṭabarī, *Ta'rīkh*, ser. i, pp. 2830–31).

The
Events of the Year
88
(December 12, 706–November 30, 707)

Among them was God's conquest for the Muslims of one of the fortresses of the Byzantines, called Ṭuwānah, in Jumādā II (May–June); they spent the winter there. In command of the army were Maslamah b. ʿAbd al-Malik and al-ʿAbbās b. al-Walīd b. ʿAbd al-Malik.

Muḥammad b. ʿUmar al-Wāqidī mentioned that Thawr b. Yazīd related to him on the authority of his companions: The conquest of Ṭuwānah was [effected] at the hands of Maslamah b. ʿAbd al-Malik and al-ʿAbbās b. al-Walīd. The Muslims inflicted an [initial] defeat on the enemy on that day. [The enemy] went to their church and then returned, and [the Muslims] suffered a defeat from which they thought they would never recover. Al-ʿAbbās remained with a party [of men], including Ibn Muḥayrīz al-Jumaḥī. He said to Ibn Muḥayrīz, "Where are the people of the Qurʾān who desire Paradise?" Ibn Muḥayrīz said, "If you call them, they will come to you." Al-ʿAbbās called, "O people of the Qurʾān!" and they all came forward. Then God defeated the enemy until they went into Ṭuwānah.[474] Al-Walīd b. ʿAbd al-Malik

[1192]

---

474. Cf. Brooks, "The Arabs in Asia Minor," p. 192; Lilie, *Byzantinische Reaktion*, pp. 116ff.

had required the people of Medina to provide levies in this year.

According to Muḥammad b. ʿUmar—his father: Makhramah b. Sulaymān al-Wālibī said: He required them to produce two thousand [levies]. They stipulated among themselves to give pay to such of them as would serve as substitutes,[475] and fifteen hundred set out and 500 stayed behind. They made the summer campaign with Maslamah and al-ʿAbbās, who were in command of the army; and they wintered at Ṭuwānah and conquered it.

In [this year] al-Walīd b. Yazīd b. ʿAbd al-Malik was born.

[Reconstruction of the Mosque of Medina]

In [this year] al-Walīd b. ʿAbd al-Malik ordered the pulling down of the mosque of the Messenger of God, may God bless and preserve him, and the pulling down of the rooms of the wives of the Messenger of God, may God bless and preserve him, and the incorporation of them into the mosque.

Muḥammad b. ʿUmar mentioned that Muḥammad b. Jaʿfar b. Wardān al-Bannāʾ (i.e., "the builder") said: I saw the messenger sent by al-Walīd b. ʿAbd al-Malik. He arrived in the month of Rabīʿ I in the year 88 (February–March 707), with a turban wound round his head. He entered into the presence of ʿUmar b. ʿAbd al-ʿAzīz bearing al-Walīd's letter ordering him to incorporate the rooms of the wives of the Messenger of God, may God bless and preserve him, into the mosque, and to buy [the land, etc.] behind it and beside it so that it might [measure] two hundred cubits by two hundred cubits. He also said to him [in the letter]: "Move the *qiblah* [wall] forward, if you are able, and you *are* able, because of the standing of your maternal uncles;[476] they will not go against you. If any of them objects, order the people of the *miṣr* to estimate a fair value for him. Then demolish and pay them the prices. You have good precedents [for this in the actions of] ʿUmar and ʿUthmān." [ʿUmar] had [the uncles] read the letter, they being with him; the people agreed to the price, and he gave them it and began to pull down the rooms of the wives of the Prophet, may God bless and preserve him, and to build the mosque. Soon afterward there arrived the workmen sent by al-Walīd.

[1193]

---

475. All of this being the sense of *tajāʿalū*; (see Lane, *Lexicon*, s.v.).
476. ʿUmar's mother being a descendant of ʿUmar b. al-Khaṭṭāb.

According to Muḥammad b. ʿUmar—Mūsā b. Yaʿqūb—his paternal uncle: I saw ʿUmar b. ʿAbd al-ʿAzīz pulling down the mosque; with him were [such] leading people [as] al-Qāsim, Sālim, Abū Bakr b. ʿAbd al-Raḥmān b. al-Ḥārith, ʿUbaydallāh b. ʿAbdallāh b. ʿUtbah, Khārijah b. Zayd, and ʿAbdallāh b. ʿAbdallāh b. ʿUmar, showing him key features (al-aʿlām) in the mosque and taking measurements. They laid its foundation.

According to Muḥammad b. ʿUmar—Yaḥyā b. al-Nuʿmān al-Ghifārī—Ṣāliḥ b. Kaysān: When al-Walīd's letter came from Damascus—it took fifteen [nights][477]—with the order to pull down the mosque, ʿUmar b. ʿAbd al-ʿAzīz applied himself to the task with vigor.

Ṣāliḥ said: He put me in charge of pulling it down and [re-]building it. We pulled it down using the workers of Medina, [1194] and we began to pull down the rooms of the wives of the Prophet, may God bless and preserve him. [This went on] until there came to us the workmen sent by al-Walīd.

According to Muḥammad—Mūsā b. Abī Bakr—Ṣāliḥ b. Kaysān: We started pulling down the mosque of the Messenger of God, may God bless and preserve him, in Ṣafar in the year 88 (January–February 707). Al-Walīd sent [word] to the Byzantine Emperor informing him that he had ordered the pulling down of the mosque of the Messenger of God, may God bless and preserve him, and [asking him] to help him in [that regard]. [The Byzantine Emperor] sent to him one hundred thousand mithqāls of gold, one hundred workers, and forty loads of mosaic; he ordered that mosaic be sought in cities that had been ruined and sent it to al-Walīd. Al-Walīd sent [all] that on to ʿUmar b. ʿAbd al-ʿAzīz.[478]

In this year ʿUmar b. ʿAbd al-ʿAzīz began building the mosque.[479]

In it, too, Maslamah campaigned against the Byzantines. Three fortresses were conquered at his hands: the fortress of Qusṭanṭīn, [the fortress of] Ghazālah, and the fortress of al-Akhram; and he killed about a thousand of the mustaʿribah,[480] along with taking

---

477. Following the suggestions made in the Addenda et Emendanda.

478. On this locus classicus, see Gibb, "Arab-Byzantine Relations under the Umayyad Caliphate," pp. 52ff.

479. Al-Yaʿqūbī (Taʾrīkh, vol. II, p. 340 [where the same figures are given for mithqāls, etc.]) notes that the work was finished in A.H. 90.

480. See above, n. 460.

the offspring captive and appropriating wealth.[481]

In this year Qutaybah campaigned against Tūmushkath and Rāmīthanah.[482]

[Qutaybah's] Campaign [against Tūmushkath and Rāmīthanah]

According to 'Alī b. Muḥammad—al-Mufaḍḍal b. al-Muhallab— his father and Muṣ'ab b. Ḥayyān—a mawlā of theirs: Qutaybah [1195] campaigned against Tūmushkath in the year 88, having deputed over Marw Bashshār b. Muslim. Its people met him, and he made peace with them. Then he went to Rāmīthanah and its people made peace with him, and he departed from them. [At this point], the Turks, accompanied by the Soghdians and the people of Farghānah, marched on him and tried to intercept the Muslims while they were on their way. They caught up with 'Abd al-Raḥmān b. Muslim al-Bāhilī, who was in command of the rear guard, there being a [distance of an Arab] mile[483] between him [on the one hand] and Qutaybah and the troops at the front [on the other]. When they drew near to him, 'Abd al-Raḥmān sent a messenger with his report to Qutaybah. The Turks came toward him and fought him. The messenger reached Qutaybah, who came back with [reinforcements] and joined 'Abd al-Raḥmān, who was [still] fighting them. The Turks had almost gained mastery over them, but when [the Muslims fighting them] saw Qutaybah, they took heart, showed fortitude, and fought them until noontime. Nīzak, who was with Qutaybah, showed valor on that day, and God defeated the Turks and dispersed them. Qutaybah went back, heading for Marw: He crossed the river by way of al-Tirmidh, heading for Balkh, and reached Marw.

The Bāhilīs said: In command of the Turks [when] they engaged the Muslims was Kūrbaghānūn[484] al-Turkī, the son of the sister

---

481. Cf. Brooks, "The Arabs in Asia Minor," p. 192, where Ghazālah is identified as Gazelon. There are problems of chronology here (see Lilie, *Byzantinische Reaktion*, p. 118n.).

482. On Tūmushkath, see above, n. 472. Rāmīthanah was one of the districts of Bukhārā and contained a fortified village of the same name (Barthold, *Turkestan*³, p. 116); cf. Khalīfah, *Ta'rīkh*, pp. 304–5.

483. Ca. two kilometers.

484. See Marquart, "Historische Glossen zu den alttürkischen Inschriften," p.

of the king of China. [His force numbered] two hundred thousand [men], over whom God gave the Muslims victory.[485]

In this year al-Walīd b. ʿAbd al-Malik wrote to ʿUmar b. ʿAbd al-Azīz concerning making the mountain passes easier and digging wells in the [Ḥijāzī] territories.

According to Muḥammad b. ʿUmar—Ibn Abī Sabrah—Ṣāliḥ b. Kaysān: Al-Walīd wrote to ʿUmar concerning making the mountain passes easier and digging wells at Medina, and his letters to that [effect] went out to [all the] Muslim territories; al-Walīd also wrote to Khālid b. ʿAbdallān [al-Qasrī] to that [effect]. [Ibn Kaysān?] said: He stopped those with elephantiasis from going out among the people and arranged for allowances to be allocated to them.

Ibn Abī Sabrah said on the authority of Ṣāliḥ b. Kaysān: Al-Walīd wrote to ʿUmar b. ʿAbd al-ʿAzīz [telling him] to construct the drinking fountain which is today at the house of Yazīd b. ʿAbd al-Malik. ʿUmar constructed it and caused its water to flow. When al-Walīd made the pilgrimage, he stopped at it, looked at the building and the drinking fountain [itself], and was pleased by them. He ordered that it should have superintendents to look after it and that the people of the mosque should be given to drink from it. That was done.

The leader of the pilgrimage in this year was ʿUmar b. ʿAbd al-ʿAzīz in the account of Muḥammad b. ʿUmar. He mentioned that Muḥammad b. ʿAbdallāh b. Jubayr, mawlā of the Banū al-ʿAbbās, related to him on the authority of Ṣāliḥ b. Kaysān: ʿUmar b. ʿAbd al-ʿAzīz took out in that year—meaning the year 88—a number of Quraysh to whom he had sent gifts and baggage camels. They entered into a state of *iḥrām* with him at Dhū al-Ḥulayfah,[486] and he led with him animals for sacrifice. When they were at al-Tanʿīm,[487] they were met by some Qurashīs, in-

---

182 (where [*pace* the *Addenda et Emendanda*] the readings Kūrbaghānūn and Kūrmaghānūn are proposed), and, more recently, Frye's remarks (Narshakhī, *The History of Bukhara*, pp. 133–34, n. 178).

485. Gibb (*Arab Conquests*, p. 35) casts doubt on the historicity of this report.

486. A settlement six or seven *mīl* (ca. twelve or fourteen km) from Medina (Yāqūt, *Muʿjam*, vol. II, p. 324).

487. A place two parasangs (ca. twelve km) from Mecca (Yāqūt, *Muʿjam*, vol. I, p. 879).

cluding Ibn Abī Mulaykah and others, who informed him that Mecca was short of water and that they feared for the pilgrims in respect of thirst; [the reason for] that [was] that the rain had been scanty. ʿUmar said, "What is wanted here is clear. Come! We shall call [upon] God." [Ṣāliḥ b. Kaysān] said: I saw them doing so, and he with them, and they were insistent in the[ir] prayer. Ṣāliḥ said: And, by God, no sooner had we reached the House on that day than it was raining, which it did into the nighttime; the heavens opened, the flash flood came down the valley, and there came about a situation that the people of Mecca feared. ʿArafah, Minā, and Jamʿ[488] were washed out, and could only [be reached] by bridging. [Ṣāliḥ] said: Mecca produced plants that year, because of the fertility.

As for Abū Maʿshar, he said: The leader of the pilgrimage in the year 88 was ʿUmar b. al-Walīd b. ʿAbd al-Malik. That was related to me by Aḥmad b. Thābit on the authority of he who mentioned it on the authority of Isḥāq b. ʿĪsā on his (i.e., Abū Maʿshar's) authority.

The governors over the *amṣār* in this year were the same as those we have mentioned as governors in the year 87.

[1197]

---

488. Jamʿ is synonymous with al-Muzdalifah (see Yāqūt, *Muʿjam*, vol. II, p. 118); Ibn al-Athīr reads "Arafah and Mecca," while Ibn Kathīr (*Bidāyah*, vol. IX, p. 75) gives "Arafah, Muzdalifah and Minā."

❦

The
Events of the Year

89

(DECEMBER 1, 707–NOVEMBER 19, 708)

❦

Among them was the conquest by the Muslims in this year of the fortress of Sūriyah; in command of the army was Maslamah b. ʿAbd al-malik.

Al-Wāqidī claimed that Maslamah campaigned in this year in Byzantine territory, accompanied by al-ʿAbbās b. al-Walīd, [that] they entered it together and then separated, and [that] Maslamah conquered the fortress of Sūriyah, while al-ʿAbbās conquered Adhrūliyyah and encountered a body of Byzantines and defeated them.

[1198] [An authority] other than al-Wāqidī has said that Maslamah headed for ʿAmmūriyyah, where he encountered a large body of Byzantines. God defeated them, and he conquered Hiraqlah and Qamūdiyyah. Al-ʿAbbās made the summer campaign from the direction of al-Budandūn.[489]

In this year Qutaybah campaigned in Bukhārā and conquered Rāmīthanah.

ʿAlī b. Muḥammad mentioned on the authority of the Bāhilīs

---

489. The identifications are Isauria, Dorylaion, Amorion, Herakleia, Kamouliana, and Podendon, respectively (see Brooks, "The Arabs in Asia Minor," pp. 192–93; Lilie, *Byzantinische Reaktion*, pp. 118, 134 [map]).

that they said that and [that they said] that he returned, after he had conquered it, by way of Balkh. When he was at al-Fāryāb, there came to him al-Ḥajjāj's letter telling him to go to Wardān Khudhāh;[490] Qutaybah accordingly went back in the year 89. He went to Zamm, crossed the river, and was encountered on the desert road by the Soghdians and the people of Kish and Nasaf. They fought him, and he defeated them, went to Bukhārā, and stopped at Lower Kharqānah,[491] on Wardān's right. They engaged him with a large force, and he fought them for two days and nights; then God granted victory over them. Nahār b. Tawsiʿah said (ṭawīl):[492]

They had a [long] night from us at Kharqān,
    and our night at Kharqān was [even] longer.

ʿAlī [b. Muḥammad] said: According to (i) Abū al-Dhayyāl—al-Muhallab b. Iyās, and (ii) Abū al-ʿAlāʾ—Idrīs b. Ḥanẓalah: Qutaybah campaigned against Wardān Khudhāh, the king of Bukhārā, in the year 89, made no headway against him, and did not conquer any of his territory. He returned to Marw and wrote to al-Ḥajjāj about that. Al-Ḥajjāj wrote to him, "Portray [the terrain] to me," and [Qutaybah] sent him a representation of it. Al-Ḥajjāj wrote to him, "Return to your wallowing place, repent to God for what you have done, and make your approach from such-and-such a place"; and it has been said [that] al-Ḥajjāj wrote to him, "Outwit Kish, smash Nasaf, and reach Wardān;[493] beware of beating about the bush and spare me the byways."[494]

In this year Khālid b. ʿAbdallāh al-Qasrī became governor of Mecca, according to what al-Wāqidī claimed. He mentioned that ʿUmar b. Ṣāliḥ related to him on the authority of Nāfiʿ, mawlā of the Banū Makhzūm, who said: I heard Khālid b. ʿAbdallāh say on the pulpit of Mecca, while he was delivering a sermon, "O people, who is greater? A man's deputy (khalīfah) over his people or his

[1199]

---

490. "The rulers of Wardāna, who bore the title of Wardān-Khudāts, were until the beginning of the eighth century the rivals of the Bukhār-Khudāts" (Barthold, Turkestan³, p. 113).

491. One of the districts of Bukhārā (Barthold, Turkestan³, p. 114).

492. Also cited by Ibn Kathīr, Bidāyah, vol. IX, p. 76.

493. There is a play on words here; in addition, the text gives the vocalization wa-rid Wardān, which Gibb (Arab Conquests, p. 35) understood as "and drive Wardān back" (i.e., he read wa-rudda Wardān).

494. Wa-daʿnī min bunayyāt al-ṭarīq; cf. Freytag, Arabum Proverbia, vol. I, p. 483.

messenger (*rasūl*) to them?[495] If you were not to know the superiority of the caliphate, [I would tell you] that Abraham, the friend of the Merciful, prayed for water, and He gave him bitter salt to drink, and the Caliph prayed to Him for water, and He gave him sweet water," ⟨meaning by "salt" Zamzam and by "sweet water"⟩[496] a well dug by al-Walīd b. ʿAbd al-Malik between[497] the two mountain passes of Ṭawā and al-Ḥajūn.[498] The water [of this well] used to be transported and placed in a tank made of leather beside Zamzam, so that its superiority over [the water of] Zamzam might be known. [Al-Wāqidī] said: Then the well caved in and disappeared; today it is not known where it is.

[1200]

In [this year] Maslamah b. ʿAbd al-Malik campaigned against the Turks until he reached al-Bāb[499] in the region of ʿAdharbayjān; he conquered fortresses and cities there.

The pilgrimage was led in this year by ʿUmar b. ʿAbd al-ʿAzīz: thus it was related to me by Aḥmad b. Thābit on the authority of him who mentioned it on the authority of Isḥāq b. ʿĪsā on the authority of Abū Maʿshar. The governors of the *amṣār* in this year were [the same as] the governors in the preceding year; we have mentioned them already.

---

495. For discussion of the significance of this, see Crone and Hinds, *God's Caliph*, p. 29.

496. The words in brackets have been added from Ibn al-Athīr.

497. The text reads *bi-*, "at." The parallel passage in *Aghānī*², vol. XXII, p. 18, reads *bayna*.

498. Al-Ḥajūn is identified as a mountain one and a half *mīl* (3 km) from the Kaʿbah (Yāqūt, *Muʿjam*, vol. II, p. 215). Ṭawā (Dhū Ṭuwā in the *Aghānī*) is more problematic: Yāqūt knows it as the "most famous wādī at Mecca" (vol. III, p. 554), while Dhū Ṭuwā is simply "a place at Mecca" (vol. III, p. 553).

499. I.e., Bāb al-Abwāb (see *EI*², s.v.), modern Derbent, which could have been more accurately described as being in the region of Arrān.

The
Events of the Year

90
(November 20, 708–November 8, 709)

In this year, according to what Muḥammad b. ʿUmar mentioned, Maslamah campaigned in Byzantine territory in the region of Sūriyah and conquered the five fortresses there.

In it, too, al-ʿAbbās b. al-Walīd campaigned, as far as al-Arzan according to some, and as far as Sūriyah according to others. Muḥammad b. ʿUmar said: It is sounder to say that he went as far as Sūriyah.[500]

In [this year] Muḥammad b. al-Qāsim al-Thaqafī, who was in command of an army on behalf of al-Ḥajjāj, killed Dāhir b. Ṣaṣṣah,[501] the king of Sind.

In it, too, al-Walīd appointed Qurrah b. Sharīk[502] over Egypt in place of ʿAbdallāh b. ʿAbd al-Malik.

In [this year] the Byzantines took prisoner Khālid b. Kaysān, the sea commander, and took him to their king; the king of the By-

[1201]

---

500. Cf. Brooks, "The Arabs in Asia Minor," p. 193; Lilie, *Byzantinische Reaktion*, pp. 118. "Al-Arzan" seems to constitute a problem: Brooks says that it "should be Arzanene or its chief town, but this is clearly out of place here."

501. I.e., Dāhir the son of Chach (for detailed discussion of this expedition, see F. Gabrieli, "Muḥammad ibn Qāsim ath-Thaqafī and the Arab Conquest of Sind," *East and West*, n.s. 15 (1965), pp. 281–95).

502. See *EI²*, s.v. Ḳurra b. Sharīk.

zantines gave him to al-Walīd b. ʿAbd al-Malik.[503]

In it, too, Qutaybah conquered Bukhārā and defeated the armies of the enemy there.[504]

[Qutaybah's Conquest of Bukhārā]

ʿAlī b. Muḥammad said: According to (i) Abū al-Dhayyāl—al-Muhallab b. Iyās, and (ii) Abū al-ʿAlāʾ—Idrīs b. Ḥanẓalah: When there reached Qutaybah al-Ḥajjāj's letter—[the letter in which] he ordered him to repent of having departed from Wardān Khudhāh, the king of Bukhārā, before defeating him, [and ordered him] to go against [Wardān], informing him of the place from which he should proceed to [Wardān's] territory—Qutaybah went out to Bukhārā on campaign in the year 90. Wardān Khudhāh sent [word] to the Soghdians and the Turks and those who were around them, requesting their help, and they came. Qutaybah, however, reached [Bukhārā] first and besieged [it], and, when the reinforcements arrived, [the Muslims] went out to fight them. The Azd said, "Keep us on our own and let us fight them." Qutaybah said, "Go forward," and they went forward, fighting them, while Qutaybah sat wearing a yellow ridāʾ[505] over his weapons. They all showed fortitude for a long time; then the Muslims wheeled round, and the polytheists came at them, broke them, entered Qutaybah's camp, and crossed it until the women struck the faces of [the polytheists'] horses and wept. Then they returned to the charge, and the two wings of the Muslims closed in on the Turks and fought them until they repelled them to their positions.

[1202]

The Turks stood on an elevation, and Qutaybah said, "Who will dislodge them from this place for us?" No one came forward; all the clans stood [stock-still]. Qutaybah went to the Banū Tamīm and said, "O Banū Tamīm, you are in the position of the ḥuṭamiyyah.[506] [All I need is one] battle day like the battle days [in your glorious past], may my father be your ransom." [ʿAlī b. Muḥammad] continued: Wakīʿ [b. Abī Sūd][507] took the standard

---

503. Cf. Lilie, *Byzantinische Reaktion*, p. 119.
504. Cf. Gibb, *Arab Conquests*, pp. 35–36.
505. See below, n. 596 (first part).
506. "Coat of mail on which swords break" (see the *Glossarium*).
507. A leading Tamīmī in Khurasan (see Caskel, *Ǧamharat an-nasab*, register, s.v. Wakīʿ b. Ḥassān).

in his hand and said, "O Banū Tamīm, will you abandon me today?" They said, "No, O Abū Muṭarrif." Huraym b. Abī Ṭaḥmah al-Mujāshiʿī[508] was in command of the cavalry of the Banū Tamīm, and Wakīʿ was their chief. The people were standing, and all of them held back. Wakīʿ said, "Forward, O Huraym," and he gave him the banner, "take your cavalry forward," and Huraym went forward, while Wakīʿ walked slowly behind with the infantry. Huraym got as far as a river that was between him and the enemy and then stopped. Wakīʿ said to him, "Press on, O Huraym."

[ʿAlī b. Muḥammad] continued: Huraym gave Wakīʿ the look of a fierce camel and said, "Am I to impel my cavalry across this river? If they are defeated, that will be the end of them. By God, you are stupid!" [Wakīʿ] said, "You son of a stinking woman![509] I'm not going to see you disobey my order," and he struck him with an iron bar he had with him. [At this,] Huraym whipped his horse and impelled it [across the river], saying, "There can't be anything harder to take than this," and he crossed with the cavalry. Wakīʿ came to the river, called for wood, and bridged it. He said to his companions, "Whoever of you has accustomed himself to [the idea of] death, let him cross; he who has not, let him stay in his place." Only eight infantrymen crossed with him. He walked slowly with them until, when they were tired, he sat them down and they rested, while he went near the enemy. He made the cavalry into two wings and said to Huraym, "I am going to thrust at the [enemy]. Distract them from me with the cavalry." He said to the [infantrymen], "Attack!" and they charged straight at [the enemy] until they were mixed with them. Huraym attacked them with his cavalry, and they thrust at them with spears. By the time [the Muslims] desisted from [the Turks], they had dislodged them from their position. Qutaybah called out, "Do you not see the enemy defeated. No sooner did someone cross that river than the enemy fled in defeat." The [Muslims] followed them, and Qutaybah called out, "Whoever brings a[n enemy] head shall have one hundred [dirhams]."

[ʿAlī b. Muḥammad] said: Mūsā b. al-Mutawakkil al-Qurayʿī claimed: On that day eleven men from the Banū Qurayʿ came,

[1203]

---

508. Caskel, *Ǧamharat an-nasab*, register, s.v. Huraym b. ʿAdī.
509. I.e., a slave girl; note Ibn Qutaybah's observation that *al-lakhnāʾ ʿinda al-ʿarab al-amah* ("Kitāb al-ʿarab," p. 352).

each of them bringing a head; each was asked, "Who are you?" and said, "A Qurayʿī." Then a man from al-Azd brought a head and they said to him, "Who are you?" He said, "A Qurayʿī." Jahm b. Zahr[510] was sitting [nearby] and said, "He is lying, by God! May God cause you to prosper, he is my cousin." Qutaybah said to [the Azdī], "Woe to you! What induced you to [say] this?" He said, "I saw that everyone who came said, 'A Qurayʿī,' and thought that everyone who brought a head had to say, 'A Qurayʿī.'" Qutaybah laughed.

[ʿAlī b. Muḥammad] said: On that day Khāqān[511] and his son were wounded.

Qutaybah returned to Marw and wrote to al-Ḥajjāj, "I sent ʿAbd al-Raḥmān b. Muslim and God conquered at his hands." [ʿAlī b. Muḥammad] continued: A mawlā of al-Ḥajjāj's had witnessed the conquest, and he came and told [al-Ḥajjāj] what had [really] happened. Al-Ḥajjāj was angry with Qutaybah, and [Qutaybah] grieved at that. The people said to [Qutaybah], "Send a delegation of the Banū Tamīm to [al-Ḥajjāj]; give [generously] to them and please them, and they will tell the amīr that the matter was as you [described it when you] wrote." [Qutaybah] accordingly sent [some] men, including ʿUrām b. Shutayr al-Ḍabbī, and, when they reached al-Ḥajjāj, he shouted at them and stigmatized them. He called for the cupper, [who had his] scissors in his hand, and said, [1204] "I'll cut off your tongues if you don't tell me the truth." They said, "The amīr is Qutaybah, and he sent ʿAbd al-Raḥmān in command of them; the conquest belongs to the amīr and the one who is head of the people." It was ʿUrām b. Shutayr who spoke these words to him. Al-Ḥajjāj quietened down.

In this year Qutaybah renewed the peace between himself and Ṭarkhūn, the king of Soghd.

[Renewed Peace between Qutaybah and the Soghdians]

According to ʿAlī [b. Muḥammad]—Abū al-Sarī al-Marwazī—al-Jahm al-Bāhilī: When Qutaybah fell upon the people of Bukhārā and broke them up, the people of Soghd feared him. Ṭarkhūn, the

---

510. Al-Juʿfī, brother of Jabalah (Caskel, *Ğamharat an-nasab*, register).
511. See above, n. 79.

king of Soghd, went back accompanied by two horsemen until he stood near Qutaybah's camp, with the Bukhārā river between the two of them. He asked [Qutaybah] to send to him a man to whom he might talk. Qutaybah ordered a man [to go], and [this man] drew near to [Ṭarkhūn].

As for the Bāhilīs, they say that Ṭarkhūn called to Ḥayyān al-Nabaṭī,[512] who went to them. [Ṭarkhūn] asked for a peace in return for tribute that he would pay to them, and Qutaybah agreed to his request, made peace with him, and took from him hostages [to remain with him] until [such time as] Ṭarkhūn might send to him [the tribute] on the basis of which he had made peace with him. Ṭarkhūn departed to his country, and Qutaybah returned [sc. to Marw], accompanied by Nīzak.

In this year Nīzak broke the peace between himself and the Muslims, held out in his fortress, and reverted to war. Qutaybah campaigned against him.[513]

[Nīzak's] Perfidy and Why He Was Vanquished

'Alī [b. Muḥammad] said: According to (i) Abū al-Dhayyāl—al-Muhallab b. Iyās, (ii) al-Mufaḍḍal al-Ḍabbī—his father, (iii) 'Alī b. Mujāhid, and (iv) Kulayb b. Khalaf al-'Ammī—each mentioned something and I have put [what they said] together [in a single account]; and the Bāhilīs mentioned something, and I have annexed [that] to the report of these [others] and have put it in [with the rest]: Qutaybah left Bukhārā accompanied by Nīzak, who had been alarmed by the conquests he had seen and who feared Qutaybah. [Nīzak] said to his companions and his intimates among them,[514] "I am with this [fellow], and I don't feel safe with him, for the Arab is like a dog: If you beat him, he barks, and if you feed him, he wags his tail. If you campaign against him and then give him something, he is pleased and forgets what you have done to him. Ṭarkhūn fought him several times, and when he gave him tribute, he accepted it and was pleased. He is a dissolute brute. The best thing will be for me to take my leave and return." They said, "Take your leave of him," and, when Qutaybah was at Āmul, [Nīzak] sought leave of him to return to Ṭukhāristān.

[1205]

---

512. On him, see Shaban, *The 'Abbāsid Revolution*, pp. 65.
513. Cf. Gibb, *Arab Conquests*, pp. 36ff.
514. Reading the variant *minhum* in preference to *muttaham*.

[Qutaybah] gave him leave, and, when he left his camp heading for Balkh, [Nīzak] said to his companions, "Hasten," and they went at great speed until they reached al-Nawbahār. He stopped to pray in it and regarded it as a blessing, and said to his companions, "I do not doubt that Qutaybah regretted it when we left his camp with his permission to me and [that] his messenger will at any moment reach al-Mughīrah b. ʿAbdallāh, ordering him to detain me. So set up a lookout, and if you see [that] the messenger has passed through the city and has gone out of the gate, he will not reach al-Barūqān before we reach Ṭukhāristān. Al-Mughīrah will send a man, but he will not catch up with us before we enter the Khulm pass." They did so.

[ʿAlī b. Muḥammad] said: A messenger set off from Qutaybah to al-Mughīrah with orders to him to detain Nīzak. When the messenger passed [on his way] to al-Mughīrah, who was at al-Barūqān[515]—the city of Balkh being in ruins at that time—Nīzak and his companions rode off and went on their way. The messenger reached al-Mughīrah, and [al-Mughīrah] himself went in search of [Nīzak]. [But] he found that he had entered the Khulm pass, and departed.

Nīzak [now] openly disavowed [Qutaybah]. He wrote to the Iṣbahbadh of Balkh, to Bādhām, the king of Marw Rūdh, to Suhrak,[516] the king of al-Ṭālaqān, to Tūsik,[517] the king of al-Fāryāb, and to al-Jūzjānī, the king of al-Jūzjān, calling upon them to disavow Qutaybah. They responded positively to him, and he appointed the spring as the time for them to join forces and campaign against Qutaybah. He also wrote to the Kābul Shāh, seeking his help, sent to him his baggage and money, and asked him to give him permission—if he was driven to it—to go to him and receive a safe-conduct in his country; [the Kābul Shāh] agreed to that and held his baggage.

[ʿAlī b. Muḥammad] said: Jabghūyah, the king of Ṭukhāristān,

[1206]

---

515. Following the destruction of Balkh, "the Arabs built a new town in the locality of Barūqān, two farsakhs from Balkh" (Barthold, *Turkestan*,[3] p. 77).

516. The *Addenda et Emendanda* point to the form S.hr.b (sc. Suhrab) below (pp. 1566, 1569 of the Arabic text), but Justi is ready to settle for Suhrak (*Iranisches Namenbuch*, p. 292, sub Εατράκης).

517. Following the *Addenda at Emendanda* and G. Schlegel, *La stèle funéraire du Teghin Giogh*, p. 23.

whose name was al-Shadh,[518] was weak. Nīzak took him and put him in a gold fetter, for fear that he might stir up discord against him, Jabghūyah being the king of Ṭukhāristān, and Nīzak [one] of his slaves. When he was sure [that Jabghūyah could not cause him trouble], he set watchmen over him and expelled Qutaybah's governor, Muḥammad b. Sulaym al-Nāṣiḥ, from Jabghūyah's territories. [News of] his disavowal reached Qutaybah [just] before the winter, [at a time when] the troops had gone their separate ways; only the people of Marw remained with Qutaybah. He sent his brother ʿAbd al-Raḥmān to [the district of] Balkh, to al-Barūqān, with [an army of] twelve thousand [men], saying to him, "Stay there and do not initiate anything. When the winter is over, gather the army and go to Tukhāristān (sic); know that I [shall be] near you." ʿAbd al-Raḥmān went off and stopped at al-Barūqān, and Qutaybah took his time until, late in the winter, he wrote to Abrashahr,[519] Bīward,[520] Sarakhs, and the people of Herat [instructing them] to come to him. They did so, this being at an earlier time than usual.

[1207]

In this year Qutaybah fell upon the people of al-Ṭālaqān, according to one of the collectors of historical reports [ahl al-akhbār], and killed them on a massive scale; he crucified them in two straight parallel rows four parasangs long.[521]

[Qutaybah's Retribution against the People of al-Ṭālaqān]

The reason for that, according to what has been mentioned, was that, when Nīzak Ṭarkhān acted treacherously, disavowed Qutaybah, and resolved to make war on him, the king of al-Ṭālaqān concurred with [Nīzak] in making war on [Qutaybah],

---

518. As Gibb points out (*Arab Conquests*, p. 9), this identification of the Shadh with the Jabghūyah "is obviously impossible." Gibb takes the Shadh in question here (see below, pp. 1224–25 of the Arabic text) to be "the chief prince in Lower Ṭukhāristān," a description which "best suits the king of Chaghāniān." For more recent discussion of these titles, see Bosworth and Clauson, "Al-Xwārazmī on the Peoples of Central Asia," pp. 6, 9; Bombaci, "On the Ancient Turkish Title 'Šaδ'"; Bosworth, "The Rulers of Chaghāniyān in Early Islamic Times," p. 1.

519. I.e., Nishapur (see Le Strange, *Lands of the Eastern Caliphate*, p. 383).

520. I.e., Abīward (ibid., p. 394).

521. Concerning al-Ṭālaqān at this point, Gibb (*Arab Conquests*, p. 37) remarks that "the traditions are hopelessly confused."

and he appointed a time for going to him along with those of the [other] kings who had agreed to rise with him to make war on Qutaybah. When, however, Nīzak fled from Qutaybah and entered the Khulm pass, which leads to Ṭukhāristān, he knew that he was impotent against Qutaybah, and fled. Qutaybah went to al-Ṭālaqān, fell upon its people, and did what I have mentioned earlier.

The person who said [all] this has been contradicted in what he has said; I shall come back to this in [dealing with] the events of the year 91.

[1208]   The leader of the pilgrimage in this year was ʿUmar b. ʿAbd al-ʿAzīz: Thus it was related to me by Aḥmad b. Thābit on the authority of him who mentioned it on the authority of Isḥāq b. ʿĪsā on the authority of Abū Maʿshar; and so too said Muḥammad b. ʿUmar. ʿUmar b. ʿAbd al-ʿAzīz was in this year al-Walīd b. ʿAbd al-Malik's governor of Mecca, Medina, and al-Ṭāʾif. Over Iraq and the East was al-Ḥajjāj b. Yūsuf; al-Ḥajjāj's governor of al-Baṣrah was al-Jarrāḥ b. ʿAbdallāh, and in charge of its judiciary was ʿAbd al-Raḥmān b. Udhaynah; over al-Kūfah was Ziyād b. Jarīr b. ʿAbdallāh, and in charge of its judiciary was Abū Bakr b. Abī Mūsā. Over Khurasan was Qutaybah b. Muslim, and over Egypt was Qurrah b. Sharīk.

In this year Yazīd b. al-Muhallab and his brothers who were in prison with him fled with others and joined Sulaymān b. ʿAbd al-Malik, seeking protection through him from al-Ḥajjāj b. Yūsuf and al-Walīd b. ʿAbd al-Malik.[522]

The Reason for [the Muhallabids'] Escape from al-Ḥajjāj's Prison and Their Going to Sulaymān

According to Hishām [b. Muḥammad]—Abū Mikhnaf—Abū al-Mukhāriq al-Rāsibī: Al-Ḥajjāj went out to Rustāqubādh to send [1209]   out troops, for the Kurds had gained control over the whole of the territory of Fārs. He took with him Yazīd and his brothers al-Mufaḍḍal and ʿAbd al-Malik, brought them to Rustāqubādh, placed them in his camp, put around them something like a trench, housed them in a tent near his own quarters, placed them

---

522. Similar accounts of this appear in Ibn Khallikān, *Wafayāt al-aʿyān*, vol. VI, pp. 291ff.; Ibn Aʿtham, *Futūḥ*, vol. VII, pp. 209ff; Ibn Kathīr, *Bidāyah*, vol. IX, pp. 78–79.

under Syrian guard, fined them six million [dirhams], and began to torture them. Yazīd showed great fortitude, which vexed al-Ḥajjāj. Then [al-Ḥajjāj] was told that [Yazīd] had been shot by an arrow, the head of which had lodged in his leg; if anything touched it he would scream, and if it was moved, however slightly, you would hear him exclaim. He ordered that [Yazīd] be tortured and that his leg be subjected to severe pressure;[523] when that was done to him, he screamed. His sister, Hind bt. al-Muhallab, was married to al-Ḥajjāj; when she heard Yazīd's screaming, she screamed and wailed, and al-Ḥajjāj divorced her. Then he desisted from them and started to try to get them to pay up. They started to pay, while at the same time working at escaping from their situation.

They sent [word] to Marwān b. al-Muhallab, who was at al-Baṣrah, instructing him to prepare horses for them by reducing them to scanty food; he was to make people think that he wanted to sell them, to exhibit them for sale, and overprice them so that they would not be bought, "so that they will be ready for us if we are able to escape from what is here." Marwān did that. Ḥabīb was in al-Baṣrah [too], also being tortured.

Yazīd ordered that much food be made for the guards, and they ate. He ordered drink, and they were provided with it and diverted one another's attention with it. Yazīd [then] put on the clothes of his cook, put a white beard over his [own] beard, and went out. One of the guards said, "[It is] as if this is the gait of Yazīd," and he went until he stood in front of him [to see] his face in the night, saw the whiteness of the beard, and departed from him; he said, "This is an old man." Al-Mufaḍḍal went out in [Yazīd's] footsteps undetected, and they reached their boats, which had been pre- [1210] pared for them in the Baṭā'iḥ.[524] They were eighteen parasangs from al-Baṣrah. When they got to the boats, 'Abd al-Malik was slow in reaching them and was diverted from them. Yazīd said to al-Mufaḍḍal, who had the same mother as 'Abd al-Malik, she being Bahlah, an Indian woman, "No, by God. I shall not leave until he comes, even if it were to mean going back to the prison." Yazīd stayed put until he came to them, and at that they embarked on the boats and traveled that night until morning. In the morning, the guards knew that they had gone, and that was re-

---

523. *Yudhaq*: See the *Glossarium*.
524. The swamps of southern Iraq between the Tigris and the Euphrates (see *EI²*, s.v. al-Baṭīḥa).

ferred to al-Ḥajjāj. Al-Farazdaq said concerning their exodus (ṭawīl):[525]

I have not seen [anything] like the group who followed
     one another
        on the palm trunk,[526] while the guards were not
        sleeping.
They went off convinced that their allotted spans
     [were headed] for [immediate] destiny and death.
Not one of them did not quieten his fear
     with a sharp, cutting, burnished sword,[527]
And when they met, they did not meet a faint-hearted
     old man, nor a soft-boned youth;
[1211] They were like their father when they grew up,
        fifty [of them,], one after the other, [each
        of them replete with] courage and perfection.

Al-Ḥajjāj became fearful at [the escape] and imagined that they had gone in the direction of Khurasan. He sent the official courier to Qutaybah b. Muslim, warning him of their arrival and instructing him to be ready for them. He sent [word] to the amīrs of the frontier ways of access and the districts to be on the look out for them and to be ready for them, and he wrote to al-Walīd b. ʿAbd al-Malik informing him of their flight and [of the fact] that he did not think that they were heading [for anywhere] but Khurasan. Al-Ḥajjāj continued to suspect Yazīd for what he had done; he used to say, "I suspect that he is telling himself [to do] the like of what Ibn al-Ashʿath did."

When Yazid drew near to Mawqūʿ[528] in the Baṭāʾiḥ, he was met by the horses that had been prepared for him and his brothers. They went off on them, accompanied by a guide of theirs from Kalb called ʿAbd al-Jabbār b. Yazīd b. al-Rabʿah;[529] he took them by way of al-Samāwah.[530] Al-Ḥajjāj was brought [information]

---

525. *Dīwān*, vol. II, p. 265.

526. *ʿAlā ʾl-jidhʿi*, which must refer to the boats.

527. The *Dīwān* reads *bi-qalbin* in place of *bi-ʿaḍbin*.

528. Yāqūt (*Muʿjam*, vol. IV, p. 688) knew this as a watering place or well (*māʾ*) in the region of al-Baṣrah.

529. See Caskel, *Ǧamharat an-nasab*, register and chart 283, where the name of his grandfather is given as Rabīʿah.

530. The name of the desert (and of a watering place or well) between al-Kūfah and Syria (Yāqūt, *Muʿjam*, vol. III, p. 131).

two days later and was told, "The man has taken the Syria road, and these horses [have become] tired on the way; someone has come who has seen them going along in the desert." [Al-Ḥajjāj] sent [word] to al-Walīd, informing him of that.

Yazīd went on until he reached Palestine and stopped with Wuhayb b. ʿAbd al-Raḥmān al-Azdī, who was held in high estimation by Sulaymān; he lodged some of his baggage and family with Sufyān b. Sulaymān al-Azdī. Wuhayb b. ʿAbd al-Raḥmān went and entered into the presence of Sulaymān and said, "This [man] Yazīd b. al-Muhallab and his brothers are in my house. They have come to you as fugitives from al-Ḥajjāj, taking refuge with you." [Sulaymān] said, "Bring them to me, for they are safe. They will never be got at as long as I am alive." [Wuhayb] brought them and conducted them into his presence; they were in a secure position. Their guide, the Kalbī, said concerning their journey (ṭawīl): [1212]

Surely God has made all good friends
    a ransom for Ibn al-Muhallab, irrespective of what has
    happened!
What a fine young man [he is], O grouping of al-Azd!
Your riding camels
    drew near to al-Wahb,[531] to the east of a
    mountain pass,
They [then] turned to the right, [?alongside] the
    sand of ʿĀlij,[532]
    while on the right of the people were the
    heights of Ghurrab.[533]
If our riding camels do not reach Sulaymān in the
    morning after five [nights]
    from the people of al-Liwā,[534] they will
    return by night.[535]

---

531. Not known to Yāqūt.

532. Yāqūt (Muʿjam, vol. III, p. 591) knew ʿĀlij as "sands between Fayd and al-Qurayyāt . . . adjoining al-Thaʿlabiyyah on the Mecca road."

533. According to Yāqūt (Muʿjam, vol. III, p. 783), Ghurrab is "a mountain this side of Syria in the diyār of the Banū Kalb."

534. In addition to meaning "a place where the sand stops," al-Liwā is a place name signifying "one of the valleys of the Banū Sulaym" (Yāqūt, Muʿjam, vol. IV, p. 366).

535. The sense of this is not clear to me.

We flee like[536] the sun from what is behind us
　　and go, in the darkness of blackest night,
With people who were kings. I guided them
　　in the gloom in which no light of a star could be seen,
Nor a moon, save faintly, as if it were
　　a gilded bracelet, fashioned by a bracelet smith.

[1213] According to Hishām—al-Ḥasan b. Abān al-ʿUlaymī: While ʿAbd al-Jabbār b. Yazīd b. al-Rabʿah was journeying with them, Yazīd's turban fell off, and he missed it. He said, "O ʿAbd al-Jabbār, go back and seek it for us." [ʿAbd al-Jabbār] said "Someone like me should not be ordered [to do] this." [Yazīd] repeated [the order], and [ʿAbd al-Jabbār] refused. [Yazīd] caught him with [his] whip, and ʿAbd al-Jabbār proclaimed his genealogy to him; [Yazīd] felt ashamed, and that [is the context in which ʿAbd al-Jabbār] said:

Surely God has made all good friends
　　a ransom for Ibn al-Muhallab, irrespective of what has
　　happened!

Al-Ḥajjāj wrote, "The family of al-Muhallab have embezzled God's money and have fled from me and joined Sulaymān." The family of al-Muhallab reached Sulaymān after the order had been given for people to be gathered to be sent to Khurasan, [since the authorities were sure] that Yazīd had gone in the direction of Khurasan in order to rouse those who were there to rebellion. When it reached al-Walīd that he was with Sulaymān, that made some of what he felt easier for him, [but he remained] angry about the money which [Yazīd] had taken.

Sulaymān wrote to al-Walīd, "Yazīd b. al-Muhallab is with me, and I have given him a safe-conduct. He owes three million [dirhams], al-Ḥajjāj having fined them six million and they having paid three million; I shall pay the remaining three million." [Al-Walīd] wrote to him, "No, by God, I shall not give him a safe-conduct until you send him to me." [Sulaymān] wrote to him, "If I send him to you, I shall come with him [myself]. I beseech you by God not to disgrace me and not to violate my [protection]." [Al-Walīd] wrote to him, "If you come to me, I shall not give him

---

536. Reading, with Ms B, *nafirru furāra*, rather than *taqarru qarāra*.

a safe-conduct." Yazīd said [to Sulaymān], "Send me to him, by God. I do not want to occasion enmity and war between you and him, nor [do I want] the people to see a bad omen for the two of you in me. Send me to him, and send your son with me, and write to [al-Walīd] in the kindest terms you can manage"; [Sulaymān] accordingly sent his son Ayyūb with him.

Al-Walīd had ordered [Sulaymān] to send [Yazīd] to him in bonds, and he sent him to him saying to his son, "When you are about to enter [al-Walīd's] presence, you and Yazīd are to bind yourselves with a chain and go in to al-Walīd's presence together." [Ayyūb] did that with [Yazīd] when they got to al-Walīd, and they went into his presence [together]. When al-Walīd saw his nephew in a chain, he said, "By God, we have gone rather far with Sulaymān." Then the young man handed his father's letter over to his uncle and said, "O Commander of the Faithful, may I be your ransom, do not violate my father's protection, you being the most worthy of those who have defended it, and do not cut short the hope of one who has hoped for safety in taking refuge with us because of our [good] standing with you; do not abase one who has hoped for high rank in resorting to us because of our high rank with you."

[1214]

[Al-Walīd] read the letter: "To 'Abd Allāh al-Walīd, the Commander of the Faithful, from Sulaymān b. 'Abd al-Malik. To continue: I used to think that, even if an enemy who had thwarted you and striven against you sought my protection and I lodged him and gave him protection, you would neither abase my protégé nor violate my protection. As it is, I have only protected an obedient and compliant [man]—he and his father and his family have contributed much to Islam—and I have sent him to you. If you intend cutting off relations with me, violating my protection, and going to excess in doing me harm, you are [of course] able to do that if you want; but I would wish you to seek preservation by God from [any] intention of cutting off relations with me, violating my honor, and ignoring my solicitous regard [for you] and my connection [with you]. By God, O Commander of the Faithful, you know neither how much longer either of us has to live nor when death will part us. If the Commander of the Faithful, may God perpetuate his joy, is able [to bring it about] that the appointed time of death does not come to us but that he is [still] respect-

[1215] ing our blood tie, giving me my due, and refraining from harming me, let him do so. By God, O Commander of the Faithful, nothing on earth—after piety to God—pleases me more than pleasing you. Your pleasure is part of that through which I seek God's pleasure. If for once, O Commander of the Faithful, you desire my joy, my friendly connection, my honor, and the exaltation of my due, pass over Yazīd for me without punishing him; everything you seek of him will be my responsibility."

When [al-Walīd] had read the letter, he said, "We have been burdensome to Sulaymān; and he summoned his nephew and brought him near to him. [Then] Yazīd spoke. He praised God and extolled Him, blessed His Prophet, may God bless him, and then said, "O Commander of the Faithful, our benefit through you is the best. Whoever may forget that, we shall not forget it; and whoever may deny that, we shall not deny it. There has issued from our benefit as a family, in [our] obedience to you, [in our] thrusting at the eyes of your enemies in great battlefields east and west, that in which there is for us a mighty grace." [Al-Walīd] said to him, "Sit," and he sat, and [al-Walīd] gave him safe-conduct and desisted from him.

[Yazīd] returned to Sulaymān, and his brothers strove to acquire the money he owed. [Al-Walīd] wrote to al-Ḥajjāj, "I could not make any headway with Yazīd. His family is with Sulaymān. Desist from them, and stop writing to me about them." When al-Ḥajjāj saw that, he desisted from them. Abū ʿUyaynah b. al-Muhallab owed al-Ḥajjāj one hundred thousand [dirhams, which al-Ḥajjāj] left to him; and he desisted from Ḥabīb b. al-Muhallab.

[1216] Yazīd returned to Sulaymān b. ʿAbd al-Malik and stayed with him, teaching him how to dress well,[537] making delicious dishes for him, and giving him large presents. He was one of those held in [Sulaymān's] highest regard. No gift reached Yazīd b. al-Muhallab but that he sent it to Sulaymān; and no gift or benefit reached Sulaymān but that he sent half of it to Yazīd b. al-Muhallab. No slave girl pleased him but that he sent her to Yazīd, except for the slave girl Khaṭīʾah.[538]

That reached al-Walīd b. ʿAbd al-Malik, who summoned al-

---

537. If this is how we are to understand *yuʿallimuhu al-hayʾah*. Ibn al-Athīr omits it, while Ibn Kathīr (*Bidāyah*, vol. IX, p. 79) reads *ḥasan al-hayʾah*.

538. About whom no more information seems to be available.

Ḥārith b. Mālik b. Rabīʿah al-Ashʿarī and said [to him], "Go off to
Sulaymān and say to him, 'O you who are inimical to your family. It has reached the Commander of the Faithful that no gift or
benefit comes to you but that you send half of it to Yazīd, and that
one of your slave girls comes to you, and no sooner does her state
of purity come to an end than you send her to Yazīd.' Show him
the foulness of that and revile him for it. Do you think you can
convey what I have instructed you to do?" [Al-Ḥārith] said, "Obedience [consists of] obeying you. I am simply a messenger." [Al-
Walīd] said, "Go to him, say that to him, and stay with him. I
shall send him a present. Hand it over to him and take from him a
receipt for what you hand over to him."

[Al-Ḥārith] went until he reached [Sulaymān], who had a copy
of the Qurʾān in front of him and was reciting. He entered into his
presence and greeted him; [Sulaymān] did not return his greeting
until he had finished his recitation. Then [al-Ḥārith] raised his
head to him and said everything that al-Walīd had instructed him
to say. [Sulaymān's] face became distorted [with] anger. Then he
said, "By God, if I am able to get hold of you one of these days, I
shall cut part of you off!" [Al-Ḥārith] said to him, "Obedience was
incumbent upon me," and he went out of his presence.

When that [present] sent by al-Walīd to Sulaymān arrived, al-
Ḥārith b. Rabīʿah al-Ashʿarī entered into [Sulaymān's] presence
and said to him, "Give me the receipt for what I have handed over
to you." [Sulaymān] said, "What did you say to me?" He said, "I
shall never repeat it to you.539 Obedience was incumbent upon
me in respect of it." [Sulaymān] was quiet and knew that the man
had told him the truth. Then he went out and [those present]
went out with him, and he said, "Take half of these bundles and
baskets and send them to Yazīd."

[Hishām] continued: The man knew that [Sulaymān] would not
obey anyone in respect of Yazīd. Yazīd stayed with Sulaymān for
nine months; and al-Ḥajjāj died in the year 95, on Friday, 20
Shawwāl (July 8, 714).540

[1217]

---

539. Following Ibrāhīm's *ilayka abadᵃⁿ* in preference to the text's seemingly
unintelligible ʿāl.mā abadᵃⁿ.

540. The suspicion that something is wrong here is fortified by Ibn Kathīr's
version (*Bidāyah*, vol. IX, p. 79): "Yazīd b. al-Muhallab stayed with Sulaymān b.
ʿAbd al-Malik until al-Ḥajjāj died in the year 95."

⚜

The
Events of the Year

9I

⚜

In it, according to what Muḥammad b. ʿUmar and others have mentioned, ʿAbd al-ʿAzīz b. al-Walīd made the summer campaign. In command of the army was Maslamah b. ʿAbd al-Malik.

In it, too, Maslamah campaigned against the Turks until he reached al-Bāb[541] in the region of Ādharbayjān. Cities and fortresses were conquered at his hands.

In it, Mūsā b. Nuṣayr campaigned against al-Andalus. Cities and fortresses were conquered at his hands.[542]

[Qutaybah's Capture and Killing of Nīzak]

[1218] In this year Qutaybah b. Muslim killed Nīzak Ṭarkhān.[543]

The narrative returns to that of ʿAlī b. Muḥammad and the story of Nīzak and Qutaybah's victory over him until he killed him. When there reached Qutaybah those of the people of Abrashahr, Bīward, Sarakhs, and Herat to whom he had written instructing them to join him, he went with [his entire force] to

541. See above, n. 499.
542. See *EI*², s.v. al-Andalus.
543. Cf. Gibb, *Arab Conquests*, pp. 36ff.

Marw Rūdh, having deputed [at Marw] over military affairs (*ḥarb*)
Ḥammād b. Muslim and over taxation (*kharāj*) ʿAbdallāh b. al-
Ahtam. [When news of] the advance of [Qutaybah] into his territory reached the marzbān of Marw Rūdh, he fled to the land of
the Furs.[544] Qutaybah arrived in Marw Rūdh, took two sons of
his, killed them, and crucified them. Then he went to al-Ṭālaqān,
the lord of which stayed put, not fighting him and desisting from
him. [In al-Ṭālaqān] were brigands, whom Qutaybah killed and
crucified. He appointed over al-Ṭālaqān ʿAmr b. Muslim[545] and
went on to al-Fāryāb. The king of al-Fāryāb went out to him,
submissively, and professing his obedience, and [Qutaybah] was
satisfied with that and did not kill anyone there; he appointed
over it a man from Bāhilah.

News of them reached the lord of al-Jūzjān, and he left his
territory and went out into the mountains in flight. Qutaybah
went to al-Jūzjān, and its people met him, compliant and obedient, and he accepted [that] from them and did not kill anyone
there; he appointed over it ʿĀmir b. Mālik al-Ḥimmānī. Then he
reached Balkh; the Iṣbahbadh and the people of Balkh met him,
and he entered it. He stayed in it only one day and then went on,
following ʿAbd al-Raḥmān [b. Muslim], until he reached the
Khulm pass. Nīzak had gone off and camped at Baghlān,[546] leaving fighting men at the mouth and the defiles of the pass in order
to defend it, and placing fighting men in a strong fortress behind
the pass. Qutaybah stayed for [some] days fighting them at the
defile of the pass without being able to make any progress against
them. He was unable to enter it, it being a defile through which
the valley passed, and he did not know of any way by which he
could get to Nīzak other than the pass or a desert which would
not support the troops. He remained, turning his face to right and
left in perplexity, looking for stratagems.

[ʿAlī b. Muḥammad] continued: He was in this [dilemma] when
there came to him the Ruʾb Khān, the king of al-Ruʾb[547] and

[1219]

---

544. Which does not make sense in this context; in the *Addenda et Emendan-
da*, Marquart proposes that we should understand this as *bilād al-Gharsh*, i.e.,
Gharshistān, a territory in the mountains to the east of Herat (see *EI²*, s.v.
Ghardjistān).

545. This appointment (together with that of ʿĀmir b. Mālik—see the next
paragraph) is also mentioned in the account of Ibn Aʿtham (*Futūḥ*, vol. VII, p. 232).

546. Two days' journey from Siminjān (Barthold, *Turkestan³*, p. 67).

547. A town near Siminjān (Le Strange, *Lands of the Eastern Caliphate*, p. 427).

Siminjān,[548] seeking a safe-conduct from him on the basis that he would show him a way of getting into the fortress that was behind this pass. Qutaybah gave him a safe-conduct, gave him what he asked for, and sent with him at night men with whom he got to the fortress which was behind the Khulm pass. They fell upon [the men of the fortress] at night, they feeling perfectly secure [from attack], and killed them; those who survived and those who were in the pass fled, and Qutaybah and [his army] entered the pass and reached the fortress. Then he went on to Siminjān, Nīzak being at Baghlān, at a spring called Fanj Jāh;[549] between Siminjān and Baghlān is a desert that is not particularly difficult.

[ʿAlī b. Muḥammad] continued: Qutaybah stayed in Siminjān for [some] days and then went off to Nīzak; he sent his brother ʿAbd al-Raḥmān on ahead, and he reached Nīzak. [At this,] Nīzak set off from his house, crossed the Farghānah valley,[550] sent his baggage and wealth to the Kābul Shāh, and went on until he stopped at al-Kurz,[551] being followed [all the while] by ʿAbd al-Raḥmān b. Muslim. ʿAbd al-Raḥmān stopped and took control of the defiles of al-Kurz, and Qutaybah stopped at Iskīmisht,[552] two parasangs away. Nīzak took refuge in al-Kurz, having no way out save in one direction, which was difficult, since it could not be negotiated by riding animals.

[1220]

Qutaybah besieged Nīzak for two months, until Nīzak's stock of grain became scanty and they were afflicted by smallpox, which Jabghūyah caught. Qutaybah feared the winter, and he summoned Sulaym al-Nāṣiḥ[553] and said, "Go off to Nīzak and use artifice to get him to come to me without a safe-conduct. If he gives you trouble and refuses, give him a safe-conduct. Know that, if I see you and you don't have him with you, I shall crucify you. So work for your own sake." [Sulaym] said, "Write for me to

---

548. Two days' journey from Khulm (Barthold, *Turkestan*[3], p. 67).

549. Rendered *Panǧ-čāh*, "Schneebrunnen" (rather than "Five Wells"), by Marquart (*Ērānšahr*, p. 219).

550. As Marquart points out (*Ērānšahr*, p. 220), this Farghānah must have been to the south of Baghlān.

551. Not even Marquart knows any more about this place.

552. Rendered thus by Marquart (*Ērānšahr*, pp. 219–20); if Wellhausen's identification (*Kingdom*, p. 435, n. 1) is correct, it was not far southeast of Baghlān.

553. In a roughly similar account, Ibn Aʿtham (*Futūḥ*, vol. VII, p. 226) identifies Sulaym al-Nāṣiḥ as Sulaym b. ʿAbdallāh.

'Abd al-Raḥmān, [telling him] not to disobey me." [Qutaybah] said, "Yes," and he wrote for him to 'Abd al-Raḥmān. [Sulaym] then went to ['Abd al-Raḥmān] and said to him, "Send men to be [stationed] at the mouth of the pass and, when Nīzak and I come out, let them slip round behind us, interposing themselves between us and the pass."

['Alī b. Muḥammad] continued: 'Abd al-Raḥmān sent cavalry, and they were [stationed] where Sulaym instructed them [to be]. Sulaym [now] went off, carrying with him foodstuffs to last for days and loads of khabīṣ,[554] until he reached Nīzak. Nīzak said to him, "You have abandoned me, O Sulaym." Sulaym said, "I haven't abandoned you, but you disobeyed me and did harm to yourself. You disavowed [Qutaybah] and acted perfidiously." [Nīzak] said, "What is the right thing to do?" [Sulaym] said, "The right thing to do now is to go to him. You have angered him with your contention, and he is not going to leave this place of his. He is resolved to winter in situ, whether he perishes or survives." [Nīzak] said, "Am I to go to him without a safe-conduct?" [Sulaym] said, "I don't think that he will give you one, on account of what [he holds] against you in his heart, for you have filled him with wrath. I think that you should place your hand in his before he is aware of you, and I hope that, if you do that, he will be ashamed and will forgive you." [Nīzak] said, "You think that?" He said, "Yes." [Nīzak] said, "I can't bring myself to accept that. If Qutaybah sees me, he will kill me." Sulaym said to him, "I have only come to advise you to do this. If you do it, I hope that you will be safe and that your position with him will revert to what it was. If you refuse, I shall be off." [Nīzak] said, "Then let us give you lunch." [Sulaym] said, "I suspect that you (pl.) are too busy to prepare food; we have plenty of food with us."

['Alī b. Muḥammad] continued: Sulaym called for lunch [to be served], and [his servants] brought abundant food, the like of which [Nīzak's men] had been unfamiliar with since they had been besieged. The Turks devoured it, and that grieved Nīzak. Sulaym said, "O Abū al-Hayyāj, I am one of your [most] sincere advisers. I see that your companions have been worn out. If the siege goes on for a long time and you stay as you are, I can't be

[1221]

---

554. Lane (Lexicon, p. 697c) defines this as "a kind of food, sweet, well known, made of dates and clarified butter, mixed together."

sure that they won't make use of you in order to gain safe-conduct. Set off and go to Qutaybah." [Nīzak] said, "I have never felt safe with him, and I shall not go to him without a safe-conduct. My feeling about him is that he is going to kill me even if he does give me a safe-conduct, but the safe-conduct gives me more excuse from blame and more hope." [Sulaym] said, "He has given you a safe-conduct: do you have any doubts about me?" Nīzak said, "No." [Sulaym] said, "So set off with me." His companions said to him, "Accept what Sulaym has said; he would not have said but what is true." So he called for his riding animals and went with Sulaym.

When he reached the steps by which he might descend to the plain, he said, "O Sulaym, whoever may not know when he will die, I [for one] know when I shall die. I shall die when I see Qutaybah." [Sulaym] said, "By no means. Will he kill when you have a safe-conduct?" Then [Nīzak] rode, accompanied by Jabghūyah, who had recovered from smallpox, and Ṣūl and ʿUthmān, the sons of Nīzak's brother, and Ṣūl Ṭarkhān, [who was] Jabghūyah's deputy, and Kh.n.s.[555] Ṭarkhān, [who] was the police chief.

[ʿAlī b. Muḥammad] said: When he emerged from the pass, the cavalry left by Sulaym at the mouth of the pass slipped around and interposed themselves between the Turks and the exit. Nīzak said to Sulaym, "This is the first bad [sign]." [Sulaym] said, "Don't think that.[556] The [fact that] these people are staying behind[557] you is better for you." Sulaym went on, together with Nīzak and those who had had gone out with him, until they entered into the presence of ʿAbd al-Raḥmān b. Muslim, who sent a messenger to Qutaybah informing him [of this]. Qutaybah sent ʿAmr b. Abī Mih-zam to ʿAbd al-Raḥmān [with the message], "Bring them to me," and ʿAbd al-Raḥmān brought them to him. Qutaybah imprisoned the companions of Nīzak and handed Nīzak [himself] over to Ibn Bassām al-Laythī. He wrote to al-

[1222]

---

555. Or "H.b.s.," as in Ms P and Ibn al-Athīr.

556. So understanding *lā tafʿal* in the text; Ibn Aʿtham (*Futūḥ*, vol. VII, p. 227) reads *lā ʿalayka*, "don't worry," at this point.

557. Reading *takhallufu* in place of *tukhallifu* (*pace* the *Addenda et Emendanda*).

Ḥajjāj asking his permission to kill Nīzak.

Ibn Bassām placed Nīzak in his yurt, dug a trench around the yurt, and set guards over him. Qutaybah sent off Muʿāwiyah b. ʿĀmir b. ʿAlqamah al-ʿUlaymī, who removed what goods and people there were in al-Kurz and brought them to Qutaybah. [Qutaybah] imprisoned [these people], pending [the arrival of] al-Ḥajjāj's letter concerning what he had written to him about. Al-Ḥajjāj's letter instructing him to kill Nīzak reached him after forty days.

[ʿAlī b. Muḥammad] said: [Qutaybah] called for [Nīzak] and said, "Do you have any commitment from me or from ʿAbd al-Raḥmān or from Sulaym?" He said, "I have one from Sulaym." [Qutaybah] said, "You are lying," and he stood up and went into [an inner chamber]. He returned Nīzak to his prison and remained [indoors] for three days without appearing to the people.

According to [ʿAlī b. Muḥammad]—Al-Muhallab b. Iyās al-ʿAdawī: The people talked about the matter of Nīzak. Some of them said, "It is not lawful for [Qutaybah] to kill him," while others said, "It is not lawful for him to let him be." Much was said about this.

[ʿAlī b. Muḥammad] continued: On the fourth day Qutaybah came out, sat, and gave permission to the people [to come into his presence]. He said, "What do you think about killing Nīzak?" They held differing opinions: There were those who said, "Kill him," those who said, "You have given him a commitment; do not kill him," and those who said, "We are not sure [that he will not do harm] to the Muslims," Ḍirār b. Ḥusayn entered, and [Qutaybah] said to him, "What do you say, O Ḍirār?" He said, "I say that I heard you say that you had given God a covenant that if He delivered [Nīzak] into your hands, you would kill him, and that if you did not do so, [you wished that] God would never help you." Qutaybah sat silently and with downcast eyes for a long time and then said, "By God, if there were to remain of my allotted span no more than three words, I would say, 'Kill him, kill him, kill him.'" He sent for Nīzak and ordered that he and his companions be killed; he was killed along with seven hundred [others].

As for the Bāhilīs, they say that neither [Qutaybah] nor Sulaym gave him a safe-conduct. When [Qutaybah] intended to kill him,

[1223]

he called for him and for a Ḥanafī sword.[558] He unsheathed it, lengthened[559] his sleeves, and executed him with his [own] hand. He ordered ʿAbd al-Raḥmān to behead Ṣūl, and he ordered Ṣāliḥ to kill ʿUthmān, called Shaqrān, the son of Nīzak's brother. He said to Bakr b. Ḥabīb al-Sahmī, from Bāhilah, "Have you [enough] strength [to deal with the rest]?" He said, "Yes, more than enough";[560] there was roughness in Bakr. [Qutaybah] said [to him], "Take these dihqāns."

[ʿAlī b. Muḥammad] continued: When he was brought a man, he would behead him and say, "Begin and keep at it."[561] Those who were killed on that day [numbered] twelve thousand, according to what the Bāhilīs say. [Qutaybah] crucified Nīzak and the two sons of his brother at the source of a spring called Wakhsh Khāshān[562] in Iskīmisht. Al-Mughīrah b. Ḥabnāʾ said, mentioning that in a long piece (ṭawīl):[563]

By my life, what a good campaign by the army that was;
    it put an end to Nīzak and became lofty [in merit].

[1224]   According to ʿAlī—Muṣʿab b. Ḥayyān—his father: Qutaybah sent the head of Nīzak with Miḥfan b. Jazʾ al-Kilābī and Sawwār b. Zahdam al-Jarmī. Al-Ḥajjāj said, "Qutaybah should have sent Nīzak's head with one of the sons of Muslim."[564] Sawwār said (wāfir):

I say to Miḥfan, when an auspicious [bird]
    has flown [from on my left]
    and another [bird], an inauspicious one,
    from my right,
And disasters have begun to
    rise up all around him, and stop short of me,

---

558. According to Lane (*Lexicon*, p. 658), Ḥanafī swords were "*certain swords, so called in relation to El-Aḥnaf Ibn-Ḳeys; because he was the first who ordered to make them.*"

559. Sic: unrolled? One might rather have expected him to roll his sleeves up.

560. Following the preference of the *Glossarium* and of the *Addenda et Emendanda* for *wa-azīdu* (rather than *wa-urīdu*).

561. *Awridū wa-aṣdirū*: cf. al-Zamakhsharī, *Asās*, s.v. ṣ.d.r.

562. Not even Marquart has anything to say about this place.

563. On the poet, see Sezgin, *GAS*, vol. II, pp. 374–75. The following verse is given (in mangled form) by Ibn Aʿtham (*Futūḥ*, vol. VII, p. 229); Ibn al-Athīr ascribes it to Nahār b. Tawsiʿah.

564. I.e., one of his brothers.

"I beseech you, does it please you that my saddle and yours are
    on Bādhibīn[565] mules?"

Miḥfan said, "Yes, [both here] and in China."

'Alī said: According to (i) Ḥamzah b. Ibrāhīm, (ii) 'Alī b. Mujāhid—Ḥanbal b. Abī Ḥuraydah—the marzbān of Qūhistān, and
(iii) [an authority/authorities] other than those two: Qutaybah
called for Nīzak one day, while he was imprisoned, and said,
"What is your opinion about al-Sabal and al-Shadh? Do you think
that they will come if I send to them [to come]?" [Nīzak] said,
"No."

['Alī] continued: Qutaybah sent to them, and they came to him.
He summoned Nīzak and Jabghūyah, and they entered, and there
were al-Sabal and al-Shadh sitting in front of him. [Nīzak and
Jabghūyah] sat down opposite them, and al-Shadh said to
Qutaybah, "Jabghūyah, even though he is an enemy of mine, is
older that I; and he is the king, while I am as his slave. Give me
permission to draw near to him." [Qutaybah] gave him permission, and he drew near to him, kissed his hand, and prostrated
himself before him.

['Alī] continued: Then al-Sabal[566] asked [Qutaybah's] permission [in respect of Jabghūyah]; [Qutaybah gave him permission,
and he drew near to him and kissed his hand. Nīzak said to
Qutaybah, "Give me permission to draw near to al-Shadh, for I
am his slave." He gave him permission, and he drew near to him   [1225]
and kissed his hand. Then Qutaybah gave leave to al-Sabal and al-
Shadh, and they departed to their lands; he joined to al-Shadh['s
party] al-Ḥajjāj al-Qaynī, who was a leading Khurasani.

Qutaybah killed Nīzak, and al-Zubayr, the mawlā of 'Ābis[567]
al-Bāhilī, took a boot of Nīzak's in which there was a jewel.
Owing to that jewel, which he had acquired in [Nīzak's] boot, he
became the richest and most landed person in his territory.
Qutaybah allowed him it, and he remained rich until he died at
Kābul in the governorship of Abū Dāwūd.[568]

---

565. A place in Iraq to the east of Wāsiṭ (see Cornu).

566. Following Ms B. (*Thumma ista'dhanahu al-sabal*) in preference to the
version that inserts *fī* before *al-sabal*; the latter version would involve al-Shadh's
paying homage to al-Sabal, which seems less likely.

567. Ibn al-Athīr reads "'Abbās."

568. Abū Dāwūd Khālid b. Ibrāhīm al-Dhuhlī, who was governor of Khurasan
from 137/754–55 to 140/757–58 (see Omar, *The 'Abbāsid Caliphate, 132/750–
170/786*, pp. 203–4).

[ʿAlī] continued: Qutaybah set Jabghūyah free, gave generously to him, and sent him to al-Walīd; he stayed in Syria until al-Walīd died. Qutaybah returned to Marw, and appointed his brother ʿAbd al-Raḥman over Balkh. The people used to say that Qutaybah behaved perfidiously toward Nīzak. Thābit Quṭnah[569] said (ṭawīl):

Do not consider perfidy [to be the equal of] resolution;
    with it feet may ascend one day and then slip.

[ʿAlī] said: Al-Ḥajjāj used to say, "I sent Qutaybah as an inexperienced young man: Whenever I gave him an extra dhirāʿ, he gave me an extra bāʿ."[570]

ʿAlī said: According to (i) Ḥamzah b. Ibrāhīm—Khurasani shaykhs, (ii) ʿAlī b. Mujāhid—Ḥanbal b. Abī Ḥuraydah—the marzbān of Qūhistān, and (iii) [an authority/authorities] other than those two: When Qutaybah b. Muslim had returned to Marw and killed Nīzak, he sought the king of al-Jūzjān, who had fled from his country. [The king] sent [word to Qutaybah], requesting a safe-conduct, and [Qutaybah] gave him one on condition that he come to him and make peace with him. [The king] requested hostages, to be held by him, while he [in turn] would give hostages. Qutaybah gave [him] Ḥabīb b. ʿAbdallāh b. ʿAmr b. Ḥuṣayn al-Bāhilī, and the king of al-Jūzjān gave [him] hostages from his family. The king of al-Jūzjān left Ḥabīb in al-Jūzjān, in one of his fortresses, and came to Qutaybah and made peace with him. Then he returned and died in al-Ṭālaqān. The people of al-Jūzjān said, "They have poisoned him," and they killed Ḥabīb; [at this,] Qutaybah killed the hostages who were with him. Nahār b. Tawsiʿah said to Qutaybah (wāfir):[571]

[1226]

May God show you a judgment concerning the Turks
    like [His] judgment concerning Qurayẓah and al-Naḍīr![572]
A decree from Qutaybah, not tyrannical,
    through which thirsting bosoms are cured.

---

569. Thābit (b. ʿAbd al-Raḥmān) b. Kaʿb al-ʿAtakī (see Sezgin, GAS, vol. II, pp. 376–77).

570. I.e., he repaid him amply or fourfold. Dhirāʿ signifies "forearm, cubit," and the dhirāʿ sharʿiyyah is the canonical ell of 49.875 cm; bāʿ signifies the "span of two outstretched arms" and is the equivalent of four canonical ells.

571. The first two of the following verses are given also by Ibn Aʿtham (Futūḥ, vol. VII, p. 233).

572. Two of the Jewish groupings at Yathrib against whom the Prophet took harsh measures (EI², s.v. Ḳurayẓa).

If Nīzak sees disgrace and abasement,
    then how many amīrs have been rendered stupid
    in the war?

    Al-Mughīrah b. Ḥabnā' said, eulogizing Qutaybah and men-
tioning the killing of Nīzak, Ṣūl, and Nīzak's nephew [called]
'Uthmān or Shaqrān (kāmil):[573]

For whom have the abodes effaced at the foot of
    a piece [of land]
    [everything] except for what remains of dry
    herbage and panic grass?
The winds have violently blown about the dust and
    rubbish there and have obliterated them,
    sweeping right across their open spaces.
An abode of a slave girl, whose saliva is
    as if it were musk, the mixture of which is
    mingled with wine.
Inform Abū Ḥafṣ Qutaybah of my eulogy,
    and recite to him my greeting and salutation.
O sword, convey it, for its praise is
    good, and you are witness to my deed.
He is elevated, and, when he is elevated, men are humbled
    to Qutaybah, the protector of the preserve of Islam.
The finest one, the one who is chosen for a matter
    of moment,
    the experienced one, through whom the numerous
    enemy is taken.
He goes forth when the coward fears and the war has
    become hot, its fire kindled with blazing
    kindling grass.
The spear, with the standard before it, is given to drink
    blood, under flashing [weapons] and [gushing]
    throats;
Heads are cut off by swords as if they were   [1227]
    broken ostrich eggs, when you see them in
    the hole.
You see slender steeds readied

---

573. The first of the following verses appears also (in mangled form) in Ibn
A'tham (Futūḥ, vol. VII, p. 224).

in his courtyard for whatever may befall;
With them he brought Nīzak down from a high place
    and al-Kurz, where [Nīzak] was doing what he
    wanted.
You gave to his brother, Shaqrān, to drink from
    his cup,
    and you gave their two cups to Bādhām to
    drink from.
You left Ṣūl, when he attacked, knocked down,
    with the horses treading on him with the
    backs and edges of their hooves.

In this year—I mean the year 91—Qutaybah made his second campaign in Shūmān, Kish, and Nasaf, and he made peace with Ṭarkhān.[574]

[Qutaybah's Campaign in Transoxania]

ʿAlī said: According to (i) Bishr b. ʿĪsā—Abū Ṣafwān, (ii) Abū al-Sarī and Jabalah b. Farrūkh—Sulaymān b. Mujālid, (iii) al-Ḥasan b. Rushayd—Ṭufayl b. Mirdās al-ʿAmmī, (iv) Abū al-Sarī al-Marwazī—his paternal uncle, (v) Bishr b. ʿĪsā and ʿAlī b. Mujāhid—Ḥanbal b. Abī Ḥuraydah—the marzbān of Qūhistān, (vi) ʿAyyāsh b. ʿAbdallāh al-Ghanawī—Khurasani shaykhs, and (vii) my foster father—"each has mentioned something, and I have put it [all] together and have inserted some parts into other parts": Qaybishtasbān[575]—one of them said Ghushtāsbān[576]—the king of Shūmān, threw out Qutaybah's governor and withheld the tribute on the basis of which he had made peace with Qutaybah. [1228] Qutaybah sent to him ʿAyyāsh al-Ghanawī, accompanied by one of the Khurasani ascetics, to induce the king of Shūmān to pay the tribute on the basis of which he had made peace with Qutaybah. They reached the country, and [the people] came out to them and shot at them. [The ascetic] turned back, while ʿAyyāsh al-Ghanawī stayed [where he was]. He said, "Is there no

---

574. Cf. Gibb, *Arab Conquests*, pp. 38ff.

575. Following the proposal of Marquart in the *Addenda et Emendanda* (see also *Ērānšahr*, p. 226 [= Kai-Bištaspān; cf. Justi, *Iranisches Namenbuch*, p. 372]).

576. Following the proposal of Marquart in the *Addenda et Emendanda* (see also *Ērānšahr*, loc. cit. = Ghuštāspān, and cf. above, p. 128 and n. 442).

Muslim here?" and a man came out of the city to him and said, "I am a Muslim; what do you want?" ['Ayyāsh] said, "[I want] you to help me make holy war (jihād) against them." [The man] said, "Yes." 'Ayyāsh said to him, "Be behind me to protect my back," and he stood behind him; the man's name was al-Muhallab. 'Ayyāsh fought them; he charged them, and they scattered away from him. [Then] al-Muhallab attacked 'Ayyāsh from behind and killed him. They found sixty wounds on him, and his death grieved them; they said, "We have killed a brave man."

[News of this] reached Qutaybah, who went to them in person, taking the Balkh road. When he reached [Balkh], he sent his brother 'Abd al-Raḥmān on ahead and placed 'Amr b. Muslim over Balkh. The king of Shūmān was a friend of Ṣāliḥ b. Muslim's, and Ṣāliḥ sent to him a man to order him to [render] obedience and guarantee him Qutaybah's pleasure if he reverted to the [terms of the] peace. [The king] refused and said to Ṣāliḥ's messenger, "With what will you make me frightened of Qutaybah? I, among the kings, have the strongest fortress. When I shoot at the top of it—I, the strongest of people with the bow and the strongest of them in shooting—my arrow does not [even] get halfway up my fortress. I do not fear Qutaybah."

Qutaybah went on from Balkh, crossed the river, and reached Shūmān, where the king had fortified himself. Qutaybah set up mangonels against it and pounded it. When [the king] feared that he would be vanquished and saw what had befallen him, he gathered all the money and jewels he had and dropped them in a spring in the middle of the fortress, the bottom of which was not known.

['Alī] said: Then [Qutaybah] conquered the fortress. [The king] went out to them, fought them, and was killed. Qutaybah took the fortress by force of arms, killed the fighting men, and took the offspring captive. Then he returned to Bāb al-Ḥadīd,[577] and passed from there to Kish and Nasaf. Al-Ḥajjāj had written to him, "Outwit Kish, and smash Nasaf; and beware of beating about the bush."[578] He conquered Kish and Nasaf, [but] F.ryāb[579] held out

[1229]

---

577. The famous Iron Gate, i.e., the Buzgala pass, on the road from al-Tirmidh to Kish and Nasaf (Barthold, *Turkestan*³, p. 186; Le Strange, *Lands of the Eastern Caliphate*, pp. 441–42).

578. Cf. above, p. 147.

579. Thus, too, in Ibn Kathīr (*Bidāyah*, vol. IX, p. 83), but this cannot be the

against him; so he burned it, and it was called "The Burnt."[580] From Kish and Nasaf, Qutaybah sent his brother ʿAbd al-Raḥmān b. Muslim to Ṭarkhūn in Soghd. [ʿAbd al-Raḥmān] went along until he stopped at a meadow near [Ṭarkhūn and his followers], that being at the time of the afternoon prayer. [His army] broke up into groups and drank until they became silly and made mischief. ʿAbd al-Raḥmān ordered Abū Mardiyyah, a mawlā of theirs (sc. the Bāhilīs), to prevent the people from drinking the [fermented] juice;[581] he beat them, broke their vessels, and poured out their wine, which flowed into the valley. It was called "Wine Meadow." One of their poets said (kāmil):

As for wine, I do not drink it;
   I fear the dog Abū Mardiyyah,
Going vigorously and violently with his ax handle,[582]
   jumping over walls, [looking] for drink.

ʿAbd al-Raḥmān took from Ṭarkhūn something on the basis of which Qutaybah had made peace with him, handed over to him [some] hostages that were with him, and departed [heading] for Qutaybah, who was at Bukhārā. They then returned to Marw.

The Soghdians said to Ṭarkhūn, "You have been satisfied with humiliation, and you have deemed the [paying of] tax agreeable; you are an old man, and we have no need of you."

[ʿAlī] said: They put Ghūrak[583] in charge and imprisoned Ṭarkhūn. Ṭarkhūn said, "There is nothing after being stripped of kingship other than being killed; I prefer that that should be by my [own] hand rather than that someone other than myself should take charge of it in respect of me"; and he leaned on his

[1230]   sword until it came out of his back.[584] [ʿAlī] said: They did this to

---

well-known Fāryāb, since the context is Transoxanian; see Barthold, *Turkestan*[3], p. 138 (also Wellhausen, *Kingdom*, pp. 435 [n. 3], 466).

580. As Barthold (*Turkestan*[3], p. 138, citing al-Ṭabarī, *Taʾrīkh*, ser. ii, p. 1041) notes, a village in this area had become known as "The Burnt" as a result of the earlier activities of Ḥabīb b. al-Muhallab.

581. So rendering al-ʿaṣīr, which was clearly alcoholic in this case (Dr. D. F. Waines has informed me that this sense of ʿaṣīr is not uncommon).

582. Preferring bi-shikkatihi, as proposed by the *Addenda et Emendanda*.

583. Following the *Addenda et Emendanda*, rather than the text (see also Gibb, *Arab Conquests*, p. 42 and n. 15 thereto); Ibn Kathīr (*Bidāyah*, vol. IX, p. 84) gives this form and says that Ghūrak was Ṭarkhūn's brother.

584. According to al-Yaʿqūbī (*Taʾrīkh*, vol. II, p. 344), Ghūrak killed Ṭarkhūn.

Ṭarkhūn when Qutaybah went out to Sijistān; and they put Ghūrak in charge.

As for the Bāhilīs, they say: Qutaybah besieged the king of Shūmān and set mangonels against his fortress. He set up a mangonel that they used to call "The Pigeon-Toed," shot the first stone, and hit the [city] wall; he shot another, and it landed in the city. Then the stones followed one another, landing in the city. One of them landed in the king's court, hitting a man and killing him. [Qutaybah] conquered the fortress by force of arms. Then he returned to Kish and Nasaf, and thence to Bukhārā. He stopped at a village in which there were a fire temple and a house of gods; in [this village] there were peacocks, and they called it "The Dwelling Place of the Peacocks."[585] Then he went to Ṭarkhūn in Soghd, in order to collect from him that on the basis of which he had made peace with him. When he looked out on the valley of Soghd and saw how good it was, he recited (basīṭ):

A green and fertile valley that has been protected
    from people, out of caution against death and battle.[586]
I have come to it with fine horses, that are urged along,
    bringing at a run tousle-headed [fighters]
    thirsty for blood.

['Alī] said: [Qutaybah] took from Ṭarkhūn his [tribute as stipulated in the] peace. Then he returned to Bukhārā. He made a young man Bukhārā Khudhāh, and killed those he feared would oppose him. Then he went by way of Āmul to Marw.

According to ['Alī]—the Bāhilīs—Bashshār b. 'Amr—a man from Bāhilah: [Qutaybah's men] kept on bombarding their buildings until the fortress was conquered.

[Khālid al-Qasrī's Strict Governorship of Mecca]

In this year al-Walīd b. 'Abd al-Malik appointed over Mecca Khālid b. 'Abdallāh al-Qasrī, who remained governor there until al-Walīd died.   [1231]

---

585. *Manzil al-ṭawāwīs.* See Barthold, *Turkestan*[3], pp. 98–99.
586. Reading *ḥadhāru 'l-mawti wa-'l-rahaji*, with Ms B.

According to Muḥammad b. 'Umar al-Wāqidī—Ismā'īl b. Ibrāhīm b. 'Uqbah—Nāfi', mawlā of the Banū Makhzūm: I heard Khālid b. 'Abdallāh say, "O people, you are in the most sacrosanct of God's lands. God chose it from [all] the lands and put His House in it. Then He prescribed for His servants the making of pilgrimage to it, 'he who is able to make his way there.'[587] O people, incumbent upon you are obedience and cleaving to the collective body. Beware of uncertainties. By God, no one who impugns his imām (that is, the Caliph) will be brought to me but that I shall crucify him in the Ḥaram. God has placed the caliphate in relation to Him in the position in which He has placed it. Assent, obey, and do not say, 'Thus and thus.' The only [right] view concerning what the Caliph writes about or opines is to put it into effect. Know that it has reached me that some of those [given to] disobedience are coming to you and staying in your land. Beware not to accommodate anyone you know to be deviating from the collective body. I shall not find any one of them in the house of any one of you but that I shall demolish his house. Look [carefully] at those you accommodate in your houses. Incumbent upon you are the collective body and obedience. Disunity is the great affliction."

According to Muḥammad b. 'Umar—Ismā'īl b. Ibrāhīm—Mūsā b. 'Uqbah—Abū Ḥabībah: I performed the lesser pilgrimage and stopped at the residences of the Banū Asad, in the houses of al-Zabīr. Suddenly, there was [Khālid], calling me. I went into his presence, and he said to me, "Who are you from?" I said, "From the people of Medina." He said, "What made you stop in the houses of the one who went against obedience?" I said, "It is where I stay, if I stay for a day or so. Then I go back to my [own] house. There is no disobedience in me. I am one of those who exalt the matter of the caliphate. I claim that he who disowns it will be destroyed." He said, "Where you stayed will not be held against you. But it is disliked that there stays [here] anyone who is scornful of the Caliph." I said, "God forbid!" [In addition,] I heard him one day saying, "By God, if I were to know that this wild animal that is safe in the Ḥaram had spoken without acknowledging obedience, I would expel it from the Ḥaram. No one who goes

[1232]

---

587. Qur'ān, 3:97 = 91.

against the collective body, who scoffs at [the caliphs], may dwell in the Ḥaram of God." I said, "May God grant the amīr success."

[Al-Walīd's Visit to Medina]

The leader of the pilgrimage in this year was al-Walīd b. ʿAbd al-Malik. Aḥmad b. Thābit related to me on the authority of him who mentioned it on the authority of Isḥāq b. ʿĪsā on the authority of Abū Maʿshar, who said: Al-Walīd made the pilgrimage in the year 91.

Similarly, Muḥammad b. ʿUmar said: Mūsā b. Abī Bakr related to me: Ṣaliḥ b. Kaysān related to us: When the arrival of al-Walīd took place, ʿUmar b. ʿAbd al-ʿAzīz ordered twenty men from Quraysh to go out with him to meet al-Walīd b. ʿAbd al-Malik; they included Abū Bakr b. ʿAbd al-Raḥmān b. al-Ḥārith b. Hishām, his brother Muḥammad b. ʿAbd al-Raḥman, and ʿAbdallāh b. ʿAmr b. ʿUthmān b. ʿAffān. They went out until they reached al-Suwaydāʾ,[588] they being with ʿUmar b. ʿAbd al-ʿAzīz; with them on that day were riding animals and horses. They met al-Walīd, who was mounted. The chamberlain said, "Dismount for the Commander of the Faithful," and they dismounted. Then [al-Walīd] gave them an order, and they rode. [Al-Walīd] summoned ʿUmar and went with him until he stopped at Dhū Khushub.[589] Then they were presented: [Al-Walīd] summoned them one by one, and they greeted him. [After this, al-Walīd] called for lunch, and they lunched with him; he left Dhū Khushub in the evening.

When he entered Medina, he went in the morning to the mosque, to look at its building. The people were cleared out of it, and no one was left in it except[590] Saʿīd b. al-Musayyab, whom none of the guards dared to send out. [Saʿīd] was in his place of prayer wearing only two thin garments, worth no more than five dirhams. Someone said to him, "If only you would stand," and he said, "I shall not stand until there comes the time when I usually stand." Someone said to him, "If only you would greet the Commander of the Faithful," and he said, "No, by God. I shall not

[1233]

---

588. Two stages from Medina on the way to Syria (see Cornu).
589. One stage from Medina on the way to Syria (see Cornu).
590. Literally, ". . . no one was left in it. Saʿīd b. al-Musayyab remained. . . ."

stand up for him." ʿUmar b. ʿAbd al-ʿAzīz said, "I began to steer al-Walīd to the side of the mosque, hoping that he would not see Saʿīd until he stood up." But al-Walīd happened to glance toward the *qiblah* and said, "Who is that [person] sitting? Is he the shaykh Saʿīd b. al-Musayyab?" ʿUmar said, "Yes, O Commander of the Faithful, he's unpredictable.[591] If he knew that you were here, he would stand up and greet you, [but] his sight is weak." Al-Walīd said, "I know about him. We shall go to him and greet him." He took a turn in the mosque until he stopped at the grave [of the Prophet], and then advanced until he stood before Saʿīd. He said, "How are you, O shaykh?" Saʿīd neither moved nor stood, and [then] said, "Well, praise be to God. And how is the Commander of the Faithful?" Al-Walīd said, "Well, praise be to God," and he departed, saying to ʿUmar, "This is the last of the old school."[592] I said, "Yes, O Commander of the Faithful."

[Muḥammad b. ʿUmar] said: Al-Walīd distributed in Medina many foreign slaves,[593] vessels of gold and silver, and wealth. He gave the sermon in Medina on the Friday and led the prayer.

According to Muḥammad b. ʿUmar—Isḥāq b. Yaḥyā: I saw al-Walīd delivering the sermon on the pulpit of the Messenger of God, may God bless and preserve him, on Friday in the year when he made the pilgrimage. His troops were lined up in two rows from the pulpit to the back wall of the mosque; in their hands were iron rods, and on their shoulders were iron bars. I saw him ascend it wearing a *durrāʿah*[594] and a *qalansuwwah*,[595] without a *ridāʾ*.[596] He went up the pulpit, and, when he reached the top, he

[1234]

---

591. *Wa-min ḥālihi wa-min ḥālihi*: Ibn al-Athīr has *wa-min ḥālihi kadhā wa-kadhā*, while Ibn Kathīr's version (*Bidāyah*, vol. IX, p. 82) is somewhat different at this point.

592. So rendering *baqiyyat al-nās* (thus, too, in al-Yaʿqūbī [*Taʾrīkh*, vol. II, p. 341] and Ibn al-Athīr); Ibn Kathīr (*Bidāyah*, vol. IX, p. 82) more prosaically reads *faqīh al-nās*.

593. *Raqīqan kathīran ujman*. Ibn al-Athīr has *daqīqan kathīran*, but al-Ṭabarī's *ujman* is the clincher as far as the *raqīqan* reading is concerned.

594. A "[garment of the kind called] *jubba*, slit in the fore part" (Lane, *Lexicon*, p. 872b, s.v. *midraʿa*), lined, according to *EI*[2], s.v. Libās (vol. V, p. 737a); see also Dozy, *Dictionnaire détaillé des noms des vêtements chez les arabes*, pp. 177–81.

595. Originally a close-fitting cap, this could also designate a hood or cowl (*EI*[2], s.v. Libās (vol. V, pp. 734b–735a); see also Dozy, *Noms des vêtements*, pp. 365–71.

596. "Garment covering the upper half of the body" (Lane, *Lexicon*, s.v.); al-Yaʿqūbī (*Taʾrīkh*, vol. II, p. 341) provides an abbreviated version of this report.

proclaimed a greeting. Then he sat, and the muezzins made the call to prayer. Then they were quiet, and he delivered the first sermon sitting; then he stood, and delivered the second standing. Isḥāq said: I met Rajā' b. Ḥaywah,[597] who was accompanying [al-Walīd], and said, "Do they [always] do it this way?" He said, "Yes. Mu'āwiyah did it in this way, and so on." I said, "Aren't you going to speak to him [about it]?" He said, "Qabīṣah b. Dhu'ayb informed me that he spoke to 'Abd al-Malik b. Marwān [about it], and he refused to do [anything different], saying, "Uthmān delivered sermons in this way.'" I said, "By God, he did not deliver sermons in this way; 'Uthmān only delivered sermons standing up." Rajā' said, "They were told this and took to it." Isḥāq said: We did not see any [Umayyad caliph] more proud than [al-Walīd].

Muḥammad b. 'Umar said: [al-Walīd] brought the incense of the mosque of the Messenger of God, may God bless and preserve him, its thurible, and the covering of the Ka'bah. [The covering] was spread out on ropes in the mosque, [it being made] of good brocade. The like of it had never been seen. He spread it out one day, and then folded [it] and moved [it].

The governors of the *amṣār* in this year were [the same as] those who were their governors in the year 90, except for Mecca, the governor of which in this year was Khālid b. 'Abdallāh al-Qasrī, according to al-Wāqidī. [An authority/authorities] other than al-Wāqidī said: The governorship of Mecca was 'Umar b. 'Abd al-'Azīz's in this year too.

---

597. On him, see Bosworth, "Rajā' b. Ḥaywa al-Kindī and the Umayyad Caliphs," *The Islamic Quarterly* 16 (1972), pp. 36–80.

The
Events of the Year

92

 (OCTOBER 29, 710–OCTOBER 18, 711)

Among them was the campaign of Maslamah b. ʿAbd al-Malik and ʿUmar b. al-Walīd in Byzantine territory. Three fortresses were conquered at the hands of Maslamah; the people of Sūsanah migrated to the inner part of Byzantine territory.

In this year Ṭāriq b. Ziyād, the mawlā of Mūsā b. Nuṣayr, campaigned in al-Andalus with twelve thousand [men]. He encountered the king of al-Andalus—al-Wāqidī claimed that he was called Adrīnūq[598]—who was one of the people of Iṣbahān. He (?al-Wāqidī) said: They are the kings of the foreigners of al-Andalus.[599] Ṭāriq marched on him with all his forces, and al-Adrīnūq went forward on the king's throne, wearing his crown, his gloves, and all the adornments kings used to wear. They fought a hard battle until God killed al-Adrīnūq. Al-Andalus was conquered in the year 92.

---

598. I.e., Roderic; "al-Adrīq" in al-Yaʿqūbī (Taʾrīkh, vol. II, p. 341) and both "Adhrīqūn" and "Adrūnīq" in Ibn Kathīr (Bidāyah, vol. IX, p. 83).

599. Al-Yaʿqūbī's version of what is clearly the same report (Taʾrīkh, vol. II, p. 341) is to be taken to mean at this point "they are the Goths, the kings of al-Andalus."

In [this year], according to what one of the biographers (*ahl al-siyar*) claimed, Qutaybah campaigned in Sijistān, heading for the great Zunbīl and al-Zābul.[600] When he stopped in Sijistān, the messengers of the Zunbīl met him with [a proposal for] a peace agreement.[601] [Qutaybah] accepted that, departed, and appointed over them ʿAbd Rabbihi b. ʿAbdallāh b. ʿUmayr al-Laythī.

The leader of the pilgrimage in this year was ʿUmar b. ʿAbd al-ʿAzīz, who was over Medina: Thus it was related to me by Aḥmad b. Thābit on the authority of he who mentioned it on the authority of Isḥāq b. ʿĪsā on the authority of Abū Maʿshar; and al-Wāqidī and [an authority/authorities] other than him said the same. The governors of the *amṣār* in this year were [the same as] their governors in the preceding year.

[1236]

---

600. I.e., Zābulistān (see Marquart, *Ērānšahr*, p. 247).
601. Ibn Aʿtham (*Futūḥ*, vol. VII, p. 234) provides some details.

The
Events of the Year

93

(OCTOBER 19, 711–OCTOBER 6, 712)

Among [the events] in [this year] was the campaign of al-ʿAbbās b. al-Walīd in Byzantine territory. God conquered Samasṭiyyah[602] at his hands.

In it, too, was the campaign of Marwān b. al-Walīd against the Byzantines. He reached Khanjarah.[603]

In it was the campaign of Maslamah b. ʿAbd al-Malik in Byzantine territory. He conquered Māsah,[604] and Ḥiṣn al-Ḥadīd, Ghazālah, and Tarḥamah[605] in the region of Malaṭyah.

In it Qutaybah killed the king of Khām Jird and made a renewed peace with the king of Khwārazm.[606]

---

602. Sabasṭiyya, according to Ibn al-Athīr. Brooks ("The Arabs in Asia Minor," p. 193n.) and Lilie (*Byzantinische Reaktion*, p. 120n.) take it to signify Mistheia.

603. I.e., Gangra.

604. I.e., Amaseia.

605. Following the Mss. and Brooks ("The Arabs in Asia Minor," p. 194n); Khālifah's version (*Taʾrīkh*, p. 309) is even more mangled.

606. Cf. Gibb, *Arab Conquests*, pp. 42ff.; Ibn Aʿtham, *Futūḥ*, vol. VII, pp. 235–37. It looks as if it remains for Khām Jird to be identified, but Gibb rightly points out that its king is to be identified with Khurrazādh (who figures in the account that follows here), "or at least with his party" (p. 43).

[The Killing of the King of Khām Jird and
Renewed Peace with Khwārazm]

'Alī b. Muḥammad said: According to (i) Abū al-Dhayyāl—al-
Muhallab b. Iyās, (ii) al-Ḥasan b. Rushayd—Ṭufayl b. Mirdās
al-'Ammī, (iii) 'Alī b. Mujāhid—Ḥanbal b. Abī Ḥuraydah—the   [1237]
marzbān of Qūhistān, (iv) Kulayb b. Khalaf, (v) the Bāhilīs, and (vi)
[an authority/authorities] other than [the foregoing]—some of
them mentioned what others did not mention, and I have put it
all together: The king of Khwārazm was weak, and his younger
brother Khurrazādh seized power. If it reached him that anyone
who concerned himself with the king had a slave girl or a riding
animal or fine goods, he sent and took it [from him]; or [if] it
reached him that any one of them had a daughter or a sister or a
beautiful wife, he sent to him and constrained him by force, taking what he wanted and withholding what he wanted. No one
could hold out against him, nor could the king protect [anyone].
When [the king] was spoken to [about this], he said, "I am not
strong [enough to deal] with him." [Khurraz]madh] had nonetheless filled him with anger, and, when that had gone on for a long
time on the part of [Khurrazādh], to the detriment of [the king], he
wrote to Qutaybah, calling him to his land [and] desiring to hand
it over to him. He sent to him the keys of the cities of Khwārazm—three keys of gold—and he stipulated that [Qutaybah]
should hand over to him his brother and all who had opposed
him, so that he might judge concerning [them] as he saw fit. He
sent messengers concerning [all] that, and he did not apprise any
of his marzbāns or dihqāns of what he had written about to
Qutaybah. His messengers reached Qutaybah in the last part of
the winter, at the time [when] campaigning [started]; Qutaybah
had [already] prepared himself for campaigning, and he made it
look as if he were heading for Soghd. The Khwārazm Shāh's messengers returned to him with welcome news from Qutaybah, who
went and deputed over Marw Thābit al-A'war, Muslim's mawlā.

[ʿAlī] said: [The Khwārazm Shāh] gathered together his kings, his
religious leaders (aḥbār), and his dihqāns, and said, "Qutaybah is
heading for Soghd and won't be campaigning against you; come, let
us take our ease in this spring of ours," and they began drinking
and taking their ease, thinking themselves safe from campaigning.

[ʿAlī] said: The next thing they knew was that Qutaybah had   [1238] stopped at Hazārasp,[607] on the other side of the river. The Khwā-razm Shāh said to his companions, "What do you think?" They said, "We think that we should fight him." He said, "But I do not think that. People stronger and more powerful than we are have been helpless before him. I think that we should turn him away by giving him something. We'll turn him away for this year and [then] see what we think." They said, "We agree with your view." The Khwārazm Shāh accordingly set off and stopped at the city of al-Fīl on the other side of the river.[608] [ʿAlī] said: The cities of the Khwārazm Shāh [were] three [in number], surrounded by a single moat;[609] the city of al-Fīl is the most strongly fortified of them.

The Khwārazm Shāh stopped at [al-Fīl] while Qutaybah was at Hazārasp, on the other side of the river; he had not crossed it, and [indeed] only the Balkh river (that is, the Oxus) lay between him and the Khwārazm Shah. [The latter] made peace with Qutaybah for ten thousand slaves,[610] for gold and goods, and on the condi-tions that [Qutaybah] would help him against the king of Khām Jird and would fulfill what he had written for him. Qutaybah accepted that from him and fulfilled [what he had said he would do] for him. [He] sent to the king of Khām Jird—who had been hostile to the Khwārazm Shāh—his brother ʿAbd al-Raḥmān, who fought him, killed him, and gained mastery over his land. He then came to Qutaybah from [there] with four thousand prisoners; [Qutaybah] killed them. When his brother ʿAbd al-Raḥmān brought them, Qutaybah ordered that his throne be brought out, and he appeared before the people [sitting on it].

[ʿAlī] said: He ordered that the prisoners be killed: One thou-sand were killed in front of him, one thousand to his right, one thousand to his left, and one thousand behind him.

According to [ʿAlī]—al-Muhallab b. Iyās: The swords of the

---

607. *EI*², s.v.

608. I.e., at Kāth, the ancient capital of Khwārazm; "at the time of the Arab invasion the town consisted of three parts, of which the most strongly fortified, *i.e.*, the citadel, bore the name of Fīl or Fīr" (Barthold, *Turkestan*³, p. 144).

609. *Fārqīn*, which is defined in the *Glossarium* as "fossa quae cingit murum urbis"; according to the *Glossarium* (p. 82) accompanying al-Balādhurī's *Futūḥ*, this is the arabized form of Persian *bārgīn* or *pārgīn*.

610. Translated thus here and below; literally, "heads."

nobles were taken on that day, and heads were cut off with them. Among them were [swords] that could neither cut nor wound. [1239] They took my sword, with which nothing had been struck without being cut clean through. One of Qutaybah's family envied me [it], and he indicated to the one who was performing the executions that he should cut to one side with it; he cut a little to one side and it hit the molar of the dead man and was notched. Abū al-Dhayyāl said: I have the sword.

['Alī] said: Qutaybah handed over to the Khwārazm Shāh his brother and those who had gone against him, and he killed them, appropriated their wealth, and sent it to Qutaybah. Qutaybah entered the city of Fīl[611] and accepted from the Khwārazm Shāh that on the basis of which he had made peace with him. Then he returned to Hazārasp. Ka'b al-Ashqarī said (basīṭ):[612]

Fīl has cast to you what is in it and has not transgressed;
    before you, the boastful babbler[613] wanted it.
He who is weak with the spear will not suffice
    for the frontier, nor
    will the one who is soft when put to the test,
    [the one with] a palpitating heart.
Do you remember the nights when you were killing
    Turks
    on the other side of Kāzah,[614] while the
    babbler was wrapped in his sheet?
They only rode horses once they were grown men,
    heavy [men], hard on their backs.
You (pl.) are Sh.bās and Mardādhān, [who is] despicable,
    and Baskharā', tombs filled with foreskins.[615]   [1240]

---

611. Which has now lost its definite article.

612. Verses 1, 4, 5, and 7 occur in *Aghānī*[2], vol. XIV, p. 299; verse 6 occurs in Ibn A'tham, *Futūḥ*, vol. VII, p. 237; verses 4 and 5 occur in Yāqūt, *Mu'jam*, vol. II, p. 387, and verse 1 in vol. III, p. 933.

613. Presumably, Yazīd b. al-Muhallab is meant.

614. Yāqūt, *Mu'jam*, vol. IV, p. 226 ult., knows this as one of the villages of Marw.

615. This verse calls for several comments: (i) As will become clear and as was noted by Hell ("al-Farazdaḳ's Lieder auf die Muhallabiten," p. 591 n.), the purpose of the verse is to point to the non-Arab origins of the Muhallabids. The Persian names come in various forms: (a) Sh.bās (Ṭab.), Shunās (*Agh.*), and B.shāsh (Yāqūt),

I have seen that the battle days of Abū Ḥafṣ (that is,
    Qutaybah) prefer him,
    while the efforts of the people differ.
[He is] the pure Qaysite,[616] while some of the
    people[617] are allotted to
    villages and countryside, those with real
    genealogies and those with fake ones.
If you had obeyed the people of weakness, they would
    not have shared
    seventy thousand [slaves], with the glory of Soghd
    commencing anew.
In Samarqand there is more [booty]: you are the one
    to divide it up,
    if death hangs back from your soul.
You have been ahead with whatever good people have
    preferred, and no nobility of what they have left misses
    you.

[ʿAlī] said: ʿAlī b. Mujāhid recited to me [as the wording of the
beginning of the first line], "Fīl has cast to you what is beyond
Kāzah"; [ʿAlī] said: And so too said al-Ḥasan b. Rushayd al-Jūzjānī. As for [someone] other than those two, he said, "Fīl has cast

---

while Ibn Ḥajar (Iṣābah, vol. II, p. 241) opts for Sanās; (b) M.rdādhān (Ṭab.), Mardādhā' (Agh.), B.hbwdhān (Yāqūt; and Ibn Rustah [al-Aʿlāq al-nafīsah, p. 206]); (c)
B.skharā' (Ṭab.), Faskharā' (Agh.), Baskharah (Yāqūt and Ibn Rustah), and Y.sf.rwḥ
or B.sf.rwḥ (Kitāb al-ʿuyūn wa'l-ḥadā'iq, p. 49). The compiler of the Aghānī (vol.
XIV, p. 300) cites the view that Shunās was the Persian name of al-Muhallab's
father, Abū Ṣufrah Ẓālim b. Sarrāq, while Mardādhā' was the name of Abū Ṣufrah's
father, and Faskharā' was the name of Abū Ṣufrah's grandfather. On the other
hand, Ibn Rustah and Yāqūt identify Abū ʿUbaydah [Maʿmar b. al-Muthannā] as
their source for the information that Abū Ṣufrah's original name was Baskharah b.
Bahbūdhān (and that he was a Zoroastrian weaver from Khārg Island who went to
Oman, attached himself to the Azd, became a groom for ʿUthmān b. Abī al-ʿĀṣ al-
Thaqafī, etc.); and it is pretty clear that the information in the Kitāb al-ʿuyūn wa'l-
ḥadā'iq comes from the same source.
  (ii) The reference to "foreskins" is of course an unambiguous suggestion that
Muhallabid origins were non-Arab. (It can be noted that Ibn Ḥajar [Iṣābah, vol. I, p.
345] knew that Abū Ṣufrah was not circumcised until he was a shaykh, in the
caliphate of ʿUmar b. al-Khaṭṭāb; and it can be added that, according to the
Aghānī[2] [vol. XXIII, p. 230], even right at the end of the Umayyad period,
"Quraysh did not think that any one of the Azd from Oman was an Arab.")
  (iii) Where in al-Ṭabarī's version the word following M.rdādhān is muḥtaqarun,
in the Aghānī it is naʿrifuhu, and in Yāqūt it is mukhtabarun.
  616. Preferring the Aghānī's ṣarīḥu Qaysin to al-Ṭabarī's Qaysun ṣarīḥun.
  617. I.e., Yemen.

to you what is in it." They [all] said: Fīl is the [principal] city of
[the region of] Samarqand.[618] ['Alī] said: In my opinion, what 'Alī
b. Mujāhid said is sounder.

According to ['Alī]—the Bāhilīs: Qutaybah acquired one hundred thousand slaves from Khwārazm.[619]

['Alī] said: Qutaybah's intimates spoke to him in the year 93
saying, "The people are becoming weary," they had come from   [1241]
Sijistān, "let them rest this year." He refused.

['Alī] said: When [Qutaybah] had made peace with the people of
Khwārazm, he went to Soghd. Al-Ashqarī said:

If you had obeyed the people of weakness, they would
    not have shared
    seventy thousand [slaves], with the glory of Soghd
    commencing anew.

Abū Jaʿfar said: In this year Qutaybah, on his departure form
Khwārazm, campaigned against Samarqand and conquered it.[620]

[Qutaybah's Conquest of Samarqand]

We have already referred to the chain of authorities (*isnād*) of the
people from whom ʿAlī b. Muḥammad mentioned that he took
[material concerning events] when Qutaybah made peace with
the lord of Khwārazm. Then he mentioned, by way of insertion
into that [account], that, when he took the peace [tribute] of the
lord of Khwārazm, al-Mujashshar[621] b. al-Muzāḥim al-Sulamī
said, "I need [to say something to you]; let me be alone with you."
[Qutaybah] did so, and [al-Mujashshar] said, "If you want [to conquer] the Soghdians one of these days, do so now, for they feel
secure from your moving against them this year. They are only
ten days away." [Qutaybah] said, "Has anyone advised you [to
suggest] this?" He said, "No." [Qutaybah] said, "Have you informed anyone of it?" He said, "No." [Qutaybah] said, "If anyone
speaks of it, I shall execute you."

---

618. Where al-Ṭabarī has *qālū: Fīl madīnat Samarqand*, al-Balādhurī (*Futūḥ*, p.
421) has *qāla ʿAlī b. Mujāhid: innamā madīnat Fīl Samarqand*.
619. Khalīfah (*Taʾrīkh*, p. 309) says ten million, which is amended in the margin
to ten thousand.
620. Cf. Gibb, *Arab Conquests*, pp. 44–45; Ibn Aʿtham, *Futūḥ*, vol. VII, pp.
238ff.
621. Following the emendation proposed in the *Addenda et Emendanda*.

[Qutaybah] stayed put that day. On the morning of the next day he summoned ʿAbd al-Raḥmān [b. Muslim] and said, "Go with the horsemen and archers and take the baggage[622] to Marw." The baggage was sent off in the direction of Marw, and ʿAbd al-Raḥmān spent all that day following it, heading for Marw. In the evening, [Qutaybah] wrote to him, "In the morning, send the baggage to Marw and go with the horsemen and archers to Soghd. Keep [this] information secret. I shall be following [you]." [ʿAlī] said: When [this instruction] reached ʿAbd al-Raḥmān, he ordered the people in charge of the baggage to go on to Marw, and he went where he [himself] had been ordered to go.

[1242]

Qutaybah addressed [his army] and said, "God has conquered this place for you at a time when campaigning in it is possible. Now this [region of] Soghd has no one to defend it. They have broken the covenant that was between us. They have withheld that on the basis of which we made peace with Ṭarkhūn, and have done to him that which has reached you. God has said, 'Whosoever breaks his oath breaks it but to his own hurt.'[623] Go with God's blessing. I hope that Khwārazm and Soghd will be like al-Naḍīr and Qurayẓah,[624] for God has said, 'And other [spoils] you were not able to take; God has encompassed them already.'"[625]

[ʿAlī] said: Qutaybah reached Soghd—ʿAbd al-Raḥān had reached it before him—with twenty thousand [men].[626] Qutaybah reached it, accompanied by Khwārazmians and Bukhārans, three or four nights after ʿAbd al-Raḥmān had stopped there, and said, "When we light on a people's courtyard, how evil will be the morning of them that are warned."[627] He besieged them for a month; in the course of being besieged, [the Soghdians] fought [Qutaybah's men] several times from a single direction. Fearful throughout the siege, the Soghdians wrote to the king of al-Shāsh and the Ikhshād[628] of Farghānah, "If the Arabs vanquish us, they will visit upon you the like of what they brought us."

---

622. See above, n. 343.
623. Qurʾān 48:10.
624. See above, n. 572.
625. Qurʾān 48:21.
626. Alternatively, the 20,000 men were with ʿAbd al-Raḥmān.
627. Cf. Qurʾān 37:177.
628. Rather than the more usual "Ikhshīd" (see *EI*[2], s.f.); for further discussion of this form, see Bombaci, "On the Ancient Turkish Title 'Šaδ,'" pp. 182–83.

[The king of al-Shāsh and the Ikhshād and their followers] agreed to go to [the Soghdians] and sent [word] to them: "Send [against the Arabs] those who may distract them, so that we may make a night attack on their camp."

['Alī] said: They chose horsemen from [among] the sons of the marzbāns, the Asāwirah,[629] and heroic men of strength, and sent them off, having ordered them to stage a night attack on the [Arab] camp. The spies of the Muslims came bearing information [of this], and Qutaybah chose three hundred—or six hundred—men of courage, put Ṣāliḥ b. Muslim in charge of them, and sent them along the road from which he feared that he might be approached. Ṣāliḥ sent out spies to bring him information [about the enemy], while he [himself] stopped two parasangs away from their camp. The spies returned and informed him that [the enemy] would be coming to him that night. Ṣāliḥ split his cavalry into three groups, kept two of them hidden, and [himself] stayed on the main road. The polytheists came by night, unaware of the position of Ṣāliḥ and confident that no one would engage them before [they reached Qutaybah's] camp. They did not know about Ṣāliḥ until they ran into him. [1243]

['Alī] said: [Ṣāliḥ and his men] charged them and, when spear thrusts were being exchanged, the two hidden groups came out and fought.

According to ['Alī]—one of the Barājim:[630] I was present [on that occasion], and I have never seen people fighting more strongly or with more fortitude in adversity than the sons of those kings; only a few of them fled. We gathered together their weapons, cut off their heads, and took prisoners. We asked them about those whom we had killed, and they said, "You have killed none other than [here] a son of a king, or [here] one of the nobles, or [here] one of the heroes. You have killed men [among whom were those who were each] the equal of a hundred men; [in those cases,] we have written [their names] on their ears."[631] Then we entered the camp in the morning, and there was not a single man

---

629. Persian knights, "who under Persian rule were exempt of taxes together with the other higher classes" (Løkkegaard, *Islamic Taxation in the Classic Period*, p. 171).

630. A name applied to two separate clan groupings, one in Tamīm and one in 'Abd al-Qays (Caskel, *Ǧamharat an-nasab*, vol. II, p. 224).

631. The syntax is complicated here; Ibn al-Athīr simplifies and changes it.

among us who did not hang up[632] a head known by name. We took as plunder excellent weapons, fine goods, and brisk riding animals, and Qutaybah let us have all that as *nafal*.[633]

[1244] That broke the Soghdians. Qutaybah set up mangonels against [the Soghdians], and shot at them, fighting them without desisting. He was well advised by those of the Bukharans and Khwārazmians who were with him; they fought hard and gave of themselves unstintingly. Ghūrak[634] sent [word] to [Qutaybah]: "You are fighting me with my brothers and family from [among] the non-Arabs. Send Arabs out to me." Qutaybah became angry, summoned al-Jadalī, and said, "Review the [army] and pick out the bravest people," and [al-Jadalī] gathered the [army] together. Then Qutaybah set, reviewing them himself. He summoned the platoon commanders (*ʿurafāʾ*) and began to call for one man after another, saying, "What do you have?" The platoon commander would say, "[This is] a brave [man]." "And what is this?" "[This is] one of limited ability." "And what is this?" "[This is] a coward." Qutaybah called the cowards "the Stinkers," took their good weapons, and gave them to the brave men and those of limited ability, and left them the most worn-out weapons. Then Qutaybah took them forward and fought [the enemy] with them, [using both] horsemen and infantrymen. He bombarded the city with the mangonels and made a breach [in the wall] which [the enemy] blocked with sacks of millet. There emerged a man who stood on top of the breach and shouted abuse at Qutaybah. Qutaybah said to the archers who were with him, "Choose two of your number," and they did so. Qutaybah said, "Which of the two of you will shoot at this man [on the understanding that,] if he hits him, he will receive ten thousand [dirhams] and, if he misses him, his hand will be cut off?" One of them held back, while the other came forward and shot him, right in the eye. [Qutaybah] ordered that he be given ten thousand [dirhams].

According to [ʿAlī]—the Bāhilīs—Yaḥyā b. Khālid—his father, Khālid b. Bāb, the mawlā of Muslim b. ʿAmr: I was among the

---

632. Preferring Ibrāhīm's *muʿalliq*[un] to Guidi's *muʿallaq*[un].

633. "That part of the booty which was left to the free disposal of the leader, when distributing the portions of booty that were due to the soldiers" (Løkkegaard, *Islamic Taxation in the Classic Period*, p. 19).

634. See above, n. 583.

archers of Qutaybah. When we conquered the city, I climbed up
the wall and reached the place in which that man was. I found
him dead on the wall; the arrow had gone right through his eye
and come out the nape of his neck.

On the morning of the next day, they bombarded the city and   [1245]
breached it [again]. Qutaybah said, "Press on to [the breach], so
that you may cross on it." They fought [the enemy] until they
were on the breach, and the Soghdians shot them with arrows.
[The Arabs] put up their shields—a man would put his shield up
over his eye and then charge—until they were on the breach. [The
Soghdians] said to [Qutaybah], "Depart from us today, so that we
may make peace with you tomorrow."

As for Bāhilah, they say: Qutaybah said, "We shall not make
peace with you without our men being on the breach and our
mangonels moving up and down [bombarding] your heads and
your city."

As for [authorities] other than [Bāhilah], they say: Qutaybah
said, "The slaves have become frightened. Depart victorious,"
and they departed. He made peace with them the next day, on [the
following terms]: [1] 2,200,000 [dirhams] *per annum*; [2] in that
year, 30,000 slaves free of defect and including neither young boys
nor old men;[635] [3] that they would empty the city for Qutaybah,
and would not have in it any fighting men; [4] that there would be
built for Qutaybah in it a mosque, so that he might enter [it] and
pray, and [that] a pulpit would be set up in it, so that he might
preach a sermon, eat lunch, and go forth.

['Alī] said: When the peace had been concluded, Qutaybah sent
ten men—two from each fifth—and they took receipt of that on
the basis of which [the Soghdians] had made peace with him.
Qutaybah said, "Now they have been humbled—now that their
brethren and children have fallen into our hands." Then they
emptied the city, built a mosque, and set up a pulpit. Qutaybah
went into the city with four thousand [men] he had chosen. When

---

635. The first of the two preceding figures is also given by al-Balādhurī (*Futūḥ*,
p. 421), and both of them are given by Khalīfah (*Ta'rīkh*, p. 309); but Ibn A'tham
(*Futūḥ*, vol. VII, p. 243) mentions [1a] an immediate payment of 2,000,000 dirhams; [1b] an annual payment of 200,000 dirhams; and [2] 3,000 (sic) slaves including neither young boys nor old men (see also what purports to be the 'ahd docu-
ment formalizing the peace arrangements (pp. 244–46).

he had entered it, he went to the mosque and prayed and preached a sermon. Then he ate lunch and sent [word] to the Soghdians: "Whoever of you wants to take his goods may do so, for I am not going out of [the city]. I have done this for you, and I shall not take from you more than that on the basis of which I made peace with you; but the troops will stay in [the city]."

[1246]

[ʿAlī] said: As for the Bāhilīs, they say: Qutaybah made peace with them in return for one hundred thousand slaves, the fire temples, and the adornments of the idols. He took receipt of that on the basis of which he had made peace with them, and he was brought the idols, which were despoiled and then placed before him; gathered together, they were like an enormous edifice. He ordered that they be burned, and the non-Arabs said to him, "Among them are idols the burner of which will be destroyed." Qutaybah said, "I shall burn them with my [own] hand." Ghūrak came, knelt before him, and said, "Devotion to you is a duty incumbent upon me. Do not expose yourself to these idols." Qutaybah called for fire, took a brand in his hand, went out, proclaimed "God is great," and set fire to them; [others then also] set fire [to them], and they burned fiercely. In the remains of the gold and silver nails that had been in them, they found fifty thousand *mithqāl*s.[636]

According to [ʿAlī]—Makhlad b. Ḥamzah b. Bīḍ—his father—someone who witnessed the conquest of Samarqand, or one of the districts of Khurasan: They brought out of it [some] huge copper cooking pots, and Qutaybah said to Ḥuḍayn, "O Abū Sāsān, do you think that Raqāsh[637] ever had cooking pots like these?" He said, "No, but ʿAylān[638] had a pot like these." Qutaybah laughed and said, "You have gained your revenge."

[ʿAlī] said: Muḥammad b. Abī ʿUyaynah[639] said to Salm b. Qutaybah in the presence of Sulaymān b. ʿAlī,[640] "The non-Arabs revile Qutaybah for perfidy; he acted perfidiously at Khwārazm

---

636. See above, n. 469, and cf. the story given at that point.

637. I.e., Ḥuḍayn's own clan.

638. ʿAylān being the grouping to which Bāhilah belonged; the wordplay seems to be that ʿaylān can signify "hungry, going about looking for sustenance."

639. I.e., Muḥammad b. Abī ʿUyaynah b. al-Muhallab (Ibn Ḥazm, *Jamharah*, p. 369).

640. I.e., Sulaymān b. ʿAlī b. ʿAbdallāh al-ʿAbbāsī, governor of al-Baṣrah from 133 (750–51) to 137 (754–55) (de Zambaur, *Manuel*, p. 40).

and Samarqand."

According to ['Alī]—a shaykh from the Banū Sadūs—Ḥamzah
b. Bīḍ:[641] Qutaybah acquired in Khurasan—in Soghd—a slave girl   [1247]
who was one of the descendants of Yazdajird. He said, "Do you
think that the son of this [girl] will be *hajīn?*"[642] They said, "Yes,
he will be *hajīn* through his father." He sent her to al-Ḥajjāj, who
sent her to al-Walīd; she bore him Yazīd b. al-Walīd.

According to ['Alī]—one of the Bāhilīs—Nahshal b. Yazīd—his
paternal uncle, who was contemporary with all that: When
Ghūrak saw Qutaybah's pressure against them, he wrote to the
king of al-Shāsh, the Ikhshād of Farghānah, and Khāqān, "We are
between you and the Arabs. If we are reached [by them], you will
be weaker.[643] Exert whatever strength you have." They took
stock and said, "We shall be outmaneuvered [if we use] our common people, for they do not have our ability. We, the grouping of
the kings, are the ones to be concerned with this matter. Choose
the sons of the kings and the people of valor from [among] the
young men of their kings, and let them go forth until they reach
Qutaybah's camp, which should be subjected to a night attack
while he is distracted with besieging the Soghdians."

They did [this], put in command a son of Khāqān's, and went
off, having agreed to make a night attack on the camp. [News of
this] reached Qutaybah, who chose people of valor and courage
and leading figures—among them Shu'bah b. Ẓuhayr[644] and
Zuhayr b. Ḥayyān; there were four hundred of them. He said to
them, "Your enemies have seen God's favor with you and His
support of you in your fighting and your contending. [In view of]
all that, God will give you mastery over them. They have decided
to use your heedlessness as an expedient and to attack you by
night, and have chosen their dihqāns and kings. You are the dihqāns and horsemen of the Arabs, and God has favored you with   [1248]
His religion, so do Him a good deed,[645] and you will thereby merit
reward, together with defense of your honor."

['Alī] said: Qutaybah set spies on the enemy [and was informed

---

641. *EI*², s.v.; Sezgin, *GAS*, vol. II, p. 333–34.
642. Baseborn, having an Arab father and a non-Arab slave mother.
643. So rendering *aḍ'af wa-adhall.*
644. Guidi renders this "Ẓahīr."
645. So transposing the Qur'ānic expression *ablāhu Allāhu balā'an ḥasanan.*

by them] until, when [the enemy] were near [enough] to him to be able to reach his camp in the course of the night, he brought in those whom he had chosen, spoke to them, exhorted them, and placed Ṣāliḥ b. Muslim in charge of them. They went out of the camp at sunset, proceeded [on their way], and stopped two parasangs from the camp on the road of the [enemy] described to them by [the spies]. Ṣāliḥ split his cavalry into groups, placing one in hiding on his right and one in hiding on his left; halfway—or two-thirds of the way—through the night, the enemy came, together, quickly, and silently. Ṣāliḥ stood with his cavalry, and when they saw him they attacked him. When spear thrusts were exchanged, the two hidden groups attacked from right and left, and we heard only battle cries. We have never seen people tougher than they.

According to [ʿAlī]—one of the Barājim—Zuhayr or Shuʿbah: We were repeatedly thrusting at them and smiting them when I discerned Qutaybah under the [cover of] night. I had struck a blow that had pleased me, and I looked toward Qutaybah and said, "What do you think, may you [be ransomed] by my father and mother?" He said, "Shut up, may God smash your mouth!" He continued: We killed them and only the [odd] stray escaped. We stayed, gathering plunder and cutting off heads, until morning; then we went to the camp, and I have never seen a group bring the like of what we brought. There was not a [single] man among us who did not hang up[646] a head known by name and [did not have] a prisoner in his bonds. He continued: We took the heads to Qutaybah, and he said, "May God reward you with good for [what you have done for] the religion and personal honor!" Qutaybah showed me regard, without articulating anything to me [by way of special compliment]; in the presenting of gifts and the showing of regard, he joined with me Ḥayyān al-ʿAdawī and Ḥulays al-Shaybānī, and I thought that he [must have] seen from the like of what he had seen from me. That [battle] broke the people of Soghd. They sought peace and offered tribute. [But Qutaybah] refused, saying, "I am going to avenge the blood of Ṭarkhūn, who was my mawlā and one of the people under my protection."

[The main authorities all] said: ʿAmr b. Muslim related on the authority of his father, who said: Qutaybah prolonged his stay,

[1249]

---

646. See n. 632 above.

and the breach was made at Samarqand. [Muslim?] said: A crier who was eloquent in Arabic called out, abusing Qutaybah.

['Amr b. Muslim?] said: 'Amr b. Abī Zahdam said: We were around Qutaybah. When we heard the abuse, we went out in haste and waited for a long time while he persisted in [his] abuse. I went to Qutaybah's tent and looked, and, there was Qutaybah, sitting with his knees bound to his chest (*muḥtab*[in]) by a wrapper, saying, as one talking to himself, "For how much longer, O Samarqand, will Satan nest in you? By God, in the morning I shall do my damnedest with your people." I departed to my companions and said, "How many intransigent souls from among us and them will die tomorrow!" and I told them [what he had said].

['Alī] said: As for Bāhilah, they say: Qutaybah journeyed, keeping the river on his right, until he arrived in Bukhārā. He rallied [the people of Bukhārā] with him and journeyed until, when he was at the city of Arbinjān[647]—the one from which Arbinjān saddlecloths come—Ghūrak, the lord of Soghd, engaged him with a large force of Turks and people from al-Shāsh and Farghānah. There took place skirmishes between them, without [any large-scale] fighting; the Muslims won all of these, and [the two sides then] desisted from fighting until they drew near to the city of Samarqand. At that point they joined in fighting: The Soghdians made an all-out charge on the Muslims, broke [their ranks, and] passed through their camp; then the Muslims wheeled round on them [and] pushed them back to their camp. God killed a large number of the polytheists; and [the Muslims] entered the city of Samarqand, [the population of which] made peace with them.

According to ['Alī]—the Bāhilīs—Ḥātim b. Abī Ṣaghīrah: I saw the cavalry on that day exchanging spear thrusts with the Muslims. Qutaybah had given the order on that day for his throne to be brought out, and he sat on it. [The enemy] exchanged spear thrusts with [the Muslims] until they got as far as Qutaybah, who was sitting with his knees up to his chest, [propping himself] with his sword; he stayed just like that, and the two wings of the Muslims swept in on those who had defeated the center, defeated them, and pushed them back to their camp. Many polytheists

[1250]

---

647. Also called Rabinjān, to the west of Samarqand (Barthold, *Turkestan*[3], p. 97).

were killed. [The Muslims] entered the city of Samarqand, [the population of which] made peace with them. Ghūrak prepared food and invited Qutaybah [to partake of it with him]; [Qutaybah] went to him with a number of his companions and, when he had finished lunch, [Qutaybah] asked [Ghūrak] to give him Samarqand. He said to the king, "Depart from it," and he did so; Qutaybah recited, "And that He destroyed ʿĀd, the ancient, and Thamūd, and He did not spare [them]."[648]

According to [ʿAlī]—Abū al-Dhayyāl—ʿUmar b. ʿAbdallāh al-Tamīmī: The person sent by Qutaybah to al-Ḥajjāj with [news of] the conquest of Samarqand related to me: I reached al-Ḥajjāj, and he sent me to Syria. I reached Syria, entered the mosque [of [1251] Damascus], and sat, [it being] before sunrise. Next to me was a blind man, and I asked him something about Syria. He said to me, "You are a stranger." I said, "Yes." He said, "Where are you from?" I said, "From Khurasan." He said, "What brought you?" and I told him. He said, "By Him Who sent Muḥammad with the truth, you have only[649] conquered it by perfidy. You, O people of Khurasan, are those who will strip the Banū Umayyah of their dominion, and pull Damascus down stone by stone."

[ʿAlī] said: Al-ʿAlāʾ b. Jarīr informed us: It has reached me that, when Qutaybah conquered Samarqand, he stood on its hill, looked at the people scattering in the meadows of Soghd, and recited the words of Ṭarafah (ṭawīl):[650]

And peoples pastured; had we not alighted
    at Makhshiyyah, they would have taken their
    camels off and their tents down.

[ʿAlī] said: Khālid b. al-Aṣfaḥ informed us: Al-Kumayt said (basīṭ):[651]

Samarqand was Yamanī for [many] years;
    now Muḍar are giving it a Qaysī lineage.

---

648. Qurʾān, 53:50–51 = 51–52.

649. Reading illā in place of the misprint in the text (which is noted in the Addenda et Emendanda).

650. This line is not to be found in Ṭarafah's Dīwān (ed. D. al-Khaṭīb and L. al-Ṣaqqāl, Damascus, 1975).

651. Judging by Shiʿr al-Kumayt, no. 188, the following verse survives only here and in Ibn al-Athīr.

['Alī] said: Abū al-Ḥasan al-Jushamī said: When Qutaybah made peace with the people of Soghd, he summoned Nahār b. Tawsi'ah and said, "[Well now,] O Nahār, what about your words (ṭawīl):[652]

The campaigning that brought riches nigh has ended,
    and generosity and munificence have died
    after al-Muhallab.
They have stayed at Marw al-Rūdh as two pledges
    at his sepulcher,
    and have been rendered totally absent from
    both east and west.

Is this campaigning, O Nahār?" [Nahār] said, "No, this is the congregation,[653] and I am he who says (ṭawīl):

Neither in our own lifetimes, nor before us,
    nor after us, is the like of Ibn Muslim.
He killed Turks hither and yon with his sword,
    and made abundant divisions of spoil among us,
    one division after another."

['Alī] said: Then Qutaybah set off, returning to Marw. He depu-   [1252]
ted 'Abdallāh b. Muslim[654] over Samarqand, and left with him massive [numbers of] troops and much war matériel, saying to him, "Do not let [any] polytheist enter any of Samarqand's gates without having a seal on his hand. If the clay has dried before he goes out, kill him. If you find on him a piece of iron, [or] a knife, [or] anything else, kill him. If you close the gate at night and find any one of them in [the city], kill him." Ka'b al-Ashqarī—or, it has been said: a man from Ju'fī—said (Khafīf):[655]

---

652. Cf. above, p. 32 and n. 144; Ibn A'tham (Futūḥ, vol. VII, pp. 241–42) wrong-ly takes the poet in question to have been Ka'b b. Ma'dān al-Ashqarī.

653. I.e., on the day of resurrection (reading al-ḥashr, as proposed in the Adden-da et Emendanda); cf. Ibn Qutaybah, al-Shi'r wa'l-shu'arā', p. 538; Ibn Khallikān, Wafayāt al-a'yān, vol. IV, p. 87.

654. According to al-Ya'qūbī (Ta'rīkh, vol. II, p. 344) and Ibn A'tham (Futūḥ, vol. VII, p. 246), Qutaybah appointed his brother 'Abd al-Raḥmān b. Muslim. It can be added that al-Ya'qūbī's account of this episode is rather muddled and that he thought that the peace was concluded in A.H. 94.

655. Thus, too, in Ibn Kathīr (Bidāyah, vol. IX, p. 86). The Kitāb al-'uyūn wa'l-ḥadā'iq (pp. 2–3) also says that the poet was Ka'b al-Ashqarī and cites all the following verses; but al-Balādhurī (Futūḥ, p. 421) says that the poet was al-Mukhtār b. Ka'b al-Ju'fī and cites only verse 3.

Every day Qutaybah gathers plunder
   and increases wealth even more
A Bāhilī who has been given a crown to wear until
   partings of the hair that were black have
   become gray.
He subdued Soghd with the squadrons until
   he left it stripped and prone.
The infant weeps at the loss of his father,
   and a pained father cries for his infant.
Whenever [Qutaybah] stops in, or reaches, a place,
   his cavalry leaves [its] mark there.

[ʿAlī] said: Qutaybah said, "This is [real] succession, not [just] successive killing of a couple of asses [*lā ʿidāʾ ʿayrayn*]," because he conquered Khwārazm and Samarqand in a single year. [The explanation of] that [expression is] that, when a horseman fells two asses in a single heat, people say, "He made a succession, one to the other, between the two asses."[656] Then [Qutaybah] departed from Samarqand and stayed at Marw. His governor over Khwārazm was Iyās b. ʿAbdallāh b. ʿAmr, over its military affairs (*ḥarb*)—he was weak—and over its taxation (*kharāj*) was ʿUbaydallāh b. Abī ʿUbaydallāh, the mawlā of the Banū Muslim.[657]

[ʿAlī] said: The people of Khwārazm thought Iyās to be weak and gathered together against him. ʿUbaydallāh wrote to Qutaybah, and Qutaybah sent ʿAbdallāh b. Muslim in the winter as governor, saying [to him], "Flog Iyās b. ʿAbdallāh and Ḥayyān al-Nabaṭī, and shave [their heads]. Draw ʿUbaydallāh b. ʿUbaydallāh, the mawlā of the Banū Muslim, close to you, and listen to him, for he is loyal." [ʿAbdallāh] went on until, when he was one stage from Khwārazm, Iyās was clandestinely informed and warned, and withdrew. ʿAbdallāh then arrived, took Ḥayyān, gave him a hundred lashes, and shaved [his head].

[ʿAlī] said: Then Qutaybah sent al-Mughīrah b. ʿAbdallāh with troops to Khwārazm, after ʿAbdallāh. [News of] that reached them, and, when, al-Mughīrah arrived, the sons of those whom

[1253]

---

656. Cf. Lane, *Lexicon*, p. 1978b, where my source of translational inspiration will be obvious.

657. According to al-Balādhurī (*Futūḥ*, p. 421), Qutaybah appointed over Khwārazm "his brother ʿUbaydallāh b. Muslim."

[the] Khwārazm Shāh had killed said, "We shall not help you," and he fled to the land of the Turks. Al-Mughīrah arrived, and took captives and killed. Those who survived made peace with him; he took the tax and went to Qutaybah, who appointed him over Nishapur.

In this year Mūsā b. Nuṣayr dismissed Ṭāriq b. Ziyād from al-Andalus and sent him to Toledo.

[Mūsā b. Nuṣayr's Dismissal of Ṭāriq b. Ziyād]

Muḥammad b. ʿUmar mentioned that Mūsā b. Nuṣayr became angry with Ṭāriq in the year 93 and went to him in Rajab of that year (April–May 712), accompanied by Ḥabīb b. ʿUqbah b. Nāfiʿ al-Fihrī. When he went off, he deputed over Ifrīqiyah his son, ʿAbdallāh b. Mūsā b. Nuṣayr. Mūsā crossed [the sea] to Ṭāriq with [a force of] ten thousand [men] and met him. [Ṭāriq] sought to please [1254] him, and he was pleased with him and accepted his excuse from him. [Mūsā] sent [Ṭāriq] from [where he was] to the city of Toledo, which was one of the great cities of al-Andalus, twenty days' [journey] from Cordova. There he acquired the table of Solomon the son of David, containing God knows how much [by way of] gold and jewels.[658]

[Muḥammad b. ʿUmar] said: In [this year] the people of Ifrīqiyah suffered a terrible drought. Mūsā b. Nuṣayr went out and prayed for rain,[659] making invocations until the middle of that day, and preaching a sermon to the people. When he wanted to step down, he was asked whether he was going to make an invocation to the Commander of the Faithful. He said, "This is not a day for that." They were given to drink that which sufficed them for a time.

In this year ʿUmar b. ʿAbd al-ʿAzīz was dismissed from Medina.

Why al-Walīd Dismissed [ʿUmar b. ʿAbd al-ʿAzīz]

The reason for that, according to what has been mentioned, is that ʿUmar b. ʿAbd al-ʿAzīz wrote to al-Walīd informing him of the harshness of al-Ḥajjāj toward the people of his governorship in Iraq, of his aggression toward them and his oppression of them,

---

658. Cf. al-Yaʿqūbī, Taʾrīkh, vol. II, p. 341.
659. See EI[2], s.v. Istiskāʾ.

without any right [on his part] or offense [on theirs], and that
reached al-Ḥajjāj, who held it against ʿUmar and wrote to al-
Walīd, "I have with me the deviant elements of the Iraqis and the
people of schism. They have emigrated from Iraq and have taken
refuge in Medina and Mecca. That [constitutes a point of] weakness." Al-Walīd wrote to al-Ḥajjāj, "Suggest to me [the names of]
two men," and [al-Ḥajjāj] wrote to him suggesting ʿUthmān b.
Ḥayyān[660] and Khālid b. ʿAbdallāh. Al-Walīd appointed Khālid
over Mecca, and ʿUthmān over Medina, and dismissed ʿUmar b.
ʿAbd al-ʿAzīz.

Muḥammad b. ʿUmar said: ʿUmar b. ʿAbd al-ʿAzīz went out of
Medina and stayed at al-Suwaydāʾ, saying to [his mawlā]
Muzāḥim, "Does it make you fearful that you are one of those
whom Ṭaybah has expelled?"[661]

[1255]   In this year ʿUmar b. ʿAbd al-ʿAzīz flogged Khubayb b. ʿAbdallāh
b. al-Zubayr on al-Walīd's order to him and poured on his head a
skin of cold water.[662]

Muḥammad b. ʿUmar mentioned that Abū al-Mulayḥ related to
him on the authority of someone who was present when ʿUmar b.
ʿAbd al-ʿAzīz gave Khubayb b. ʿAbdallāh b. al-Zubayr fifty lashes,
poured a skin of water on his head on a wintry day, and made him
stand at the door of the mosque; he stayed [there] all that day and
then died.

The leader of the pilgrimage in this year was ʿAbd al-ʿAzīz b. al-
Walīd b. ʿAbd al-Malik: Thus it was related to me by Aḥmad b.
Thābit on the authority of him who mentioned it on the authority of Isḥāq b. ʿĪsā on the authority of Abū Maʿshar. The governors
of the amṣār in this year were [the same as] the governors in the
preceding years, except for the case of Medina, where the governor was ʿUthmān b. Ḥayyān al-Murrī, who took over, so it has
been said, in Shaʿbān of the year 93 (May–June 712). As for al-

---

660. Caskel, Ǧamharat an-nasab, register.

661. The reference being to the [Prophetic] ḥadīth, "innahā Ṭaybah wa-innahā
tanfī al-khabath," "It is Ṭaybah (i.e., Medina) and it expels/will expel dross"
(Wensinck, Concordance, vol. IV, p. 69). Ibn al-Athīr spells it out: "When ʿUmar b.
ʿAbd al-ʿAzīz went out [of Medina], he said, 'I fear that I shall be one of those whom
Medina has expelled,' meaning by that the saying of the Messenger of God, may
God bless and preserve him, 'It will expel its dross.'"

662. Al-Yaʿqūbī explains (Taʾrīkh, vol. II, pp. 339–40) that Khubayb had objected
to the pulling down of the rooms of the wives of the Prophet (cf. above pp. 141–
42).

Wāqidī, he said that ʿUthmān reached Medina on Shawwāl 27 in the year 94 (July 26, 713). One of [the authorities] said: ʿUmar b. ʿAbd al-ʿAzīz departed from Medina, dismissed, in Shaʿbān of the year 93, and campaigned in [the same year]. When he went off, he deputed over it Abū Bakr b. Muḥammad b. ʿAmr b. Ḥazm al-Anṣārī. ʿUthmān b. Ḥayyān reached Medina on Shawwāl 27 (August 6, 712).

The
Events of the Year

94
(OCTOBER 7, 712–SEPTEMBER 25, 713)

Among them was the campaign of al-ʿAbbās b. al-Walīd in Byzantine territory. It has been said that he conquered Anṭākyah[663] in [this year].

[1256]   In [this year], according to what has been said, ʿAbd al-ʿAzīz b. al-Walīd campaigned in Byzantine territory until he reached Ghazālah; al-Walīd b. Hishām al-Muʿayṭī reached the land of Burj al-Ḥamām,[664] and Yazīd b. Abī Kabshah [reached] the land of Sūriyah.

In it there was an earthquake in Syria.

In it, too, al-Qāsim b. Muḥammad al-Thaqafī conquered the land of al-Hind.[665]

In [this year] Qutaybah campaigned in al-Shāsh and Farghānah

---

663. I.e., Antiocheia in Pisidia (Wellhausen, "Die Kämpfe der Araber," p. 437; Lilie, *Byzantinische Reaktion*, pp. 121, 134 [map]).

664. Not identified. As Wellhausen has pointed out ("Die Kämpfe der Araber," p. 437n.), it may be interchangeable with al-Yaʿqūbī's *"marj al-shaḥm"* (s.p.; *Taʾrīkh*, vol. II, p. 337), which was between Malaṭyah and al-Maṣṣīṣah.

665. I.e., parts of Sind. Clearly Muḥammad b. al-Qāsim should be understood in place of al-Qāsim b. Muḥammad (see above, p. 141).

until he reached Khujandah and Kāsān,[666] the two [principal] cities of Farghānah.[667]

Qutaybah's Campaign [in al-Shāsh and Farghānah]

'Alī b. Muḥammad said that Abū al-Fawāris al-Tamīmī informed
him on the authority of Māhān and Yūnus b. Abī Isḥāq that
Qutaybah campaigned in the year 94. When he crossed the river,
he imposed a levy of twenty thousand fighting men on the people
of Bukhārā, Kish, Nasaf, and Khwārazm. ['Alī] said: They went
with him to Soghd; they were then sent to al-Shāsh, while
[Qutaybah] himself went to Farghānah. He went as far as Khujandah, the people of which gathered against him and engaged him.
They fought several times, with the Muslims being victorious on
each occasion. One day [the Muslims] were unoccupied and rode
their horses [about, here and there]; one man went to the top of an
elevated place and said, "By God, I haven't seen [anything] like
today [for us to be caught] off guard. If there were any commotion
today, with us as spread about as I see, we would be shamefully
[defeated]." A man beside him said, "By no means; we are as 'Awf
b. al-Khari'[668] said (mutaqārib):

We betake ourselves to the land because of love   [1257]
    of engaging [in fighting],
    and we do not guard against a bird of omen
    when it flies;
Whether it be auspicious or inauspicious,
    either way we meet with prosperity."

Saḥbān Wā'il[669] said, mentioning their fighting at Khujandah
(kāmil):

Ask the horsemen in Khujandah,
    [who are] beneath sharp/slim spears,
"Wasn't I the one who used to gather them together

---

666. Reading this, as in Ms B, rather than Kāshān, as in the text; Kāshān is in
Jūzjān, not Farghānah (see Cornu).
667. Cf. Gibb, Arab Conquests, pp. 48–49.
668. Sezgin, GAS, vol. II, pp. 206–7.
669. The following verses are also given by Ibn Kathīr (Bidāyah, vol. IX, pp. 95–
96), who says that Ibn al-Jawzī says in his Munaẓẓam that Saḥbān died in the
caliphate of Mu'āwiyah some time after A.H. 50. Al-Ṭabarī makes no other reference to Saḥbān.

[again] when
    they were defeated, and came forward to fight?
Wasn't I the one who smote the head of
    the insolent and endured the spears?"
This, and you are the hero of all
    Qays, giving out on a large scale.
You have excelled Qays in generosity,
    [just as] your father did in past years.
The justice of your judgment among
    them in all money [matters] has become clear.
Your (pl.) manliness is complete and your (pl.)
    glory has risen up to the loftiest of mountains.

[ʿAlī] said: Then Qutaybah went to Kāsān,[670] the [principal] city of Farghānah, [where] he was joined by the troops he had sent to al-Shāsh, which they had conquered and most of which they had burnt; [from Kāsān,] Qutaybah departed to Marw. Al-Ḥajjāj wrote to Muḥammad b. al-Qāsim, "Send such Iraqis as you have with you to Qutaybah, and send to (i.e., with) them Jahm b. Zaḥr b. Qays, for he is better with Iraqis than with Syrians." Muḥammad was fond of Jahm b. Zaḥr; when Jahm bade him farewell, he wept and said, "O Jahm, [this is] the [moment of] parting." [Jahm] said, "It cannot be avoided." [ʿAlī] said: [Jahm] reached Qutaybah in the year 95 (713–14).

[1258]   In this year ʿUthmān b. Ḥayyān al-Murrī arrived in Medina as governor for al-Walīd b. ʿAbd al-Malik.

[ʿUthmān b. Ḥayyān al-Murrī's] Governorship

We have already mentioned the reason for al-Walīd's dismissal of ʿUmar b. ʿAbd al-ʿAzīz from Medina and Mecca and his appointment of ʿUthmān b. Ḥayyān as amīr of Medina.

Muḥammad b. ʿUmar claimed that ʿUthmān reached Medina as amīr on 27 Shawwāl in the year 94 (July 26, 713) and stopped there at Dār Marwān,[671] saying, "By God, [this is] a repellent place;[672] he who is [really] deceived is he who is deceived by you"; and he placed Abū Bakr b. Ḥazm in charge of the judiciary.

---

670. See n. 666 above.
671. See above, n. 447.
672. So rendering miẓʿān: See the *Glossarium*.

According to Muḥammad b. ʿUmar—Muḥammad b. ʿAbdallāh b. Abī Ḥurrah—his paternal uncle: I saw ʿUthmān b. Ḥayyān take Riyāḥ b. ʿUbaydallāh and Munqidh al-ʿIrāqī; he imprisoned them, punished them, and then sent them in neck collars[673] to al-Ḥajjāj b. Yūsuf. He let no Iraqi, whether a merchant or anyone else, [stay] in Medina. He ordered [all of] them out, from every place [in the area under his control], and I saw them in neck collars. He hounded the nonconformists and arrested Hayṣam, on whom he inflicted amputation,[674] and Manḥūr; the two of them were from Khawārij.

[The same authority] said: I heard [ʿUthmān] deliver a sermon on the pulpit, saying, "O people, we have found you, both long since and more recently, to be insincere to the Commander of the Faithful. [Now] there have taken refuge with you those who will increase your unsoundness. The people in Iraq are people of schism and hypocrisy. By God, they are the nest of hypocrisy and the egg that split apart and produced it! By God, I have never put an Iraqi to the test but that I have found him who thinks most of himself to be him who says about the family of Abū Ṭālib what he says.[675] They are not [in reality] partisans of [the family of Abū Ṭālib]; [rather,] they are enemies of them and of [persons] other than them. Because of what God desires by way of spilling their blood, I shall not, by God, be brought anyone who has given refuge to any one of them, or has rented him a house, or has accommodated him, but that I shall demolish his house and shall cause to befall him what he deserves. When ʿUmar b. al-Khaṭṭāb garrisoned[676] the territories, striving after what was good for his subjects, those who wanted to make holy war would stop by him and seek his advice, [asking,] 'Is Syria dearer to you or Iraq?' and he would say, 'Syria is dearer to me. I think that Iraq is an incurable disease; in it Satan has hatched [his brood] and they have made things difficult for me.[677] I can see myself scattering them

[1259]

---

673. See n. 303 above.

674. The text reads simply *fa-qaṭaʿahu*. According to the *Kitāb al-ʿuyūn waʾl-ḥadāʾiq* (p. 16), ʿUthmān was ordered by al-Walīd to cut off his hand and his foot and then kill him.

675. Apparently a roundabout way of suggesting that the most arrogant and hypocritical of the Iraqis professed themselves to be extreme philo-Ṭālibids.

676. So rendering *maṣṣara*.

677. *La-qad aʿḍalū bī*: Lane, *Lexicon*, p. 2074, renders this "[the people of El-Koofeh have caused that] the means of effecting my object in their affair . . . have

in the [various] territories. [But] then I say, "If I were to scatter them, they would corrupt those into whose presence they enter by [using] argument and contention, [saying,] 'How?' and 'Why?' and by [their] swiftness of entering into sedition.'" If they are put to the test with swords, no superiority on their part emerges. They did no good for ʿUthmān, who met with death and disaster from them. They were the first of the people to occasion this enormous breach, undoing the loops of Islam one by one and spoiling [its] territories. By God, I shall draw nearer to God with everything I do to them, because of what I know of their view[s] and their tenets. Then the Commander of the Faithful Muʿāwiyah took charge of them; he cajoled them and they did him no good. [Next,] a real man[678] took charge of them, flogging them and extending [his] sword over them; he made them fearful, and they became orderly for him, whether willingly or otherwise, that being because he tested them and knew them. O people, by God, we have never considered [any] rallying cry to be the like of security; nor have we considered [any] basis [for life] to be worse than fear. So cleave to obedience. O people of Medina, I have experience of disobedience. By God, you are not people given to

[1260]   fighting; keep to your houses and grit your teeth. For I have sent to your gathering (*majālis*) those who will hear [what you say] and will inform me about you. [Something] other than unnecessary talk is more requisite for you. Leave off the stigmatizing of governors; for [such stigmatizing causes] the situation gradually to deteriorate, until sedition comes about. Sedition is an affliction; seditions destroy the religion, property, and children."

According to Muḥammad b. ʿUmar—Khālid b. al-Qāsim—Saʿīd b. ʿAmr al-Anṣārī: I saw ʿUthmān b. Ḥayyān's crier call out among us, "O Banū Umayyah b. Zayd,[679] God's protection will be removed from anyone who gives refuge to an Iraqi." There was with us a Baṣran of some merit, one of the pious people, called Abū Sawādah, and he said, "By God, I do not want to occasion something unpleasant for you. Convey me to somewhere where I may

---

become strait to me . . . and the treating them with gentleness has become difficult to me."

678. *Rajul min al-nās*: Presumably, al-Ḥajjāj is meant.

679. Presumably, the Aws and Anṣār clan of Umayyah b. Zayd b. Mālik is meant.

be safe." I said, "There is no good for you in going out. God will protect both you and us." [Sa'īd b. 'Amr] continued: I took him into my house, and [news of that] reached 'Uthmān b. Ḥayyān, who sent guards. I removed him to my brother's house, and [the guards] came across nothing; [the person] who had got me into trouble was an enemy. I said to the amīr, "May God cause the amīr to prosper! He is bringing [to your attention] a falsehood. Do not punish on the basis of it." He continued: ['Uthmān] gave the person who had got me into trouble twenty lashes. We got the Iraqi out. He used to perform the ritual prayer with us, not missing a single day. The people of our house showed kindness to him and said to him, "We shall die in defense of you." He did not leave until 'Uthmān was dismissed.

According to Muḥammad b. 'Umar—'Abd al-Ḥakīm[680] b. 'Abdallāh b. Abī Farwah: Al-Walīd sent 'Uthmān b. Ḥayyān to   [1261] Medina to expel those Iraqis who were there and to scatter the nonconformists and those who controlled them and those who espoused their cause. He did not send him as governor; he neither ascended the pulpit nor gave a sermon on it. When ['Uthmān] had done what he did to the Iraqis and to Manḥūr and others, [al-Walīd] established him over Medina [as governor], and he [thenceforward] used to ascend the pulpit.

In this year al-Ḥajjāj killed Saʿīd b. Jubayr.[681]

The Report of [Saʿīd b. Jubayr's] Death

The reason why al-Ḥajjāj killed him was that he had gone against [al-Ḥajjāj], together with 'Abd al-Raḥmān b. Muḥammad b. al-Ashʿath. Al-Ḥajjāj had put [Saʿīd] in charge of the troops' stipends when he sent 'Abd al-Raḥmān to fight the Zunbīl. When 'Abd al-Raḥmān disavowed al-Ḥajjāj, Saʿīd was among those who disavowed him with him; and, when 'Abd al-Raḥmān was defeated and fled to the Zunbīl's country, Saʿīd [also] fled.

According to Abū Kurayb—Abū Bakr b. 'Ayyāsh: Al-Ḥajjāj wrote to so-and-so, who was in charge of Iṣbahān—and Saʿīd was [there]: Abū Jaʿfar said: I think that, when he fled from al-Ḥajjāj,

---

680. Following the *Addenda et Emendanda*.
681. For other versions, see Sayed, *Revolte*, p. 353 and n. 546 thereto.

he went to Iṣbahān. [Al-Ḥajjāj] wrote to [this governor], "Saʿīd is with you. Arrest him." The order came to a man who held himself aloof from doing wrong, and he sent [word] to Saʿīd, "Move yourself away from me." Saʿīd did so and went to Ādharbayjān, where he remained [for some time]. Then he felt that he had been there long enough, and he made the lesser pilgrimage; he went out to Mecca and stayed there. [In Mecca] there were people of his sort, lying low and not revealing their names.

[1262]   [Abū Kurayb?] continued: Abū Ḥusayn said, relating this to us: It reached us that so-and-so had been made amīr of Mecca, and I said to [Saʿīd], "O Saʿīd, this man cannot be trusted; he is a man of evil nature, and I am on my guard against him for you. Go off! Depart!" [Saʿīd] said, "O Abū Ḥusayn, by God, I have been a fugitive until I have become ashamed before God. Let there come to me what God has prescribed for me." I said, "By God, I think that you are happy (saʿīd), just as your mother named you." [Abū Ḥusayn] continued: That man came to Mecca and sent [for Saʿīd], who was arrested. Then he treated [Saʿīd] gently and spoke to him and tried him this way and that.[682]

According to Abū ʿĀsim—ʿAmr b. Qays: Al-Ḥajjāj wrote to al-Walīd, "The people of hypocrisy and schism have taken refuge in Mecca. If the Commander of the Faithful sees fit to allow me [to get] at them[, that will be a good thing]." Al-Walīd wrote to Khālid b. ʿAbdallāh al-Qasrī, who arrested ʿAṭāʾ, Saʿīd b. Jubayr, Mujāhid, Ṭalq b. Ḥabīb, and ʿAmr b. Dīnār.[683] As for ʿAmr b. Dīnār and ʿAṭāʾ, they were released, since they were Meccans. As for the others, they were sent by [Khālid] to al-Ḥajjāj; Ṭalq died on th eway, Mujāhid was held in prison until al-Ḥajjāj died, and Saʿīd b. Jubayr was killed.

According to Abū Kurayb—Abū Bakr—al-Ashjaʿī: When the two guards brought Saʿīd b. Jubayr, he was accommodated in a house near to al-Rabadhah.[684] One of the guards went off to answer a call of nature, while the other remained. The one who was with [Saʿīd] woke up, having had a dream, and said, "O Saʿīd, by

---

682. Reading yudīruhu, as proposed by the Addenda et Emendanda.

683. ʿAṭāʾ b. Abī Rabāḥ (d. 114/732), Mujāhid b. Jabr (d.±102/721), ʿAmr b. Dīnār (d.125/742)—see Juynboll, Muslim Tradition, p. 40; on Ṭalq, cf. Ibn Ḥajar, Tahdhīb, vol. V, pp. 31–32.

684. Near Dhāt al-ʿIrq on the road from Fayd to Mecca (Yāqūt, Muʿjam, vol. II, p. 749); see S. A. A. al-Rashid, Al-Rabadhah. A Portrait of Early Islamic Civilization in Saudi Arabia, Riyadh, 1985.

God, I'll have nothing to do with killing you. In my dream I was
told, 'Woe to you, have nothing to do with killing Saʿīd b. Jubayr.'   [1263]
Go where you want. I shall never pursue you." Saʿīd said, "I hope
for well-being and [keep on] hoping," and he refused. Then [the
other guard] came, and on the next day he had a similar dream and
was told, "Have nothing to do with killing Saʿīd." He said, "O
Saʿīd, go where you wish. I'll have nothing to do with killing
you," [and he kept on saying this?] until he brought him to his
house; the house in which Saʿīd was is this house of theirs.⁶⁸⁵

According to Abū Kurayb—Abū Bakr—Yazīd b. Abī Ziyād, the
mawlā of the Banū Hāshim: I entered into [Saʿīd's] presence in
this house of Saʿīd's, and he was brought in fettered. Then the
Kūfan *qurrāʾ* entered into his presence. I said, "O Abū ʿAbdallāh,
did he speak to you?" ⁶⁸⁶ He said, "Yes, by God," laughing and
talking to us, with a little daughter of his on his lap. She glanced
and saw the fetter, and wept. I heard him say, "My daughter, be
careful not to take [it] as a bad omen," and, by God, that was hard
on him. We followed him, saying goodbye to him, until we got to
the bridge with him. The two guards said, "We shall never take
him across until he gives us a surety. We are afraid that he may
drown himself." [Yazīd] continued: We said, "Saʿīd drown himself?" but they did not cross until we made ourselves responsible
for him.

According to Wahb b. Jarīr—his father—al-Faḍl b. Suwayd: Al-
Ḥajjāj sent me off for something. Saʿīd b. Jubayr was brought [in
my absence], and I then returned and said [to myself], "I'll see   [1264]
what [al-Ḥajjāj] does," and I stood by al-Ḥajjāj's head. Al-Ḥajjāj
said to him, "O Saʿīd, did I not cause you to partake of my trust?
Did I not appoint you? Did I not do [such-and-such]?" until I
thought that he was going to let him go. [Saʿīd] said, "Yes." "Then
what induced you to go against me?" [Saʿīd] said, "It was enjoined
upon me [to do so]." [The narrator] continued: [At this, al-Ḥajjāj]
flew into a rage and said, "Hah! You thought that the enjoining of
the Enemy of the Merciful⁶⁸⁷ [constituted] a duty incumbent
upon you, and you did not think that you had any duty to God, to
the Commander of the Faithful, and to me. Behead him!" and he

---

685. Presumably, the narrator was in, or in sight of, the relevant house at this
juncture in his narrative. The text is rather tangled here.
686. The identity of the subject here is unclear.
687. *ʿAduww al-raḥmān*: Cf. above, n. 95.

was beheaded; his head fell, attired in a small white item of headgear.

According to Abū Ghassān Mālik b. Ismāʿīl—Khalaf b. Khalīfah—a man who said: When Saʿīd b. Jubayr was killed and his head fell, he called out "There is no god but God" three times; the first time he articulated it clearly, and the next two times he said something like that, without clear articulation.

According to Abū Bakr[688] al-Bāhilī—Anas b. Abī Shaykh: When al-Ḥajjāj was brought Saʿīd b.Jubayr, he said, "May God curse the son of the Christian woman"—[Anas] said: Meaning Khālid al-Qasrī, who had sent [Saʿīd] from Mecca—"didn't I know the place where he was? Yes, by God, and the [very] house in Mecca where he was." The he advanced upon Saʿīd and said, "What induced you to go out against me?" He said, "May God cause the amīr to prosper, I am simply a Muslim man who makes a mistake on one occasion and gets it right on another." [Anas] continued: Al-Ḥajjāj cheered up, and his face brightened, and he hoped that he might find a way out of [this] situation. [Anas] continued: Then he came back at [Saʿīd] about something, and Saʿīd said, "But I was bound by an oath of allegiance to [ʿAbd al-Raḥmān]." [Anas] continued: Then [al-Ḥajjāj] became filled with rage, to the extent that one of the ends of his *ridāʾ*[689] fell from his shoulder, and he said, "O Saʿīd, did I not go to Mecca and kill Ibn al-Zubayr, and then take its people's oath of allegiance and your oath of allegiance to the Commander of the Faithful, ʿAbd al-Malik?" He said, "Yes." [Al-Ḥajjāj] said, "And did I not then arrive in al-Kūfah as governor of Iraq and renew the oath of allegiance to the Commander of the Faithful and take your oath of allegiance to him for a second time?" He said, "Yes." [Al-Ḥajjāj] said, "And you then forswear two oaths of allegiance to the Commander of the Faithful and fulfill one to the weaver, the son of the weaver? Behead him!" [Anas?] said: It was [Saʿīd] that Jarīr meant with his words (*kāmil*):[690]

[1265]

How many a breaker of two oaths of allegiance have you left,
  with his beard dyed with the blood of [his]
  jugular veins.

---

688. Following the *Addenda et Emendanda.*
689. See above, n. 596.
690. *Dīwān,* p. 90.

According to ʿAttāb b. Bishr—Sālim al-Afṭas: Al-Ḥajjāj was brought Saʿīd b. Jubayr when he was about to go riding and had put one of his feet in the stirrup.[691] He said, "By God, I shall not ride until you occupy your sitting place in hellfire. Behead him!" and he was beheaded. Then al-Ḥajjāj's mind became confused on the spot, and he started saying, "Our fetters, our fetters."[692] [The people present] thought that he was referring to the fetters on Saʿīd b. Jubayr; they cut his legs at the knees and removed the fetters.

Muḥammad b. Ḥātim said: ʿAbd al-Malik b. ʿAbdallāh related to us on the authority of Hilāl b. Khabbāb:[693] Saʿīd b. Jubayr was brought to al-Ḥajjāj, who said [to him], "Did you write to Muṣʿab b. al-Zubayr?" He said, "No, Muṣʿab wrote to me." [Al-Ḥajjāj] said, "By God, I shall kill you." [Saʿīd] said, "In that case I shall be happy (saʿīd), just as my mother named me."

[The narrator] said: [Al-Ḥajjāj] killed him and then [himself] lasted only about forty days after him. When he slept, he would see [Saʿīd] in his sleep, taking hold of the front part of his clothing and saying, "O enemy of God, what did you kill me for?" and he would say, "What concern is Saʿīd b. Jubayr of mine? What concern is Saʿīd b. Jubayr of mine?"

Abū Jaʿfar said: This year was called the year of the specialists in religious law (fuqahāʾ), [for] in it most of the Medinan fuqahāʾ died, [starting with] ʿAlī b. al-Ḥusayn, peace be upon him, at the beginning of it, then ʿUrwah b. al-Zubayr, and then Saʿīd b. al-Musayyab and Abū Bakr b. ʿAbd al-Raḥmān b. al-Ḥārith b. Hishām.[694]

In this year al-Walīd placed Sulaymān b. Ḥabīb[695] in charge of the judiciary in Syria.

There is disagreement about who led the pilgrimage in this year. Abū Maʿshar said, according to what Aḥmad b. Thābit related to me on the authority of him who mentioned it on the author-

[1266]

---

691. Thus rendering simply al-gharz aw al-rikāb.

692. Quyūdunā quyūdunā, and thus, too, in the Kitāb al-ʿuyūn wa'l-ḥadāʾiq (p. 10) and Ibn Kathīr (Bidāyah, vol. IX, p. 97); the variants suggest an alternative possible reading qayyidūnā qayyidūnā, "fetter us, fetter us!"

693. Following the Addenda et Emendanda.

694. Cf. Juynboll, Muslim Tradition, pp. 41–42.

695. Al-Muḥāribī. Cf. Wakīʿ, Akhbār al-quḍāh, vol. III, pp. 210–12, where we are told that he was ʿAbd al-Malik's judge over Ḥimṣ and that he was a judge for ʿUmar II and Hishām, but where no mention is made of al-Walīd.

ity of Isḥāq b. ʿĪsā on his (Abū Maʿshar's) authority: Maslamah b. ʿAbd al-Malik led the pilgrimage in the year 94. [However,] al-Wāqidī said: In the year 94 ʿAbd al-ʿAzīz b. al-Walīd b. ʿAbd al-Malik led the pilgrimage. [Al-Wāqidī] added: It is said [that] Maslamah b. ʿAbd al-Malik [did so].

The governor of Mecca in [this year] was Khālid b. ʿAbdallāh al-Qasrī; over Medina was ʿUthmān b. Ḥayyān al-Murrī; over al-Kūfah was Ziyād b. Jarīr, with Abū Bakr b. Abī Mūsā in charge of the judiciary; over al-Baṣrah was al-Jarrāḥ b. ʿAbdallāh, with ʿAbd al-Raḥmān b. Udhaynah over the judiciary; over Khurasan was Qutaybah b. Muslim; and over Egypt was Qurrah b. Sharīk. Over Iraq and the East in its entirety was al-Ḥajjāj.

The
Events of the Year

95

(SEPTEMBER 26, 713–SEPTEMBER 15, 714)

In it there took place the campaign of al-ʿAbbās b. al-Walīd b. ʿAbd
al-Malik in Byzantine territory. At his hands God conquered   [1267]
three fortresses, according to what has been said, they being
Ṭūlus, al-Marzbānayn,[696] and Hiraqlah.

In it the rest of al-Hind was conquered, except for al-Kayraj and
al-Mandal.[697]

In it Wāsiṭ al-Qaṣab was built, in the month of Ramaḍān (May–
June 714).

In it Mūsā b. Nuṣayr left al-Andalus for Ifrīqiyah. He performed
the rites of the Feast of the Sacrifice (10 Dhū al-Ḥijjah/August 26,
714) at Qaṣr al-Māʾ, one [Arab] mile from al-Qayrawān.

In it Qutaybah b. Muslim campaigned against al-Shāsh.

---

696. It remains for these two places to be identified with any certainty (Brooks,
"The Arabs in Asia Minor," p. 194; Lilie, *Byzantinische Reaktion*, p. 121).

697. Yāqūt knows Mandal (sic) as a place in al-Hind from which fine aloes come
(*Muʿjam*, vol. IV, p. 660); he does not mention al-Kayraj. Both places figure in al-
Balādhurī's account of Arab operations in Sind (*Futūḥ*, pp. 440, 442).

The Report of [Qutaybah's] Campaign [in al-Shāsh]

The narrative returns to that of ʿAlī b. Muḥammad, who said: Al-Ḥajjāj sent from Iraq an army that joined Qutaybah in the year 95; and [Qutaybah] went on campaign. When he was at al-Shāsh or at Kushmāhan,[698] [news of] the death of al-Ḥajjāj in Shawwāl reached him. That grieved him; he turned back to Marw and recited (*ṭawīl*):[699]

> By my life, how good is the man from the Āl Jaʿfar,
>   who was caught by snares in Ḥawrān.
> If you live, I shall not tire of my [own] life, and if you die,
>   there will be no avail in life after your death.

[ʿAlī b. Muḥammad] said: He returned with [his army] and dispersed them; he left some people in Bukhārā and sent some people to Kish and Nasaf. Then he reached Marw and stayed there. There came to him al-Walīd's letter: "The Commander of the Faithful knows your testing and your striving in the waging of holy war against the enemies of the Muslims, and the Commander of the Faithful raises you[r station] and does to you what ought to be done. [Now] consolidate your campaigns and await the reward of your Lord; let not your letters to the Commander of the Faithful fall short, so that it may be as if I can see your territory and the frontier on which you are."

[1268]

In [this year] al-Ḥajjāj b. Yūsuf died in Shawwāl (mid-June–mid-July 713), aged fifty-four years, also put at fifty-three years; it has [also] been said that his death took place in this year on 25 Ramaḍān (June 13, 713).

In it, when death was imminent, al-Ḥajjāj deputed over the ritual prayer his son ʿAbdallāh b. al-Ḥajjāj. According to al-Wāqidī, al-Ḥajjāj's rule over Iraq lasted for twenty years.

In this year al-ʿAbbās b. al-Walīd conquered Qinnasrīn.[700]

---

698. One stage from Marw on the Bukhārā road (Le Strange, *Lands of the Eastern Caliphate*, p. 400).

699. The poet is al-Ḥuṭayʾah. Cf. *Aghānī*², vol. XVI, p. 295 (where an extra verse is given); Yāqūt, *Muʿjam*, vol. II, p. 358 (where two extra verses are given).

700. This cannot be right (and is ignored by Brooks, Wellhausen, and Lilie); there is no evidence that Qinnasrīn (see *EI*², s.v. Ḳinnasrīn) had fallen out of Arab control. Possibly this is a mangled version of the report that al-ʿAbbās raised levies from Qinnasrīn (see al-Balādhurī, *Futūḥ*, p. 189).

In it, al-Waḍḍāḥī[701] and about one thousand men with him were killed in Byzantine territory.

In it, according to what has been mentioned, al-Manṣūr, ʿAbdallāh b. Muḥammad b. ʿAlī was born.

In it al-Walīd b. ʿAbd al-Malik put Yazīd b. Abī Kabshah in charge of military affairs (ḥarb) and civilian affairs (ṣalāt) in the two miṣrs of al-Kūfah and al-Baṣrah; and he put Yazīd b. Abī Muslim in charge of their taxation (kharāj). And it has been said that, when his death was imminent, al-Ḥajjāj deputed Yazīd b. Abī Kabshah over the military affairs of the two places and [over] the civilian affairs of their people and Yazīd b. Abī Muslim over their taxation and [that], after the death of al-Ḥajjāj, al-Walīd confirmed them [in their positions] over what al-Ḥajjāj had depu-   [1269] ted them over. He did the same with all of al-Ḥajjāj's governors; after [his death], he confirmed them [in their positions] over the governorships they occupied during his lifetime.

The leader of the pilgrimage in this year was Bishr b. al-Walīd b. ʿAbd al-Malik: Thus it was related to me by Aḥmad b. Thābit on the authority of him who mentioned it on the authority of Isḥāq b. ʿĪsā on the authority of Abū Maʿshar; and al-Wāqidī said the same. The governors of the amṣār in this year were the same as those who were [governors] in the preceding year, except for al-Kūfah and al-Baṣrah, which were joined to those whom I have mentioned, after the death of al-Ḥajjāj.

---

701. This (together with the parallel reference in Ibn al-Athīr) appears to be the sole reference to him; presumably, he was one of the lieutenants of al-Waḍḍāḥ, the Berber freedman of ʿAbd al-Malik who commanded the force known as the Waḍ-ḍāḥiyyah (Crone, *Slaves on Horses*, p. 38).

   The
Events of the Year

96

(September 16, 714–September 4, 715)

In it there took place, according to what al-Wāqidī said, the
winter campaign of Bishr b. al-Walīd; he returned after al-Walīd
had died.

[The Death of al-Walīd b. ʿAbd al-Malik]

In it there took the place the death of al-Walīd b. ʿAbd al-Malik on
Saturday in the middle of Jumādā II in the year 96 (late February
715), according to what all the biographers (ahl al-siyar) say.
There has been disagreement about the length of his caliphate.
According to Ibn Wahb—Yūnus—al-Zuhrī: Al-Walīd ruled for
ten years less one month. According to Aḥmad b. Thābit—Isḥāq
b. ʿĪsā—Abū Maʿshar: The caliphate of al-Walīd lasted for nine
[1270]   years and seven months. Hishām b. Muḥammad said: The rule of
al-Walīd lasted for eight years and six months. Al-Wāqidī said:
His caliphate lasted for nine years, eight months, and two nights.
There has also been disagreement about the length of his life.
   Muḥammad b. ʿUmar said: He died at Damascus aged forty-six
years and six months. Hishām b. Muḥammad said: He died aged
forty-five. ʿAlī b. Muḥammad said: He died aged forty-two and a

few months. 'Alī said: The death of al-Walīd took place at Dayr Murrān;[702] he was buried outside Bāb al-Ṣaghīr,[703] and it has been said: in the al-Farādīs graveyards.[704] And it has [also] been said that he died aged forty-seven.

According to what 'Alī said, he had nineteen sons: 'Abd al-'Azīz, Muḥammad, al-'Abbās, Ibrāhīm, Tammām, Khālid, 'Abd al-Raḥmān, Mubashshir, Masrūr, Abū 'Ubaydah, Ṣadaqah, Manṣūr, Marwān, 'Anbasah, 'Umar, Rawḥ, Bishr, Yazīd, and Yaḥyā. The mother of 'Abd al-'Azīz and Muḥammad was Umm al-Banīn bt. 'Abd al-'Azīz b. Marwān, and the mother of Abū 'Ubaydah was a Fazāriyyah; the rest of [the sons] were by various mothers.[705]

Report of Some of What He Did

[1271]

According to 'Umar [b. Shabbah]—'Alī: In the opinion of the Syrians, al-Walīd b. 'Abd al-Malik was the worthiest of their caliphs. He built mosques—the mosque of Damascus and the mosque of Medina—set up pulpits,[706] gave out to the people, and gave to those afflicted with elephantiasis, telling them not to beg from the people; he gave every cripple a servant and every blind person a guide. During his rule massive conquests were effected: Mūsā b. Nuṣayr conquered al-Andalus, Qutaybah conquered Kāshghar, and Muḥammad b. al-Qāsim conquered al-Hind. [The narrator] continued: Al-Walīd would stop by at the greengrocer's, take a bunch of greens, and say, "How much is this?" [The greengrocer] would say, "[One] *fals*,"[707] and [al-Walīd] would say, "Put more [greens] in it."

[The narrator] continued: A man from the Banū Makhzūm came to him asking him [for help] in respect of a debt of his. [Al-Walīd] said, "Yes, if you are deserving of that." [The Makhzūmī] said, "O Commander of the Faithful, how can I not be deserving

---

702. A monastery near Damascus (see *EI²*, s.v.).

703. A gate on the south side of Damascus (*EI²*, s.v. Dimashḳ, vol. II, p. 279a; for the graveyard in question, p. 281a).

704. Yāqūt (*Mu'jam*, vol. III, p. 862) says that al-Farādīs is "a place near Damascus"; presumably, what is meant here is the graveyard near the Bāb al-Farādīs, on the north side of Damascus (*EI²*, s.v. Dimashḳ, vol. II, pp. 279a, 281a).

705. Cf. *Kitāb al-'uyūn wa'l-ḥadā'iq*, p. 12; Ibn 'Abd Rabbihi, *'Iqd*, vol. IV, p. 422; al-Mas'ūdī, *Murūj*, vol. V, p. 361 = par. 2114.

706. Reading *al-manābir* with the *'Iqd* (vol. IV, p. 424); the text has *al-manār*.

707. A copper or bronze coin (*EI²*, s.v.).

of that, given my relationship [to you]?"[708] [Al-Walīd] said, "Have you recited the Qurʾān?" He said, "No." [Al-Walīd] said, "Draw near to me." He drew near, and al-Walīd knocked off his turban with a rod he had in his hand and struck him several times with it; he said to a man [in attendance], "Keep this [fellow] with you, and do not let him part from you until he has recited the Qurʾān."

ʿUthmān b. Yazīd b. Khālid b. ʿAbdallāh b. Khālid b. Asīd[709] betook himself to [al-Walīd] and said, "O Commander of the Faithful, I have a debt." [Al-Walīd] said, "Have you recited the Qurʾān?" He said, "Yes," and [al-Walīd] asked him to recite ten verses from [the Sūrah of] the Spoils and ten from Repentance. He did so, and [al-Walīd] said, "Yes, we'll pay up for you, and we shall make close our ties of relationship thereby."

[1272]   [The narrator] continued: Al-Walīd became ill and fell unconscious. He remained most of that day thought by [those who were in attendance] to be dead. He was wept over, and the official couriers went off with [news of] his death. When a messenger reached al-Ḥajjāj, [the latter] said, "We belong to God and to Him shall we return!" and called for a rope, which was tied to his hand and then secured to a pillar; he said, "O God, do not empower over me one who has no mercy; how often have I asked you to make my death [take place] before his!" and he began to make invocations. He was thus engaged when an official courier reached him with [the news of al-Walīd's] regaining of consciousness.

ʿAlī said: When al-Walīd regained consciousness, he said, "No one will be happier at the well-being of the Commander of the Faithful than al-Ḥajjāj." ʿUmar b. ʿAbd al-ʿAzīz said, "How great is God's bounty to us through your well-being! In my mind's eye I envisage a letter coming to you from al-Ḥajjāj, in which he mentions that, when [news of] your recovery reached him, he sank to the ground prostrating himself to God, freed every mamlūk of his, and sent out [as gifts] bottles of Indian preserved fruit." A few days later there arrived a letter saying just that.

[ʿAlī] said: Al-Ḥajjāj did not die before becoming burdensome to

---

708. Presumably, because the mother of Hishām, al-Walīd's brother, was a Makhzūmiyyah.

709. Of the Banū Abī'l-ʿĪṣ of ʿAbd Shams of Quraysh (see Caskel, *Ǧamharat an-nasab*, chart 8).

al-Walīd. A servant of al-Walīd's said: One day I was washing al-Walīd for lunch. He stretched out his hand, and I began pouring the water on him; he was inattentive, the water was flowing, and I couldn't speak. Then he splashed the water in my face and said, "Are you dozing?" and he raised his head up to me and said, "You don't know what happened last night?" I said, "No." He said, "Woe to you! Al-Ḥajjāj died." I said, "We belong to Him and to Him shall we return!" He said, "Be quiet. It wouldn't please your master [any more] if he had an apple in his hand to smell."

ʿAlī said: Al-Walīd was an enthusiast for building and making constructions and estates. When people met in his time, they would ask one another about building and constructions. Then there took charge Sulaymān, who was an enthusiast for sexual intercourse and food, and people took to asking one another about coupling and slave girls; and, when ʿUmar b. ʿAbd al-ʿAzīz took charge, they would meet, and one man would say to another "What is your *wird*[710] tonight? How much of the Qurʾān have you memorized? When will you complete memorizing [it]? When did you complete memorizing [it]? For how much of the month will you fast?" Jarīr said, elegizing al-Walīd (*basīṭ*):[711]

[1273]

O eye, weep copious tears aroused by remembrance;
    after today there is no point in your tears' being stored.
The Caliph's noble qualities have been concealed by
    earth in which a burial niche has been dug,
    a niche the side of which inclines.
When the catastrophe had become clear, his sons were
    like stars whose central moon has fallen.
They were all [together]; neither ʿAbd al-ʿAzīz,
    nor Rawḥ, nor ʿUmar, repelled his fate.

According to ʿUmar—ʿAlī: Al-Walīd b. ʿAbd al-Malik made the pilgrimage, and Muḥammad b. Yūsuf[712] did likewise from the Yemen, carrying presents for al-Walīd. Umm al-Banīn said to [her husband] al-Walīd, "O Commander of the Faithful, make Muḥammad b. Yūsuf's present over to me!" and he ordered that it should be delivered to her. The messengers of Umm al-Banīn

---

710. A section of the Qurʾān recited privately.
711. *Dīwān*, pp. 296–97 (where two additional verses are given).
712. The brother of al-Ḥajjāj (see *EI*², s.v. al-Ḥadjdjāj b. Yūsuf [p. 42a]).

reached Muḥammad concerning [this matter], and Muḥammad refused [to hand the presents over], saying, "Not until the Commander of the Faithful takes a look at them and decides," for there were many presents. [Umm al-Banīn] said, "O Commander of the Faithful, you ordered that Muḥammad's presents were to be delivered to me; I have no need of them." [Al-Walīd] said, "Why?" She said, "It has reached me that he took them from [1274] people by force, required them to make them, and oppressed them." Muḥammad transported the goods to al-Walīd, who said, "It has reached me that you acquired [these] by force." [Muḥammad] said, "God forbid." [Al-Walīd] gave the order, and [Muḥammad] was required to swear fifty oaths by God, between the Corner [in which the Black Stone is accommodated] and the Standing Place [of Abraham],[713] that he had not taken any of [the gifts] by force, had not oppressed anyone, and had only acquired them lawfully. He swore; al-Walīd accepted [his oaths] and handed [the presents] over to Umm al-Banīn. Then Muḥammad b. Yūsuf died in the Yemen, afflicted by a disease from which he became decomposed.[714]

[Al-Walīd's Desire to Remove Sulaymān from the Succession]

In this year al-Walīd had wanted to go to his brother Sulaymān to remove him from the succession, desiring [that] the oath of allegiance [be taken] to his son as his successor; that was before the illness from which he died.

According to ʿUmar—ʿAlī: Al-Walīd and Sulaymān were the two designated successors of ʿAbd al-Malik. When power passed to al-Walīd, he wanted to have the oath of allegiance taken to his son ʿAbd al-ʿAzīz [as his successor] and to remove Sulaymān from the succession. [Sulaymān] refused, and [al-Walīd then] endeavored to induce him [to agree] on the basis that he would make the succession his after [ʿAbd al-ʿAzīz]. [Sulaymān] refused, and [al-Walīd] offered him large amounts of money. [Sulaymān still] refused. [Al-Walīd] wrote to his governors, [instructing them] to take the oath of allegiance to ʿAbd al-ʿAzīz. No one responded to

---

713. See *EI²*, s.v. Maḳām Ibrāhīm.
714. Which is presumably intended to suggest that he had sworn a false oath.

that except for al-Ḥajjāj and Qutaybah and some of the notables of the people. ʿAbbād b. Ziyād[715] said [to al-Walīd], "The people are not responding to you positively in this matter; and, even if they were to do so, I would not be sure that they would not act perfidiously toward your son. Write to Sulaymān to come to you, for he does owe you obedience, and endeavor to induce him [to agree] to the oath of allegiance being taken to ʿAbd al-ʿAzīz as his successor. He won't be able to hold out while he is with you; and, if he does refuse, the people will be against him." Al-Walīd accordingly wrote to Sulaymān, ordering him to come [to him]. [Sulaymān] delayed, and al-Walīd resoled to go to him and remove him from the succession. He ordered [his retinue] to get ready, and he gave the order for his mare,[716] which was brought out. Then he became ill, and died before he could go, still desiring that.

According to ʿUmar—ʿAlī—Abū ʿĀṣim al-Ziyādī—al-Hilwāth al-Kalbī: We were in al-Hind with Muḥammad b. al-Qāsim. God killed Dāhir, and a letter came to us from al-Ḥajjāj [instructing us] to disavow Sulaymān. When Sulaymān had taken charge, a letter came to us from him: "Sow and till; no Syria for you." We stayed in that land until ʿUmar b. ʿAbd al-ʿAzīz came to power. Then we returned.   [1275]

According to ʿUmar—ʿAlī: Al-Walīd wanted to build the mosque of Damascus, in which there was a church.[717] He said to his companions, "I beg of you nothing but that each of you bring me one brick," and each man began to do so. An Iraqi brought him two bricks, and he said to him, "Whom are you from?" He said, "From the people of Iraq." [Al-Walīd] said, "O people of Iraq, you go to excess in everything, even in obedience." They demolished the church and built it into a mosque. When ʿUmar b. ʿAbd al-ʿAzīz took charge, [some of the Christians] complained to him of that. It was said [to him], "Everything outside the city was conquered by force of arms," and he said to [the people who had complained], "We'll return your church to you and demolish the church of Thomas, which was conquered by force of arms, and

---

715. ʿAbbād b. Ziyād b. Abī Sufyān (see *EI*[2], s.v.).

716. Reading *ḥajr* or *ḥijr*, where Guidi has understood *ḥujar*; Ibn al-Athīr gives *khiyām*.

717. This is what the text says. In fact, al-Walīd wanted to enlarge the existing mosque onto adjoining land occupied by the church of St. John the Baptist (see *EI*[2], s.v. Dimashḳ, at vol. II, pp. 280–81).

build it into a mosque." When he said that to them, they said, "Never mind. We'll leave you to what al-Walīd demolished and you leave the church of Thomas to us." ʿUmar did that.

In that year Qutaybah conquered Kāshghar and campaigned in China.[718]

[Qutaybah in Kāshghar and China]

The narrative returns to that of ʿAlī b. Muḥammad with the list of authorities I mentioned earlier. He said: Then Qutaybah campaigned in the year 96, taking with [his troops] their dependents and desiring to afford his dependents a safe refuge in Samarqand, out of fear of Sulaymān. When he had crossed the river, he put one of his mawlās, a man called al-Khwārazmī, in charge of the river crossing and said, "No one may cross except with a pass." He went to Farghānah and sent [ahead] to the ʿIṣām pass[719] [troops] to facilitate for him the road to Kāshghar, the nearest of the cities of China; [news of] the death of al-Walīd reached him while he was at Farghānah.

[1276]

According to [ʿAlī]—Abū al-Dhayyāl—al-Muhallab b. Iyās—Iyās b. Zuhayr: When Qutaybah crossed the river, I went to him and said to him, "I didn't know your view about the dependents, so that we might make preparations in that regard. My older sons are with me, but there are dependents I have left behind, and an old mother, and they do not have with them anyone to take care of them. If you see fit, [I hope] that you will write a letter for me [to go] with one of my sons, whom I shall send to bring me my family." He wrote the letter and gave it to me. I then reached the river, the man in charge of the [crossing] being on the other side. I beckoned with my hand, and some people came [across] in a boat. They said, "Who are you, and where is your pass?" I informed them, and some of them sat with me while others took the boat back to the man in charge and informed him. [Iyās] went on: Then they returned to me and transported me, and I reached [the people

---

718. Cf. Gibb, *Arab Conquests*, pp. 52–53, and "The Arab Invasion of Kashgar in A.D. 715," *Bulletin of the School of Oriental Studies*, 2 (1923), pp. 467–74, who disputes the historicity of this report; also Ibn Aʿtham, *Futūḥ*, vol. VII, p. 251.

719. Named after ʿIṣām b. ʿAbd Allāh al-Bāhilī, who is reported to have been appointed in this area by Qutaybah (Barthold, *Turkestan*³, p. 186, and Gibb, *Arab Conquests*, p. 49, both citing al-Ṭabarī, *Taʾrīkh*, ser. ii, p. 1440).

on the other side]; they were eating, and I was hungry, so I hurled myself [at the food]. [The man in charge] asked me things while I was eating and not answering him. He said, "This bedouin is [half-] dead from hunger." Then I rode, reached Marw, transported my mother, and returned, heading for the camp. [News of] the death of al-Walīd came, and I departed for Marw.

According to ['Alī]—Alū Mikhnaf—his father: Qutaybah sent Kathīr[720] b. fulān to Kāshghar; he took captives from it and sealed their necks [with the words] "Part of what God has granted to Qutaybah." Then Qutaybah returned, and [news of] the death of al-Walīd reached them.

['Alī] said: According to (i) Yaḥyā b. Zakariyyā' al-Hamdānī—Khurasani shaykhs, and (ii) al-Ḥakam b. 'Uthmān—a Khurasani shaykh: Qutaybah penetrated far, until he drew near to China. ['Alī] continued: The king of China wrote to [Qutaybah], "Send to us one of the nobles who are with you, [that] he may tell us about you and we may ask him about your religion." Qutaybah chose twelve—one of them said: ten—men from his army, from assorted tribes,[721] good-looking, beefy men, eloquent, hirsute, and brave, [this being] after he had asked about them and found them to be the best of those from among whom they came. Qutaybah spoke to them and contended with them in sagacity; he perceived intellects and good looks, and he ordered that they be well equipped with weapons, fine silks, embroidered garments, soft delicate white clothing, sandals, and perfume. He mounted them on fine horses, to be led with them, and riding animals for them to ride.

['Alī] said: Hubayrah b. al-Mushamraj al-Kilābī was eloquent, unconstrained with his tongue. [Qutaybah] said to him, "O Hubayrah, how are you going to conduct [this]?" [Hubayrah] said, "May God cause the amīr to prosper! I have a sufficiency of self-discipline. Say what you wish, and I shall say [that] and hold to it." [Qutaybah] said, "Go with God's blessing; through God comes success. Do not remove your turbans until you reach [the king's] country. When you enter into his presence, inform him that I have sworn that I shall not depart until I tread on their land, seal [the necks of] their kings, and collect their tax."

['Alī] said: They went off, led by Hubayrah b. al-Mushamraj.

[1277]

---

720. Ibn al-Athīr has "Kabīr."
721. Taking this to be the sense of *min afnā' al-qabā'il* here.

When they arrived, the king of China sent to them, summoning them. They entered the bathhouse, and then emerged and donned white clothes with tunics underneath; they applied ghāliyah[722] perfume to themselves, censed themselves, put on sandals and ridāʾ's,[723] and entered into [the king's] presence; with him were the grandees of his kingdom. They sat down, and neither the king nor any of those sitting with him spoke to them; then they stood up [and went out]. The king said to those who were present with him, "What do you think of these [people]?" They said, "We think they are people who are nothing but women; there was not one of us who, on seeing them and smelling their perfume, did not have an erection."

[ʿAlī] said: On the next day the king sent for them, and they donned embroidered garments, silken turbans, and maṭārif[724] and went to him in the morning. When they entered into his presence, they were told, "Return." [The king said to his companions, "What do you think of this attire?" They said, "This attire is more like the attire of men than that first one was. They are [indeed men]."

On the third day the king sent for them, and they strapped on their weapons, donned their head mail and helmets, girded themselves with their swords, took up their spears, shouldered their bows, mounted their horses, and went [to him] in the morning. The king of China looked at them, and he saw what resembled mountains advancing. When they drew near [to him], they fixed their spears into the ground. Then they advanced toward [the king and his companions], tucking up their garments. Before they could enter, they were told, "Return," on account of the fear of the [Arabs] that had entered the hearts of [the king and his companions].

---

722. Which is variously defined as "a sort of perfume, well known"; "a certain compound of perfumes"; "musk mixed or boiled [with other perfumes]"; and "a perfume composed of musk and ambergris and camphor and oil of ben" (Lane, *Lexicon*, s.v.).

723. See above, n. 596.

724. The *miṭraf* is defined by Lane (*Lexicon*, s.v.) as "a garment, . . . or [such as is termed] *ridāʾ*, . . . of [the kind of cloth called] *khazz*, . . . square, or four-sided . . . having ornamental or coloured or figured, borders (*aʿlam*): . . . or a garment having, in its two ends, or sides, (*fī ṭarafayhi*) two such borders (*ʿalamā-n*): . . . or a square, or four-sided, garment of *khazz*."

['Alī] said: They departed; they mounted their horses, pulled up their spears, and urged on their horses, as if pursuing one another with them. The king said to his companions, "What do you think of them?" They said, "We have never seen the like of these." In the evening the king sent [word] to them: "Send me your leader, the worthiest of you as a man." They sent Hubayrah to him. When [Hubayrah] had entered into his presence, [the king] said to him, "You have seen the might of my dominion and that no one can protect you from me while you are in my country. You are in the position of an egg in the palm of my hand. I am going to ask you about something, and, if you do not tell me the truth, I shall kill you." [Hubayrah] said, "Ask!" He said, "Why did you do what you did with [your] dress on the first, second, and third days?" [Hubayrah] said, "As for our dress on the first day, that is what we wear among our families, and the perfume we use when with them. As for the second day, [that is what we wear] when we go to our amīrs. As for the third day, [that is] our dress for our enemies. When we are aroused and provoked, we [dress] thus." [The king] said, "How well you organize your customs. Depart to your mas-   [1279] ter and tell him to depart, for I know his cupidity and the small number of his companions; otherwise I shall send against you someone who will destroy both you and him." Hubayrah said, "How can one whose front cavalry are in your country, while the last of them are in the places where the olive trees grow, be said to have a small number of companions? How can one who has left the world behind him, under his control, and has campaigned against you, be charged with cupidity? As for your [attempt] to frighten us with being killed, we have allotted spans; when [their ends] come about, the noblest of them [involves] being killed. We do not dislike [that], nor do we fear it." [The king] said, "What then will satisfy your master?" [Hubayrah] said, "He has sworn an oath that he will not depart until he treads your land, seals your kings, and is given tax." [The king] said, "We shall extricate him from his oath. We shall send some soil from the soil of our land, so that he may tread on it; we shall send him some of our sons so that he may seal [their necks]; and we shall send him some tax, so that he may be pleased with it." [The narrator] said: He called for some dishes of gold with soil in them, and he sent silk and gold and four young men from [among] the sons of their kings; he gave them leave [to depart] and presented them with fine gifts, and they went off and reached [Qutaybah] with what [the king] had sent. Qutaybah accepted the tax, sealed the young men and returned them, and trod on the soil. Sawādah b. ʿAbdallāh al-Salūlī said (kāmil):[725]

There is no disgrace in the delegation you sent
     to China, if they followed the right way.
They broke their eyelids against the motes, out
     of fear of death,
          except for the noble Hubayrah b. Mushamraj.
He wanted nothing but to seal their necks
     and [to take] hostages, handed over [as a pledge]
     for the remission of tax.
[1280] He transmitted the message you asked him to be
     mindful of,
          and brought a way out of violating the oath.

[ʿAlī] said: Qutaybah sent Hubayrah to al-Walīd, and he died at Qaryah[726] in Fārs. Sawādah elegized him, saying (kāmil):

To God be attributed [the excellence of] the
     grave of Hubayrah b. Mushamraj;
          what generosity and beauty it contains!
And eloquence that the eloquent fall short of,
     when people gather to witness what men say.
He was [like] spring, when the droughts had
     followed one another,
          and [like] a lion, when heroes quailed.
May clouds raining torrents give water
     to Qaryah, where his grave is.
The pawing[727] steeds wept at the loss of him,
     as did every straight and waving spear,

---

725. Both the poet and the verses that follow are apparently known only here (and in the parallel passage in Ibn al-Athīr).

726. In her entries on Fārs, Cornu (Atlas: Répertoires, p. 55) lists twelve place names in which the first component is Qaryah.

727. Ṣāfināt. More exactly, Lane (Lexicon, s.v.) defines ṣāfin as [a horse] "standing upon three legs and the extremity of the hoof of the fourth leg: . . . or standing upon three legs, and turning back the extremity of the fore part of the fourth hoof, that of his foreleg: . . . or standing upon three legs. . . ."

And there wept for him tousle-headed women, who did
    not find anyone to console them
    in the year that was affected by drought and
    barrenness.

According to ['Alī]—The Bāhilīs: When Qutaybah returned
from campaigning each year, he would buy twelve fine mares and
twelve dromedaries, paying no more than four thousand
[dirhams] per mare, and have them looked after until the time for
campaigning [came round again]. When he was ready for the campaign and was encamped, he had [the mares] tethered and made
lean; he would not cross a river with horses until their flesh was
lean. He used to mount his advance parties on them; he used to
send on his advance parties horsemen from [among] the *ashrāf*,
together with non-Arabs he thought to be faithful, [these latter
being mounted] on the dromedaries. When he sent out an advance
scout, he would order that a tablet be inscribed; then he would
break it into two pieces and give him one piece and keep the
other, which he would not be able to simulate, and would order   [1281]
him to bury [his piece] in a place that he would describe to him,
such as a well-known ford or tree, or a ruin. Then he would send
someone to search it out, so that he might know whether his
advance scout was telling the truth or not. Thābit Quṭnah
al-'Atakī said, concerning those of the kings of the Turks whom
[Qutaybah] killed (*wāfir*):[728]

The killing of Kāz.r.nk and K.shbyz gladdened
    the eye, as did what B.yār encountered.[729]

Al-Kumayt said, concerning the campaign in Soghd and Khwārazm (*basīṭ*):[730]

Afterwards, in a campaign that was blessed,
    [a campaign that] destroys peoples' agriculture
    and reaps,

---

728. Cf. above, n. 569; the following verse appears not to occur elsewhere.
729. The forms and significations (if any) of these names/titles remain to be
elucidated ("B.yār" is given in the *Addenda et Emendanda* in preference to the
"Y.bād" given in the text).
730. If we are to judge by *Shi'r al-Kumayt*, no. 146, the following verses are
found only here.

The cloud [of this campaign] brought Fīl its heavy rain,
    and Soghd, when its cold shower poured on them.
[Fīl] still has plunder to give as booty
    at the divisions of spoil—[and] nothing
    mean or paltry.
Those [are the] conquests by which the Caliph is afforded
    the proof that we are people who exert our
    fullest efforts.
You did not avert your face from [any] people in
    [any] campaign against them,
    until they were told, "May you die!" and they
    were killed.
You were not pleased with any fortress of theirs
    if it was holding out,
    until the One, the Everlasting, could be proclaimed
    in it with the words "God is great!"

Bibliography of Cited Works

Aghānī, see al-Iṣfahānī.

A'shā Hamdān, see Geyer; von Goutta.

al-Balādhurī, Aḥmad b. Yaḥyā. *Anonyme arabische Chronik*. Edited by W. Ahlwardt. Greifswald, 1883.

———. *Futūḥ al-buldān*. Edited by M. J. de Goeje. Leiden, 1866.

Barthold, W. *Turkestan Down to the Mongol Invasion*. 3rd ed. London, 1968.

Bombaci, A. "On the Ancient Turkish Title 'Šaδ,'" in *Gururajāmañjarikā: Studi in onore di Giuseppe Tucci*, Vol. I. Naples, 1974. pp. 163–93.

Bosworth, C. E. "Rajā' b. Ḥaywa al-Kindī and the Umayyad Caliphs," *The Islamic Quarterly* 16 (1972), pp. 36–80.

———. "The Rulers of Chaghāniyān in Early Islamic Times," *Iran* 19 (1981), pp. 1–20.

———. *Sīstān under the Arabs, from the Islamic Conquest to the Rise of The Ṣaffārids (30–250/651–864)*. Rome, 1968.

——— and G. Clauson. "Al-Xwārazmī on the Peoples of Central Asia," *Journal of the Royal Asiatic Society* (1965), pp. 1–12.

Brooks, E. W. "The Arabs in Asia Minor (641–750) from Arabic Sources," *Journal of Hellenic Studies* 18 (1898), pp. 182–208.

Brunschvig, R. "Métiers vils en Islam," *Studia Islamica* 16 (1962), pp. 41–60.

Bulliet, R. W. "Naw Bahār and the Survival of Iranian Buddhism," *Iran* 14 (1976), pp. 140–45.

Caskel, W. *Ǧamharat an-nasab: Das genealogische Werk des Hišām ibn Muḥammad al-Kalbī*. 2 vols. Leiden, 1966.

Cornu, G. *Atlas du monde arabo-islamique a l'époque classique, ixe–xe siècles*. Leiden, 1985.

Crone, P. *Meccan Trade and the Rise of Islam.* Princeton, 1987.

———. *Slaves on Horses: The Evolution of the Islamic Polity.* Cambridge, 1980.

——— and M. Hinds. *God's Caliph: Religious Authority in the First Centuries of Islam.* Cambridge, 1986.

al-Dhahabī, Abū ʿAbd Allāh Muḥammad b. Aḥmad. *Taʾrīkh al-Islām.* Cairo, 1327–.

al-Dīnawarī, Abū Ḥanīfah Aḥmad b. Dāwūd. *al-Akhbār al-ṭiwāl.* Edited by V. Guirgass. Leiden, 1888.

Dixon, ʿA. ʿA. *The Umayyad Caliphate (65–86/684–705): A Political Study.* London, 1971.

Dozy, R. P. A. *Dictionnaire détaillé des noms des vêtements chez les arabes.* Amsterdam, 1845.

———. *Supplément aux dictionnaires arabes.* Leiden, 1881.

Dunlop, D. M. "Arab Relations with Tibet in the 8th and Early 9th Centuries A.D.," *İslâm Tetkikleri Enstitüsü Dergisi* 5 (1973), pp. 301–18.

The Encyclopaedia of Islam (EI[1]). 5 vols. and Supplement. Leiden, 1913–38.

The Encyclopaedia of Islam (EI[2]). New ed. Leiden, 1960–.

Fahd, T. *Le panthéon de l'Arabie centrale à la veille de l'hégire.* Beirut, 1968.

al-Farazdaq, Tammām b. Ghālib. *Dīwān.* Beirut, 1960.

Freytag, G. W. *Arabum Proverbia.* 3 vols. Bonn, 1838–43.

Gabrieli, F. "Muḥammad ibn Qāsim and the Arab Conquest of Sind," *East and West,* N.S. 15 (1965), pp. 281–95.

Geyer, R. *The Díwán of al-Aʿshà.* London, 1928.

Ghirshman, R. *Les Chionites-Hephtalites.* Cairo, 1948.

Gibb, H. A. R. "Arab-Byzantine Relations under the Umayyad Caliphate," in *Studies on the Civilization of Islam.* Edited by S. J. Shaw and W. R. Polk. London, 1962. Pp. 47–61.

———. *The Arab Conquests in Central Asia.* London, 1923.

———. "The Arab Invasion of Kashgar in A.D. 715," *Bulletin of the School of Oriental Studies* 2 (1923), pp. 467–74.

Goeje, M. J. de. *Mémoire sur les Carmathes du Bahraïn et les Fatimides.* 2nd ed. Leiden, 1886.

von Goutta, G. *Der Aġaniartikel über ʾAʿšā von Hamdān.* Kirchhain, 1912.

Hawting, G. R. *The First Dynasty of Islam: The Umayyad Caliphate, AD 661–750.* London, 1986.

Hell, J. "Al-Farazdaḳ's Lieder auf die Muhallabiten," *Zeitschrift der Deutschen Morgenländischen Gesellschaft* 59 (1905), pp. 589–621; 60 (1906), pp. 1–48.

Hinds, M. *An Early Islamic Family from Oman: Al-ʿAwtabī's Account of the Muhallabids.* Journal of Semitic Studies Monograph 12. Forthcoming.

————. "Kûfan Political Alignments and Their Background in the Mid-Seventh Century A.D.," *International Journal of Middle East Studies* 2 (1971), pp. 346–67.

Ibn ʿAbd Rabbihi, Abū ʿUmar Aḥmad b. Muḥammad. *al-ʿIqd al-farīd.* Edited by A. Amīn, A. al-Zayn, and I. al-Abyārī. 8 vols. Cairo, 1940–65.

Ibn Aʿtham, Abū Muḥammad Aḥmad. *Kitāb al-futūḥ.* 8 vols. Hyderabad, 1968–75.

Ibn al-Athīr, ʿIzz al-Din ʿAlī. *al-Kāmil fī al-taʾrīkh.* Edited by C. J. Tornberg. 13 vols. Leiden, 1851–56; reset, Beirut, 1965–67.

Ibn Durayd, Abū Bakr Muḥammad b. al-Ḥasan. *al-Ishtiqāq.* Edited by ʿA.-S. M. Hārūn. Cairo, 1958.

Ibn Ḥajar al-ʿAsqalanī, Abū al-Faḍl Aḥmad b. ʿAlī. *al-Iṣābah fī tamyīz al-ṣaḥābah.* Cairo, 1328 (1910).

————. *Tahdhīb al-tahdhīb.* 12 vols. Hyderabad, 1325–27 (1907–9).

Ibn Ḥamdūn, Muḥammad b. al-Ḥasan b. Muḥammad b. ʿAlī. *al-Tadhkirah al-ḥamdūniyyah.* Edited by I. ʿAbbās. Beirut, 1983–.

Ibn Ḥazm, Abū Muḥammad ʿAlī b. Aḥmad. *Jamharat ansāb al-arab.* Edited by ʿA.-S. M. Hārūn. Cairo, 1962.

Ibn al-ʿImād, Abū al-Falāḥ ʿAbd al-Ḥayy. *Shadharāt al-dhahab fī akhbār man dhahab.* 8 vols. Cairo, 1350–51 (1931–32).

Ibn al-Jawzī, Jamāl al-Dīn Abū al-Faraj ʿAbd al-Raḥmān b. Abī al-Ḥusayn ʿAlī. *Sīrat ʿUmar b. ʿAbd al-ʿAzīz.* Edited by Muḥibb al-Dīn al-Khaṭīb. Cairo, 1331 (1913).

Ibn al-Kalbī, see Caskel.

Ibn Kathīr, ʿImād al-Dīn Abū al-Fidāʾ Ismāʿīl b ʿUmar. *al-Bidāyah wa-al-nihāyah fī al-taʾrīkh.* 14 vols. Cairo, 1351–58 (1932–37).

Ibn Khallikān, Shams al-Dīn Abū al-ʿAbbās Aḥmad b. Muḥammad. *Wafāyat al-aʿyān wa-anbāʾ abnāʾ al-zamān.* Edited by I. ʿAbbās. 8 vols. Beirut, 1968–72.

Ibn Khurradādhbih, ʿUbaydallāh b. ʿAbdallāh. *Kitāb al-masālik wa-al-mamālik.* Edited by M. J. de Goeje. Leiden, 1889.

Ibn Manẓūr, Jamāl al-Dīn Abu al-Faḍl Muḥammad b. Mukarram. *Lisān al-ʿarab.* 20 vols. Būlāq, 1300–7 (1883–91).

Ibn Qays al-Ruqayyāt, ʿUbayd Allāh. *Dīwān.* Edited by N. Rhodokanakis. Vienna, 1902.

Ibn Qutaybah, ʿAbd Allāh b. Muslim. "Kitāb al-ʿarab," in *Rasāʾil al-bulaghāʾ.* 4th ed. Edited by M. K. ʿAlī. Cairo, 1954. Pp. 344–77.

————. *Kitāb al-shiʿr wa-al-shuʿarāʾ.* Edited by A. M. Shākir. 2 vols. Cairo, 1966–67.

Ibn Rustah, Abū ʿAlī Aḥmad b. ʿUmar. *Kitāb al-aʿlaq al-nafīsah* (part 7). Edited by M. J. de Goeje. Bibliotheca geographorum arabicorum 7. Leiden, 1892. Pp. 1–229.

ʿIqd, see Ibn ʿAbd Rabbihi.

al-Iṣfahānī, Abū al-Faraj ʿAlī b. al-Ḥusayn. *Kitāb al-Aghānī.* 1st ed. Vol. XXI. Edited by R. E. Brünnow. Leiden, 1888. 2nd ed. 24 vols. Cairo, 1929–74.

Jarīr B. ʿAṭiyyah b. al-Khaṭafā. *Dīwān.* Edited by M. I. ʿA. al-Ṣāwī. Cairo, 1353 (1933–34).

Justi, F. *Iranisches Namenbuch.* Marburg, 1895.

Juynboll, G. H. A. *Muslim Tradition: Studies in Chronology, Provenance and Authorship of Early Ḥadīth.* Cambridge, 1983.

Kennedy, H. *The Prophet and the Age of the Caliphates.* London, 1986.

Khalīfah b. Khayyāṭ. *Taʾrīkh.* Edited by A. D. al-ʿUmarī. al-Najaf, 1967.

Kitāb al-ʿuyūn wa-al-ḥadāʾiq. Edited by M. J. de Goeje. Leiden, 1871.

al-Kumayt b. Zayd al-Asadī. *Shiʿr al-Kumayt.* Collected by D. Sallūm. 3 vols. Baghdad, 1969–70.

Lammens, H. "Le califat de Yazid Ier," *Mélanges de la Faculté orientale de l'Université St.-Joseph de Beyrouth* 5/2 (1911–12), pp. 588–724.

Lane, E. W. *An Arabic-English Lexicon.* 8 vols. London, 1863–93.

Le Strange, G. *The Lands of the Eastern Caliphate.* Cambridge, 1905.

Lévi-Provençal, E. *Histoire de l'Espagne musulmane.* New ed. 3 vols. Leiden, 1950–53.

Lilie, R.-J. *Die byzantinische Reaktion auf die Ausbreitung der Araber.* Miscellanea Byzantina Monacensia 22. Munich, 1976.

Løkkegard, F. *Islamic Taxation in the Classic Period with Special Reference to Circumstances in Iraq.* Copenhagen, 1950.

Marquart, J. *Ērānšahr nach der Geographie des Ps. Moses Xorenacʿi.* Abhandlungen der königlichen Gesellschaft der Wissenschaften zu Göttingen, philologisch-historische Klasse, N.F. 3/2. Berlin, 1901.

———. "Historische Glossen zu den alttürkischen Inschriften," *Vienna Oriental Journal* 12 (1898), pp. 157–200.

al-Masʿūdī, Abū al-Ḥasan ʿAlī b. al-Ḥusayn. *Kitāb al-tanbīh wa-al-ishrāf.* Edited by M. J. de Goeje. Leiden, 1894.

———. *Murūj al-dhahab wa-maʿādin al-jawhar.* 9 vols. Edited by C. Barbier de Meynard and Pavet de Courteille. Paris, 1861–77. Revised and corrected by C. Pellat. 7 vols. Beirut, 1966–79. References are, first, to the volume and page of the Paris edition as given by Pellat and, second, to the paragraph number of Pellat's edition.

al-Mubarrad, Abū al-ʿAbbās Muḥammad b. Yazīd. *al-Kitāb al-Kāmil.* Edited by W. Wright. 3 vols. Leipzig, 1864–92.

Naqā'iḍ Jarīr wa-al-Farazdaq. Edited by A. A. Bevan. 3 vols. Leiden, 1905–12.

Narshakhī, Muḥammad b. Jaʿfar. *The History of Bukhara.* Translated by R. N. Frye. Cambridge, Mass., 1954.

Nöldeke, T. Review of Marquart's *Ērānšahr, Zeitschrift der Deutschen Morgenländischen Gesellschaft* 56 (1902), pp. 427–36.

Omar, F. *The ʿAbbāsid Caliphate, 132/750–170/786.* Baghdad, 1969.

Pellat, C. *Le milieu baṣrien et la formation de Ǧāḥiẓ.* Paris, 1953.

Périer, J. *Vie d'al-Hadjdjadj ibn Yousof.* Paris, 1904.

Qur'ān. Where two different numbers are given for a verse, the first is that of the official Egyptian edition, the second that of G. Flügel's text (Leipzig, 1883).

al-Rashid, S. A. A. *Al-Rabadhah, a Portrait of Early Islamic Civilization in Saudi Arabia.* Riyadh, 1985.

Sayed, R. *Die Revolte des Ibn Ašʿaṯ und die Koranleser: Ein Beitrag zur Religions- und Sozialgeschichte der frühen Umayyadenzeit.* Freiburg im Breisgau, 1977.

Schacht, J. *An Introduction to Islamic Law.* Oxford, 1964.

Schlegel, G. *La stèle funéraire du Teghni Giogh.* Helsinki, 1892.

Sezgin, F. *Geschichte des arabischen Schrifttums.* Vol. II. Leiden, 1975.

Shaban, M. A. *The ʿAbbāsid Revolution.* Cambridge, 1970.

———. *Islamic History A.D. 600–750 (A.H. 132): A new Interpretation.* Cambridge, 1971.

al-Siyar wa-al-jawābāt li-ʿulamā' wa-a'immat ahl ʿUmān. Edited by S. I. Kāshif. Oman, 1986.

al-Ṭabarī, Abū Jaʿfar Muḥammad b. Jarīr. *Ta'rīkh al-Ṭabarī: Ta'rīkh al-rusul wa-al-mulūk.* 10 vols. Cairo, 1960–69 (referred to for some variant readings).

Ṭarafah b. al-ʿAbd. *Dīwān.* Edited by D. al-Khaṭīb and L. al-Ṣaqqāl. Damascus, 1975.

al-Thaʿālibī, Abū Manṣūr ʿAbd al-Malik b. Muḥammad b. Ismāʿīl. *Laṭā'if al-maʿārif.* Edited by I. al-Abyārī and H. K. al-Ṣayrafī. Cairo, 1960. English translation by C. E. Bosworth. Edinburgh, 1968.

al-ʿUyūn wa-al-ḥadā'iq, see *Kitāb al-ʿuyūn wa-al-ḥadā'iq.*

Wakiʿ, Abū Bakr Muḥammad b. Khalaf. *Akhbār al-quḍāh.* Edited by ʿA. M. al-Marāghī. 3 vols. Cairo, 1947–50.

Wellhausen, J. *The Arab Kingdom and Its Fall.* Calcutta, 1927.

———. "Die Kämpfe der Araber mit den Romäern in der Zeit der Umaijiden," *Nachrichten von der königlischen Gesellschaft der Wissenschaften zu Göttingen, philologische-historische Klasse* (1901), pp. 414–47.

Wensinck, A. J., et. al. *Concordance et indices de la tradition musulmane.* 6 vols. Leiden, 1936–69.

al-Ya'qūbī, Aḥmad b. Abī Ya'qūb. *Kitāb al-buldān.* Edited by M. J. de Goeje. Bibliotheca geographorum arabicorum 7, Leiden, 1891. Pp. 231–373.

———. *Ta'rīkh.* Edited by M. T. Houtsma. Leiden, 1883.

Yāqūt b. 'Abdallāh al-Rūmī. *Mu'jam al-buldān.* Edited by F. Wüstenfeld. 6 vols. Leipzig, 1866–73.

al-Zabīdī, Abū al-Fayḍ Muḥammad Murtaḍā b. Muḥammad. *Sharḥ al-qāmūs al-musammā tāj al-'ārūs.* 10 vols. Būlāq, 1306–7.

al-Zamakhsharī, Abū al-Qāsim Muḥammad b. 'Umar. *Asās al-balāghah.* Cairo, 1922.

Zambaur, E. de. *Manuel de généalogie et de chronologie pour l'histoire de l'Islam.* Hanover, 1927.

al-Zubayr b. Bakkār. *al-Akhbār al-muwaffaqiyyāt.* Edited by S. M. al-'Ānī. Baghdad, 1972.

Index

For purposes of alphabetization, b. (son), bt. (daughter), and the definite article al- have been ignored; tribal names beginning with Banū have, however, been alphabetized under that word.

A

Abān b. ʿUthmān (b. ʿAffān) 13, 33–34, 71
Abazqubādh 68
ʿAbbād b. Ziyād 223
al-ʿAbbās b. al-Walīd b. ʿAbd al-Malik 140–41, 146, 149, 184, 204, 215–16, 219
ʿAbd al-ʿAzīz b. Marwān 80, 108–14
ʿAbd al-ʿAzīz b. al-Walīd b. ʿAbd al-Malik xiv, 164, 202, 204, 214, 219, 221, 222–23
ʿAbd al-Ḥakīm b. ʿAbdallāh b. Abī Farwah (narrator) 209
ʿAbd al-Jabbār b. Yazīd b. al-Rabʿah al-Kalbī 158–60
ʿAbd al-Malik b. ʿAbdallāh (narrator) 213
ʿAbd al-Malik b. Marwān xi, xiv, 6–10, 12, 21–24, 32–33, 52, 57, 66, 71, 79–81, 83–86, 88, 97, 108–21, 126, 181, 212, 222
ʿAbd al-Malik b. al-Muhallab 47, 86, 129, 156–57

ʿAbd al-Muʾmin b. Shabath b. Ribʿī al-Tamīmī 5
ʿAbd al-Qays 49, 53–54
ʿAbd Rabbihi b. ʿAbdallāh b. ʿUmayr al-Laythī 183
ʿAbd al-Raḥmān b. ʿAbbās b. Rabīʿah b. al-Ḥārith b. ʿAbd al-Muṭṭalib (al-Hāshimī) 17, 21–22, 25, 52–56, 60, 89, 97
ʿAbd al-Raḥmān b. ʿAbdallāh b. ʿĀmir al-Ḥaḍramī, ḥalīf of Ḥarb b. Umayyah 20
ʿAbd al-Raḥmān b. Abī Laylā 25, 35, 48
ʿAbd al-Raḥmān b. Abī al-Zinād (narrator) 131
ʿAbd al-Raḥmān b. ʿAwf al-Ruʾāsī, Abū Ḥumayd 39
ʿAbd al-Raḥmān b. ʿAwsajah, Abū Sufyān al-Nihmī 15
ʿAbd al-Raḥmān b. Ḥabīb al-Ḥakamī 25
ʿAbd al-Raḥmān b. Muḥammad b. al-Ashʿath xi–xiii, 3–12, 14–26, 35, 38, 42–43, 46–53, 57–58, 62–63,

'Abd al-Raḥmān b. Muḥammad b. al-
　　Ash'ath (cont.)
　　66–69, 72, 77–83, 88, 97, 103,
　　111, 158, 209, 212
'Abd al-Raḥmān b. Mundhir b. Bishr
　　b. Ḥārithah; see 'Abd al-Raḥmān
　　b. al-Mundhir b. al-Jārūd
'Abd al-Raḥmān b. al-Mundhir b. al-
　　Jārūd 53–54, 56
'Abd al-Raḥmān b. Muslim al-Bāhilī
　　143, 152, 155, 165–72, 175–76,
　　186, 190
'Abd al-Raḥmān b. Sulaym al-Kalbī 25
'Abd al-Raḥmān b. Ṭalḥah b.
　　'Abdallāh b. Khalaf 57, 64
'Abd al-Raḥmān b. Udhaynah (b. al-
　　Ḥārith al-'Abdī) 13, 156, 214
'Abd al-Raḥmān b. al-Walīd b. 'Abd al-
　　Malik 219
'Abdallāh b. Abān al-Ḥārithī 10
'Abdallāh b. 'Abd al-Malik b. Marwān
　　23–24, 44, 72, 109, 118, 149
'Abdallāh b. 'Abdallāh b. 'Umar 132,
　　142
'Abdallāh b. al-Ahtam 165
'Abdallāh b. 'Āmir b. Misma' (al-
　　Shaybānī) 11–12, 15
'Abdallāh b. 'Āmir al-Na''ār al-Tamīmī
　　al-Mujāshi'ī 6, 50–52, 66
'Abdallāh b. 'Āmir b. Rabī'ah 132
'Abdallāh b. 'Amr b. 'Uthmān b. 'Affān
　　179
'Abdallāh b. Budayl b. 'Abdallāh b.
　　Budayl b. Warqā' 103, 107
'Abdallāh b. Dhu'āb al-Sulamī 24, 43
'Abdallāh b. Fuḍāla al-Zahrānī 56
'Abdallāh b. al-Ḥajjāj al-Tha'labī 120
'Abdallāh b. al-Ḥajjāj b. Yūsuf 216
'Abdallāh b. Hammām al-Salūlī 125
'Abdallāh b. Ja'far (narrator) 114
'Abdallāh b. Khāzim 90, 95
'Abdallāh b. Mu'ammar b. Shumayr
　　al-Yashkurī 27
'Abdallāh b. Muḥammad b. 'Alī; see
　　al-Manṣūr
'Abdallāh b. Mulayl al-Hamdānī 38

'Abdallāh b. Mūsā b. Nuṣayr 201
'Abdallāh b. Muslim, al-Faqīr 129,
　　199–200
'Abdallāh b. Rizām al-Ḥārithī 15, 25,
　　39–40, 43
'Abdallāh b. Rumaythah al-Ṭā'ī 10
'Abdallāh b. Shaddād b. al-Hād 69
'Abdallāh b. 'Umar 65
'Abdallāh b. Wahb; see Ibn Wahb
'Abdallāh b. Wa'lān al-'Adawī 137
'Abdallāh b. Yazīd b. al-Mughaffal 43
'Abdallāh b. al-Zubayr 88, 114, 116–
　　17, 121, 212
'Ābis al-Bāhilī 171
al-Abrad b. Qurrah al-Tamīmī 25, 42–
　　43
Abraham 148
Abrashahr 155, 164
Abū al-'Alā' (narrator) 147, 150
Abū al-Āṣ 120
Abū 'Āṣim (al-Ḍaḥḥāk b. Makhlad al-
　　Nabīl) (narrator) 210
Abū 'Āṣim al-Ziyādī (narrator) 223
Abū al-Bakhtarī al-Ṭā'ī 25, 36, 37, 42, 48
Abū Bakr b. 'Abd al-'Azīz b. Marwān
　　111
Abū Bakr b. 'Abd al-Malik b. Marwān
　　118
Abū Bakr b. 'Abd al-Raḥmān (b. al-
　　Ḥārith b. Hishām) 132, 142, 179,
　　213
Abū Bakr b. Abī Mūsā al-Ash'arī 139,
　　156, 214
Abū Bakr b. 'Amr b. Ḥazm; see Abū
　　Bakr b. Muḥammad b. 'Amr
Abū Bakr b. 'Ayyāsh (narrator) 209–11
Abū Bakr al-Bāhilī (narrator) 212
Abū Bakr b. Ḥazm; see Abū Bakr b.
　　Muḥammad b. 'Amr
Abū Bakr al-Hudhalī (narrator) 67
Abū Bakr b. Muḥammad b. 'Amr b.
　　Ḥazm al-Anṣārī 139, 203, 206
Abū Bakr b. Sulaymān b. Abī
　　Ḥathmah 132
Abū Burdah b. Abī Mūsā 13
Abū al-Dardā' al-Khath'amī 39

Abū Dāwūd (Khālid b. Ibrāhīm al-
    Dhuhlī) 171
Abū al-Dhayyāl (Zuhayr b. Hunayd
    al-ʿAdawī) (narrator) 134, 137–38,
    147, 150, 153, 185, 187, 198, 224
Abū Dhibbān (= ʿAbd al-Malik b.
    Marwān) 8
Abū al-Fawāris al-Tamīmī (narrator)
    205
Abū Ghassān Mālik b. Ismāʿīl
    (narrator) 212
Abū Ḥabībah (narrator) 178
Abū al-Ḥasan al-Jushamī (narrator)
    133, 199
Abū Ḥusayn (narrator) 210
Abū al-ʿIlj, mawlā of ʿUbaydallāh b.
    Maʿmar 56
Abū Isḥāq (ʿAmr b. ʿAbdallāh) al-Sabīʿī
    7–8
Abū (al-)Jahḍam al-Azdī (narrator) 47–
    48
Abū al-Jahm b. Kinānah al-Kalbī 45–
    46
Abū Jildah al-Yashkurī 49
Abū Kaʿb b. ʿUbayd b. Sarjis 11
Abū Kurayb (Muḥammad b. al-ʿAlāʾ)
    (narrator) 209–11
Abū Mardiyyah 176
Abū Maʿshar (Najīḥ al-Sindī) (narrator)
    13, 34, 71, 76, 115–17, 129–39,
    145, 148, 156, 179, 183, 202, 213–
    14, 217–18
Abū Mikhnaf Lūṭ b. Yaḥyā (narrator)
    3–5, 6–8, 10–12, 14, 19–20, 24,
    26, 35–37, 39, 42, 44, 46–49, 57–
    59, 63, 68, 77–79, 81, 88, 156,
    225
Abū Muḥammad al-Zammī 27–28
Abū al-Mukhāriq al-Rāsibī (narrator)
    3–4, 42, 88, 156
Abū al-Mulayḥ (al-Hudhalī) (narrator)
    202
Abū Muslim 99
Abū Qaṭīfah ʿAmr b. al-Walīd b.
    ʿUqbah b. Abī Muʿayṭ 119
Abū Ṣafwān (narrator) 174

Abū Saʿīd; see al-Muhallab b. Abī
    Ṣufrah
Abū al-Ṣalt (al-Aʿwar al-Taymī)
    (narrator) 8
Abū al-Ṣalt b. Kanārā 63
Abū al-Saqr 20
Abū al-Sarī al-Marwazī (narrator) 152,
    174
Abū Sawādah 208
Abū Ṭālib 207
Abū ʿUbaydah Maʿmar b. al-Muthannā
    (narrator) 63, 79
Abū ʿUbaydah b. al-Walīd b. ʿAbd al-
    Malik 219
Abū ʿUyaynah b. al-Muhallab 162
Abū Yazīd al-Saksakī (narrator) 24, 26,
    37, 42, 46
Abū Zayd (ʿUmar b. Shabbah)
    (narrator); see ʿUmar (b. Shabbah,
    Abū Zayd)
Abū al-Zubayr al-Hamdānī al-Arḥabī
    (narrator) 10, 12, 14–15, 20, 35–
    36
ʿĀd 198
Ādharbayjān 148, 164, 210
Adhrūliyyah (Dorylaion) 146
al-Adrīnūq (Roderic) 182
Afr. y. dh 68
aḥbār 185
ahl al-akhbār 155
ahl al-dhimmah 67
ahl al-siyar 117, 183, 218
Aḥmad b. Thābit (narrator) 13, 34, 71,
    76, 115–16, 129, 139, 145, 148,
    156, 179, 183, 202, 213, 217–18
al-Ahwāz 12, 76
ʿĀʾishah bt. ʿAbd al-Malik b. Marwān
    118
ʿĀʾishah bt. Hishām; see Umm
    Hishām bt. Hishām
ʿĀʾishah bt. Muʿāwiyah b. al-Mughīrah
    b. Abī al-ʿĀṣ b. Umayyah, mother
    of ʿAbd al-Malik b. Marwān 117–
    18
ʿĀʾishah bt. Mūsā b. Ṭalḥah, wife of
    ʿAbd al-Malik b. Marwān 118

Akharūn 89, 126, 128
al-Akhram 134, 142
'Akk 50
Āl Abī 'Aqīl (a man from) 56
Āl Ja'far 216
Āl Sa'īd (b. al-'Āṣ al-'Umarī) 14
al-'Alā' b. Jarīr (narrator) 198
a'lāj; see 'ilj
a'lām 142
'Alī b. Abī Ṭālib 35, 118
'Alī b. al-Ḥusayn (b. 'Alī) 132–33, 213
'Alī b. al-Muhājir al-Khuzā'ī 101, 103–4
'Alī b. Muḥammad; see al-Madā'inī
'Alī b. Mujāhid (narrator) 153, 171–72, 174, 185, 188, 189
'Ālij 159
'Alqamah b. 'Amr al-Awdī 77
'Āmir b. Mālik al-Ḥimmānī 165
'Āmir al-Sha'bī; see al-Sha'bī
'Āmir b. Wāthilah al-Kinānī, Abū al-Ṭufayl 5, 18
'Ammūriyyah (Amorion) 146
'Amr b. Abī Mihzam 168
'Amr b. Abī Qurrah al-Kindī 58
'Amr b. Abī Zahdam (narrator) 197
'Amr b. Dīnār 210
'Amr b. Ḥurayth 21
'Amr b. Khālid b. Ḥuṣayn (al-Kilābī) 94–96
'Amr b. Khālid al-Zuraqī 34
'Amr b. Laqīṭ al-'Abdī 49
'Amr b. Mulim (narrator) 196–97
'Amr b. Muslim (al-Bāhilī) 165, 175
'Amr b. Qays (narrator) 210
'Amr b. Sa'īd al-Ashdaq 109
amṣār; see miṣr
Āmul 90, 128, 135, 138, 153, 177
Anas b. Abī Shaykh (narrator) 212
'Anbasah b. 'Abd al-Malik b. Marwān 118
'Anbasah b. Sa'īd b. al-'Āṣ al-Umawī 14 n. 49, 71, 76
'Anbasah b. al-Walīd b. 'Abd al-Malik 219
al-Andalus 164, 182, 201, 215, 219
Anṭākiyah 134, 204

'Arafah 145
arbā' 95
Arbinjān 197
al-Arzan 149
Asāwirah 191
A'shā Banī Shaybān 120
A'sha Hamdān 6, 7, 59–63, 82
Ash'arīs 50
al-Ash'ath b. Qays 25, 58, 79
al-Ashja'ī (narrator) 210
al-Ashqarī; see Ka'b b. Ma'dān al-Ashqarī
ashrāf; see sharīf
al-Ashtar 23
'Aṭā' b. Abī Rabāḥ 210
'Aṭā' b. Abī al-Sā'ib (al-Laythī) 56
(al-)'Atīk 27, 53, 75
'Ātikah bt. Yazīd b. Mu'āwiyah b. Abī Sufyān, wife of 'Abd al-Malik b. Marwān 118
'Aṭiyyah, mawlā of 'Atīk 27
'Aṭiyyah b. 'Amr al-'Anbarī 7
'Attāb b. Bishr (narrator) 213
'Awānah (b. al-Ḥakam) al-Kalbī (narrator) 39, 73, 118
'Awf b. al-Khari' 205
'Aylān 194
'Ayn al-Tamr 22
'Ayyāsh b. 'Abdallāh al-Ghanawī (narrator) 174
'Ayyāsh b. al-Aswad b. 'Awf al-Zuhrī 56
'Ayyāsh al-Ghanawī 174–75
Ayyūb b. al-Ḥakam b. Abī 'Aqīl (to be understood as al-Ḥakam b. Ayyūb, q.v.) 19, 46, 130
Ayyūb b. al-Qirriyyah 72–73
Ayyūb b. Sulaymān b. 'Abd al-Malik 161
al-Azd 150, 152, 159

B

bā' 172
al-Bāb (= Bāb al-Abwāb) 148, 164

Bāb al-Ḥadīd (the Iron Gate) 175
Bāb al-Jābiyah 125–26
Bāb al-Ṣaghīr 219
Bādghīs 74–75, 88, 133
Bādhām, king of Marw al-Rūdh 154, 174
Bādhibīn 171
Baghlān 165, 166
Bahallah; see Bahlah
Bāhilah 165, 170, 177, 193, 197
Bāhilīs 128, 143, 146, 153, 169, 170, 177, 185, 192, 194–95, 197, 229
Bahlah/Bahallah 86, 157
al-Bakhtarī (narrator) 108
Bakkār b. ʿAbd al-Malik; see Abū Bakr b. ʿAbd al-Malik b. Marwān
Bakr b. Ḥabīb al-Sahmī al-Bāhilī 170
Bakr b. Wāʾil 17, 33, 50
Balkh 29, 101, 105, 106, 127–29, 143, 147, 154–55, 165, 172, 175
Balkh river; see Oxus
al-Baltaʿ al-Saʿdī 17
al-Bāmiyān 99
Banū al-ʿAbbās 144
Banū Abī al-ʿĀṣ 25
Banū ʿAdī 138
Banū ʿĀmir (of Kalb) 39, 45
Banū al-ʿAnbar 17
Banū Anf al-Nāqah 17
Banū Ḍubayʿah 139
Banū Ḥanīfah 57
Banū Hāshim 211
Banū Jaʿfar b. Qurayʿ 17
Banū Jaḥdar 18
Banū Makhzūm 147, 178, 219
Banū al-Malakān 137
Banū Marwān 24, 61
Banū Mujāshiʿ b. Dārim 50
Banū Naṣr b. Muʿāwiyah 63, 65
Banū Qays b. Thaʿlabah 17
Banū Qurayʿ 151, 152
Banū Riyāḥ b. Yarbūʿ 19
Banū Sadūs 6, 195
Banū Taym Allāh b. Thaʿlabah 8
Banū Umayyah 198
Banū Umayyah b. Zayd 208
Banū Yarbūʿ 19

al-Barāʾ (b. Qabīṣah b. Abī ʿAqīl al-Thaqafī) 14
al-Barājim 191, 196
Barmak 129
al-Barūqān 154–55
Bashshār b. ʿAmr (narrator) 177
Bashshār b. Muslim al-Bāhilī 143
Baskharāʾ 187
al-Baṣrah xiii, 9–19, 21, 34, 46–49, 67, 69, 130, 139, 156–57, 214, 217
al-Baṭāʾiḥ 157–58
bayna al-ashajj wa-bayna Qays 59, 62
Bishr b. ʿĪsā (narrator) 174
Bishr b. al-Mundhir b. al-Jārūd al-ʿAbdī 69
Bishr b. al-Walīd b. ʿAbd al-Malik 217–19
Bisṭām b. Maṣqalah b. Hubayrah 37, 38, 43–44, 47–48, 69
Bīward 155, 164
al-Budandūn (Podendon) 146
Bukayr b. Rabīʿah b. Tharwān al-Ḍabbī 48, 70
Bukayr b. Wishāḥ 94
Bukhārā 90–91, 96–97, 100, 135, 137–38, 146–47, 150, 152, 176–77, 197, 205, 216
Bukhārā Khudhāh 177
Būlaq 134
Būlus (and Qumqum) 134
Burj al-Ḥamām 204
Bust 6, 50
B.yār 229
Byzantine Emperor/king 142, 149–50
Byzantines xiv, 72, 134, 140, 142, 146, 149–50, 184

C

China 144, 171, 224–26, 228
Chosroes 7
Cordova 201
Ctesiphon 7 n. 14

D

al-Ḍaḥḥāk b. Yazīd b. Huzayl 102
Dāhir b. Ṣaṣṣah 149, 223
Damascus 126, 142, 198, 218–19, 223
Ḍamrah b. Rabīʿah (narrator) 67
Dār Marwān 132, 206
Dastawā 12
Dāwūd b. Jubayr (narrator) 132
Dayr al-Jamājim, battle 8, 20–26, 35–
    44, 46, 58, 72
Dayr Murrān 219
Dayr Qurrah 22
Dharr b. ʿAbdallāh al-Hamdānī 6
dhirāʿ 172
Dhū al-Ḥulàyfah 144
Dhū Khushub 179
Dhū Ṭawā 148 n 498
Dhubāb 113
Dīnār al-Sijistānī 27
Ḍirār b. Ḥuṣayn al-Ḍabbī 135, 169
Dujayl (river = Kārūn) 10, 47, 69
durrāʿah 180

E

Egypt xii, 80, 109, 111–12, 114, 149,
    156, 214
Euphrates 44, 75

F

al-Faḍl b. ʿAbbās b. Rabīʿah b. al-
    Ḥārith b. ʿAbd al-Muṭṭalib (al-
    Hāshimī) 16
al-Faḍl b. Suwayd (narrator) 211
Fahm b. ʿAmr (tribe) 119
al-Falālīj 22
al-Fallūjah 43
fals 219
Fanj Jāh 166
faqīh, pl. fuqahāʾ 35, 213
al-Farādīs graveyards 219
al-Farazdaq 64–65, 84, 158

Farghānah 143, 190, 195, 197, 204–6,
    224
Farghānah valley (south of Baghlān)
    166
Fārs 7–8, 16, 18, 24, 65, 156, 228
Fartanā 90
al-Fāryāb 147, 154, 165
Fāṭimah bt. ʿAbd al-Malik b. Marwān
    118
Fayrūz Ḥusayn, Abū ʿUthmān 56, 64,
    67
the Fazāriyyah, mother of Abū
    ʿUbaydah b. al-Walīd b. ʿAbd al-
    Malik 219
(al-)Fīl 186–89, 229
fitnah 8
fityān 105
F.ryāb (a place in Transoxania) 175
Fuḍayl b. Khadīj (al-Kindī) 10
fuqahāʾ; see faqīh
Furs 165

G

ghāliyah 226
al-Gharriyān 16
Gharshistān 165 n. 544
Ghazalah (Gazelon) 142, 184, 204
Ghazwān al-Iskāf, lord of Zamm 27
ghulām 30, 64
Ghūrak 176, 177, 192, 194–95, 197–
    98
Ghurrab 159
Ghushtāsbān 128, 174
Guftān 95, 98, 106, 128

H

Ḥāʾ, mīm 104
Ḥabīb b. ʿAbdallāh b. ʿAmr b. Ḥuṣayn
    al-Bāhilī 172
Ḥabīb b. al-Muhallab 31–32, 63–64,
    129, 157, 162

Ḥabīb b. 'Uqbah b. Nāfi' al-Fihrī 201
Ḥafṣ b. 'Umar b. Qabīṣah (narrator) 56
hajīn 195
al-Ḥajjāj b. 'Abd al-Malik b. Marwān 118
al-Ḥajjāj b. Jāriyah al-Khath'amī 25, 39
al-Ḥajjāj b. Marwān 107
al-Ḥajjāj al-Qaynī 171
al-Ḥajjāj b. Yūsuf al-Thaqafī xi–xv, 3–27, 32–34, 38–42, 44–48, 50–51, 57–71, 72–73, 76–88, 105, 109, 111–12, 115, 126, 128–30, 135, 138–40, 147, 149, 150, 152, 156–60, 162–63, 169–70, 172, 175, 195, 198, 201, 202, 206–7, 209–14, 216–17, 220–21, 223
al-Ḥajūn 148
al-Ḥakam b. 'Abd al-Malik b. Marwān 118
al-Ḥakam b. Ayyūb (sometimes wrongly Ayyūb b. al-Ḥakam) b. Abī 'Aqīl al-Thaqafī 11–12, 19, 46, 130
al-Ḥakam b. Makhramah al-'Abdī 69
al-Ḥakam b. 'Uthmān (narrator) 225
ḥalīf 19, 76
Hamdān 7, 21
Ḥamīdah (or Ḥumaydah), the daughter (or sister) of Ziyād b. Muqātil 17
Ḥammād b. Muslim (al-Bāhilī) 165
Ḥammām 'Umar 70
Ḥamzah b. Bīḍ 194–95
Ḥamzah b. Ibrāhīm (narrator) 171–72
Ḥanafī sword 169
Ḥanbal b. Abī Ḥuraydah (narrator) 171–72, 174, 185
Ḥanẓalah b. al-Warrād al-Tamīmī 19
al-Ḥaram 178–79
ḥarb 13, 127, 130, 139, 164, 200, 217
al-Ḥarīsh b. Hilāl al-Sa'dī 17–18
al-Ḥārith (b. Muḥammad) (narrator) 114, 116–17
al-Ḥārith b. Mālik b. Rabī'ah al-Ash'arī 163
al-Ḥārith b. Munqidh, uterine brother

of Ḥurayth and Thābit, the sons of Quṭbah 96
al-Ḥārith b. Rabī'ah; see al-Ḥārith b. Mālik
al-Ḥārith b. Wa'lah 8
Hārūn b. 'Īsā (narrator) 134
al-Ḥasan b. Abān al-'Ulaymī 160
al-Ḥasan b. Rushayd al-Jurjānī (narrator) 126, 137, 174, 185, 188
al-Hāshimī; see 'Abd al-Raḥmān b. 'Abbās b. Rabī'ah
Ḥātim b. Abī Ṣaghīrah (narrator) 197
Ḥawrān 216
Hawshab (an executioner) 66
Hawshab b. Yazīd 72, 73
Hayṣam al-Khārijī 207
al-Haytham b. al-Munakhkhal al-Jurmūzī 27
Ḥayyān (b. Iyās) al-'Adawī 196
Ḥayyān al-Nabaṭī 153, 200
Hazārasp 186–87
Hephthalites 97
Herat 52–53, 64, 77, 155, 164
Hilāl b. Khabbāb (narrator) 213
al-Hilqām b. Nu'aym b. al-Qa'qā' b. Ma'bad b. Zurārah 56–57, 66
al-Hilwāth al-Kalbī (narrator) 223
al-Hind 204, 215, 219, 223
Hind bt. al-Muhallab 157
Hiraqlah (Herakleia) 146, 215
Hishām b. 'Abd al-Malik b. Marwān xv, 118, 134
Hishām b. Ayyūb b. 'Abd al-Raḥmān b. Abi 'Aqīl (al-Thaqafī) 19, 49, 57
Hishām b. Ḥassān 68
Hishām b. Ismā'īl al-Makhzūmī 33, 71, 76, 113–15, 129, 131–33
Hishām b. Muḥammad; see Ibn al-Kalbī
Ḥiṣn al-Ḥadīd 184
Ḥīt 22
Horsemen of Soghd 91
Ḥ.shwrā 100
Hubayrah b. al-Mushamraj al-Kilābī 225, 227–28

(al-)Ḥuḍayn b. al-Mundhir, Abū Sāsān
    86–87, 194
Hudhayl 76
Hulays (b. Ghālib) al-Shaybānī 56
Ḥumayd al-Arqaṭ 82
Ḥumaydah; see Ḥamīdah
Huraym b. Abi Ṭaḥmah al-Mujāshiʿī
    151
Ḥurayth b. Quṭbah, mawlā of
    Khuzāʿah 29–31, 96–99
Ḥusayn (b. ʿAlī) 65
Ḥusayn b. Mujāhid al-Rāzī (narrator)
    134
ḥuṭamiyyah 150

I

Ibn Abī Dhiʾb 13
Ibn Abī Mulaykah (ʿAbdallāh b.
    ʿUbaydallāh) 145
Ibn Abī Sabrah (narrator) 40, 144
Ibn ʿAffān; see ʿUthmān b. ʿAffān
Ibn ʿĀʾishah (narrator) 81
ibn ʿamm 39, 45
Ibn al-Ashʿath; see ʿAbd al-Raḥmān b.
    Muḥammad b. al-Ashʿath
Ibn ʿAttāb b. Warqāʾ (= Khālid b.
    ʿAttāb?) 19
Ibn Bahlah; see al-Mufaḍḍal b. al-
    Muhallab
Ibn Bassām al-Laythī 168
Ibn al-Ḥaḍramī; see ʿAbd al-Raḥmān
    b. ʿAbdallāh b. ʿĀmir al-Ḥaḍramī
Ibn Jaʿdah b. Hubayrah 43
Ibn Juʿdubah (narrator) 113
Ibn al-Kalbī, Hishām b. Muḥammad
    (narrator) 4, 14, 20, 35, 39, 46,
    56–57, 73, 77, 81, 88, 156, 160,
    218
Ibn Kāwān island 103
Ibn Muḥammad b. al-Ashʿath; see
    ʿAbd al-Raḥmān b. Muḥammad b.
    al-Ashʿath
Ibn Muḥayriz al-Jumaḥī 140
Ibn al-Qalammas 119

Ibn Qays al-Ruqayyāt 117
Ibn al-Qirriyyah; see Ayyūb b. al-
    Qirriyyah
Ibn Saʿd (narrator) 114, 116–17
Ibn Shawdhab (narrator) 67
Ibn Ṭalḥah; see ʿAbd al-Raḥmān b.
    Ṭalḥah
Ibn ʿUbaydallāh b. ʿAbd al-Raḥmān b.
    Samurah 66
Ibn ʿUmar; see ʿAbdallāh b. ʿUmar
Ibn Wahb (ʿAbdallāh) (narrator) 218
Ibn Ziyād (ʿUbaydallāh b. Ziyād) 103
Ibn al-Zubayr; see ʿAbdallāh b. al-
    Zubayr
Ibrāhīm b. al-Walīd b. ʿAbd al-Malik
    219
Idrīs b. Ḥanẓalah (narrator) 147, 150
Ifrīqiyah 201, 215
iḥrām 144
Ikhshād of Farghānah 190–91, 195
ʿilj, pl. *aʿlāj* 25, 68
imātat al-ṣalāt 36 n. 151
ʿImrān b. Faḍīl al-Burjumī 139
ʿImrān b. ʿIṣām al-ʿAnazī 109–11
Iraq xi–xiii, xv, 6, 9–10, 13, 23, 44,
    60, 66, 72, 88, 97, 102, 115–16,
    129, 139, 156, 201, 207, 214, 216,
    223
ʿIṣām al-ʿAnazī 111
ʿIṣām pass 224
Iṣbahān 182, 209
Iṣbahbadh of Balkh 154, 165
Isḥāq b. ʿĪsā (narrator) 13, 34, 71, 76,
    115–16, 129, 139, 145, 148, 156,
    179, 183, 202, 214, 217
Isḥāq b. Muḥammad b. al-Ashʿath 4
Isḥāq b. Yaḥyā 180–81
Iskīmisht 166, 170
Island of ʿUthmān 106
Ismāʿīl b. Ibrāhīm b. ʿUqbah (narrator)
    178
isnād 189
Īwān 7
ʿIyāḍ b. ʿAmr 6 n. 12, 50 n. 188
ʿIyāḍ b. Himyān al-Bakrī 6, 50
ʿIyāḍ b. Ḥuḍayn b. al-Mundhir 87

Iyās b. ʿAbdallāh b. ʿAmr 127, 200
Iyās b. Bayhas al-Bāhilī 137
Iyās b. al-Zuhayr (narrator) 224

J

Jabalah b. Farrūkh (narrator) 133, 174
Jabalah b. Zaḥr b. Qays al-Juʿfī 25–26, 35–37, 39
Jabghūyah 154–55, 166, 168, 172
Jābir b. al-Aswad b. ʿAwf al-Zuhrī 114
Jābir b. ʿUmārah of the Banū Ḥanīfah (narrator) 56
al-Jadalī 192
al-Jahm al-Bāhilī (narrator) 152
Jahm b. Zaḥr 152, 206
Jamʿ 145
jamāʿah 31
al-Jamājim; see Dayr al-Jamājim
Janūb 16
Jarāmiqah 40
Jarīr (b. ʿAṭiyyah b. al-Khaṭafā) 212, 221
Jarm 8
al-Jarrāḥ b. ʿAbdallāh al-Ḥakamī 26, 39–40, 139, 156, 214
al-Jazīrah 22
Jerusalem 84
jihād 175
jinn 93
jizā 74
Judayʿ b. Yazīd 54
Juʿfī 199
al-Jūzjān 154, 165, 172
al-Jūzjānī, king of al-Jūzjān 154

K

Kaʿb b. Maʿdān al-Ashqarī 28, 74, 89, 187, 189, 199
Kaʿbah 181
Kabul 53, 97, 171
Kābul Shāh 154, 166
Kalb 158

al-Kalbī, Muḥammad b. al-Sāʾib (narrator) 24, 39, 44
al-Kallāʾ 11
al-Kāmil, Yazīd b. al-Muhallab's horse 54
al-Karkh 69
Kāsān 205, 206
Kāshghar xiii, 219, 224, 225
Kaskar 71
Kathīr b. fulān 225
al-Kayraj 215
Kāzah 187, 188
Kāz.r.nk 229
khabīṣ 167
Khalaf b. Khalīfah (narrator) 212
Khālid b. ʿAbdallāh al-Qasrī xv, 144, 147, 177–78, 181, 202, 210, 212, 214
Khālid b. Abī Barzah 106, 107
Khālid b. al-Aṣfaḥ (narrator) 198
Khālid b. Bāb, mawlā of Muslim b. ʿAmr (narrator) 192
Khālid b. Barmak 129
Khālid b. Jarīr b. ʿAbdallāh al-Qasrī 47
Khālid b. Kaysān 149
Khālid b. al-Qāsim (al-Bayāḍī) (narrator) 208
Khālid b. Qaṭan al-Ḥārithī (narrator) 59
Khālid b. al-Walīd b. ʿAbd al-Malik 219
Khālid b. Yazīd b. Muʿāwiyah 9
khalīfah 147
Kham Jird 184, 186
Khanjarah (Gangra) 184
Khāqān 18, 152, 195
kharāj 6, 13, 54, 127, 164, 200, 217
Kharashah b. ʿAmr al-Tamīmī 8
Khārijah b. Zayd 132, 142
Khārijī(s) 27, 92, 207
Kharqān 147
Kharqānah 147
Khathʿam 39, 45
Khaṭīʾah, a slave girl 162
khaṭīb 5, 6, 44
Khawārij; see Khārijī(s)

Khāzim b. ʿAbdallāh b. Khāzim 99,
    108
khazz 101
Kh.dāsh 68
al-Khiyār b. Sabrah b. Dhuʾayb b.
    ʿArfajah b. Muḥammad b. Sufyān
    b. Mujāshiʿ 85
Kh.n.s Ṭarkhān 168
Khubayb b. ʿAbdallāh b. al-Zubayr 202
Khujandah 205
Khulayd ʿAynayn 55
Khulm 154, 156, 165–66
khums 17
Khurasan, xii–xiii, 10, 13, 26, 33, 34,
    47, 52–53, 67, 70, 76, 83, 85–88,
    92, 94, 96–97, 102, 104, 126–27,
    130, 136–38, 139, 156, 158, 160,
    194–95, 198, 214
Khurasani shaykh(s) (narrator[s]) 133,
    174, 225
Khurrazādh 185
Khushaynah b. al-Walīd (narrator) 6
Khuzāʿah 29, 103
Khuzāʿī (anonymous), opponent of
    Mūsā b. ʿAbdallāh b. Khāzim 94–
    96
Khwārazm 87, 104–9, 190, 194, 200,
    205, 229
Khwārazm Shāh 185–87, 201
al-Khwārazmī, mawlā of Qutaybah b.
    Muslim 224
Kilāb 39
Kirmān 8, 10, 16, 49, 79
Kish 27, 29, 31, 91–93, 100, 147, 174–
    77, 205, 216
K.shbyz 229
al-Kūfah xiii, 13, 16, 19 ff., 26, 34, 44,
    46, 48, 72, 130, 139, 156, 212,
    214, 217
Kulayb b. Khalaf al-ʿAmmī (narrator)
    87, 126, 153, 185
Kumayl b. Ziyād al-Nakhaʿī 26, 45
al-Kumayt b. Zayd al-Asadī 137, 198,
    229
kunyah 117
Kūrbaghānūn al-Turkī 143

Kurds 48, 156
al-Kurz 166, 169, 174
Kushmāhan 216

L

lā ʿidāʾ ʿayrayn 200
al-Liwā 159
Lower Kharqānah 147

M

Maʿadd b. ʿAdnān 7, 33
al-Madāʾin 19, 46
al-Madāʾinī, ʿAlī b. Muḥammad
    (narrator) 26–31, 53–56, 74, 76,
    83–88, 91–108, 109–13, 117–19,
    126, 133–39, 143, 147, 150–54,
    164–72, 174–77, 185–200, 216,
    218–29
Madhḥij 7
Maghrāʾ b. al-Mughīrah b. Abī Ṣufrah
    108
Māhān (narrator) 205
al-Mahdī 129
Maḥmiyah al-Sulamī 104
majlis, pl. *majālis* 139, 208
Makhlad b. Ḥamzah b. Bīḍ (narrator)
    194
Makhramah b. Sulaymān al-Wālibī
    (narrator) 141
Makhshiyyah 198
maktab 10
Malaṭyah 184
Mālik b. Ismāʿīl; see Abū Ghassān
al-Mandal 215
al-Manṣūr, ʿAbdallāh b. Muḥammad b.
    ʿAlī 217
Manṣūr b. Jumhūr al-Kalbī 46
Manṣūr al-Khārijī 207, 209
Manṣūr b. al-Walīd b. ʿAbd al-Malik
    219
Maʿqil, a shaykh of ʿAbd al-Qays 49

Mardādhān 187
Marw 26–27, 29, 31–32, 54, 56, 90,
	94, 102, 127–28, 135, 137, 143,
	147, 152, 164, 171–72, 176–77,
	185, 190, 199–200, 206, 216, 225
Marw (al-)Rūdh 31, 33, 54, 87, 135,
	154, 165, 199
Marwān b. ʿAbd al-Malik b. Marwān
	118
Marwān al-Akbar b. ʿAbd al-Malik b.
	Marwān 118
Marwān b. al-Muhallab 157
Marwān b. al-Walīd b. ʿAbd al-Malik
	184, 219
Marzbān of Qūhistān (narrator) 171–
	72, 174, 185
al-Marzbānayn 215
Māsabadhān 38
Māsah (Amaseia) 184
Masāmiʿah 11 n. 38
Maskin 47 n. 178
Maskin, battle 46–48, 53, 63, 68, 69
Maslamah b. ʿAbd al-Malik b. Marwān
	118, 129, 133–34, 140–42, 146,
	148–49, 164, 182, 184, 214
Maṣqalah b. Karib b. Raqabah al-ʿAbdī
	44
Masrūr b. al-Walīd b. ʿAbd al-Malik
	219
al-Maṣṣīṣah 72, 134
Maṭar b. Nājiyah al-Yarbūʿī 19–21
maṭārif 226
maʿūnah 19
Mawdūd al-Naḍrī al-ʿAnbarī 78–79
Mawqūʿ 158
al-Mawṣil 23, 44
Maymūn al-Jurjumānī 134
Maysān 84
Mecca xv, 145, 147, 156, 177, 181,
	202, 206, 210, 212, 214
Medina xiv, 13, 33, 71, 113, 114, 131–
	32, 139, 141–42, 144, 156, 178,
	179, 180, 183, 201, 202–3, 206–7,
	209, 214, 219
Miḥfan b. Jazʾ al-Kilābī 170
Minā 145

al-Mirbad 17
Mismaʿ b. Mālik b. Mismaʿ 70
miṣr, pl. amṣār 16, 22, 48, 62, 71, 76,
	88, 135, 141, 145, 148, 181, 183,
	202, 217
mithqāl 137, 142, 194
Moses 105
Mosul; see al-Mawṣil
Muʿāwiyah b. ʿAbd al-Malik b.
	Marwān 118
Muʿāwiyah b. Abī Sufyān 181, 208
Muʿāwiyah b. ʿĀmir b. ʿAlqamah
	al-ʿUlaymī 169
Muʿāwiyah b. Khālid b. Abī Barzah
	106
al-Mubashshir b. al-Walīd b. ʿAbd al-
	Malik 219
Muḍar 66, 133, 198
Mudrik b. al-Muhallab 105–7
al-Mufaḍḍal al-Ḍabbī; see al-Mufaḍḍal
	b. Muḥammad
al-Mufaḍḍal b. al-Muhallab xiii, 32,
	54–55, 83, 86, 88, 105, 108, 126,
	156–57
al-Mufaḍḍal b. Muḥammad al-Ḍabbī
	(narrator) 26, 29, 31, 53, 74, 83,
	88–89, 143, 153
al-Mughīrah b. ʿAbdallāh, subgovernor
	of Qutaybah's 154, 200–1
al-Mughīrah b. ʿAbdallāh b. Abī ʿAqīl
	130
al-Mughīrah b. Ḥabnāʾ 170, 173
al-Mughīrah b. al-Muhallab 13, 26–28
al-Muhallab, a Muslim of Shūmān
	175
al-Muhallab b. Abi Ṣufrah, Abū Saʿīd
	xiii, 9–11, 13, 26–33, 64, 89, 96,
	139, 160, 199
al-Muhallab b. Iyās al-ʿAdawī
	(narrator) 134, 137, 147, 150, 153,
	169, 185–86, 224
Muhallabids xiii, xv, 84–85, 88
Muḥammad, the Prophet 8–9, 61,
	141, 198
Muḥammad b. Abān b. ʿAbdallāh 10
	n. 30

Muḥammad b. ʿAbd al-Malik b.
Marwān 118
Muḥammad b. ʿAbd al-Raḥmān b. al-
Ḥārith b. Hishām 179
Muḥammad b. ʿAbdallāh b. Abī
Ḥurrah (narrator) 207
Muḥammad b. ʿAbdallāh b. Jubayr,
mawlā of the Banū al-ʿAbbās
(narrator) 144
Muḥammad b. ʿAbdallāh b. Marthad
al-Khuzāʿī 99
Muḥammad b. ʿAbdallāh b.
Muḥammad b. ʿUmar (narrator)
132
Muḥammad b. Abī ʿUyaynah 194
Muḥammad b. al-Ashʿath 58
Muḥammad b. al-Ḥajjāj 16, 48
Muḥammad b. Ḥātim (narrator) 213
Muḥammad b. Jaʿfar b. Wardān al-
Bannāʾ (narrator) 141
Muḥammad b. Marwān 24, 44
Muḥammad b. al-Muthannā (narrator)
133
Muḥammad b. al-Qāsim al-Thaqafī
xiii, 149, 204, 206, 219, 223
Muḥammad b. Saʿd b. Abī Waqqāṣ 25,
46, 56–57, 65
Muḥammad b. al-Sāʾib; see al-Kalbī
Muḥammad b. Sulaym al-Nāṣiḥ 155
Muḥammad b. ʿUmar; see al-Wāqidī
Muḥammad b. al-Walīd b. ʿAbd al-
Malik 219
Muḥammad b. Yazīd al-Anṣārī 112
Muḥammad b. Yūsuf al-Thaqafī 221–
22
al-Muḥill al-Ṭufāwī 101
muhtab[in] 197
Mujāhid (b. Jabr) 210
al-Mujashshar b. Muzāḥim al-Sulamī
189
Mujjāʿah b. ʿAbd al-Raḥmān al-ʿAtakī
27–28
Mujjāʿah b. Siʿr al-Saʿdī 85
al-Mukhtār b. Abī ʿUbayd 7 n. 15
Mulaykah, wife of ʿAbd al-Raḥmān b.
Muḥammad b. al-Ashʿath 43, 78

al-Munakhkhal b. Ḥābis al-ʿAbdī
(narrator) 6, 49
al-Mundhir b. ʿAbd al-Malik b.
Marwān 118
al-Mundhir b. al-Jārūd 15
Munqidh al-ʿIrāqī 207
Murrah b. ʿAṭāʾ b. Abī al-Sāʾib 56
Mūsā, a man reproved in a line of
verse 105
Mūsā b. ʿAbdallāh b. Khāzim al-
Sulamī xiii, 31, 56, 90–108
Mūsā b. Abī Bakr (narrator) 142, 179
Mūsā b. al-Mutawakkil al-Qurayʿī
(narrator) 151
Mūsā b. Nuṣayr xiv, 164, 182, 201,
215, 219
Mūsā b. ʿUqbah 178
Mūsā b. Yaʿqūb (narrator) 142
Muṣʿab (b. ʿAbdallāh b. Abī ʿAqīl al-
Thaqafī) 14–15
Muṣʿab b. Ḥayyān (narrator) 143, 170
Muṣʿab b. al-Zubayr 116, 213
Muslim b. ʿAmr al-Bāhilī, father of
Qutaybah 138–39, 192
Muslim b. Qutaybah 129
mustaʿribah 134, 142
Muṭahhar b. Ḥurr al-ʿAkkī (or al-
Judhāmī) 10–12
Muṭarrif b. ʿĀmir b. Wāthilah al-
Kinānī 5
Muzāḥim, mawlā of ʿUmar b. ʿAbd
al-ʿAzīz 202

N

al-Naḍīr 172, 190
al-Naḍr b. Shumayl (narrator) 68
al-Naḍr b. Sulaymān b. ʿAbdallāh b.
Khāzim 106–7
nafal 192
Nāfiʿ, mawlā of the Banū Makhzūm
(narrator) 147, 178
Nāfiʿ b. ʿAlqamah 84
Nahār b. Tawsiʿah al-Taymī 32, 147,
172, 199

Nahr Tīrā 68
Nahshal b. Yazīd (narrator) 195
Nasaf 27, 100, 147, 174–77, 205, 216
Naṣr b. ʿAbd al-Ḥamīd al-Khuzāʿī 99
Naṣr b. Sayyār 128
al-Nawbahār 129, 154
Nawfal b. Musāḥiq al-ʿĀmirī 33
Nile 75
Nishapur 90, 201
Nīzak, Abū al-Hayyāj 74–76, 96–97,
    103–4, 133–34, 143, 153–56,
    164–74
Nūḥ b. ʿAbdallāh b. Khāzim 99, 103–
    4, 108
al-Nujayr 62
Nūqān 91
Nuṣayr, mawlā of al-Faḍl b. ʿAbbās 16

O

Oxus 29, 90, 99, 186

P

Palestine xv, 84, 159
Paykand 134–37
Pharaoh 6, 46

Q

Qabīṣah b. Dhuʾayb, Abū Isḥāq 108–9,
    181
al-Qādisiyyah 21
Qaḥṭān 7, 33, 64
qalansuwwah 180
Qamūdiyyah (Kamouliana) 146
Qaryah, in Fārs 228
al-Qāsim b. Muḥammad 132, 142
al-Qāsim b. Muḥammad b. al-Ashʿath
    6, 79–80
al-Qāsim b. Muḥammad al-Ḥaḍramī
    (narrator) 56
Qaṣr al-Māʾ 215

qāṣṣ 6
Qaybishtasbān 174
al-Qayrawān 215
Qays 44, 85, 96, 97, 206
qiblah 141, 180
Qinnasrīn 216
qubbah 99 n. 370, 110
Quḍāʿah 61
Qudāmah b. al-Ḥarīsh al-Tamīmī 40–
    42
Qudāmah b. Yazīd b. Huzayl 102
Qūmis 105
Qumqum 134
Qurʾān 32, 140, 163, 220–21
Quraysh 14, 21–22, 25, 61, 81, 110,
    121, 144
Qurayẓah 172, 190
qurrāʾ 12, 15, 22, 25–26, 35–37, 67,
    211
Qurrah b. Sharīk 149, 156, 214
Qusṭanṭīn 142
Qutaybah b. Muslim al-Bāhilī, Abū
    Ḥafṣ xii–xiii, 38, 58, 63, 85, 87,
    108, 126–30, 133, 134–39, 143,
    146–47, 150–56, 158, 164–77,
    183–201, 204–6, 214–16, 219,
    223, 224–25, 228–29

R

al-Rabadhah 210
Rabīʿah 38, 97
rafāghah 22
Rajāʾ b. Ḥaywah (al-Kindī) 181
rajaz poet 28
Rāmithanah 143, 146
Raqabah b. al-Ḥurr al-ʿAnbarī 100–1,
    103, 107
Raqāsh 194
rasūl 148
Rawḥ b. al-Walīd b. ʿAbd al-Malik
    219, 221
Rawḥ b. Zinbāʿ al-Judhāmī, Abū
    Zurʿah 108–9
al-Rayy 38, 58, 63, 99, 129

ridā' 150, 180, 212, 226
riṭl 54
Riyāḥ b. ʿUbaydallāh 207
Roderic; see Adrīnūq
al-Ruʾb 165
Ruʾb Khān 165
al-Rukhkhaj 80
al-Ruqād b. ʿUbayd (or Ziyād) al-Azdī
    al-ʿAtakī 53
Rustam 98
Rustāqubādh 12, 156

S

al-Sabal 96–97, 106, 171
Sabrah b. (al-)Nakhf b. Abī Ṣufrah 56
Sābūr 48
Saʿd b. Najd al-Qurdūsī 56
Saʿd b. ʿUbaydallāh (narrator) 81
Ṣadaqah b. al-Walīd b. ʿAbd al-Malik
    219
Safawān 17
Ṣaffūriyyah 25
al-Ṣaghāniyān 97, 102, 104, 127–28
Saḥbān Wāʾil 205
Sahm b. ʿAbd al-Raḥmān al-Juhanī
    (narrator) 19, 37
Saʿīd b. ʿAmr al-Anṣārī (narrator) 208–
    9
Saʿīd b. ʿAmr b. al-Aswad al-Ḥarashī
    (narrator) 40–42
Saʿīd b. al-ʿĀṣ (al-Umawī) 23
Saʿīd al-Ḥarashī; see Saʿīd b. ʿAmr b.
    al-Aswad al-Ḥarashī
Saʿīd b. Jubayr, Abū ʿAbdallāh 25, 36,
    42, 209–13
Saʿīd al-Khayr b. ʿAbd al-Malik b.
    Marwān 118
Saʿīd b. al-Musayyab 113–15, 132,
    179–80, 213
Saʿīd b. Yaḥyā b. Saʿīd b. al-ʿĀṣ (al-
    Umawī) 15
Salamah b. Zayd b. Wahb b. Nubātah
    al-Fahmī 118–19

ṣalāt 129, 217
Ṣāliḥ b. Kaysān (narrator) 40, 142,
    144–45, 179
Ṣāliḥ b. Muslim, brother of Qutaybah
    128, 170, 175, 191, 196
Sālim b. ʿAbdallāh b. ʿUmar 132, 142
Sālim al-Afṭas (narrator) 213
Salm b. Qutaybah 194
Samarqand 91, 188–200, 224
Samasṭiyyah (Mistheia) 184
al-Samāwah 158
Sarakhs 155, 164
al-Sarī b. Ismāʿīl (narrator) 58
Sawādah b. ʿAbdallāh al-Salūlī 228
Sawwār, mawlā of Mūsā b. ʿAbdallāh
    b. Khāzim 98
Sawwār b. Marwān 56
Sawwār b. Zahdam al-Jarmī 170
Sayf b. Bishr al-ʿIjlī (narrator) 6, 49
sayyid 27
al-Shaʿbī, ʿĀmir b. Sharāḥīl 25, 36, 58,
    59
al-Shadh 155, 171
shākiriyyah 31, 99, 103, 104
Shaqrāʾ bt. Salamah b. Ḥalbas al-Ṭāʾī,
    wife of ʿAbd al-Malik b. Marwān
    118
Shaqrān; see ʿUthmān (called Shaqrān)
Sharawrā 60
sharīf, pl. *ashrāf* xi–xii, 55, 58, 67,
    229
al-Shāsh 190–91, 195, 197, 204–6,
    215–16
al-Shaybānī (narrator) 67
Sh.bās 187
Shuʿbah b. Zuhayr 195–96
Shūmān 89, 126, 128, 133, 174–75,
    177
Shuraḥbīl b. Abī ʿAwn (narrator) 116
al-Sīb 68–69
Ṣiffīn 35
Sijistān xii, 5, 6, 9–10, 18, 48, 50–53,
    63, 79, 177, 183, 189
Siminjān 166
Sinān al-Aʿrābī 107
Sind xi, xiii, 56, 149

Siyāh, mawlā of Qutaybah b. Muslim
    135
Soghd 91, 106, 153, 176–77, 185, 188–
    90, 195–200, 205, 229
Soghdians 135, 143, 147, 150, 189–95,
    197
Solomon, son of David 201
Sufyān b. al-Abrad al-Kalbī 15, 25, 42,
    47–48, 61
Sufyān b. Sulaymān al-Azdī 159
Suhrak, king of al-Ṭālaqān 154
Ṣūl, son of Nīzak's brother 168, 170,
    173–74
Ṣūl Ṭarkhān 168
Sulaym al-Nāṣiḥ, mawlā of
    ʿUbaydallāh b. Abī Bakrah 133,
    136, 166–69
Sulaymān b. ʿAbd al-Malik xiv–xv, 13,
    112–14, 118, 156, 159–63, 221–
    24
Sulaymān b. Abī Rāshid (narrator) 78
Sulaymān b. ʿAlī 194
Sulaymān b. Ḥabīb (al-Muḥāribī) 213
Sulaymān b. Kathīr al-ʿAmmī
    (narrator) 126
Sulaymān b. Mujālid (narrator) 174
Sulaymān b. Yasār 132
Sumayyah (wife of ʿĀmir b.
    Wāthilah?) 18
Sūriyah (Isauria) 146, 149, 204
al-Sūs 48
Sūsanah (Sision) 134, 182
al-Suwaydāʾ 179, 202
Syria xii, 10, 22, 44, 116, 159, 172,
    198, 204, 207, 213, 223

T

al-Ṭabasayn 56
(Banū) Taghlib 33, 138
al-Ṭāʾif 156
takbīr 94, 95
al-Ṭālaqān 127, 154–56, 165, 172
Talastānah 87

Ṭalḥah b. ʿAbdallāh al-Khuzāʿī 64, 103
Ṭalq b. Ḥabīb 210
(Banū) Tamīm 21, 50, 90, 97, 150–52
Tammām b. al-Walīd b. ʿAbd al-Malik
    219
Tanʿīm 144
Ṭarafah (b. al-ʿAbd) 198
Tarḥamah 184
Ṭāriq b. ʿAbdallāh al-Asadī 38
Ṭāriq b. Ziyād, mawlā of Mūsā b.
    Nuṣayr xiv, 182, 201
Ṭarkhūn 91–92, 96–98, 100, 102–4,
    106, 152, 176–77, 190, 196
Ṭawā 148
Ṭaybah 202
Tayhān b. Abjar 8
Thābit al-Aʿwar, mawlā of Muslim
    185
Thābit b. Quṭbah 30–31, 96–97, 99–
    103, 105, 107
Thābit Quṭnah 172, 229
Thamūd 198
Thaqīf 7, 14, 45, 85
Thawr b. Yazīd (narrator) 140
Thomas, church of 224
Tibetans 97
Tīdhar 135
Tigris 68–69, 71
Tinjānah 128
al-Tirmidh xiii, 90, 92–94, 99, 100,
    106, 108, 128, 143
Tirmidh Shāh 92–93
Tīsh al-Aʿwar, king of al-Ṣaghāniyān
    127–28
Toledo 201
Transoxania xiii, 27, 97, 105
(al-)Ṭufayl b. ʿĀmir b. Wāthilah 16, 18
Ṭufayl b. Mirdās al-ʿAmmī (narrator)
    126, 137, 174, 185
Ṭukhāristān xiii, 128, 153–56
Ṭūlus 215
Tūmushkath 138, 143
Turks 27–29, 93–94, 97–98, 106, 143,
    148, 150, 164, 167–68, 172, 197,
    199, 229
Tūsik, king of al-Fāryāb 154

Tustar 10, 12, 24
Ṭuwānah (Tyana) 134, 140–41

U

ʿUbayd b. Abī Ṣubayʿ al-Tamīmī al-
    Yarbūʿī 78–80
ʿUbayd b. Mawhab 14, 84
ʿUbayd b. Sarjis 11
ʿUbaydallāh b. ʿAbd al-Raḥmān b.
    Samurah b. Ḥabīb b. ʿAbd Shams
    al-Qurashī 46, 52, 53, 56–57, 66,
    82, 108
ʿUbaydallāh b. ʿAbdallāh b. ʿUtbah
    132, 142
ʿUbaydallāh b. Abī Bakrah 133
ʿUbaydallāh b. Maʿmar 56
ʿUbaydallāh b. ʿUbaydallāh, mawlā of
    the Banū Muslim 200
ʿUdayy al-Raḥmān (= ʿAbd al-Raḥmān
    b. Muḥammad b. al-Ashʿath) 21,
    57; cf. 211
al-ʿUdhayb 21
ʿUmān 85
ʿUmar (b. Shabbah, Abū Zayd)
    (narrator) 81, 109, 117, 219, 221–
    23
ʿUmar b. ʿAbd al-ʿAzīz b. Marwān xiv–
    xv, 131–32, 139, 141–42, 144–45,
    148, 156, 179–81, 183, 201–3,
    220–21, 223
ʿUmar b. ʿAbdallāh al-Tamīmī
    (narrator) 198
ʿUmar b. Abī al-Ṣalt b. Kanārā, mawlā
    of the Banū Naṣr b. Muʿāwiyah
    63, 65
ʿUmar b. Dharr b. ʿAbdallāh al-
    Hamdānī 6
ʿUmar b. Ḍubayʿah al-Raqāshī 69
ʿUmar b. al-Khaṭṭāb 141, 207
ʿUmar b. Mūsā b. ʿUbaydallāh b.
    Maʿmar 57–58, 65
ʿUmar b. Ṣāliḥ (narrator) 147
ʿUmar b. al-Walīd b. ʿAbd al-Malik
    145, 182, 219, 221
ʿUmārah b. Tamīm al-Lakhmī 25, 49,
    52, 68, 78–80

ʿUmayr b. Tayhān 24
Umayyah b. ʿAbdallāh b. Khālid b.
    Asīd 94, 96
Umm Abīhā bt. ʿAbdallāh b. Jaʿfar,
    wife of ʿAbd al-Malik b. Marwān
    118
Umm Ayyūb bt. ʿAmr b. ʿUthmān b.
    ʿAffān, wife of ʿAbd al-Malik b.
    Marwān 118
Umm al-Banīn bt. ʿAbd al-ʿAzīz b.
    Marwān 219, 221–22
Umm Ḥafṣ, daughter of Thābit b.
    Quṭbah 96
Umm Hishām bt. Hishām b. Ismāʿīl b.
    Hishām b. al-Walīd b. al-
    Mughīrah al-Makhzūmī, wife of
    ʿAbd al-Malik b. Marwān 118
Umm Kulthūm bt. ʿAbd al-Malik b.
    Marwān 118
Umm al-Mughīrah bt. al-Mughīrah b.
    Khālid b. al-ʿĀṣ b. Hishām b. al-
    Mughīrah, wife of ʿAbd al-Malik
    b. Marwān 118
umm walad 118, 132
Upper Bukhārā 135
ʿUqbah b. ʿAbd al-Ghāfir al-Azdī al-
    Jahḍamī 12, 15
ʿurafāʾ 192
ʿUrām b. Shutayr al-Ḍabbī 152
ʿUrwah b. al-Zubayr 132, 213
ʿUthmān (called Shaqrān), the son of
    Nīzak's brother 168, 170, 173–74
ʿUthmān b. ʿAffān 23, 45, 117, 141,
    181
ʿUthmān b. Ḥayyān al-Murrī 202–3,
    206–9, 214
ʿUthmān island 106
ʿUthmān b. Masʿūd (al-Nājī?) 105–8
ʿUthmān b. al-Saʿdī 127
ʿUthmān b. Yazīd b. ʿAbdallāh b.
    Khālid b. Asīd 220

W

al-Waḍḍāḥī 217
Wādī al-Sibāʿ 21
al-Wahb 159

Wahb b. Jarīr (b. Ḥāzim) (narrator) 211
Wakīʿ b. Abī Sūd, Abū Muṭarrif 150–
      51
Waksh Khāshān 170
Waʾlān al-ʿAdawī 138, 139
al-Walīd b. ʿAbd al-Malik xi, xiv–xv,
      109–14, 118, 125–26, 131–32,
      140–42, 144, 148–50, 156, 158,
      160–63, 172, 177, 179–81, 195,
      201–2, 206, 209–10, 213, 216–25,
      228
al-Walīd b. Hishām al-Muʿaytī 204
al-Walīd b. Hishām b. Qaḥdham
      (narrator) 67
al-Walīd b. Naḥīt al-Kalbī 39
al-Walīd b. Yazīd b. ʿAbd al-Malik 141
Wallādah bt. al-ʿAbbās b. Jazʾ b. al-
      Ḥārith b. Zubayr b. Jadhīmah b.
      Rawāḥah b. Rabīʿah b. Māzin b.
      al-Ḥārith b. Qutayʿah b. ʿAbs b.
      Baghīḍ, wife of ʿAbd al-Malik b.
      Marwān 118
al-Wāqidī, Muḥammad b. ʿUmar
      (narrator) 3, 13, 20, 33, 40, 71, 72,
      108, 114–17, 125, 129, 131, 132,
      134, 140–42, 144, 146, 147, 149–
      50, 156, 164, 178–83, 201–3, 207,
      208, 209, 214, 216–18
Wardān Khudāh 147, 150
Wāṣil b. Ṭaysalah al-ʿAnbarī 107
Wāsiṭ/Wāsiṭ al-Qasab xiii, 64, 70–71,
      84, 215
wird 221
Wuhayb b. ʿAbd al-Raḥmān al-Azdī
      159

Y

Yaḥyā b. al-Ḥakam 33
Yaḥyā b. Khālid (narrator) 192
Yaḥyā b. al-Nuʿmān al-Ghifārī
      (narrator) 142
Yaḥyā b. al-Walīd b. ʿAbd al-Malik
      219
Yaḥyā b. Yaʿmar al-ʿAdwānī 76
Yaḥyā b. Zakariyyāʾ al-Hamdānī
      (narrator) 225

Yamaniyyah 63
Yawm al-Dār 117
Yazdajird 195
Yazīd b. ʿAbd al-Malik b. Marwān
      118, 144
Yazīd b. Abī Kabshah 84, 204, 217
Yazīd b. Abī Muslim 58, 217
Yazīd b. Abī Ziyād, mawlā of the
      Banū Hāshim (narrator) 211
Yazīd b. Dīnār 84
Yazīd b. Ḥuṣayn b. Numayr 84
Yazīd b. Huzayl 101–3
Yazīd b. Jubayr 133
Yazīd b. Muʿāwiyah 65
Yazīd b. al-Muhallab xiii, xv, 26–29,
      32–34, 52–57, 63–64, 67, 74–76,
      83–88, 97, 105, 129, 156–63
Yazīd b. al-Walīd b. ʿAbd al-Malik
      195, 219
Yemen 97, 221–22
Yūnus b. Abī Isḥāq (narrator) 19, 20,
      134, 205, 218

Z

Zabārā bridge 20
al-Zabīr (b. ʿAbdallāh b. al-Zubayr?)
      178
al-Zābul 183
Zābulistān 7
Zāghūl 31
Zamm 27, 90, 135, 138, 147
Zamzam 148
Zaranj 6, 50
al-Zāwiyah 11, 24, 49, 67
Zawraq, a herdsman and guide 68
Ziyād, a man with al-Ḥajjāj at al-
      Zāwiyah 15
Ziyād b. Ghunaym al-Qaynī 47
Ziyād b. Jarīr b. ʿAbdallāh al-Bajalī 82,
      130, 139, 156, 214
Ziyād b. Muqātil b. Mismaʿ (al-
      Shaybānī) 17
Ziyād al-Qaṣīr al-Khuzāʿī 102
al-Zubayr, mawlā of ʿĀbis al-Bāhilī
      171
Zubayrids xi–xii, 85, 88

Ẓuhayr, Abū Saʿīd, companion of
  Thābit b. Quṭbah 101–3
Zuhayr b. Ḥayyān 195–96
Zuhayr b. Hunayd; see Abū al-
  Dhayyāl

al-Zuhrī, Ibn Shihāb (narrator) 218
Zunbīl 3, 6, 50–53, 63, 77–81, 183,
  209
Zurʿah b. ʿAlqamah al-Sulamī 90, 92,
  107